NICCOLO MACHIAVELLI

THE ART OF WAR

THE COMPLETE BOOKS

The Original Text with English Translation

Constantin Vaughn

Erebus Society

First published in Great Britain in 2017
by Erebus Society

First Edition

Editor: Constantin Vaughn

ISBN: 978-1-912461-00-4

TABLE OF CONTENTS

PREFACE

Many, Lorenzo, have held and still hold the opinion, that there is nothing which has less in common with another, and that is so dissimilar, as civilian life is from the military. Whence it is often observed, if anyone designs to avail himself of an enlistment in the army, that he soon changes, not only his clothes, but also his customs, his habits, his voice, and in the presence of any civilian custom, he goes to pieces; for I do not believe that any man can dress in civilian clothes who wants to be quick and ready for any violence; nor can that man have civilian customs and habits, who judges those customs to be effeminate and those habits not conducive to his actions; nor does it seem right to him to maintain his ordinary appearance and voice who, with his beard and cursing, wants to make other men afraid: which makes such an opinion in these times to be very true. But if they should consider the ancient institutions, they would not find matter more united, more in conformity, and which, of necessity, should be like to each other as much as these (civilian and military); for in all the arts that are established in a society for the sake of the common good of men, all those institutions created to (make people) live in fear of the laws and of God would be in vain, if their defense had not been provided for and which, if well arranged, will maintain not only these, but also those that are not well established. And so (on the contrary), good institutions without the help of the military are not much differently disordered than the habitation of a superb and regal palace, which, even though adorned with jewels and gold, if it is not roofed over will not have anything to protect it from the rain. And, if in any other institutions of a City and of a Republic every diligence is employed in keeping men loyal, peaceful, and full of the fear of God, it is doubled in the military; for in what man ought the country look for greater loyalty than in that man who has to promise to die for her? In whom ought there to be a greater love of peace, than in him who can only be injured by war? In whom ought there to be a greater fear of God than in him who, undergoing infinite dangers every day, has more need for His aid? If these necessities in forming the life of the soldier are well considered, they are found to be praised by those who gave the laws to the Commanders and by those who were put in charge of military training, and followed and imitated with all diligence by others.

But because military institutions have become completely corrupt and far removed from the ancient ways, these sinister opinions have arisen which make the military hated and intercourse with those who train them avoided. And I, judging, by what I have seen and read, that it is not impossible to restore its ancient ways and return some form of past virtue to it, have decided not to let this leisure time of mine pass without doing something, to write what I know of the art of war, to the satisfaction of those who are lovers of the ancient deeds. And although it requires courage to treat of those matters of which others have made a profession, none the less, I do not believe that it is a mistake to occupy a position with words, which may, with greater presumption, have been occupied with deeds; for the errors which I should make in writing can be corrected without injury to anyone, but those which are made with deeds cannot be found out except by the ruin of the Commanders.

You, Lorenzo, will therefore consider the quality of these efforts of mine, and will give in your judgement of them that censure or praise which will appear to you to be merited. I send you these, as much as to show myself grateful for all the benefits I have received from you, although I will not include in them the (review) of this work of mine, as well as also, because being accustomed to honor similar works of those who shine because of their nobility, wealth, genius, and liberality, I know you do not have many equals in wealth and nobility, few in ingenuity, and no one in liberality.

PROEMIO

Hanno, Lorenzo, molti tenuto, e tengono questa opinione, che e' non sia cosa alcuna che minore convenienza abbia con un'altra, nè che sia tanto dissimile, quanto la vita civile dalla militare. Donde si vede spesso, se alcuno disegna nello esercizio del soldo prevalersi, che subito, non solamente cangia abito, ma ancora ne' costumi, nelle usanze, nella voce e nella presenza da ogni civile uso si disforma; perchè non crede potere vestire uno abito civile colui che vuole essere espedito e pronto a ogni violenza; nè i civili costumi e usanze puote avere quello il quale giudica e quegli costumi essere effeminati e quelle usanze non favorevoli alle sue operazioni; nè pare conveniente mantenere la presenza e le parole ordinarie a quello che con la barba e con le bestemmie vuole fare paura agli altri uomini, il che fa in questi tempi tale opinione essere verissima. Ma se si considerassino gli antichi ordini, non si troverebbono cose più unite più conformi e che, di necessità, tanto l'una amasse l'altra, quanto queste, perchè tutte l'arti che si ordinano in una civiltà per cagione del bene comune degli uomini, tutti gli ordini fatti in quella per vivere con timore delle leggi e d'Iddio, sarebbono vani, se non fussono preparate le difese loro; le quali, bene ordinate mantengono quegli, ancora che non bene ordinati. E così per il contrario i buoni ordini, senza il militare ajuto, non altrimenti si disordinano, che l'abitazioni d'uno superbo e regale palazzo, ancora che ornate di gemme e d'oro, quando, senza essere coperte, non avessino cosa che dalla pioggia le difendesse. E se in qualunque altro ordine delle cittadi e de' regni si usava ogni diligenza per mantenere gli uomini fedeli, pacifici e pieni del timore d'Iddio nella milizia si raddoppiava; perchè in quale uomo debbe ricercare la patria maggiore fede, che in colui che le ha a promettere di morire per lei? In quale debbe essere più amore di pace, che in quello che solo dalla guerra puote essere offeso? In quale debbe essere più timore d'Iddio, che in colui che ogni dì, sottomettendosi a infiniti pericoli, ha più bisogno degli ajuti suoi? Questa necessità considerata bene, e da coloro che davano le leggi agli imperj, e da quegli che agli esercizi militari erano preposti, faceva che la vita de' soldati dagli altri uomini era lodata e con ogni studio seguitata e imitata. Ma per essere gli ordini militari al tutto corrotti e, di gran lunga, dagli antichi modi separati, ne sono nate queste sinistre opinioni, che fanno odiare la milizia e fuggire la conversazione di coloro che la esercitano. E giudicando io, per quello che io ho veduto e letto, ch'e' non sia impossibile ridurre quella negli antichi modi e renderle qualche forma della passata virtù, diliberai, per non passare questi mia oziosi tempi senza operare alcuna cosa, di scrivere, a sodisfazione di quegli che delle antiche azioni sono amatori, della arte della guerra quello che io ne intenda. E benchè sia cosa animosa trattare di quella materia della quale altri non ne abbia fatto professione, nondimeno io non credo sia errore occupare con le parole uno grado il quale molti, con maggiore prosunzione, con le opere hanno occupato; perchè gli errori che io facessi, scrivendo, possono essere senza danno d'alcuno corretti, ma quegli i quali da loro sono fatti, operando, non possono essere se non con la rovina degli imperj conosciuti. Voi pertanto, Lorenzo, considererete le qualità di queste mie fatiche e darete loro, con il vostro giudizio, quel biasimo o quella lode la quale vi parrà ch'elle abbiano meritato. Le quali a voi mando sì per dimostrarmi grato, ancora che la mia possibilità non vi aggiunga, de' benefizi ho ricevuto da voi, sì ancora, perchè essendo consuetudine onorare di simili opere coloro i quali per nobiltà, ricchezze, ingegno e liberalità risplendono, conosco voi di ricchezze e nobiltà non avere molti pari, d'ingegno pochi, e di liberalità niuno.

Book One

BOOK ONE

As I believe that it is possible for one to praise, without concern, any man after he is dead since every reason and supervision for adulation is lacking, I am not apprehensive in praising our own Cosimo Ruccelai, whose name is never remembered by me without tears, as I have recognized in him those parts which can be desired in a good friend among friends and in a citizen of his country. For I do not know what pertained to him more than to spend himself willingly, not excepting that courage of his, for his friends, and I do not know of any enterprise that dismayed him when he knew it was for the good of his country. And I confess freely not to have met among so many men whom I have known and worked with, a man in whom there was a mind more fired with great and magnificent things. Nor does one grieve with the friends of another of his death, except for his having been born to die young unhonored within his own home, without having been able to benefit anyone with that mind of his, for one would know that no one could speak of him, except (to say) that a good friend had died. It does not remain for us, however, or for anyone else who, like us, knew him, to be able because of this to keep the faith (since deeds do not seem to) to his laudable qualities. It is true however, that fortune was not so unfriendly to him that it did not leave some brief memory of the dexterity of his genius, as was demonstrated by some of his writings and compositions of amorous verses, in which (as he was not in love) he (employed as an) exercise in order not to use his time uselessly in his juvenile years, in order that fortune might lead him to higher thoughts. Here, it can be clearly comprehended, that if his objective was exercise, how very happily he described his ideas, and how much he was honored in his poetry. Fortune, however, having deprived us of the use of so great a friend, it appears to me it is not possible to find any other better remedy than for us to seek to benefit from his memory, and recover from it any matter that was either keenly observed or wisely discussed. And as there is nothing of his more recent than the discussions which the Lord Fabrizio Colonna had with him in his gardens, where matters pertaining to war were discussed at length by that Lord, with (questions) keenly and prudently asked by Cosimo, it seemed proper to me having been present with other friends of ours, to recall him to memory, so that reading it, the friends of Cosimo who met there will renew in their minds the memory of his virtue, and another part grieving for not having been there, will learn in part of many things discussed wisely by a most sagacious man useful not only to the military way of life, but to the civilian as well. I will relate, therefore, how Fabrizio Colonna, when he returned from Lombardy where he had fought a long time gloriously for the Catholic King, decided to pass through Florence to rest several days in that City in order to visit His Excellency the Duke, and see again several gentlemen with whom he had been familiar in the past. Whence it appeared proper to Cosimo to invite him to a banquet in his gardens, not so much to show his generosity as to have reason to talk to him at length, and to learn and understand several things from him, according as one can hope to from such a man, for it appeared to him to give him an opportunity to spend a day discussing such matters as would satisfy his mind.

Fabrizio, therefore, came as planned, and was received by Cosimo together with several other loyal friends of his, among whom were Zanobi Buondelmonti, Battista Della Palla, and Luigi Alamanni, young men most ardent in the same studies and loved by him, whose good qualities, because they were also praised daily by himself, we will omit. Fabrizio, therefore, was honored according to the times and the place, with all the highest honors they could give him. As soon as the convivial pleasures were past and the table cleared and every arrangement of feasting finished, which, in the presence of great men and those who have their minds turned to honorable thoughts is soon accomplished, and because the day was long and the heat intense, Cosimo, in order to satisfy their desire better, judged it would be well to take the opportunity to escape the heat by leading them to the more secret and shadowy part of his garden: when they arrived there and chairs brought out, some sat on the grass which was most fresh in the place, some sat on chairs placed in those parts under the shadow of very high trees; Fabrizio praised the place as most delightful, and looking especially at the trees, he did not recognize one of them, and looked puzzled. Cosimo, becoming aware of this said: Perhaps you have no knowledge of some of these trees, but do not wonder about them, because here are some which were more widely known by the ancients than are those commonly seen today. And giving him the name of some and telling him that Bernardo, his grandfather, had worked hard in their culture, Fabrizio replied: I was thinking that it was what you said I was, and this place and this study make me remember several Princes of the Kingdom, who delighted in their ancient culture and the shadow they cast. And stopping speaking of this, and somewhat upon himself as though in suspense, he added: If I did not think I would offend you, I would give you my opinion: but I do not believe in talking and discussing things with friends in this manner that I insult them. How much better would they have done (it is said with peace to everyone) to seek to imitate the ancients in the strong and rugged things, not in the soft and delicate, and in the things they did under the sun, not in the shadows, to adopt the honest and perfect ways of antiquity, not the false and corrupt; for while these practices were pleasing to my Romans, my country (without them) was ruined. To which Cosimo replied (but to avoid the necessity of having to repeat so many times who is speaking, and what the other adds, only the names of those speaking will be noted, without repeating the others). Cosimo, therefore, said: You have opened the way for a discussion which I desired, and I pray you to speak without regard, for I will question you without regard; and if, in questioning or in replying, I accuse or excuse anyone, it will not be for accusing or excusing, but to understand the truth from you.

FABRIZIO: And I will be much content to tell you what I know of all that you ask me; whether it be true or not, I will leave to your judgement. And I will be grateful if you ask me, for I am about to learn as much from what you ask me, as you will from me replying to you, because many times a wise questioner causes one to consider many things and understand many others which, without having been asked, would never have been understood.

COSIMO: I want to return to what you first were saying, that my grandfather and those of yours had more wisely imitated the ancients in rugged things than in delicate ones, and I want to excuse my side because I will let you excuse the other (your side). I do not believe that in your time there was a man who disliked living as softly as he, and that he was so much a lover of that rugged life which you praise: none the less he recognized he could not practice it in his personal life, nor in that of his sons, having been born in so corrupted an age, where anyone who wanted to depart from the common usage would be deformed and despised by everyone. For if anyone in a naked state should thrash upon the sand under the highest sun, or upon the snow in the most icy months of winter, as did Diogenes, he would be considered mad. If anyone (like the Spartan) should raise his children on a farm, make them sleep in the open, go with head and feet bare, bathe in cold water in order to harden them to endure vicissitudes, so that they then might love life less and fear death less, he would be praised by few and followed by none. So that dismayed at these ways of living, he presently leaves the ways of the ancients, and in imitating antiquity, does only that which he can with little wonderment.

FABRIZIO: You have excused him strongly in this part, and certainly you speak the truth: but I did not speak so much of these rugged ways of living, as of those other more human ways which have a greater conformity to the ways of living today, which I do not believe should have been difficult to introduce by one who is numbered among the Princes of a City. I will never forego my examples of my Romans. If their way of living should be examined, and the institutions in their Republic, there will be observed in her many things not impossible to introduce in a Society where there yet might be something of good.

COSIMO: What are those things similar to the ancients that you would introduce?

FABRIZIO: To honor and reward virtu, not to have contempt for poverty, to esteem the modes and orders of military discipline, to constrain citizens to love one another, to live without factions, to esteem less the private than the public good, and other such things which could easily be added in these times. It is not difficult to persuade (people) to these ways, when one considers these at length and approaches them in the usual manner, for the truth will appear in such (examinations) that every common talent is capable of undertaking them. Anyone can arrange these things; (for example), one plants trees under the shadow of which he lives more happily and merrily than if he had not (planted them).

COSIMO: I do not want to reply to anything of what you have spoken, but I do want leave to give a judgment on these, which can be easily judged, and I shall address myself to you who accuse those who in serious and important actions are not imitators of the ancients, thinking that in this way I can more easily carry out my intentions. I should want, therefore, to know from you whence it arises that, on the one hand you condemn those who do not imitate the ancients in their actions, on the other hand, in matters of war which is your profession and in which you are judged to be excellent, it is not observed that you have employed any of the ancient methods, or those which have some similarity.

FABRIZIO: You have come to the point where I expected you to, for what I said did not merit any other question, nor did I wish for any other. And although I am able to save myself with a simple excuse, none the less I want, for your greater satisfaction and mine, since the season (weather) allows it, to enter into a much longer discussion. Men who want to do something, ought first to prepare themselves with all industry, in order ((when the opportunity is seen)) to be prepared to achieve that which they have proposed. And whenever the preparations are undertaken cautiously, unknown to anyone, no none can be accused of negligence unless he is first discovered by the occasion; in which if it is not then successful, it is seen that either he has not sufficiently prepared himself, or that he has not in some part given thought to it. And as the opportunity has not come to me to be able to show the preparations I would make to bring the military to your ancient organization, and it I have not done so, I cannot be blamed either by you or by others. I believe this excuse is enough to respond to your accusation.

COSIMO: It would be enough if I was certain that the opportunity did not present itself.

FABRIZIO: But because I know you could doubt whether this opportunity had come about or not, I want to discuss at length ((if you will listen to me with patience)) which preparations are necessary to be made first, what occasion needs to arise, what difficulty impedes the preparations from becoming beneficial and the occasion from arriving, and that this is ((which appears a paradox)) most difficult and most easy to do.

COSIMO: You cannot do anything more pleasing for me and for the others than this. But if it is not painful for you to speak, it will never be painful for us to listen. But at this discussion may be long, I want help from these, my friends, and with your permission, and they and I pray you one thing, that you do not become annoyed if we sometimes interrupt you with some opportune question.

FABRIZIO: I am most content that you, Cosimo, with these other young people here, should question me, for I believe that young men will become more familiar with military matters, and will more easily understand what I have to say. The others, whose hair (head) is white and whose blood is icy, in part are enemies of war and in part incorrigible, as those who believe that the times and not the evil ways constrain men to live in such a fashion. So ask anything of me, with assurance and without regard; I desire this, as much because it will afford me a little rest, as because it will give me pleasure not to leave any doubts in your minds. I want to begin from your words, where you said to me that in war ((which is my profession)) I have not employed any of the ancient methods. Upon this I say, that this being a profession by which men of every time were not able to live honestly, it cannot be employed as a profession except by a Republic or a Kingdom; and both of these, if well established, will never allow any of their citizens or subjects to employ it as a profession: for he who practices it will never be judged to be good, as to gain some usefulness from it at any time he must be rapacious, deceitful, violent, and have many qualities, which of necessity, do not make him good: nor can men who employ this as a profession, the great as well as the least, be made otherwise, for this profession does not provide for them in peace. Whence they are obliged, either to hope that there will be no peace or to gain so much for themselves in times of war, that they can provide for themselves in times of peace. And wherever one of these two thoughts exists, it does not occur in a good man; for, from the desire to provide for oneself in every circumstance, robberies, violence and assassinations result, which such soldiers do to friends as well as to enemies: and from not desiring peace, there arises those deceptions which Captains perpetrate upon those whom they lead, because war hardens them: and even if peace occurs frequently, it happens that the leaders, being deprived of their stipends and of their licentious mode of living, raise a flag of piracy, and without any mercy sack a province.

Do you not have within the memory of events of your time, many soldiers in Italy, finding themselves without employment because of the termination of wars, gathered themselves into very troublesome gangs, calling themselves companies, and went about levying tribute on the towns and sacking the country, without there being any remedy able to be applied? Have you not read how the Carthaginian soldiers, when the first war they engaged in with the Romans under Matus and Spendius was ended, tumultuously chose two leaders, and waged a more dangerous war against the Carthaginians than that which they had just concluded with the Romans? And in the time of our fathers, Francesco Sforza, in order to be able to live honorably (comfortably) in times of peace, not only deceived the Milanese, in whose pay he was, but took away their liberty and became their Prince. All the other soldiers of Italy, who have employed the military as their particular profession, have been like this man; and if, through their malignity, they have not become Dukes of Milan, so much more do they merit to be censured; for without such a return ((if their lives were to be examined)), they all have the same cares. Sforza, father of Francesco, constrained Queen Giovanna to throw herself into the arms of the King of Aragon, having abandoned her suddenly, and left her disarmed amid her enemies, only in order to satisfy his ambition of either levying tribute or taking the Kingdom. Braccio, with the same industry, sought to occupy the Kingdom of Naples, and would have succeeded, had he not been routed and killed at Aquilla. Such evils do not result from anything else other than the existence of men who employ the practice of soldiering as their own profession. Do you not have a proverb which strengthens my argument, which says: War makes robbers, and peace hangs them? For those who do not know how to live by another practice, and not finding any one who will support them in that, and not having so much virtu that they know how to come and live together honorably, are forced by necessity to roam the streets, and justice is forced to extinguish them.

COSIMO: You have made me turn this profession (art) of soldiering back almost to nothing, and I had supposed it to be the most excellent and most honorable of any: so that if you do not clarify this better, I will not be satisfied; for if it is as you say, I do not know whence arises the glory of Caesar, Pompey, Scipio, Marcellus, and of so many Roman Captains who are celebrated for their fame as the Gods.

FABRIZIO: I have not yet finished discussing all that I proposed, which included two things: the one, that a good man was not able to undertake this practice because of his profession: the other, that a well established Republic or Kingdom would never permit its subjects or citizens to employ it for their profession. Concerning the first, I have spoken as much as has occurred to me: it remains for me to talk of the second, where I shall reply to this last question of yours, and I say that Pompey and Caesar, and almost all those Captains who were in Rome after the last Carthaginian war, acquired fame as valiant men, not as good men: but those who had lived before them acquired glory as valiant and good men: which results from the fact that these latter did not take up the practice of war as their profession; and those whom I named first as those who employed it as their profession. And while the Republic lived immaculately, no great citizen ever presumed by means of such a practice to enrich himself during (periods of) peace by breaking laws, despoiling the provinces, usurping and tyrannizing the country, and imposing himself in every way; nor did anyone of the lowest fortune think of violating the sacred agreement, adhere himself to any private individual, not fearing the Senate, or to perform any disgraceful act of tyranny in order to live at all times by the profession of war. But those who were Captains, being content with the triumph, returned with a desire for the private life; and those who were members (of the army) returned with a desire to lay down the arms they had taken up; and everyone returned to the art (trade or profession) by which they ordinarily lived; nor was there ever anyone who hoped to provide for himself by plunder and by means of these arts. A clear and evident example of this as it applies to great citizens can be found in the Regent Attilio, who, when he was captain of the Roman armies in Africa, and having almost defeated the Carthaginians, asked the Senate for permission to return to his house to look after his farms which were being spoiled by his laborers. Whence it is clearer than the sun, that if that man had practiced war as his profession, and by means of it thought to obtain some advantage for himself, having so many provinces which (he could) plunder, he would not have asked permission to return to take care of his fields, as each day he could have obtained more than the value of all his possessions. But as these good men, who do not practice war as their profession, do not expect to gain anything from it except hard work, danger, and glory, as soon as they are sufficiently glorious, desire to return to their homes and live from the practice of their own profession. As to men of lower status and gregarious soldiers, it is also true that every one voluntarily withdrew from such a practice, for when he was not fighting would have desired to fight, but when he was fighting wanted to be dismissed. Which illustrates the many ways, and especially in seeing that it was among the first privileges, that the Roman people gave to one of its Citizens, that he should not be constrained unwillingly to fight. Rome, therefore, while she was well organized ((which it was up to the time of the Gracchi)) did not have one soldier who had to take up this practice as a profession, and therefore had few bad ones, and these were severely punished. A well ordered City, therefore, ought to desire that this training for war ought to be employed in times of peace as an exercise, and in times of war as a necessity and for glory, and allow the public only to use it as a profession, as Rome did. And any citizen who has other aims in (using) such exercises is not good, and any City which governs itself otherwise, is not well ordered.

COSIMO: I am very much content and satisfied with what you have said up to now, and this conclusion which you have made pleases me greatly: and I believe it will be true when expected from a Republic, but as to Kings, I do not yet know why I should believe that a King would not want particularly to have around him those who take up such a practice as their profession.

FABRIZIO: A well ordered Kingdom ought so much the more avoid such artifices, for these only are the things which corrupt the King and all the Ministers in a Tyranny. And do not, on the other side, tell me of some present Kingdom, for I will not admit them to be all well ordered Kingdoms;

for Kingdoms that are well ordered do not give absolute (power to) Rule to their Kings, except in the armies, for only there is a quick decision necessary, and, therefore, he who (rules) there must have this unique power: in other matters, he cannot do anything without counsel, and those who counsel him have to fear those whom he may have near him who, in times of peace, desire war because they are unable to live without it. But I want to dwell a little longer on this subject, and look for a Kingdom totally good, but similar to those that exist today, where those who take up the profession of war for themselves still ought to be feared by the King, for the sinews of armies without any doubt are the infantry. So that if a King does not organize himself in such a way that his infantry in time of peace are content to return to their homes and live from the practice of their own professions, it must happen of necessity that he will be ruined; for there is not to be found a more dangerous infantry than that which is composed of those who make the waging of war their profession; for you are forced to make war always, or pay them always, or to risk the danger that they take away the Kingdom from you. To make war always is not possible: (and) one cannot pay always; and, hence, that danger is run of losing the State. My Romans ((as I have said)), as long as they were wise and good, never permitted that their citizens should take up this practice as their profession, notwithstanding that they were able to raise them at all times, for they made war at all times: but in order to avoid the harm which this continuous practice of theirs could do to them, since the times did not change, they changed the men, and kept turning men over in their legions so that every fifteen years they always completely re-manned them: and thus they desired men in the flower of their age, which is from eighteen to thirty five years, during which time their legs, their hands, and their eyes, worked together, nor did they expect that their strength should decrease in them, or that malice should grow in them, as they did in corrupt times.

Ottavianus first, and then Tiberius, thinking more of their own power than the public usefulness, in order to rule over the Roman people more easily, begun to disarm them and to keep the same armies continually at the frontiers of the Empire. And because they did not think it sufficient to hold the Roman People and the Senate in check, they instituted an army called the Praetorian (Guard), which was kept near the walls of Rome in a fort adjacent to that City. And as they now begun freely to permit men assigned to the army to practice military matters as their profession, there soon resulted that these men became insolent, and they became formidable to the Senate and damaging to the Emperor. Whence there resulted that many men were killed because of their insolence, for they gave the Empire and took it away from anyone they wished, and it often occurred that at one time there were many Emperors created by the several armies. From which state of affairs proceeded first the division of the Empire and finally its ruin. Kings ought, therefore, if they want to live securely, have their infantry composed of men, who, when it is necessary for him to wage war, will willingly go forth to it for love of him, and afterwards when peace comes, more willingly return to their homes; which will always happen if he selects men who know how to live by a profession other than this. And thus he ought to desire, with the coming of peace, that his Princes return to governing their people, gentlemen to the cultivation of their possessions, and the infantry to their particular arts (trades or professions); and everyone of these will willingly make war in order to have peace, and will not seek to disturb the peace to have war.

COSIMO: Truly, this reasoning of yours appears to me well considered: none the less, as it is almost contrary to what I have thought up to now, my mind is not yet purged of every doubt. For I see many Lords and Gentlemen who provide for themselves in times of peace through the training for war, as do your equals who obtain provisions from Princes and the Community. I also see almost all the men at arms remaining in the garrisons of the city and of the fortresses. So that it appears to me that there is a long time of peace for everyone.

FABRIZIO: I do not believe that you believe this, that everyone has a place in time of peace; for other reasons can be cited for their being stationed there, and the small number of people who remain in the places mentioned by you will answer your question. What is the proportion of infantry needed to be employed in time of war to that in peace? for while the fortresses and the city are garrisoned in times of peace, they are much more garrisoned in times of war; to this should be added the soldiers kept in the field who are a great number, but all of whom are released in time of peace. And concerning the garrisons of States, who are a small number, Pope Julius and you have shown how much they are to be feared who do not know any other profession than war, as you have taken them out of your garrisons because of their insolence, and placed the Swiss there, who are born and raised under the laws and are chosen by the community in an honest election; so do not say further that in peace there is a place for every man. As to the men at arms continued in their enlistment in peace time, the answer appears more difficult. None the less, whoever considers everything well, will easily find the answer, for this thing of keeping on the men at arms is a corrupt thing and not good. The reason is this; as there are men who do not have any art (trade or profession), a thousand evils will arise every day in those States where they exist, and especially so if they were to be joined by a great number of companions: but as they are few, and unable by themselves to constitute an army, they therefore, cannot do any serious damage. None the less, they have done so many times, as I said of Francesco and of Sforza, his father, and of Braccio of Perugia. So I do not approve of this custom of keeping men at arms, both because it is corrupt and because it can cause great evils.

COSIMO: Would you do without them?, or if you keep them, how would you do so?

FABRIZIO: By means of an ordinance, not like those of the King of France, because they are as dangerous and insolent as ours, but like those of the ancients, who created horsemen (cavalry) from their subjects, and in times of peace sent them back to their homes to live from the practice of their own profession, as I shall discuss at length before I finish this discussion. So, if this part of the army can now live by such a practice even when there is peace, it stems from a corrupt order. As to the provisions that are reserved for me and the other leaders, I say to you that this likewise is a most corrupt order, for a wise Republic ought not to give them to anyone, rather it ought to employ its citizens as leaders in war, and in time of peace desire that they return to their professions. Thus also, a wise King ought not to give (provisions) to them, or if he does give them, the reasons ought to be either as a reward for some excellent act, or in order to avail himself of such a man in peace as well as in war. And because you have mentioned me, I want the example to include me, and I say I have never practiced war as a profession, for my profession is to govern my subjects, and defend them, and in order to defend them, I must love peace but know how to make war; and my King does not reward and esteem me so much for what I know of war, as because I know also how to counsel him in peace. Any King ought not, therefore, to want to have next to him anyone who is not thusly constituted, if he is wise and wants to govern prudently; for if he has around him either too many lovers of peace or too many lovers of war, they will cause him to err. I cannot, in this first discussion of mine and according to my suggestion, say otherwise, and if this is not enough for you, you must seek one which satisfies you better. You can begin to recognize how much difficulty there is in bringing the ancient methods into modem wars, and what preparations a wise man must make, and what opportunities he can hope for to put them into execution. But little by little you will know these things better if the discussion on bringing any part of the ancient institutions to the present order of things does not weary you.

COSIMO: If we first desired to hear your discussion of these matters, truly what you have said up to now redoubles that desire. We thank you, therefore, for what we have had and ask you for the rest.

FABRIZIO: Since this is your pleasure, I want to begin to treat of this matter from the beginning being able in that way to demonstrate it more fully, so that it may be better understood. The aim of those who want to make war is to be able to combat in the field with every (kind) of enemy, and to be able to win the engagement. To want to do this, they must raise an army. In raising an army, it is necessary to find men, arm them, organize them, train them in small and large (battle) orders, lodge them, and expose them to the enemy afterwards, either at a standstill or while marching. All the industry of war in the field is placed in these things, which are the more necessary and honored (in the waging of war). And if one does well in offering battle to the enemy, all the other errors he may make in the conduct of the war are supportable: but if he lacks this organization, even though he be valiant in other particulars, he will never carry on a war to victory (and honor). For, as one engagement that you win cancels out every other bad action of yours, so likewise, when you lose one, all the things you have done well before become useless. Since it is necessary, therefore, first to find men, you must come to the Deletto (Draft) of them, as thus the ancients called it, and which we call Scelta (Selection): but in order to call it by a more honored name, I want us to preserve the name of Deletto. Those who have drawn up regulations for war want men to be chosen from temperate countries as they have spirit and are prudent; for warm countries give rise to men who are prudent but not spirited, and cold (countries) to men who are spirited but not prudent. This regulation is drawn up well for one who is the Prince of all the world, and is therefore permitted to draw men from those places that appear best to him: but wanting to draw up a regulation that anyone can use, one must say that every Republic and every Kingdom ought to take soldiers from their own country, whether it is hot, cold, or temperate. For, from ancient examples, it is seen that in every country, good soldiers are made by training; because where nature is lacking, industry supplies it, which, in this case, is worth more than nature: And selecting them from another place cannot be called Deletto, because Deletto means to say to take the best of a province, and to have the power to select as well those who do not want to fight as those who do want to. This Deletto therefore, cannot be made unless the places are subject to you; for you cannot take whoever you want in the countries that are not yours, but you need to take those who want to come.

COSIMO: And of those who want to come, it can even be said, that they turn and leave you, and because of this, it can then be called a Deletto.

FABRIZIO: In a certain way, you say what is true: but consider the defects that such as Deletto has in itself, for often it happens that it is not a Deletto. The first thing (to consider), is that those who are not your subjects and do not willingly want to fight, are not of the best, rather they are of the worst of a province; for if nay are troublesome, idle, without restraint, without religion, subject to the rule of the father, blasphemous, gamblers, and in every way badly brought up, they are those who want to fight, (and) these habits cannot be more contrary to a true and good military life. When there are so many of such men offered to you that they exceed the number you had designated, you can select them; but if the material is bad, it is impossible for the Deletto to be good: but many times it happens that they are not so many as (are needed) to fill the number you require: so that being forced to take them all, it results that it can no longer be called the making of a Deletto, but in enlisting of infantry. The armies of Italy and other places are raised today with these evils, except in Germany, where no one is enlisted by command of the Prince, but according to the wishes of those who want to fight. Think, therefore, what methods of those ancients can now be introduced in an army of men put together by similar means.

COSIMO: What means should be taken therefore?

FABRIZIO: What I have just said: select them from your own subjects, and with the authority of the Prince.

COSIMO: Would you introduce any ancient form in those thus selected?

FABRIZIO: You know well it would be so; if it is a Principality, he who should command should be their Prince or an ordinary Lord; or if it is a Republic, a citizen who for the time should be Captain: otherwise it is difficult to do the thing well.

COSIMO: Why?

FABRIZIO: I will tell you in time: for now, I want this to suffice for you, that it cannot be done well in any other way.

COSIMO: If you have, therefore, to make ibis Deletto in your country, whence do you judge it better to draw them, from the City or the Countryside?

FABRIZIO: Those who have written of this all agree that it is better to select them from the Countryside, as they are men accustomed to discomfort, brought up on hard work, accustomed to be in the sun and avoid the shade, know how to handle the sword, dig a ditch, carry a load, and are without cunning or malice. But on this subject, my opinion would be, that as soldiers are of two kinds, afoot and on horseback, that those afoot be selected from the Countryside, and those on horseback from the City.

COSIMO: Of what age would you draw them?

FABRIZIO: If I had to raise an (entirely) new army, I would draw them from seventeen to forty years of age; if the army already exists and I had to replenish it, at seventeen years of age always.

COSIMO: I do not understand this distinction well.

FABRIZIO: I will tell you: if I should have to organize an army where there is none, it would be necessary to select all those men who were more capable, as long as they were of military age, in order to instruct them as I would tell them: but if I should have to make the Deletto in places where the army was (already) organized, in order to supplement it, I would take those of seventeen years of age, because the others having been taken for some time would have been selected and instructed.

COSIMO: Therefore you would want to make an ordinance similar to that which exists in our countries.

FABRIZIO: You say well: it is true that I would arm them, captain them, train them, and organize them, in a way which I do not know whether or not you have organized them similarly.

COSIMO: Therefore you praise the ordinance?

FABRIZIO: Why would you want me to condemn it?

COSIMO: Because many wise men have censured it.

FABRIZIO: You say something contrary, when you say a wise man censured the ordinance: for he can be held a wise man and to have censured them wrongly.

COSIMO: The wrong conclusion that he has made will always cause us to have such a opinion.

FABRIZIO: Watch out that the defect is not yours, but his: as that which you recognized before this discussion furnishes proof.

COSIMO: You do a most gracious thing. But I want to tell you that you should be able to justify yourself better in that of which those men are accused. These men say thusly: either that it is useless and our trusting in it will cause us to lose the State: or it is of virtue, and he who governs through it can easily deprive her of it. They cite the Romans, who by their own arms lost their liberty: They cite the Venetians and the King of France, of whom they say that the former, in order not to obey one of its Citizens employed the arms of others, and the King disarmed his People so as to be able to command them more easily. But they fear the uselessness of this much more; for which uselessness they cite two principal reasons: the one, because they are inexpert; the other, for having to fight by force: because they say that they never learn anything from great men, and nothing good is ever done by force.

FABRIZIO: All the reasons that you mention are from men who are not far sighted, as I shall clearly show. And first, as to the uselessness, I say to you that no army is of more use than your own, nor can an army of your own be organized except in this way. And as there is no debating over this, which all the examples of ancient history does for us, I do not want to lose time over it. And because they cite inexperience and force, I say ((as it is true)) that inept experience gives rise to little spirit (enthusiasm) and force makes for discontent: but experience and enthusiasm gains for themselves the means for arming, training, and organizing them, as you will see in the first part of this discussion. But as to force, you must understand that as men are brought to the army by commandment of the Prince, they have to come, whether it is entirely by force or entirely voluntarily: for if it were entirely from desire, there would not be a Deletto as only a few of them would go; so also, the (going) entirely by force would produce bad results; therefore, a middle way ought to be taken where neither the entirely forced or entirely voluntarily (means are used), but they should come, drawn by the regard they have for the Prince, where they are more afraid of of his anger then the immediate punishment: and it will always happen that there will be a compulsion mixed with willingness, from which that discontent cannot arise which causes bad effects. Yet I do not claim that an army thus constituted cannot be defeated; for many times the Roman armies were overcome, and the army of Hannibal was defeated: so that it can be seen that no army can be so organized that a promise can be given that it cannot be routed. These wise men of yours, therefore, ought not measure this uselessness from having lost one time, but to believe that just as they can lose, so too they can win and remedy the cause of the defeat. And if they should look into this, they will find that it would not have happened because of a defect in the means, but of the organization which was not sufficiently perfect. And, as I have said, they ought to provide for you, not by censuring the organization, but by correcting it: as to how this ought to be done, you will come to know little by little.

As to being apprehensive that such organization will not deprive you of the State by one who makes himself a leader, I reply, that the arms carried by his citizens or subjects, given to them by laws and ordinances, never do him harm, but rather are always of some usefulness, and preserve the City uncorrupted for a longer time by means of these (arms), than without (them). Rome remained free four hundred years while armed: Sparta eight hundred: Many other Cities have been dis-armed, and have been free less than forty years; for Cities have need of arms, and if they do not have arms of their own, they hire them from foreigners, and the arms of foreigners more readily do harm to the public good than their own; for they are easier to corrupt, and a citizen who becomes powerful can more readily avail himself, and can also manage the people more readily as he has to oppress men who are disarmed. In addition to this, a City ought to fear two enemies more than one. One which avails itself of foreigners immediately has to fear not only its citizens, but the foreigners that it enlists; and, remembering what I told you a short while ago of Francesco Sforza, (you will see that) that fear ought to exist. One which employs its own arms, has not other fear except of its own Citizens. But of all the reasons which can be given, I want this one to serve me, that no one ever established any Republic or Kingdom who did not think that it should be defended by those who lived there with arms: and if the Venetians had been as wise in this as in their other institutions, they would have created a new world Kingdom; but who so much more merit censure, because they had been the first who were armed by their founders. And not having dominion on land, they armed themselves on the sea, where they waged war with virtu, and with arms in hand enlarged their country. But when the time came when they had to wage war on land to defend Venice and where they ought to have sent their own citizens to fight (on land), they enlisted as their captain (a foreigner), the Marquis of Mantua. This was the sinister course which prevented them from rising to the skies and expanding. And they did this in the belief that, as they knew how to wage war at sea, they should not trust themselves in waging it on land; which was an unwise belief (distrust), because a Sea captain, who is accustomed to combat with winds, water, and men, could more easily become a Captain on land where the combat is with men only, than a land Captain become a sea one. And my Romans, knowing how to combat on land and not on the sea, when the war broke out with the Carthaginians who were powerful on the sea, did not enlist Greeks or Spaniards experienced at sea, but imposed that change on those citizens they sent (to fight) on land, and they won. If they did this in order that one of their citizens should not become Tyrant, it was a fear that was given little consideration; for, in addition to the other reasons mentioned a short while ago concerning such a proposal, if a citizen (skilled) in (the use of) arms at sea had never been made a Tyrant in a City situated in the sea, so much less would he be able to do this if he were (skilled) in (the use of arms) on land. And, because of this, they ought to have seen that arms in the hands of their own citizens could not create Tyrants, but the evil institutions of a Government are those which cause a City to be tyrannized; and, as they had a good Government, did not have to fear arms of their own citizens. They took an imprudent course, therefore, which was the cause of their being deprived of much glory and happiness. As to the error which the King of France makes in not having his people disciplined to war, from what has been cited from examples previously mentioned, there is no one ((devoid of some particular passion of theirs)) who does not judge this defect to be in the Republic, and that this negligence alone is what makes it weak. But I have made too great a digression and have gotten away from my subject: yet I have done this to answer you and to show you, that no reliance can be had on arms other than ones own, and ones own arms cannot be established otherwise than by way of an ordinance, nor can forms of armies be introduced in any place, nor military discipline instituted. If you have read the arrangements which the first Kings made in Rome, and most especially of Servius Tullus, you will find that the institution of classes is none other than an arrangement to be able quickly to put together an army for the defense of that City. But turning to our Deletto, I say again, that having to replenish an established (old) organization, I would take the seventeen year olds, but having to create a new one, I would take them of every age between seventeen and forty in order to avail myself of them quickly.

COSIMO: Would you make a difference of what profession (art) you would choose them from?

FABRIZIO: These writers do so, for they do not want that bird hunters, fishermen, cooks, procurers, and anyone who makes amusement his calling should be taken, but they want that, in addition to tillers of the soil, smiths and blacksmiths, carpenters, butchers, hunters, and such like, should be taken. But I would make little difference in conjecturing from his calling how good the man may be, but how much I can use him with the greatest usefulness. And for this reason, the peasants, who are accustomed to working the land, are more useful than anyone else, for of all the professions (arts), this one is used more than any other in the army: After this, are the forgers (smiths), carpenters, blacksmiths, shoemakers; of whom it is useful to have many, for their skills succeed in many things, as they are a very good thing for a soldier to have, from whom you draw double service.

COSIMO: How are those who are or are not suitable to fight chosen?

FABRIZIO: I want to talk of the manner of selecting a new organization in order to make it after wards into an army; which yet also apply in the discussion of the selection that should be made in re-manning an old (established) organization. I say, therefore, that how good the man is that you have to select as a soldier is recognized either from his experience, shown by some excellent deeds of his, or by conjecture. The proof of virtu cannot be found in men who are newly selected, and who never before have been selected; and of the former, few or none are found in an organization which is newly established. It is necessary, therefore, lacking experience to have recourse to conjecture, which is derived from their age, profession, and physical appearance. The first two have been discussed: it remains to talk of the third. And yet I say that some have wanted that the soldier be big, among whom was Pyrrhus: Some others have chosen them only from the strength of the body, as Caesar did: which strength of body is conjectured from the composition of the members and the gracefulness of aspect. And yet some of those who write say that he should have lively and merry eyes, a nervy neck, a large breast, muscular arms, long fingers, a small stomach, round hips, sleek legs and feet: which parts usually render a man strong and agile, which are the two things sought above everything else in a soldier. He ought, above all, to have regard for his habits and that there should be in him a (sense of) honesty and shame, otherwise there will be selected only an instrument of trouble and a beginning of corruption; for there is no one who believes that in a dishonest education and in a brutish mind, there can exist some virtu which in some part may be praiseworthy. Nor does it appear to me superfluous, rather I believe it necessary, in order for you to understand better the importance of this selection, to tell you the method that the Roman Consuls at the start of their Magistracy observed in selecting the Roman legions. In which Deletto, because those who had to be selected were to be a mixture of new and veteran men ((because of the continuing wars)), they proceeded from experience with regard to the old (veteran) men, and from conjecture with regard to the new. And this ought to be noted, that these Deletti are made, either for immediate training and use, or for future employment.

I have talked, and will talk, of those that are made for future employment, because my intention is to show you how an army can be organized in countries where there is no military (organization), in which countries I cannot have Deletti in order to make use of them. But in countries where it is the custom to call out armies, and by means of the Prince, these (Deletti) exist, as was observed at Rome and is today observed among the Swiss. For in these Deletti, if they are for the (selection of) new men, there are so many others accustomed to being under military orders, that the old (veteran) and new, being mixed together, make a good and united body. Notwithstanding this, the Emperors, when they began to hold fixed the (term of service of the) soldiers, placed new men in charge over the soldiers, whom they called Tironi, as teachers to train them, as is seen in the life of the Emperor Maximus: which thing, while Rome was free, was instituted, not in the army, but within the City: and as the military exercises where the young men were trained were in the City, there resulted that those then chosen to go to war, being accustomed in the method of mock warfare, could easily adapt themselves to real war. But afterwards, when these Emperors discontinued these exercises, it was necessary to employ the methods I have described to you. Arriving, therefore, at the methods of the Roman Selection, I say that, as soon as the Roman Consuls, on whom was imposed the carrying on of the war, had assumed the Magistracy, in wanting to organize their armies ((as it was the custom that each of them had two legions of Roman men, who were the nerve (center) of their armies)), created twenty four military Tribunes, proposing six for each legion, who filled that office which today is done by those whom we call Constables. After they had assembled all the Roman men adept at carrying arms, and placed the Tribunes of each legion apart from each of the others. Afterwards, by lot they drew the Tribes, from which the first Selection was to be made, and of that Tribe they selected four of their best men, from whom one was selected by the Tribunes of the first legion, and of the other three, one was selected by the Tribunes of the second legion; of the other two, one was selected by the Tribunes of the third, and that last belonged to the fourth legion. After these four, four others were selected, of whom the first man was selected by the Tribunes of the second legion, the second by those of the third, the third by those of the fourth, the fourth remained to the first. After, another four were chosen: the first man was selected by the (Tribunes of the) third (legion), the second by the fourth, the third by the first, the fourth remained to the second. And thus this method of selection changed successively, so that the selection came to be equal, and the legions equalized. And as we said above, this was done where the men were to be used immediately: and as it was formed of men of whom a good part were experienced in real warfare, and everyone in mock battles, this Deletto was able to be based on conjecture and experience. But when a new army was to be organized and the selection made for future employment, this Deletto cannot be based except on conjecture, which is done by age and physical appearance.

COSIMO: I believe what you have said is entirely true: but before you pass on to other discussion, I want to ask about one thing which you have made me remember, when you said that the Deletto which should be made where these men are not accustomed to fighting should be done by conjecture: for

I have heard our organization censured in many of its parts, and especially as to number; for many say that a lesser number ought to be taken, of whom those that are drawn would be better and the selection better, as there would not be as much hardship imposed on the men, and some reward given them, by means of which they would be more content and could be better commanded. Whence I would like to know your opinion on this part, and if you preferred a greater rather than a smaller number, and what methods you would use in selecting both numbers.

FABRIZIO: Without doubt the greater number is more desirable and more necessary than the smaller: rather, to say better, where a great number are not available, a perfect organization cannot be made, and I will easily refute all the reasons cited in favor of this. I say, therefore, first, that where there are many people, as there are for example in Tuscany, does not cause you to have better ones, or that the Deletto is more selective; for desiring in the selection of men to judge them on the basis of experience, only a very few would probably be found in that country who would have had this experience, as much because few have been in a war, as because of those few who have been, very few have ever been put to the test, so that because of this they merit to be chosen before the others: so that whoever is in a similar situation should select them, must leave experience to one side and take them by conjecture: and if I were brought to such a necessity, I would want to see, if twenty young men of good physical appearance should come before me, with what rule rule I ought to take some or reject some: so that without doubt I believe that every man will confess that it is a much smaller error to take them all in arming and training them, being unable to know (beforehand) which of them are better, and to reserve to oneself afterwards to make a more certain Deletto where, during the exercises with the army, those of greater courage and vitality may be observed. So that, considering everything, the selection in this case of a few in order to have them better, is entirely false. As to causing less hardship to the country and to the men, I say that the ordinance, whether it is bad or insufficient, does not cause any hardship: for this order does not take men away from their business, and does not bind them so that they cannot go to carry out their business, because it only obliges them to come together for training on their free days, which proposition does not do any harm either to the country or the men; rather, to the young, it ought to be delightful, for where, on holidays they remain basely indolent in their hangouts, they would now attend these exercises with pleasure, for the drawing of arms, as it is a beautiful spectacle, is thus delightful to the young men. As to being able to pay (more to) the lesser number, and thereby keeping them more content and obedient, I reply, that no organization of so few can be made, who are paid so continually, that their pay satisfies them. For instance, if an army of five thousand infantry should be organized, in wanting to pay them so that it should be believed they would be contented, they must be given at least ten thousand ducats a month. To begin with, this number of infantry is not enough to make an army, and the payment is unendurable to a State; and on the other hand, it is not sufficient to keep the men content and obligated to respect your position. So that in doing this although much would be spent, it would provide little strength, and would not be sufficient to defend you, or enable you to undertake any enterprise. If you should give them more, or take on more, so much more impossible would it be for you to pay them: if you should give them less, or take on fewer, so much less would be content and so much less useful would they be to you. Therefore, those who consider things which are either useless or impossible. But it is indeed necessary to pay them when they are levied to send to war.

But even if such an arrangement should give some hardship to those enrolled in it in times of peace, which I do not see, they are still recompensed by all those benefits which an army established in a City bring; for without them, nothing is secure. I conclude that whoever desires a small number in order to be able to pay them, or for any other reason cited by you, does not know (what he is doing); for it will also happen, in my opinion, that any number will always diminish in your hands, because of the infinite impediments that men have; so that the small number will succeed at nothing. However, when you have a large organization, you can at your election avail yourself of few or of many. In addition to this, it serves you in fact and reputation, for the large number will always give you reputation. Moreover, in creating the organization, in order to keep men trained, if you enroll a small number of men in many countries, and the armies are very distant from each other, you cannot without the gravest injury to them assemble them for (joint) exercises, and without this training the organization is useless, as will be shown in its proper place.

COSIMO: What you have said is enough on my question: but I now desire that you resolve another doubt for me. There are those who say that such a multitude of armed men would cause confusion, trouble, and disorder in the country.

FABRIZIO: This is another vain opinion for the reason I will tell you. These organized under arms can cause disorders in two ways: either among themselves, or against others; both of these can be obviated where discipline by itself should not do so: for as to troubles among themselves, the organization removes them, not brings them up, because in the organization you give them arms and leaders. If the country where you organize them is so unwarlike that there are not arms among its men, and so united that there are no leaders, such an organization will make them more ferocious against the foreigner, but in no way will make it more disunited, because men well organized, whether armed or unarmed, fear the laws, and can never change, unless the leaders you give them cause a change; and I will later tell you the manner of doing this. But if the country where you have organized an army is warlike and disunited, this organization alone is reason enough to unite them, for these men have arms and leaders for themselves: but the arms are useless for war, and the leaders causes of troubles; but this organization gives them arms useful for war, and leaders who will extinguish troubles; for as soon as some one is injured in that country, he has recourse to his (leader) of the party, who, to maintain his reputation, advises him to avenge himself, (and) not to remain in peace. The public leader does the contrary. So that by this means, the causes for trouble are removed, and replaced by those for union; and provinces which are united but effeminate (unwarlike) lose their usefulness but maintain the union, while those that are disunited and troublesome remain united; and that disordinate ferocity which they usually employ, is turned to public usefulness.

As to desiring that they do us injury against others, it should be kept in mind that they cannot do this except by the leaders who govern them. In desiring that the leaders do not cause disorders, it is necessary to have care that they do not acquire too much authority over them. And you have to keep in mind that this authority is acquired either naturally or by accident: And as to nature, it must be provided that whoever is born in one place is not put in charge of men enrolled in another place, but is made a leader in those places where he does not have any natural connections. As to accidents, the organization should be such that each year the leaders are exchanged from command to command; for continuous authority over the same men generates so much unity among them, which can easily be converted into prejudice against the Prince. As to these exchanges being useful to those who have employed them, and injurious to those who have not observed them, is known from the example of the Kingdom of Assyria and from the Empire of the Romans, in which it is seen that the former Kingdom endured a thousand years without tumult and without civil war; which did not result from anything else than the exchanges of those Captains, who were placed in charge of the care of the armies, from place to place every year. Nor, for other reasons, (did it result) in the Roman Empire; once the blood (race) of Caesar was extinguished, so many civil wars arose among the Captains of the armies, and so many conspiracies of the above mentioned Captains against the Emperors, resulting from the continuing of those Captains in their same Commands. And if any of those Emperors, and any who later held the Empire by reputation, such as Hadrian, Marcus, Severus, and others like them, would have observed such happenings, and would have introduced this custom of exchanging Captains in that Empire, without doubt they would have made it more tranquil and lasting; for the Captains would have had fewer opportunities for creating tumults, and the Emperors fewer causes to fear them, and the Senate, when there was a lack in the succession, would have had more authority in the election of Emperors, and consequently, better conditions would have resulted. But the bad customs of men, whether from ignorance or little diligence, or from examples of good or bad, are never put aside.

COSIMO: I do not know if, with my question, I have gone outside the limits you set; for from the Deletto we have entered into another discussion, and if I should not be excused a little, I shall believe I merit some reproach.

FABRIZIO: This did us no harm; for all this discussion was necessary in wanting to discuss the Organization (of an Army), which, being censured by many, it was necessary to explain it, if it is desired that this should take place before the Deletto. And before I discuss the other parts, I want to discuss the Deletto for men on horseback. This (selection) was done by the ancients from among the more wealthy, having regard both for the age and quality of the men, selecting three hundred for each legion: so that the Roman cavalry in every Consular army did not exceed six hundred.

COSIMO: Did you organize the cavalry in order to train them at home and avail yourself of them in the future?

FABRIZIO: Actually it is a necessity and cannot be done otherwise, if you want to have them take up arms for you, and not to want to take them away from those who make a profession of them.

COSIMO: How would you select them?

FABRIZIO: I would imitate the Romans: I would take the more wealthy, and give them leaders in the same manner as they are given to others today, and I would arm them, and train them.

COSIMO: Would it be well to give these men some provision?

FABRIZIO: Yes, indeed: but only as much as is necessary to take care of the horse; for, as it brings an expense to your subjects, they could complain of you. It would be necessary, therefore, to pay them for the horse and its upkeep.

COSIMO: How many would you make? How would you arm them?

FABRIZIO: You pass into another discussion. I will tell you in its place, which will be when I have said how the infantry ought to be armed, and how they should prepare for an engagement.

Libro Primo

LIBRO PRIMO

Perchè io credo che si possa lodare dopo la morte ogni uomo, senza carico, sendo mancata ogni cagione e sospetto di adulazione, non dubiterò di lodare Cosimo Rucellai nostro, il nome del quale non fia mai ricordato da me senza lagrime, avendo conosciute in lui quelle parti le quali, in uno buono amico dagli amici, in uno cittadino dalla sua patria si possono disiderare. Perchè io non so quale cosa si fusse tanto sua, non eccettuando, non ch'altro, l'anima) che per gli amici volentieri da lui non fusse stata spesa; non so quale impresa lo avesse sbigottito, dove quello avesse conosciuto il bene della sua patria. Ed io confesso, liberamente, non avere riscontro, tra tanti uomini che io ho conosciuti e pratichi, uomo nel quale fusse il più acceso animo alle cose grandi e magnifiche. Nè si dolse con gli amici d'altro, nella sua morte, se non di essere nato per morire giovane dentro alle sue case e inonorato, senza avere potuto secondo l'animo suo giovare ad alcuno perchè sapeva che di lui non si poteva parlare altro, se non che fusse morto un buono amico. Non resta però per questo, che noi, e qualunque altro che come noi lo conosceva, non possiamo fare fede, poichè l'opere non appariscono, delle sue lodevoli qualità. Vero è che non gli fu però in tanto la fortuna nemica, che non lasciasse alcun breve ricordo della destrezza del suo ingegno, come ne dimostrano alcuni suoi scritti e composizioni di amorosi versi, ne' quali, come che innamorato non fusse, per non consumare il tempo invano, tanto che a più alti pensieri la fortuna lo avesse condotto, nella sua giovanile età si esercitava. Dove chiaramente si può comprendere con quanta felicità i suoi concetti descrivesse, e quanto nella poetica si fusse onorato, se quella, per suo fine fusse da lui stata esercitata. Avendone pertanto privati la fortuna dello uso d'uno tanto amico, mi pare che non si possa farne altri rimedi che, il più che a noi è possibile cercare, di godersi la memoria di quello e repetere se da lui alcuna cosa fusse stata o acutamente detta o saviamente disputata. E perchè non è cosa di lui più fresca, che il ragionamento il quale ne' prossimi tempi il signore Fabrizio Colonna dentro a' suoi orti ebbe con seco, dove largamente fu da quel signore delle cose della guerra disputato, e acutamente e prudentemente in buona parte da Cosimo domandato,; mi è parso, essendo con alcuni altri nostri amici stato presente, ridurlo alla memoria, acciò che, leggendo quello, gli amici di Cosimo che quivi convennono, nel loro animo la memoria delle sue virtù rinfreschino, e gli altri, parte si dolgano di non vi essere intervenuti, parte molte cose utili alla vita non solamente militare, ma ancora civile, saviamente da uno sapientissimo uomo disputate, imparino.

Dico pertanto che, tornando Fabrizio Colonna di Lombardia, dove più tempo aveva per il Re cattolico con grande sua gloria militato, deliberò, passando per Firenze, riposarsi alcun giorno in quella città, per visitare l'Eccellenza del Duca e rivedere alcuni gentili uomini co' quali per lo addietro aveva tenuto qualche familiarità. Donde che a Cosimo parve convitarlo ne' suoi orti, non tanto per usare la sua liberalità quanto per avere cagione di parlar seco lungamente, e da quello intendere ed imparare varie cose, secondo che da un tale uomo si può sperare, parendogli avere occasione di spendere uno giorno in ragionare di quelle materie che allo animo suo sodisfacevano. Venne adunque Fabrizio, secondo che quello volle, e da Cosimo insieme con alcuni altri suoi fidati amici fu ricevuto, tra' quali furono Zanobi Buondelmonti, Batista della Palla e Luigi Alamanni, giovani tutti amati da lui e de' medesimi studi ardentissimi, le buone qualità de' quali, perchè ogni giorno e ad ogni ora per se medesime si lodano, ommettereno. Fabrizio adunque fu, secondo i tempi e il luogo, di tutti quegli onori che si poterono maggiori onorato; ma passati i convivali piaceri e levate le tavole e consumato ogni ordine di festeggiare, il quale, nel conspetto degli uomini grandi e che a pensieri onorevoli abbiano la mente volta si consuma tosto, essendo il dì lungo e il caldo molto, giudicò Cosimo, per sodisfare meglio al suo disiderio, che fusse bene, pigliando l'occasione dal fuggire il caldo, condursi nella più segreta e ombrosa parte del suo giardino. Dove pervenuti e posti a sedere, chi sopra all'erba che in quel luogo è freschissima, chi sopra a sedili in quelle parti ordinati sotto l'ombra d'altissimi arbori, lodò Fabrizio il luogo come dilettevole; e considerando particolarmente gli arbori e alcuno di essi non ricognoscendo stava con l'animo sopeso. Della qual cosa accortosi Cosimo, disse: Voi per avventura non avete notizia di parte di questi arbori; ma non ve ne maravigliate, perchè ce ne sono alcuni più dagli antichi, che oggi dal comune uso celebrati. E dettogli il nome di essi, e come Bernardo suo avolo in tale cultura si era affaticato, replicò Fabrizio: Io pensava che fusse quello che voi dite e questo luogo e questo studio mi faceva ricordare d'alcuni principi del Regno, i quali di queste antiche culture e ombre si dilettano. E fermato in su questo il parlare e stato alquanto sopra di se come sospeso, soggiunse: Se io non credessi offendere, io ne direi la mia opinione; ma io non lo credo fare, parlando con gli amici, e per disputare le cose e non per calunniarle. Quanto meglio avrebbono fatto quelli, sia detto con pace di tutti, a cercare di somigliare gli antichi nelle cose forti e aspre, non nelle delicate e molli, e in quelle che facevano sotto il sole, non sotto l'ombra, e pigliare i modi della antichità vera e perfetta, non quelli della falsa e corrotta; perchè, poichè questi studi piacquero ai miei Romani, la mia patria rovinò. A che Cosimo rispose: ma per fuggire il fastidio d'avere a ripigliare tante volte quel disse, e quello altro soggiunse, si noteranno solamente i nomi di chi parli, senza replicarne altro. Disse dunque.

COSIMO: Voi avete aperto la via a uno ragionamento quale io desiderava, e vi priego che voi parliate senza rispetto, perchè io senza rispetto vi domanderò; e se io, domandando o replicando, scuserò o accuserò alcuno, non sarà per scusare o per accusare, ma per intendere da voi la verità.

FABRIZIO: Ed io sarò molto contento di dirvi quel che io intenderò di tutto quello mi domanderete; il che se sarà vero o no, me ne rapporterò al vostro giudicio. E mi sarà grato mi domandiate; perchè io sono per imparare così da voi nel domandarmi, come voi da me nel rispondervi; perchè molte volte uno savio domandatore fa a uno considerare molte cose e conoscerne molte altre, le quali, senza esserne domandato, non avrebbe mai conosciute.

COSIMO: Io voglio tornare a quello che voi diceste prima: che l'avolo mio e quegli vostri avrebbero fatto più saviamente a somigliar gli antichi nelle cose aspre che nelle delicate; e voglio scusare la parte mia, perchè l'altra lascerò scusare a voi. Io non credo ch'egli fusse, ne' tempi suoi, uomo che tanto detestasse il vivere molle quanto egli, e che tanto fusse amatore di quella asprezza di vita che voi lodate; nondimeno e' conosceva non potere nella persona sua, nè in quella de' suoi figliuoli, usarla, essendo nato in tanta corruttela di secolo, dove uno che si volesse partire dal comune uso, sarebbe infame e vilipeso da ciascheduno. Perchè se uno ignudo, di state, sotto il più alto sole si rivoltasse sopr'alla rena, o di verno ne' più gelati mesi sopra alla neve, come faceva Diogene, sarebbe tenuto pazzo. Se uno, come gli Spartani, nutrisse i suoi figliuoli in villa, facessegli dormire al sereno, andare col capo e co' piedi ignudi, lavare nell'acqua fredda per indurgli a poter sopportare il male e per fare loro amare meno la vita e temere meno la morte, sarebbe schernito e tenuto piuttosto una fiera che uno uomo. Se fusse ancora veduto uno nutrirsi di legumi e spregiare l'oro, come Fabrizio, sarebbe lodato da pochi e seguito da niuno. Tal che, sbigottito da questi modi del vivere presente, egli lasciò gli antichi, e in quello che potè con minore ammirazione imitare l'antichità, lo fece.

FABRIZIO: Voi lo avete scusato in questa parte gagliardamente, e certo voi dite il vero; ma io non parlava tanto di questi modi di vivere duri, quanto di altri modi più umani e che hanno con la vita d'oggi maggiore conformità; i quali io non credo che ad uno che sia numerato tra' principi d'una città, fusse stato difficile introdurgli. Io non mi partirò mai, con lo esemplo di qualunque cosa, da' miei Romani. Se si considerasse la vita di quegli e l'ordine di quella repubblica, si vedrebbero molte cose in essa non impossibili ad introdurre in una civilità dove fusse qualche cosa ancora del buono.

COSIMO: Quali cose sono quelle che voi vorreste introdurre simili all'antiche?

FABRIZIO: Onorare e premiare le virtù, non dispregiare la povertà, stimare i modi e gli ordini della disciplina militare, constringere i cittadini ad amare l'uno l'altro, a vivere senza sette, a stimare meno il privato che il pubblico, e altre simili cose che facilmente si potrebbono con questi tempi accompagnare. I quali modi non sono difficili persuadere, quando vi si pensa assai ed entrasi per li debiti mezzi, perchè in essi appare tanto la verità, che ogni comunale ingegno ne puote essere capace; la quale cosa chi ordina, planta arbori sotto l'ombra de' quali si dimora più felice e più lieto che sotto questa.

COSIMO: Io non voglio replicare, a quello che voi avete detto, alcuna cosa, ma ne voglio lasciare dare giudicio a questi, i quali facilmente ne possono giudicare; e volgerò il mio parlare a voi, che siete accusatore di coloro che nelle gravi e grandi azioni non sono degli antichi imitatori, pensando, per questa via, più facilmente essere nella mia intenzione sodisfatto. Vorrei pertanto sapere da voi, donde nasce che dall'un canto voi danniate quegli che nelle azioni loro gli antichi non somigliano; dall'altro, nella guerra, la quale è l'arte vostra e in quella che voi siete giudicato eccellente, non si vede che voi abbiate usato alcuno termine antico, o che a quegli alcuna similitudine renda.

FABRIZIO: Voi siete capitato appunto dove io vi aspettava, perchè il parlare mio non meritava altra domanda, nè io altra ne desiderava. E benchè io mi potessi salvare con una facile scusa, nondimeno voglio entrare, a più sodisfazione mia e vostra, poichè la stagione lo comporta, in più lungo ragionamento. Gli uomini che vogliono fare una cosa, deono prima con ogni industria prepararsi, per essere, venendo l'occasione, apparecchiati a sodisfare a quello che si hanno presupposto di operare. E perchè, quando le preparazioni sono fatte cautamente elle non si conoscono, non si può accusare alcuno d'alcuna negligenza, se prima non è scoperto dalla occasione; nella quale poi, non operando, si vede o che non si è preparato tanto che basti, o che non vi ha in alcuna parte pensato. E perchè a me non è venuta occasione alcuna di potere mostrare i preparamenti da me fatti per potere ridurre la milizia negli antichi suoi ordini, se io non la ho ridotta, non ne posso essere da voi nè da altri incolpato. Io credo che questa scusa basterebbe per risposta all'accusa vostra.

COSIMO: Basterebbe, quando io fussi certo che l'occasione non fusse venuta.

FABRIZIO: Ma perchè io so che voi potete dubitare se questa occasione è venuta o no, voglio io largamente, quando voi vogliate con pazienza ascoltarmi discorrere quali preparamenti sono necessarii prima fare, quale occasione bisogna nasca, quale difficultà impedisce che i preparamenti non giovano e che l'occasione non venga; e come questa cosa a un tratto, che paiono termini contrarii, è difficilissima e facilissima a fare.

COSIMO: Voi non potete fare, e a me e a questi altri, cosa più grata di questa; e se a voi non rincrescerà il parlare, mai a noi non rincrescerà l'udire. Ma perchè questo ragionamento debbe esser lungo, io voglio aiuto da questi miei amici con licenza vostra; e loro ed io vi preghiamo d'una cosa che voi non pigliate fastidio se qualche volta, con qualche domanda importuna, vi interromperemo.

FABRIZIO: Io sono contentissimo che voi, Cosimo, con questi altri giovani qui mi domandiate, perchè io credo che la gioventù vi faccia più amici delle cose militari e più facili a credere quello che da me si dirà. Questi altri, per aver già il capo bianco e avere i sangui ghiacciati addosso, parte sogliono essere nimici della guerra, parte incorreggibili, come quegli che credono che i tempi e non i cattivi modi costringano gli uomini a vivere così. Sì che domandatemi tutti voi sicuramente e senza rispetto; il che io disidero, sì perchè mi fia un poco di riposo, sì perchè io arò piacere non lasciare nella mente vostra alcuna dubitazione. Io mi voglio cominciare dalle parole vostre, dove voi mi diceste che nella guerra, che è l'arte mia, io non aveva usato alcun termine antico. Sopra a che dico come, essendo questa una arte mediante la quale gli uomini d'ogni tempo non possono vivere onestamente, non la può usare per arte se non una repubblica o uno regno; e l'uno e l'altro di questi, quando sia bene ordinato, mai non consentì ad alcuno suo cittadino o suddito usarla per arte; nè mai alcuno uomo buono l'esercitò per sua particulare arte. Perchè buono non sarà mai giudicato colui che faccia uno esercizio che, a volere d'ogni tempo trarne utilità, gli convenga essere rapace, fraudolento, violento e avere molte qualitadi le quali di necessità lo facciano non buono; nè possono gli uomini che l'usano per arte, così i grandi come i minimi, essere fatti altrimenti, perchè questa arte non gli nutrisce nella pace; donde che sono necessitati o pensare che non sia pace, o tanto prevalersi ne' tempi della guerra, che possano nella pace nutrirsi. E qualunque l'uno di questi due pensieri non cape in uno uomo buono; perchè dal volersi potere nutrire d'ogni tempo, nascono le ruberie, le violenze, gli assassinamenti che tali soldati fanno così agli amici come a' nimici; e dal non volere la pace nascono gli inganni che i capitani fanno a quegli che gli conducono, perchè la guerra duri; e se pure la pace viene, spesso occorre che i capi, sendo privi degli stipendi e del vivere, licenziosamente rizzano una bandiera di ventura e senza alcuna piatà saccheggiano una provincia. Non avete voi nella memoria delle cose vostre come, trovandosi assai soldati in Italia senza soldo per essere finite le guerre, si ragunarono insieme più brigate, le quali si chiamarono Compagnie, e andavano taglieggiando le terre e saccheggiando il paese, senza che vi si potesse fare alcuno rimedio? Non avete voi letto che i soldati cartaginesi, finita la prima guerra ch'egli ebbero co' Romani, sotto Mato e Spendio, due capi fatti tumultuariamente da loro, ferono più pericolosa guerra a' Cartaginesi che quella che loro avevano finita co' Romani? Ne' tempi de' padri nostri, Francesco Sforza, per potere vivere onorevolmente ne' tempi della pace, non solamente ingannò i Milanesi de' quali era soldato, ma tolse loro la libertà e divenne loro principe. Simili a costui sono stati tutti gli altri soldati di Italia, che hanno usata la milizia per loro particolare arte; e se non sono, mediante le loro malignitadi, diventati Duchi di Milano, tanto più meritano di essere biasimati, perchè senza tanto utile hanno tutti, se si vedesse la vita loro, i medesimi carichi. Sforza, padre di Francesco, costrinse la reina Giovanna a gittarsi nelle braccia del Re di Ragona, avendola in un subito abbandonata e in mezzo a' suoi nimici lasciatala disarmata, solo per sfogare l'ambizione sua o di taglieggiarla o di torle il regno. Braccio, con le medesime industrie, cercò di occupare il regno di Napoli, e se non era rotto e morto a l'Aquila, gli riusciva. Simili disordini non nascono da altro che da essere stati uomini che usavano lo esercizio del soldo per loro propria arte. Non avete voi uno proverbio il quale fortifica le mie ragioni, che dice: «La guerra fa i ladri, e la pace gl'impicca?». Perchè quegli che non sanno vivere d'altro esercizio, e in quello non trovando chi gli sovvenga e non avendo tanta virtù che sappiano ridursi insieme a fare una cattività onorevole, sono forzati dalla necessità rompere la strada, e la giustizia è forzata spegnerli.

COSIMO: Voi m'avete fatto tornare questa arte del soldo quasi che nulla, ed io me la aveva presupposta la più eccellente e la più onorevole che si facesse; in modo che, se voi non me la dichiarate meglio, io non resto sodisfatto, perchè, quando sia quello che voi dite, io non so donde si nasca la gloria di Cesare, di Pompeo, di Scipione, di Marcello, e di tanti capitani romani che sono per fama celebrati come dii.

FABRIZIO: Io non ho ancora finito di disputare tutto quello che io proposi, che furono due cose: l'una, che uno uomo buono non poteva usare questo esercizio per sua arte; l'altra, che una repubblica o uno regno bene ordinato non permesse mai che i suoi suggetti o i suoi cittadini la usassono per arte. Circa la prima ho parlato quanto mi è occorso, restami a parlare della seconda, dove io verrò a rispondere a questa ultima domanda vostra, e dico che Pompeo e Cesare, e quasi tutti quegli capitani che furono a Roma dopo l'ultima guerra cartaginese, acquistarono fama come valenti uomini, non come buoni; e quegli che erano vivuti avanti a loro, acquistarono gloria come valenti e buoni. Il che nacque perchè questi non presero lo esercizio della guerra per loro arte, e quegli che io nominai prima, come loro arte la usarono. E in mentre che la repubblica visse immaculata, mai alcuno cittadino grande non presunse, mediante tale esercizio, valersi nella pace, rompendo le leggi, spogliando le provincie, usurpando e tiranneggiando la patria e in ogni modo prevalendosi; nè alcuno d'infima fortuna pensò di violare il sacramento, aderirsi agli uomini privati, non temere il senato, o seguire alcuno tirannico insulto per potere vivere, con l'arte della guerra, d'ogni tempo. Ma quegli che erano capitani, contenti del trionfo, con disiderio tornavono alla vita privata; e quelli che erano membri, con maggior voglia deponevano le armi che non le pigliavano; e ciascuno tornava all'arte sua mediante la quale si aveva ordinata la vita; nè vi fu mai alcuno che sperasse con le prede e con questa arte potersi nutrire. Di questo se ne può fare, quanto a' cittadini grandi, evidente coniettura mediante Regolo Attilio, il quale, sendo capitano degli eserciti romani in Affrica e avendo quasi che vinti i Cartaginesi, domandò al senato licenza di ritornarsi a casa a custodire i suoi poderi che gli erano guasti dai suoi lavoratori. Donde è più chiaro che il sole, che, se quello avesse usata la guerra come sua arte e, mediante quella, avesse pensato farsi utile, avendo in preda tante provincie, non avrebbe domandato licenza per tornare a custodire i suoi campi; perchè ciascuno giorno avrebbe molto più, che non era il prezzo di tutti quegli, acquistato. Ma perchè questi uomini buoni, e che non usano la guerra per loro arte, non vogliono trarre di quella se non fatica, pericoli e gloria, quando e' sono a sufficienza gloriosi disiderano tornarsi a casa e vivere dell'arte loro. Quanto agli uomini bassi e soldati gregarii, che sia vero che tenessono il medesimo ordine apparisce, che ciascuno volentieri si discostava da tale esercizio e, quando non militava, avrebbe voluto militare e, quando militava, avrebbe voluto essere licenziato. Il che si riscontra per molti modi, e massime vedendo come, tra' primi privilegi che dava il popolo romano a un suo cittadino, era che non fusse constretto fuora di sua volontà a militare. Roma pertanto, mentre ch'ella fu bene ordinata, che fu infino a' Gracchi, non ebbe alcuno soldato che pigliasse questo esercizio per arte; e però ne ebbe pochi cattivi, e quelli tanti furono severamente puniti. Debbe adunque una città bene ordinata volere che questo studio di guerra si usi ne' tempi di pace per esercizio e ne' tempi di guerra per necessità e gloria; ed al pubblico solo lasciarla usare per arte, come fece Roma. E qualunque cittadino che ha in tale esercizio altro fine, non è buono; e qualunque città si governa altrimenti, non è bene ordinata.

COSIMO: Io resto contento assai e sodisfatto di quello che insino a qui avete detto, e piacemi assai questa conclusione che voi avete fatta; e quanto si aspetta alla repubblica, io credo ch'ella sia vera; ma quanto ai re, non so già, perchè io crederrei che uno Re volesse avere intorno chi particolarmente prendesse, per arte sua, tale esercizio.

FABRIZIO: Tantopiù debbe uno regno bene ordinato fuggire simili artefici, perchè solo essi sono la corruttela del suo Re e, in tutto, ministri della tirannide. E non mi allegate all'incontro alcuno regno presente, perchè io vi negherò quelli essere regni bene ordinati. Perchè i regni che hanno buoni ordini, non danno lo imperio assoluto agli loro Re se non nelli eserciti; perchè in questo luogo solo è necessaria una subita deliberazione e, per questo, che vi sia una unica podestà. Nell'altre cose non può fare alcuna cosa senza consiglio; e hanno a temere, quegli che lo consigliano, che gli abbi alcuno appresso che ne' tempi di pace disideri la guerra, per non potere senza essa vivere. Ma io voglio in questo essere un poco più largo, nè ricercare uno regno al tutto buono, ma simile a quegli che sono oggi; dove ancora da' Re deono esser temuti quegli che prendono per loro arte la guerra, perchè il nervo degli eserciti, senza alcun dubbio, sono le fanterie. Tal che, se uno Re non si ordina in modo che i suoi fanti a tempo di pace stieno contenti tornarsi a casa e vivere delle loro arti, conviene di necessità che rovini; perchè non si truova la più pericolosa fanteria che quella che è composta di coloro che fanno la guerra come per loro arte, perchè tu sei forzato o a fare sempre mai guerra, o a pagarli sempre, o a portare pericolo che non ti tolgano il regno. Fare guerra sempre non è possibile; pagargli sempre non si può; ecco che di necessità si corre ne' pericoli di perdere lo stato. I miei Romani, come ho detto, mentre che furono savi e buoni, mai non permessero che i loro cittadini pigliassono questo esercizio per loro arte, non ostante che potessono nutrirgli d'ogni tempo, perchè d'ogni tempo fecero guerra. Ma per fuggire quel danno che poteva fare loro questo continuo esercizio, poichè il tempo non variava, ei variavano gli uomini, e andavano temporeggiando in modo con le loro legioni, che in quindici anni sempre l'avevano rinnovate; e così si valevano degli uomini nel fiore della loro età, che è da diciotto a' trentacinque anni, nel qual tempo le gambe, le mani e l'occhio rispondevano l'uno all'altro; nè aspettavano che in loro scemasse le forze e crescesse la malizia, com'ella fece poi ne' tempi corrotti. Perchè Ottaviano, prima, e poi Tiberio, pensando più alla potenza propria che all'utile pubblico, cominciarono a disarmare il popolo romano per poterlo più facilmente comandare, e a tenere continuamente quegli medesimi eserciti alle frontiere dello Imperio. E perchè ancora non giudicarono bastassero a tenere in freno il popolo e senato romano, ordinarono uno esercito chiamato Pretoriano, il quale stava propinquo alle mura di Roma ed era come una rocca addosso a quella città. E perchè allora ei cominciarono liberamente a permettere che gli uomini deputati in quelli eserciti usassero la milizia per loro arte, ne nacque subito la insolenza di quegli, e diventarono formidabili al senato e dannosi allo imperadore; donde ne risultò che molti ne furono morti dalla insolenza loro, perchè davano e toglievano l'imperio a chi pareva loro; e talvolta occorse che in uno medesimo tempo erano molti imperadori creati da varii eserciti. Dalle quali cose procedè, prima, la divisione dello Imperio e, in ultimo, la rovina di quello. Deggiono pertanto i re, se vogliono vivere sicuri, avere le loro fanterie composte di uomini che, quando egli è tempo di fare guerra, volentieri per suo amore vadano a quella, e, quando viene poi la pace, più volentieri se ne ritornino a casa. Il che sempre fia, quando egli scerrà uomini che sappiano vivere d'altra arte che di questa. E così debbe volere, venuta la pace, che i suoi principi tornino a governare i loro popoli, i gentili uomini al culto delle loro possessioni, e i fanti alla loro particolare arte: e ciascuno d'essi faccia volentieri la guerra per avere pace, e non cerchi turbare la pace per avere guerra.

COSIMO: Veramente questo vostro ragionamento mi pare bene considerato; nondimeno, sendo quasi che contrario a quello che io insino a ora ne ho pensato, non mi resta ancora l'animo purgato d'ogni dubbio; perchè io veggo assai signori e gentili uomini nutrirsi a tempo di pace mediante gli studii della guerra, come sono i pari vostri che hanno provvisioni dai principi e dalle comunità. Veggo ancora quasi tutti gli uomini d'arme rimanere con le provvisioni loro; veggo assai fanti restare nelle guardie delle città e delle fortezze, tale che mi pare che ci sia luogo, a tempo di pace, per ciascuno.

FABRIZIO: Io non credo che voi crediate questo, che a tempo di pace ciascheduno abbia luogo; perchè, posto che non se ne potesse addurre altra ragione, il poco numero che fanno tutti coloro che rimangono ne' luoghi allegati da voi, vi risponderebbe: che proporzione hanno le fanterie che bisognano nella guerra, con quelle che nella pace si adoperano? Perchè le fortezze e le città che si guardano a tempo di pace, nella guerra si guardano molto più; a che si aggiungono i soldati che si tengono in campagna, che sono un numero grande, i quali tutti nella pace si abbandonano. E circa le guardie degli stati, che sono uno piccolo numero, papa Iulio e voi avete mostro a ciascuno quanto sia da temere quegli che non vogliono sapere fare altra arte che la guerra; e gli avete per la insolenza loro privi delle vostre guardie e postovi Svizzeri, come nati e allevati sotto le leggi e eletti dalle comunità, secondo la vera elezione; sì che non dite più che nella pace sia luogo per ogni uomo. Quanto alle genti d'arme rimanendo quelle nella pace tutte con li loro soldi, pare questa soluzione più difficile; nondimeno, chi considera bene tutto, truova la risposta facile, perchè questo modo del tenere le genti d'arme è modo corrotto e non buono. La cagione è perchè sono uomini che ne fanno arte, e da loro nascerebbe ogni dì mille inconvenienti nelli stati dove ei fussono, se fussero accompagnati da compagnia sufficiente, ma sendo pochi e non potendo per loro medesimi fare un esercito, non possono fare così spesso danni gravi. Nondimeno ne hanno fatti assai volte, come io vi dissi di Francesco e di Sforza, suo padre e di Braccio da Perugia. Sì che questa usanza di tenere le genti d'arme, io non la appruovo, ed è corrotta e può fare inconvenienti grandi.

COSIMO: Vorreste voi fare senza? o, tenendone, come le vorreste tenere?

FABRIZIO: Per via d'ordinanza; non simile a quella del Re di Francia, perch'ella è pericolosa ed insolente come la nostra, ma simile a quelle degli antichi; i quali creavano la cavalleria di sudditi loro, e ne' tempi di pace gli mandavano alle case loro a vivere delle loro arti, come più largamente, prima finisca questo ragionamento, disputerò. Sì che, se ora questa parte di esercito può vivere in tale esercizio, ancora quando sia pace, nasce dall'ordine corrotto. Quanto alle provvisioni che si riserbano a me e agli altri capi, vi dico che questo medesimamente è uno ordine corrottissimo; perchè una savia repubblica non le debbe dare ad alcuno; anzi debbe operare per capi, nella guerra, i suoi cittadini e, a tempo di pace, volere che ritornino all'arte loro. Così ancora uno savio Re o e' non le debbe dare o, dandole, debbono essere le cagioni: o per premio d'alcuno egregio fatto, o per volersi valere di un uomo così nella pace come nella guerra. E perchè voi allegaste me, io voglio esemplificare sopra di me; e dico non aver mai usata la guerra per arte, perchè l'arte mia è governare i miei sudditi e defendergli, e per potergli defendere, amare la pace e saper fare la guerra. Ed il mio Re non tanto mi premia e stima per intendermi io della guerra, quanto per sapere io ancora consigliarlo nella pace. Non debbe adunque alcuno Re volere appresso di se alcuno, che non sia così fatto s'egli è savio e prudentemente si voglia governare; perchè, s'egli arà intorno, o troppi amatori della pace, o troppi amatori della guerra, lo faranno errare. Io non vi posso, in questo mio primo ragionamento e secondo le proposte mie, dire altro; e quando questo non vi basti, conviene cerchiate di chi vi sodisfaccia meglio. Potete bene avere cominciato a conoscere quanta difficultà sia ridurre i modi antichi nelle presenti guerre, e quali preparazioni ad uno uomo savio conviene fare, e quali occasioni si possa sperare a poterle esequire; ma voi di mano in mano conoscerete queste cose meglio, quando non vi infastidisca il ragionamento, conferendo qualunque parte degli antichi ordini ai modi presenti.

COSIMO: Se noi desideravamo prima di udirvi ragionare di queste cose, veramente quello che infino ad ora ne avete detto, ne ha raddoppiato il disiderio; pertanto noi vi ringraziamo di quel che noi avemo avuto, e il restante vi domandiamo.

FABRIZIO: Poichè così vi è in piacere, io voglio cominciare a trattare questa materia da principio, acciò meglio s'intenda, potendosi per quel modo più largamente dimostrare. Il fine di chi vuole fare guerra è potere combattere con ogni nimico alla campagna e potere vincere una giornata. A volere far questo, conviene ordinare uno esercito. A ordinare lo esercito, bisogna trovare gli uomini, armargli, ordinargli, e ne' piccoli e ne' grossi ordini esercitargli, alloggiargli, e al nimico dipoi, o stando o camminando, rappresentargli. In queste cose consiste tutta la industria della guerra campale, che è la più necessaria e la più onorata. E chi sa bene presentare al nimico una giornata, gli altri errori che facesse ne' maneggi della guerra sarebbono sopportabili; ma chi manca di questa disciplina, ancora che negli altri particolari valesse assai, non condurrà mai una guerra a onore; perchè una giornata che tu vinca, cancella ogni altra tua mala azione; così medesimamente, perdendola, restono vane tutte le cose bene da te avanti operate. Sendo pertanto necessario prima trovare gli uomini, conviene venire al Deletto di essi, chè così lo chiamavano gli antichi; il che noi diremmo scelta, ma, per chiamarlo per nome più onorato, io voglio gli serviamo il nome del Deletto. Vogliono coloro che alla guerra hanno dato regole, che si eleggano gli uomini de' paesi temperati, acciò ch'egli abbino animo e prudenza; perchè il paese caldo gli genera prudenti e non animosi, il freddo animosi e non prudenti. Questa regola è bene data a uno che sia principe di tutto il mondo e, per questo, gli sia lecito trarre gli uomini di quegli luoghi che a lui verrà bene; ma volendo darne una regola che ciascun possa usarla, conviene dire che ogni repubblica e ogni regno debbe scerre i soldati de' paesi suoi, o caldi o freddi o temperati che si sieno. Per che si vede, per gli antichi esempli, come in ogni paese con lo esercizio si fa buoni soldati; perchè, dove manca la natura, sopperisce la 'ndustria, la quale in questo caso vale più che la natura. Ed eleggendogli in altri luoghi, non si può chiamare Deletto, perchè Deletto vuol dire torre i migliori d'una provincia e avere potestà di eleggere quegli che non vogliono, come quegli che vogliono, militare. Non si può pertanto fare questo Deletto se non ne' luoghi a te sottoposti, perchè tu non puoi torre chi tu vuoi ne' paesi che non sono tuoi, ma ti bisogna prendere quelli che vogliono.

COSIMO: E' si può pure di quelli che voglion venire, torne e lasciarne; e per questo si può chiamare Deletto.

FABRIZIO: Voi dite il vero in uno certo modo; ma considerate i difetti che ha tale Deletto in se, perchè ancora molte volte occorre che non è Deletto. La prima cosa: quegli che non sono tuoi sudditi e che voluntarii militano, non sono de' migliori, anzi sono de' più cattivi d'una provincia; perchè se alcuni vi sono scandolosi, oziosi, senza freno, senza religione, fuggitisi dallo imperio del padre, bestemmiatori, giucatori, in ogni parte male nutriti, sono quegli che vogliono militare; i quali costumi non possono essere più contrarii a una vera e buona milizia. Quando di tali uomini ti se ne offerisce tanti che te ne avanzi al numero che tu hai disegnato, tu puoi eleggergli; ma, sendo la materia cattiva, non è possibile che il Deletto sia buono. Ma molte volte interviene che non sono tanti ch'egli adempino il numero di che tu hai bisogno; tal che, sendo forzato prendergli tutti, ne nasce che non si può chiamare più fare Deletto ma soldare fanti. Con questo disordine si fanno oggi gli eserciti in Italia e altrove eccetto che nella Magna, perchè non si solda alcuno per comandamento del principe, ma secondo la volontà di chi vuole militare. Pensate adunque ora voi che modi di quegli antichi eserciti si possano introdurre in uno esercito di uomini messi insieme per simile via.

COSIMO: Quale via si avrebbe a tenere adunque?

FABRIZIO: Quella che io dissi: scergli di suoi suggetti e con l'autorità del principe.

COSIMO: Negli scelti così introdurrebbesi alcuna antica forma?

FABRIZIO: Ben sapete che sì, quando chi li comandasse fusse loro principe o signore ordinario, quando fusse principato, o come cittadino e, per quel tempo, capitano, sendo una repubblica; altrimenti è difficile fare cosa di buono.

COSIMO: Perchè?

FABRIZIO: Io vel dirò al tempo; per ora voglio vi basti questo: che non si può operare bene per altra via.

COSIMO: Avendosi adunque a far questo Deletto ne' suoi paesi, donde giudicate voi sia meglio trarli, o della città o del contado?

FABRIZIO: Questi che ne hanno scritto, tutti s'accordano che sia meglio eleggergli del contado, sendo uomini avvezzi a' disagi, nutriti nelle fatiche, consueti stare al sole, fuggire l'ombra, sapere adoperare il ferro, cavare una fossa, portare un peso, ed essere senza astuzia e senza malizia. Ma in questa parte l'opinione mia sarebbe che, sendo di due ragioni soldati, a piè e a cavallo, che si eleggessero quegli a piè del contado e gli a cavallo delle cittadi.

COSIMO: Di quale età gli torreste voi?

FABRIZIO: Torreigli, quando io avessi a fare nuova milizia, da diciassette a quaranta anni; quando la fusse fatta ed io l'avessi a instaurare, di diciassette, sempre.

COSIMO: Io non intendo bene questa distinzione.

FABRIZIO: Dirovvi. Quando io avessi a ordinare una milizia dov'ella non fusse, sarebbe necessario eleggere tutti quegli uomini che fussero più atti, pure che fussero di età militare, per potergli instruire, come per me si dirà; ma quando io avessi a fare il Deletto ne' luoghi dove fusse ordinata questa milizia, per supplimento di essa gli torrei di diciassette anni, perchè gli altri di più tempo sarebbono scelti e descritti.

COSIMO: Dunque vorreste voi fare una ordinanza simile a quella che è ne' paesi nostri.

FABRIZIO: Voi dite bene. Vero è che io gli armerei, capitanerei, eserciterei e ordinerei in un modo, che io non so se voi gli avete ordinati così.

COSIMO: Dunque lodate voi l'ordinanza?

FABRIZIO: Perchè, volete voi che io la danni?

COSIMO: Perchè molti savi uomini l'hanno sempre biasimata.

FABRIZIO: Voi dite una cosa contraria a dire che un savio biasimi l'ordinanza, ei può bene essere tenuto savio ed essergli fatto torto.

COSIMO: La cattiva pruova ch'ella ha fatto sempre, farà avere per noi tale opinione.

FABRIZIO: Guardate che non sia il difetto vostro, non il suo, il che voi conoscerete prima che si fornisca questo ragionamento.

COSIMO: Voi ne farete cosa gratissima; pure io vi voglio dire in quello che costoro l'accusano, acciò voi possiate meglio giustificarne. Dicono costoro così: o ella fia inutile e fidandoci noi di quella ci farà perdere lo stato; o ella fia virtuosa, e, mediante quella, chi la governa ce lo potrà facilmente torre. Allegano i Romani, i quali, mediante queste armi proprie, perderono la libertà; allegano i Viniziani e il Re di Francia, de' quali quelli, per non avere ad ubbidire a un loro cittadino, usano le armi d'altri, e il Re ha disarmati i suoi popoli per potergli più facilmente comandare. Ma temono più assai la inutilità che questo. Della quale inutilità ne allegano due ragioni principali: una, per essere inesperti, l'altra, per avere a militare per forza; perchè dicano che da grande non si imparano le cose, e a forza non si fece mai nulla bene.

FABRIZIO: Tutte queste ragioni che voi dite, sono da uomini che cognoschino le cose poco discosto, come io apertamente vi mostrerrò. E prima, quanto alla inutilità, io vi dico che non si usa milizia più utile che la propria, nè si può ordinare milizia propria se non in questo modo. E perchè questo non ha disputa, io non ci voglio molto perdere tempo, perchè tutti gli esempj delle istorie antiche fanno per noi. E perchè eglino allegano la inesperienza e la forza, dico come egli è vero che la inesperienza fa poco animo e la forza fa mala contentezza; ma l'animo e l'esperienza si fa guadagnare loro con il modo dello armargli, esercitargli ed ordinargli, come nel procedere di questo ragionamento vedrete. Ma, quanto alla forza, voi avete a intendere che gli uomini che si conducono alla milizia per comandamento del principe, vi hanno a venire nè al tutto forzati, nè al tutto volontarii, perchè tutta la volontà farebbe gli inconvenienti che io dissi di sopra: che non sarebbe Deletto e sarebbono pochi quegli che andassero; e così la tutta forza partorirebbe cattivi effetti. Però si debbe prendere una via di mezzo dove non sia nè tutta forza nè tutta volontà, ma sieno tirati da uno rispetto ch'egli abbiano al principe, dove essi temano più lo sdegno di quello, che la presente pena; e sempre occorrerà ch'ella fia una forza in modo mescolata con la volontà, che non ne potrà nascere tale mala contentezza che faccia mali effetti. Non dico già, per questo, ch'ella non possa essere vinta, perchè furono vinti tante volte gli eserciti romani, e fu vinto lo esercito d'Annibale; tale che si vede che non si può ordinare uno esercito, del quale altri si prometta che non possa essere rotto. Pertanto questi vostri uomini savi non deono misurare questa inutilità dallo avere perduto una volta, ma credere che, così come e' si perde, e' si possa vincere e rimediare alla cagione della perdita. E quando ei cercassero questo, troverebbono che non sarebbe stato per difetto del modo, ma dell'ordine che non aveva la sua perfezione; e, come ho detto, dovevano provvedervi, non con biasimare l'ordinanza, ma con ricorreggerla; il che come si debbe fare, lo intenderete di mano in mano. Quanto al dubitare che tale ordine non ti tolga lo stato mediante uno che se ne faccia capo, rispondo che l'arme in dosso a' suoi cittadini o sudditi, date dalle leggi e dall'ordine, non fecero mai danno, anzi sempre fanno utile e mantengonsi le città più tempo immaculate mediante queste armi, che senza. Stette Roma libera quattrocento anni, ed era armata; Sparta, ottocento; molte altre città sono state disarmate, e sono state libere meno di quaranta. Perchè le città hanno bisogno delle armi; e quando non hanno armi proprie, soldano delle forestiere; e più presto noceranno al bene pubblico l'armi forestiere, che le proprie, perchè le sono più facili a corrompersi e più tosto uno cittadino che diventi potente se ne può valere; e parte ha più facile materia a maneggiare, avendo ad opprimere uomini disarmati. Oltre a questo una città debbe più temere due nimici che uno. Quella che si vale dell'armi forestiere, teme ad uno tratto il forestiero ch'ella solda e il cittadino; e che questo timore debba essere, ricordivi di quello che io dissi poco fa di Francesco Sforza. Quella che usa l'arme proprie, non teme se non il suo cittadino. Ma per tutte le ragioni che si potessono dire, voglio mi serva questa: che mai alcuno ordinò alcuna repubblica o regno, che non pensasse che quegli medesimi che abitavano quella, con le armi l'avessono a difendere. E se i Viniziani fussero stati savi in questo come in tutti gli altri loro ordini, eglino avrebbono fatto una nuova monarchia nel mondo. I quali tanto più meritano biasimo, sendo stati dai loro primi datori di legge, armati. Ma non avendo dominio in terra, erano armati in mare, dove ferono le loro guerre virtuosamente e, con l'armi in mano, accrebbero la loro patria. Ma venendo tempo ch'eglino ebbero a fare guerra in terra per difendere Vicenza, dove essi dovevano mandare uno loro cittadino a combattere in terra, ci soldarono per loro capitano il marchese di Mantova. Questo fu quel partito sinistro che tagliò loro le gambe del salire in cielo e dello ampliare. E se lo fecero per credere che, come che ei sapessono far guerra in mare, ei si diffidassono farla in terra, ella fu una diffidenza non savia; perchè più facilmente un capitanodi mare, che è uso a combattere con i venti, con l'acque e con gli uomini, diventerà capitano di terra, dove si combatte con gli uomini solo, che uno di terra non diventerà di mare. E i miei Romani, sapendo combattere in terra e non in mare, venendo a guerra con i Cartaginesi che erano potenti in mare, non soldarono Greci o Spagnuoli consueti in mare, ma imposero quella cura a' loro cittadini che mandavano in terra, e vinsero. Se lo ferono perchè uno loro cittadino non diventasse tiranno, ei fu uno timore poco considerato; perchè, oltre a quelle ragioni che a questo proposito poco fa dissi, se uno cittadino con l'armi di mare non si era mai fatto tiranno in una città posta in mare, tanto meno avrebbe potuto fare questo con le armi di terra. E, mediante questo, dovevano vedere che l'armi in mano a' loro cittadini non gli potevano fare tiranni, ma i malvagi ordini del governo che fanno tiranneggiare una città; e avendo quegli buono governo, non avevano a temere delle loro armi. Presero pertanto uno partito imprudente; il che è stato cagione di torre loro di molta gloria e di molta felicità. Quanto allo errore che fa il Re di Francia a non tenere disciplinati i suoi popoli alla guerra, il che quelli vostri allegano per esemplo, non è alcuno, deposta qualche sua particolare passione, che non giudichi questo difetto essere in quel regno e questa negligenza sola farlo debile. Ma io ho fatto troppa grande digressione, e forse sono uscito del proposito mio; pure lo ho fatto per rispondervi e dimostrarvi che non si può fare fondamento in altre armi che nelle proprie, e l'armi proprie non si possono ordinare altrimenti che per via d'una ordinanza, ne' per altre vie introdurre forme di eserciti in alcuno luogo nè per altro modo ordinare una disciplina militare. Se voi avete letto gli ordini che quelli primi Re fecero in Roma e massimamente Servio Tullo, troverrete che l'ordine delle classi non è altro che una ordinanza per potere di subito mettere insieme uno esercito per difesa di quella città. Ma torniamo al nostro Deletto. Dico di nuovo che, avendo ad instaurare un ordine vecchio, io gli prenderei diciassette; avendo a crearne uno nuovo, io gli prenderei d'ogni età tra diciassette e quaranta, per potermene valere subito.

COSIMO: Fareste voi differenza di quale arte voi gli scegliessi?

FABRIZIO: Questi scrittori la fanno, perchè non vogliono che si prendano uccellatori, pescatori, cuochi, ruffiani e qualunque fa arte di sollazzo; ma vogliono che si tolgano, oltre a' lavoratori di terra, fabbri, maniscalchi, legnaiuoli, beccai, cacciatori, e simili. Ma io ne farei poca differenza, quanto al conietturare dall'arte la bontà dell'uomo; ma sì bene, quanto al poterlo con più utilità usare. E per questa cagione i contadini che sono usi a lavorare la terra, sono più utili che niuno; perchè di tutte l'arti questa negli eserciti si adopera più che l'altre. Dopo questa sono i fabbri, legnaiuoli, maniscalchi, scarpellini; de' quali è utile avere assai, perchè torna bene la loro arte in molte cose, sendo cosa molto buona avere uno soldato del quale tu tragga doppio servigio.

COSIMO: Da che si conoscono quelli che sono o non sono sufficienti a militare?

FABRIZIO: Io voglio parlare del modo dello eleggere una ordinanza nuova per farne dipoi uno esercito; perchè parte si viene ancora a ragionare della elezione che si facesse ad instaurazione d'una ordinanza vecchia. Dico, pertanto, che la bontà d'uno che tu hai ad eleggere per soldato, si conosce o per esperienza, mediante qualche sua egregia opera, o per coniettura. La pruova di virtù non si può trovare negli uomini che si eleggono di nuovo e che mai più non sono stati eletti; e di questi se ne truova o pochi o niuno nell'ordinanze che di nuovo s'ordinano. È necessario pertanto, mancando questa esperienza, ricorrere alla coniettura; la quale si trae dagli anni, dall'arte e dalla presenza. Di quelle due prime si è ragionato; resta parlare della terza; e però dico come alcuni hanno voluto che il soldato sia grande, tra i quali fu Pirro; alcuni altri gli hanno eletti dalla gagliardia solo del corpo, come faceva Cesare; la quale gagliardia di corpo e d'animo si coniettura dalla composizione delle membra e dalla grazia dell'aspetto. E però dicono questi che ne scrivono, che vuole avere gli occhi vivi e lieti, il collo nervoso, il petto largo, le braccia musculose, le dita lunghe, poco ventre, i fianchi rotundi, le gambe e il piede asciutto; le quali parti sogliono sempre rendere l'uomo agile e forte, che sono due cose che in uno soldato si cercano sopra tutte l'altre. Debbesi sopratutto riguardare a' costumi, e che in lui sia onestà e vergogna, altrimenti si elegge uno instrumento di scandolo e uno principio di corruzione; perchè non sia alcuno che creda che nella educazione disonesta e nello animo brutto possa capere alcuna virtù che sia in alcuna parte lodevole. Non mi pare superfluo, anzi credo che sia necessario, perchè voi intendiate meglio la importanza di questo Deletto, dirvi il modo che i consoli romani nel principio del magistrato loro osservavono nello eleggere le romane legioni; nel quale Deletto, per essere mescolati quegli si avevono ad eleggere, rispetto alle continue guerre, d'uomini veterani e nuovi, potevano procedere con la esperienza ne' vecchi e con la coniettura ne' nuovi. E debbesi notare questo: che questi Deletti si fanno, o per usargli allora, o per esercitargli allora ed usargli a tempo. Io ho parlato e parlerò di tutto quello che si ordina per usarlo a tempo, perchè la intenzione mia è mostrarvi come si possa ordinare uno esercito ne' paesi dove non fusse milizia, ne' quali paesi non si può avere Deletti per usargli allora; ma in quegli donde sia costume trarre eserciti, e per via del principe, si può bene avergli per allora, come si osservava a Roma e come si osserva oggi tra i Svizzeri. Perchè in questi Deletti, se vi sono de' nuovi, vi sono ancora tanti degli altri consueti a stare negli ordini militari, che, mescolati i nuovi ed i vecchi insieme, fanno uno corpo unito e buono; nonostante che gli imperadori, poichè cominciarono a tenere le stazioni de' soldati ferme, avevano preposto sopra i militi novelli, i quali chiamavano Tironi, uno maestro ad esercitargli, come si vede nella vita di Massimino imperadore. La quale cosa, mentre che Roma fu libera, non negli eserciti, ma dentro nella città era ordinato; ed essendo in quella consueti gli esercizi militari dove i giovanetti si esercitavano, ne nasceva che, sendo scelti poi per ire in guerra, erano assuefatti in modo nella finta milizia, che potevano facilmente adoperarsi nella vera. Ma avendo dipoi quegli imperadori spenti questi esercizi, furono necessitati usare i termini che io v'ho dimostrati. Venendo pertanto al modo del Deletto romano, dico, poichè i consoli romani, a' quali era imposto il carico della guerra, avevano preso il magistrato, volendo ordinare i loro eserciti, perchè era costume che qualunque di loro avesse due legioni d'uomini romani, le quali erano il nervo degli eserciti loro,, creavano ventiquattro tribuni militari, e ne proponevano sei per ciascuna legione, i quali facevano quello uffizio che fanno oggi quegli che noi chiamiamo connestaboli. Facevano dipoi convenire tutti gli uomini romani idonei a portare armi, e ponevano i tribuni di qualunque legione separati l'uno dall'altro. dipoi a sorte traevano i tribi, de' quali si avesse prima a fare il Deletto, e di quello tribo sceglievano quattro de' migliori, de' quali ne era eletto uno da' tribuni della prima legione; dagli altri tre, ne era eletto uno da' tribuni della seconda legione; degli altri due, ne era eletto uno da' tribuni della terza; e quello ultimo toccava alla quarta legione. Dopo questi quattro se ne sceglieva altri quattro; de' quali, prima, uno ne era eletto da' tribuni della seconda legione; il secondo da quelli della terza; il terzo da quelli della quarta; il quarto rimaneva alla prima. dipoi se ne sceglieva altri quattro: il primo sceglieva la terza, il secondo la quarta, il terzo la prima, il quarto restava alla seconda; e così variava successivamente questo modo dello eleggere, tanto che la elezione veniva ad essere pari e le legioni si ragguagliavano. E come di sopra dicemmo, questo Deletto si poteva fare per usarlo allora, perchè si faceva d'uomini de' quali buona parte erano esperimentati nella vera milizia e tutti, nella finta, esercitati; e potevasi fare questo Deletto per coniettura e per esperienza. Ma dove si avesse ad ordinare una milizia di nuovo, e per questo a scergli per a tempo, non si può fare questo Deletto se non per coniettura, la quale si prende dagli anni e dalla presenza.

COSIMO: Io credo al tutto essere vero quanto da voi è stato detto. Ma, innanzi che voi passiate ad altro ragionamento, io vi voglio domandare d'una cosa di che voi mi avete fatto ricordare, dicendo che il Deletto che si avesse a fare dove non fussero gli uomini usi a militare, si avrebbe a fare per coniettura; perchè io ho sentito in molte parti biasimare l'ordinanza nostra, e massime quanto al numero, perchè molti dicono che se ne debbe torre minore numero, di che se ne trarrebbe questo frutto: che sarebbono migliori e meglio scelti; non si darebbe tanto disagio agli uomini; potrebbesi dar loro qualche premio mediante il quale starebbono più contenti, e meglio si potrebbono comandare. Donde io vorrei intendere in questa parte l'opinione vostra, e se voi amereste più il numero grande che il piccolo, e quali modi terreste ad eleggerli nell'uno e nell'altro numero.

FABRIZIO: senza dubbio egli è migliore e più necessario il numero grosso che il piccolo; anzi, a dire meglio, dove non se ne può ordinare gran quantità, non si può ordinare una ordinanza perfetta; e facilmente io vi annullerò tutte le ragioni assegnate da costoro. Dico pertanto in prima, che il minore numero dove sia assai popolo, come è, verbigrazia Toscana, non fa che voi gli abbiate migliori, nè che il Deletto sia più scelto. Perchè volendo, nello eleggere gli uomini, giudicargli dall'esperienza, se ne troverebbe in quel paese pochissimi i quali l'esperienza facesse probabili, sì perchè pochi ne sono stati in guerra, sì perchè, di quegli pochi, pochissimi hanno fatto pruova mediante la quale ei meritassono di essere prima scelti che gli altri; in modo che chi gli debbe in simili luoghi eleggere, conviene lasci da parte l'esperienza e gli prenda per coniettura. Riducendosi dunque altri in tale necessità, vorrei intendere, se mi vengono avanti venti giovani di buona presenza, con che regola io ne debbo prendere o lasciare alcuno; tale che, senza dubbio, credo che ogni uomo confesserà come e' fia minore errore torgli tutti per armargli ed esercitargli, non potendo sapere quale di loro sia migliore, e riserbarsi a fare poi più certo Deletto quando, nel praticargli con lo esercizio, si conoscessero quegli di più spirito e di più vita. In modo che, considerato tutto, lo scerne in questo caso pochi per avergli migliori è al tutto falso. Quanto per dare meno disagio al paese e agli uomini, dico che l'ordinanza, o molta o poca ch'ella sia, non dà alcuno disagio; perchè questo ordine non toglie gli uomini da alcuna loro faccenda, non gli lega che non possano ire a fare alcuno loro fatto, perchè gli obliga solo ne' giorni oziosi a convenire insieme per esercitarsi; la quale cosa non fa danno nè al paese nè agli uomini, anzi a' giovani arrecherebbe diletto, perchè, dove ne' giorni festivi vilmente si stanno oziosi per li ridotti, andrebbero per piacere a questi esercizi, perchè il trattare dell'armi, com'egli è bello spettacolo, così è a' giovani dilettevole. Quanto a potere pagare il minore numero e, per questo, tenergli più ubbidienti e più contenti, rispondo come non si può fare ordinanza di sì pochi, che si possano in modo continuamente pagare, che quel pagamento loro sodisfaccia. Verbigrazia, se si ordinasse una milizia di cinquemila fanti, a volergli pagare in modo che si credesse che si contentassono, converrebbe dar loro almeno diecimila ducati il mese. In prima, questo numero di fanti non basta a fare uno esercito; questo pagamento è insopportabile a uno stato, e, dall'altro canto, non è sufficiente a tenere gli uomini contenti, ed obligati da potersene valere a sua posta. In modo che, nel fare questo, si spenderebbe assai, avrebbesi poche forze, e non sarebbero a sufficienza o a defenderti o a fare alcuna tua impresa. Se tu dessi loro più, o ne prendessi più, tanta più impossibilità ti sarebbe il pagargli. Se tu dessi loro meno, o ne prendessi meno, tanta meno contentezza sarebbe in loro, o a te tanta meno utilità arrecherebbono. Pertanto quegli che ragionano di fare una ordinanza, e, mentre ch'ella si dimora a casa, pagarla, ragionano di cose o impossibili o inutili. Ma è bene necessario pagargli quando si levono per menargli alla guerra. Pure se tale ordine dessi a' descritti in quello qualche disagio ne' tempi di pace, che non ce lo veggo, e' vi sono per ricompenso tutti quegli beni che arreca una milizia ordinata in uno paese, perchè senza quella non vi è secura cosa alcuna. Conclude che, chi vuole il poco numero per poterlo pagare, o per qualunque altra delle cagioni allegate da voi, non se ne intende, perchè ancora fa per la opinione mia, che sempre ogni numero ti diminuirà tra le mani per infiniti impedimenti che hanno gli uomini, di modo che il poco numero tornerebbe a niente. Appresso, avendo l'ordinanza grossa, ti puoi a tua elezione valere de' pochi e degli assai. Oltre a questo, ella ti ha a servire in fatto e in riputazione, e sempre ti darà più riputazione il gran numero. Aggiugnesi a questo che, faccendosi l'ordinanze per tenere gli uomini esercitati, se tu scrivi poco numero di uomini in assai paesi, ei sono tanto distanti gli scritti l'uno dall'altro, che tu non puoi senza loro danno gravissimo raccozzargli per esercitargli; e senza questo esercizio l'ordinanza è inutile, come nel suo luogo si dirà.

COSIMO: Basti sopra questa mia domanda quanto avete detto; ma io disidero ora che voi mi solviate uno altro dubbio. Costoro dicono che tale moltitudine di armati è per fare confusione, scandolo e disordine nel paese.

FABRIZIO: Questa è un'altra vana opinione, per la cagione vi dirò. Questi ordinati all'armi possono causare disordine in due modi: o tra loro, o contro ad altri. Alle quali cose si può facilmente ovviare, dove l'ordine per se medesimo non ovviasse; perchè, quanto agli scandoli tra loro, questo ordine gli leva, non gli nutrisce, perchè, nello ordinarli, voi date loro armi e capi. Se il paese dove voi gli ordinate è sì imbelle che non sia, tra gli uomini di quello, armi, e sì unito che non vi sia capi, questo ordine gli fa più feroci contro al forestiero, ma non gli fa in niuno modo più disuniti, perchè gli uomini bene ordinati temono le leggi, armati come disarmati; nè mai possono alterare, se i capi che voi date loro non causano l'alterazione; e il modo a fare questo si dirà ora. Ma se il paese dove voi gli ordinate, è armigero e disunito, questo ordine solo è cagione d'unirgli, perchè costoro hanno armi e capi per loro medesimi, ma sono l'armi inutili alla guerra, e i capi nutritori di scandoli. E questo ordine dà loro armi utili alla guerra e capi estinguitori degli scandoli; perchè subito che in quel paese è offeso alcuno, ricorre al suo capo di parte, il quale, per mantenersi la reputazione, lo conforta alla vendetta, non alla pace. Al contrario fa il capo pubblico; tale che per questa via si lieva la cagione degli scandoli e si prepara quella della unione; e le provincie unite ed effeminate perdono la viltà e mantengono l'unione; le disunite e scandolose si uniscono e quella loro ferocia, che sogliono disordinatamente adoperare, si rivolta in pubblica utilità. Quanto a volere che non nuocano contro ad altri, si debbe considerare che non possono fare questo se non mediante i capi che gli governono. A volere che i capi non facciano disordine, è necessario avere cura che non acquistino sopra di loro troppa autorità. E avete a considerare che questa autorità si acquista o per natura, o per accidente. E quanto alla natura, conviene provvedere che chi è nato in un luogo, non sia preposto agli uomini descritti in quello, ma sia fatto capo di quelli luoghi dove non abbia alcuna naturale convenienza. Quanto allo accidente, si debbe ordinare la cosa in modo che ciascuno anno i capi si permutino da governo a governo; perchè la continua autorità sopra i medesimi uomini genera tra loro tanta unione, che facilmente si può convertire in preiudizio del principe. Le quali permute quanto sieno utili a quegli che le hanno usate, e dannose a chi non le ha osservate, si conosce per lo esempio del regno degli Assiri e dello imperio de' Romani; dove si vede che quel regno durò mille anni senza tumulto e senza alcuna guerra civile; il che non procedè da altro che dalle permute che facevono da luogo a luogo ogni anno quegli capitani i quali erano preposti alla cura degli eserciti. Nè per altra cagione nello imperio romano, spento che fu il sangue di Cesare, vi nacquero tante guerre civili tra' capitani degli eserciti e tante congiure da' predetti capitani contro agli imperadori, se non per tenere continuamente fermi quegli capitani ne' medesimi governi. E se in alcuni di quegli primi imperadori e di quegli poi i quali tennono l'imperio con reputazione, come Adriano, Marco, Severo e simili, fusse stato tanto vedere, che gli avessono introdotto questo costume di permutare i capitani in quello imperio, senza dubbio lo facevono più quieto e più durabile; perchè i capitani avrebbero avuta minore occasione di tumultuare, gl'imperadori minore cagione di temere, e il senato, ne' mancamenti delle successioni, avrebbe avuto nella elezione dello imperadore più autorità, e per conseguente sarebbe stata migliore. Ma le cattive consuetudini, o per la ignoranza o per la poca diligenza degli uomini, nè per i malvagi nè per i buoni esempli si possono levare via.

COSIMO: Io non so se col mio domandare io v'ho quasi che tratto fuora dell'ordine vostro, perchè dal Deletto noi siamo entrati in uno altro ragionamento; e se io non me ne fussi poco fa scusato, crederrei meritarne qualche riprensione.

FABRIZIO: Non vi dia noia questo; perchè tutto questo ragionamento era necessario volendo ragionare della ordinanza la quale, sendo biasimata da molti, conveniva la scusassi, volendo che questa prima parte del Deletto ci avesse luogo. E prima che io descenda all'altre parti, io voglio ragionare del Deletto degli uomini a cavallo. Questo si faceva, appresso agli antichi, de' più ricchi, avendo riguardo e agli anni e alla qualità dell'uomo; e ne eleggevano trecento per legione, tanto che i cavagli romani in ogni esercito consolare non passavano la somma di secento.

COSIMO: Fareste voi ordinanza di cavagli per esercitargli a casa, e valersene col tempo?

FABRIZIO: Anzi è necessario; e non si può fare altrimenti, a volere avere l'armi che sieno sue, e a non volere avere a torre di quegli che ne fanno arte.

COSIMO: Come gli eleggeresti?

FABRIZIO: Imiterei i Romani; torrei de' più ricchi, darei loro capi in quel modo che oggi agli altri si danno, e gli armerei ed eserciterei.

COSIMO: A questi sarebb'egli bene dare qualche provvisione!

FABRIZIO: Sibbene, ma tanta solamente, quanta è necessaria a nutrire il cavallo; perchè, arrecando a' tuoi sudditi spesa, si potrebbono dolere di te. Però sarebbe necessario pagare loro il cavallo e le spese di quello.

COSIMO: Quanto numero ne faresti, e come gli armeresti?

FABRIZIO: Voi passate in un altro ragionamento. Io vel dirò nel suo luogo, che fia quando io vi avrò detto come si debbono armare i fanti, o come a fare una giornata si preparano.

BOOK TWO

I believe that it is necessary, once the men are found, to arm them; and in wanting to do this, I believe it is necessary to examine what arms the ancients used, and from them select the best. The Romans divided their infantry into the heavily and lightly armed. The light armed they gave the name Veliti. Under this name they included all those who operated with the sling, cross-bow, and darts: and the greater part of them carried a helmet (head covering) and a shield on the arm for their defense. These men fought outside the regular ranks, and apart from the heavy armor, which was a Casque that came up to the shoulders, they also carried a Cuirass which, with the skirt, came down to the knees, and their arms and legs were covered by shin-guards and bracelets; they also carried a shield on the arm, two arms in length and one in width, which had an iron hoop on it to be able to sustain a blow, and another underneath, so that in rubbing on the ground, it should not be worn out. For attacking, they had cinched on their left side a sword of an arm and a half length, and a dagger on the right side. They carried a spear, which they called Pilus, and which they hurled at the enemy at the start of a battle. These were the important Roman arms, with which they conquered the world. And although some of the ancient writers also gave them, in addition to the aforementioned arms, a shaft in the hand in the manner of a spit, I do not know how a staff can be used by one who holds a shield, for in managing it with two hands it is impeded by the shield, and he cannot do anything worthwhile with one hand because of its heaviness. In addition to this, to combat in the ranks with the staff (as arms) is useless, except in the front rank where there is ample space to deploy the entire staff, which cannot be done in the inner ranks, because the nature of the battalions ((as I will tell you in their organization)) is to press its ranks continually closer together, as this is feared less, even though inconvenient, than for the ranks to spread further apart, where the danger is most apparent. So that all the arms which exceed two arms in length are useless in tight places; for if you have a staff and want to use it with both hands, and handled so that the shield should not annoy you, you cannot attack an enemy with it who is next to you. If you take it in one hand in order to serve yourself of the shield, you cannot pick it up except in the middle, and there remains so much of the staff in the back part, that those who are behind impede you in using it. And that this is true, that the Romans did not have the staff, or, having it, they valued it little, you will read in all the engagements noted by Titus Livius in his history, where you will see that only very rarely is mention made of the shaft, rather he always says that, after hurling the spears, they put their hands on the sword. Therefore I want to leave this staff, and relate how much the Romans used the sword for offense, and for defense, the shield together with the other arms mentioned above.

The Greeks did not arm so heavily for defense as did the Romans, but in the offense relied more on this staff than on the sword, and especially the Phalanxes of Macedonia, who carried staffs which they called Sarisse, a good ten arms in length, with which they opened the ranks of the enemy and maintained order in the Phalanxes. And although other writers say they also had a shield, I do not know ((for the reasons given above)) how the Sarisse and the shield could exist together. In addition to this, in the engagement that Paulus Emilius had with Perseus, King of Macedonia, I do not remember mention being made of shields, but only of the Sarisse and the difficulty the Romans had in overcoming them. So that I conjecture that a Macedonian Phalanx was nothing else than a battalion of Swiss is today, who have all their strength and power in their pikes. The Romans ((in addition to the arms)) ornamented the infantry with plumes; which things make the sight of an army beautiful to friends, and terrible to the enemy. The arms for men on horseback in the original ancient Roman (army) was a round shield, and they had the head covered, but the rest (of the body) without armor. They had a sword and a staff with an iron point, long and thin; whence they were unable to hold the shield firm, and only make weak movements with the staff, and because they had no armor, they were exposed to wounds. Afterwards, with time, they were armed like the infantry, but the shield was much smaller and square, and the staff more solid and with two iron tips, so that if the one side was encumbered, they could avail themselves of the other. With these arms, both for the infantry and the cavalry, my Romans occupied all the world, and it must be believed, from the fruits that are observed, that they were the best armed armies that ever existed.

And Titus Livius, in his histories, gives many proofs, where, in coming to the comparison with enemy armies, he says, "but the Romans were superior in virtu, kinds of arms, and discipline". And, therefore, I have discussed more in particular the arms of the victors than those of the losers. It appears proper to me to discuss only the present methods of arming. The infantry have for their defense a breast plate of iron, and for offense a lance nine armlengths long, which they call a pike, and a sword at their side, rather round in the point than sharp. This is the ordinary armament of the infantry today, for few have their arms and shins (protected by) armor, no one the head; and those few carry a halberd in place of a pike, the shaft of which ((as you know)) is three armlengths long, and has the iron attached as an axe. Among them they have three Scoppettieri (Exploders, i.e., Gunners), who, with a burst of fire fill that office which anciently was done by slingers and bow-men. This method of arming was established by the Germans, and especially by the Swiss, who, being poor and wanting to live in freedom, were, and are, obliged to combat with the ambitions of the Princes of Germany, who were rich and could raise horses, which that people could not do because of poverty: whence it happened that being on foot and wanting to defend themselves from enemies who were on horseback, it behooved them to search the ancient orders and find arms which should defend them from the fury of horses. This necessity has caused them to maintain or rediscover the ancient orders, without which, as every prudent man affirms, the infantry is entirely useless. They therefore take up pikes as arms, which are most useful not only in sustaining (the attacks of) horses, but to overcome them. And because of the virtu of these arms and ancient orders, the Germans have assumed so much audacity, that fifteen or twenty thousand of them would assault any great number of horse, and there have been many examples of this seen in the last twenty five years. And this example of their virtu founded on these arms and these orders have been so powerful, that after King Charles passed into Italy, every nation has imitated them: so that the Spanish armies have come into a very great reputation.

COSIMO: What method of arms do you praise more, this German one or the ancient Roman?

FABRIZIO: The Roman without any doubt, and I will tell you the good and the bad of one and the other. The German infantry can sustain and overcome the cavalry. They are more expeditious in marching and in organizing themselves, because they are not burdened with arms. On the other hand, they are exposed to blows from near and far because of being unarmed. They are useless in land battles and in every fight where there is stalwart resistance. But the Romans sustained and overcame the cavalry, as these (Germans) do. They were safe from blows near and far because they were covered with armor. They were better able to attack and sustain attacks having the shields. They could more actively in tight places avail themselves of the sword than these (Germans) with the pike; and even if the latter had the sword, being without a shield, they become, in such a case, (equally) useless. They (the Romans) could safely assault towns, having the body covered, and being able to cover it even better with the shield. So that they had no other inconvenience than the heaviness of the arms (armor) and the annoyance of having to carry them; which inconveniences they overcame by accustoming the body to hardships and inducing it to endure hard work. And you know we do not suffer from things to which we are accustomed. And you must understand this, that the infantry must be able to fight with infantry and cavalry, and those are always useless who cannot sustain the (attacks of the) cavalry, or if they are able to sustain them, none the less have fear of infantry who are better armed and organized than they. Now if you will consider the German and the Roman infantry, you will find in the German ((as we have said)) the aptitude of overcoming cavalry, but great disadvantages when fighting with an infantry organized as they are, and armed as the Roman. So that there will be this advantage of the one over the other, that the Romans could overcome both the infantry and the cavalry, and the Germans only the cavalry.

COSIMO: I would desire that you give some more particular example, so that we might understand it better.

FABRIZIO: I say thusly, that in many places in our histories you will find the Roman infantry to have defeated numberless cavalry, but you will never find them to have been defeated by men on foot because of some defect they may have had in their arms or because of some advantage the enemy had in his. For if their manner of arming had been defective, it was necessary for them to follow one of two courses: either when they found one who was better armed than they, not to go on further with the conquest, or that they take up the manner of the foreigner, and leave off theirs: and since neither ensued, there follows, what can be easily conjectured, that this method of arming was better than that of anyone else. This has not yet occurred with the German infantry; for it has been seen that anytime they have had to combat with men on foot organized and as obstinate as they, they have made a bad showing; which results from the disadvantage they have in trying themselves against the arms of the enemy. When Filippo Visconti, Duke of Milan, was assaulted by eighteen thousand Swiss, he sent against them Count Carmingnuola, who was his Captain at that time. This man with six thousand cavalry and a few infantry went to encounter them, and, coming hand to hand with them, was repulsed with very great damage. Whence Carmingnuola as a prudent man quickly recognized the power of the enemy arms, and how much they prevailed against cavalry, and the weakness of cavalry against those on foot so organized; and regrouping his forces, again went to meet the Swiss, and as they came near he made his men-at-arms descend from their horses, and in that manner fought with them, and killed all but three thousand, who, seeing themselves consumed without having any remedy, threw their arms on the ground and surrendered.

COSIMO: Whence arises such a disadvantage?

FABRIZIO: I have told you a little while ago, but since you have not understood it, I will repeat it to you. The German infantry ((as was said a little while ago)) has almost no armor in defending itself, and use pikes and swords for offense. They come with these arms and order of battle to meet the enemy, who ((if he is well equipped with armor to defend himself, as were the men-at-arms of Carmingnuola who made them descend to their feet)) comes with his sword and order of battle to meet him, and he has no other difficulty than to come near the Swiss until he makes contact with them with the sword; for as soon as he makes contact with them, he combats them safely, for the German cannot use the pike against the enemy who is next to him because of the length of the staff, so he must use the sword, which is useless to him, as he has no armor and has to meet an enemy that is (protected) fully by armor. Whence, whoever considers the advantages and disadvantages of one and the other, will see that the one without armor has no remedy, but the one well armored will have no difficulty in overcoming the first blow and the first passes of the pike: for in battles, as you will understand better when I have demonstrated how they are put together, the men go so that of necessity they accost each other in a way that they are attacked on the breast, and if one is killed or thrown to the ground by the pike, those on foot who remain are so numerous that they are sufficient for victory. From this there resulted that Carmingnuola won with such a massacre of the Swiss, and with little loss to himself.

COSIMO: I see that those with Carmingnuola were men-at-arms, who, although they were on foot, were all covered with iron (armor), and, therefore, could make the attempt that they made; so that I think it would be necessary to arm the infantry in the same way if they want to make a similar attempt.

FABRIZIO: If you had remembered how I said the Romans were armed, you would not think this way. For an infantryman who has his head covered with iron, his breast protected by a cuirass and a shield, his arms and legs with armor, is much more apt to defend himself from pikes, and enter among them, than is a man-at-arms (cavalryman) on foot. I want to give you a small modern example. The Spanish infantry had descended from Sicily into the Kingdom of Naples in order to go and meet Consalvo who was besieged in Barletta by the French. They came to an encounter against Monsignor D'Obigni with his men-at-arms, and with about four thousand German infantry. The Germans, coming hand to hand with their pikes low, penetrated the (ranks of the) Spanish infantry; but the latter, aided by their spurs and the agility of their bodies, intermingled themselves with the Germans, so that they (the Germans) could not get near them with their swords; whence resulted the death of almost all of them, and the victory of the Spaniards. Everyone knows how many German infantry were killed in the engagement at Ravenna, which resulted from the same causes, for the Spanish infantry got as close as the reach of their swords to the German infantry, and would have destroyed all of them, if the German infantry had not been succored by the French Cavalry: none the less, the Spaniards pressing together made themselves secure in that place. I conclude, therefore, that a good infantry not only is able to sustain the (attack) of cavalry, but does not have fear of infantry, which ((as I have said many times)) proceeds from its arms (armor) and organization (discipline).

COSIMO: Tell us, therefore, how you would arm them.

FABRIZIO: I would take both the Roman arms and the German, and would want half to be armed as the Romans, and the other half as the Germans. For, if in six thousand infantry ((as I shall explain a little later)) I should have three thousand infantry with shields like the Romans, and two thousand pikes and a thousand gunners like the Germans, they would be enough for me; for I would place the pikes either in the front lines of the battle, or where I should fear the cavalry most; and of those with the shield and the sword, I would serve myself to back up the pikes and to win the engagement, as I will show you. So that I believe that an infantry so organized should surpass any other infantry today.

COSIMO: What you have said to us is enough as regards infantry, but as to cavalry, we desire to learn which seems the more strongly armed to you, ours or that of the ancients?

FABRIZIO: I believe in these times, with respect to saddles and stirrups not used by the ancients, one stays more securely on the horse than at that time. I believe we arm more securely: so that today one squadron of very heavily (armed) men-at-arms comes to be sustained with much more difficulty than was the ancient cavalry. With all of this, I judge, none the less, that no more account ought to be taken of the cavalry than was taken anciently; for ((as has been said above)) they have often in our times been subjected to disgrace by the infantry armed (armored) and organized as (described) above. Tigranus, King of Armenia, came against the Roman army of which Lucullus was Captain, with (an army) of one hundred fifty thousand cavalry, among whom were many armed as our men-at-arms, whom they called Catafratti, while on the other side the Romans did not total more than six thousand (cavalry) and fifteen thousand infantry; so that Tigranus, when he saw the army of the enemy, said: "These are just about enough horsemen for an embassy". None the less, when they came to battle, he was routed; and he who writes of that battle blames those Catafratti, showing them to be useless, because, he says, that having their faces covered, their vision was impaired and they were little adept at seeing and attacking the enemy, and as they were heavily burdened by the armor, they could not regain their feet when they fell, nor in any way make use of their persons. I say, therefore, that those People or Kingdoms which esteem the cavalry more than the infantry, are always weaker and more exposed to complete ruin, as has been observed in Italy in our times, which has been plundered, ruined, and overrun by foreigners, not for any other fault than because they had paid little attention to the foot soldiers and had mounted all their soldiers on horses. Cavalry ought to be used, but as a second and not the first reliance of an army; for they are necessary and most useful in undertaking reconnaissance, in overrunning and despoiling the enemy country, and to keep harassing and troubling the enemy army so as to keep it continually under arms, and to impede its provisions; but as to engagements and battles in the field, which are the important things in war and the object for which armies are organized, they are more useful in pursuing than in routing the enemy, and are much more inferior to the foot soldier in accomplishing the things necessary in accomplishing such (defeats).

COSIMO: But two doubts occur to me: the one, that I know that the Parthians did not engage in war except with cavalry, yet they divided the world with the Romans: the other, that I would like you to tell me how the (attack of) the cavalry can be sustained by the infantry, and whence arises the virtu of the latter and the weakness of the former?

FABRIZIO: Either I have told you, or I meant to tell you, that my discussion on matters of war is not going beyond the limits of Europe. Since this is so, I am not obliged to give reasons for that which is the custom in Asia. Yet, I have this to say, that the army of Parthia was completely opposite to that of the Romans, as the Parthians fought entirely on horseback, and in the fighting was about confused and disrupted, and was a way of fighting unstable and full of uncertainties. The Romans, it may be recalled, were almost all on foot, and fought pressed closely together, and at various times one won over the other, according as the site (of the battle) was open or tight; for in the latter the Romans were superior, but in the former the Parthians, who were able to make a great trial with that army with respect to the region they had to defend, which was very open with a seacoast a thousand miles distant, rivers two or three days (journey) apart from each other, towns likewise, and inhabitants rare: so that a Roman army, heavy and slow because of its arms and organization, could not pursue him without suffering great harm, because those who defended the country were on horses and very speedy, so that he would be in one place today, and tomorrow fifty miles distant. Because of this, the Parthians were able to prevail with cavalry alone, and thus resulted the ruin of the army of Crassus, and the dangers to those of Marcantonio. But ((as I have said)) I did not intend in this discussion of mine to speak of armies outside of Europe; and, therefore, I want to continue on those which the Romans and Greeks had organized in their time, and that the Germans do today.

But let us come to the other question of yours, in which you desire to know what organization or what natural virtu causes the infantry to be superior to the cavalry. And I tell you, first, that the horses cannot go in all the places that the infantry do, because it is necessary for them either to turn back after they have come forward, or turning back to go forward, or to move from a stand-still, or to stand still after moving, so that, without doubt, the cavalry cannot do precisely thus as the infantry. Horses cannot, after being put into disorder from some attack, return to the order (of the ranks) except with difficulty, and even if the attack does not occur; the infantry rarely do this. In addition to this, it often occurs that a courageous man is mounted on a base horse, and a base man on a courageous horse, whence it must happen that this difference in courage causes disorders. Nor should anyone wonder that a Knot (group) of infantry sustains every attack of the cavalry, for the horse is a sensible animal and knows the dangers, and goes in unwillingly. And if you would think about what forces make him (the horse) go forward and what keep him back, without doubt you will see that those which hold him back are greater than those which push him; for spurs make him go forward, and, on the other hand, the sword and the pike retain him. So that from both ancient and modern experiences, it has been seen that a small group of infantry can be very secure from, and even actually insuperable to, the cavalry. And if you should argue on this that the Elan with which he comes makes it more furious in hurling himself against whoever wants to sustain his attack, and he responds less to the pike than the spur, I say that, as soon as the horse so disposed begins to see himself at the point of being struck by the points of the pikes, either he will by himself check his gait, so that he will stop as soon as he sees himself about to be pricked by them, or, being pricked by them, he will turn to the right or left. If you want to make a test of this, try to run a horse against a wall, and rarely will you find one that will run into it, no matter with what Elan you attempt it. Caesar, when he had to combat the Swiss in Gaul, dismounted and made everyone dismount to their feet, and had the horses removed from the ranks, as they were more adept at fleeing than fighting.

But, notwithstanding these natural impediments that horses have, the Captain who leads the infantry ought to select roads that have as many obstacles for horses as possible, and rarely will it happen that the men will not be able to provide for their safety from the kind of country. If one marches among hills, the location of the march should be such that you may be free from those attacks of which you may be apprehensive; and if you go on the plains, rarely will you find one that does not have crops or woods which will provide some safety for you, for every bush and embankment, even though small, breaks up that dash, and every cultivated area where there are vines and other trees impedes the horses. And if you come to an engagement, the same will happen to you as when marching, because every little impediment which the horse meets cause him to lose his fury. None the less, I do not want to forget to tell you one thing, that although the Romans esteemed much their own discipline and trusted very much on their arms (and armor), that if they had to select a place, either so rough to protect themselves from horses and where they could not be able to deploy their forces, or one where they had more to fear from the horses but where they were able to spread out, they would always take the latter and leave the former.

But, as it is time to pass on to the training (of the men), having armed this infantry according to the ancient and modern usage, we shall see what training they gave to the Romans before the infantry were led to battle. Although they were well selected and better armed, they were trained with the greatest attention, because without this training a soldier was never any good. This training consisted of three parts. The first, to harden the body and accustom it to endure hardships, to act faster, and more dexterously. Next, to teach the use of arms: The third, to teach the trainees the observance of orders in marching as well as fighting and encamping. These are the three principal actions which make an army: for if any army marches, encamps, and fights, in a regular and practical manner, the Captain retains his honor even though the engagement should not have a good ending. All the ancient Republics, therefore, provided such training, and both by custom and law, no part was left out. They therefore trained their youth so as to make them speedy in running, dextrous in jumping, strong in driving stakes and wrestling. And these three qualities are almost necessary in a soldier; for speed makes him adept at occupying places before the enemy, to come upon him unexpectedly, and to pursue him when he is routed. Dexterity makes him adept at avoiding blows, jumping a ditch and climbing over an embankment. Strength makes him better to carry arms, hurl himself against an enemy, and sustain an attack. And above all, to make the body more inured to hardships, they accustom it to carry great weights. This accustoming is necessary, for in difficult expeditions it often happens that the soldier, in addition to his arms, must carry provisions for many days, and if he had not been accustomed to this hard work, he would not be able to do it, and, hence, he could neither flee from a danger nor acquire a victory with fame.

As to the teaching of the use of arms, they were trained in this way. They had the young men put on arms (armor) which weighed more than twice that of the real (regular) ones, and, as a sword, they gave them a leaded club which in comparison was very heavy. They made each one of them drive a pole into the ground so that three arm-lengths remained (above ground), and so firmly fixed that blows would not drive it to one side or have it fall to the ground; against this pole, the young men were trained with the shield and the club as against an enemy, and sometime they went against it as if they wanted to wound the head or the face, another time as if they wanted to puncture the flank, sometimes the legs, sometime they drew back, another time they went forward. And in this training, they had in mind making themselves adept at covering (protecting) themselves and wounding the enemy; and since the feigned arms were very heavy, the real ones afterwards seemed light. The Romans wanted their soldiers to wound (the enemy) by the driving of a point against him, rather than by cutting (slashing), as much because such a blow was more fatal and had less defense against it, as also because it left less uncovered (unprotected) those who were wounding, making him more adept at repeating his attack, than by slashing. Do you not wonder that those ancients should think of these minute details, for they reasoned that where men had to come hand to hand (in battle), every little advantage is of the greatest importance; and I will remind you of that, because the writers say of this that I have taught it to you. Nor did the ancients esteem it a more fortunate thing in a Republic than to have many of its men trained in arms; for it is not the splendor of jewels and gold that makes the enemy submit themselves to you, but only the fear of arms. Moreover, errors made in other things can sometimes be corrected afterwards, but those that are made in war, as the punishment happens immediately, cannot be corrected. In addition to this, knowing how to fight makes men more audacious, as no one fears to do the things which appear to him he has been taught to do. The ancients, therefore, wanted their citizens to train in every warlike activity; and even had them throw darts against the pole heavier than the actual ones: which exercise, in addition to making men expert in throwing, also makes the arm more limber and stronger. They also taught them how to draw the bow and the sling, and placed teachers in charge of doing all these things: so that when (men) were selected to go to war, they were already soldiers in spirit and disposition. Nor did these remain to teach them anything else than to go by the orders and maintain themselves in them whether marching or combatting: which they easily taught by mixing themselves with them, so that by knowing how to keep (obey) the orders, they could exist longer in the army.

COSIMO: Would you have them train this way now?

FABRIZIO: Many of those which have been mentioned, like running wrestling, making them jump, making them work hard under arms heavier than the ordinary, making them draw the crossbow and the sling; to which I would add the light gun, a new instrument ((as you know)), and a necessary one. And I would accustom all the youth of my State to this training: but that part of them whom I have enrolled to fight, I would (especially) train with greater industry and more solicitude, and I would train them always on their free days. I would also desire that they be taught to swim, which is a very useful thing, because there are not always bridges at rivers, nor ships ready: so that if your army does not know how to swim, it may be deprived of many advantages, and many opportunities, to act well are taken away. The Romans, therefore, arranged that the young men be trained on the field of Mars, so that having the river Tiber nearby, they would be able after working hard in exercises on land to refresh themselves in the water, and also exercise them in their swimming.

I would also do as the ancients and train those who fight on horseback: which is very necessary, for in addition to knowing how to ride, they would know how to avail themselves of the horse (in maneuvering him). And, therefore, they arranged horses of wood on which they straddled, and jumped over them armed and unarmed without any help and without using their hands: which made possible that in a moment, and at a sign from the Captain, the cavalry to become as foot soldiers, and also at another sign, for them to be remounted. And as such exercises, both on foot and horseback, were easy at that time, so now it should not be difficult for that Republic or that Prince to put them in practice on their youth, as is seen from the experience of Western Cities, where these methods similar to these institutions are yet kept alive.

They divide all their inhabitants into several parts, and assign one kind of arms of those they use in war to each part. And as they used pikes, halberds, bows, and light guns, they called them pikemen, halberdiers, archers, and gunners. It therefore behooved all the inhabitants to declare in what order they wanted to be enrolled. And as all, whether because of age or other impediment, are not fit for war (combat), they make a selection from each order and they call them the Giurati (Sworn Ones), who, on their free days, are obliged to exercise themselves in those arms in which they are enrolled: and each one is assigned his place by the public where such exercises are to be carried on, and those who are of that order but are not sworn, participate by (contributing) money for those expenses which are necessary for such exercises. That which they do, therefore, we can do, but our little prudence does not allow us to take up any good proceeding.

From these exercises, it resulted that the ancients had good infantry, and that now those of the West have better infantry than ours, for the ancients exercised either at home as did those Republics, or in the armies as did those Emperors, for the reasons mentioned above. But we do not want to exercise at home, and we cannot do so in the field because they are not our subjects and we cannot obligate them to other exercises than they themselves want. This reason has caused the armies to die out first, and then the institutions, so that the Kingdoms and the Republics, especially the Italian, exist in such a weak condition today.

But let us return to our subject, and pursuing this matter of training, I say, that it is not enough in undertaking good training to have hardened the men, made them strong, fast and dextrous, but it is also necessary to teach them to keep discipline, obey the signs, the sounds (of the bugle), and the voice of the Captain; to know when to stand, to retire, to go forward, and when to combat, to march, to maintain ranks; for without this discipline, despite every careful diligence observed and practiced, an army is never good. And without doubt, bold but undisciplined men are more weak than the timid but disciplined ones; for discipline drives away fear from men, lack of discipline makes the bold act foolishly. And so that you may better understand what will be mentioned below, you have to know that every nation has made its men train in the discipline of war, or rather its army as the principal part, which, if they have varied in name, they have varied little in the numbers of men involved, as all have comprised six to eight thousand men. This number was called a Legion by the Romans, a Phalanx by the Greeks, a Caterna by the Gauls. This same number, by the Swiss, who alone retain any of that ancient military umbrage, in our times is called in their language what in ours signifies a Battalion. It is true that each one is further subdivided into small Battaglia (Companies), and organized according to its purpose. It appears to me, therefore, more suitable to base our talk on this more notable name, and then according to the ancient and modern systems, arrange them as best as is possible. And as the Roman Legions were composed of five or six thousand men, in ten Cohorts, I want to divide our Battalion into ten Companies, and compose it of six thousand men on foot; and assign four hundred fifty men to each Company, of whom four hundred are heavily armed and fifty lightly armed: the heavily armed include three hundred with shields and swords, and will be called Scudati (shield bearers), and a hundred with pikes, and will be called pikemen: the lightly armed are fifty infantry armed with light guns, cross-bows, halberds, and bucklers, and these, from an ancient name, are called regular (ordinary) Veliti: the whole ten Companies, therefore, come to three thousand shield bearers; a thousand ordinary pikemen, and one hundred fifty ordinary Veliti, all of whom comprise (a number of) four thousand five hundred infantry. And we said we wanted to make a Battalion of six thousand men; therefore it is necessary to add another one thousand five hundred infantry, of whom I would make a thousand with pikes, whom I will call extraordinary pikemen, (and five hundred light armed, whom I will call extraordinary Veliti): and thus my infantry would come ((according as was said a little while ago)) to be composed half of shield bearers and half among pikemen and other arms (carriers). In every Company, I would put in charge a Constable, four Centurions, and forty Heads of Ten, and in addition, a Head of the ordinary Veliti with five Heads of Ten. To the thousand extraordinary pikemen, I would assign three Constables, ten Centurions, and a hundred Heads of Ten: to the extraordinary Veliti, two Constables, five Centurions, and fifty Heads of Ten. I would also assign a general Head for the whole Battalion. I would want each Constable to have a distinct flag and (bugle) sound.

Summarizing, therefore, a Battalion would be composed of ten Companies, of three thousand shield bearers, a thousand ordinary pikemen, a thousand extraordinary pikemen, five hundred ordinary Veliti, and five hundred extraordinary Veliti: thus they would come to be six thousand infantry, among whom there would be one thousand five hundred Heads of Ten, and in addition fifteen Constables, with fifteen Buglers and fifteen flags, fifty five Centurions, ten Captains of ordinary Veliti, and one Captain for the whole Battalion with its flag and Bugler. And I have knowingly repeated this arrangement many times, so that then, when I show you the methods for organizing the Companies and the armies, you will not be confounded.

I say, therefore, that any King or Republic which would want to organize its subjects in arms, would provide them with these parties and these arms, and create as many battalions in the country as it is capable of doing: and if it had organized it according to the division mentioned above, and wanting to train it according to the orders, they need only to be trained Company by Company. And although the number of men in each of them could not be themselves provide a reasonably (sized) army, none the less, each man can learn to do what applies to him in particular, for two orders are observed in the armies: the one, what men ought to do in each Company: the other, what the Company ought to do afterwards when it is with others in an army: and those men who carry out the first, will easily observe the second: but without the first, one can never arrive at the discipline of the second. Each of these Companies, therefore, can by themselves learn to maintain (discipline in) their ranks in every kind and place of action, and then to know how to assemble, to know its (particular bugle) call, through which it is commanded in battle; to know how to recognize by it ((as galleys do from the whistle)) as to what they have to do, whether to stay put, or go forward, or turn back, or the time and place to use their arms. So that knowing how to maintain ranks well, so that neither the action nor the place disorganizes them, they understand well the commands of the leader by means of the (bugle) calls, and knowing how to reassemble quickly, these Companies then can easily ((as I have said)), when many have come together, learn to do what each body of them is obligated to do together with other Companies in operating as a reasonably (sized) army. And as such a general practice also is not to be esteemed little, all the Battalions can be brought together once or twice in the years of peace, and give them a form of a complete army, training it for several days as if it should engage in battle, placing the front lines, the flanks, and auxiliaries in their (proper) places.

And as a Captain arranges his army for the engagement either taking into account the enemy he sees, or for that which he does not see but is apprehensive of, the army ought to be trained for both contingencies, and instructed so that it can march and fight when the need arises; showing your soldiers how they should conduct themselves if they should be assaulted by this band or that. And when you instruct them to fight against an enemy they can see, show them how the battle is enkindled, where they have to retire without being repulsed, who has to take their places, what signs, what (bugle) calls, and what voice they should obey, and to practice them so with Companies and by mock attacks, that they have the desire for real battle. For a courageous army is not so because the men in it are courageous, but because the ranks are well disciplined; for if I am of the first line fighters, and being overcome, I know where I have to retire, and who is to take my place, I will always fight with courage seeing my succor nearby: If I am of the second line fighters, I would not be dismayed at the first line being pushed back and repulsed, for I would have presupposed it could happen, and I would have desired it in order to be he who, as it was not them, would give the victory to my patron. Such training is most necessary where a new army is created; and where the army is old (veteran), it is also necessary for, as the Romans show, although they knew the organization of their army from childhood, none the less, those Captains, before they came to an encounter with the enemy, continually exercised them in those disciplines. And Joseph in his history says, that the continual training of the Roman armies resulted in all the disturbance which usually goes on for gain in a camp, was of no effect in an engagement, because everyone knew how to obey orders and to fight by observing them. But in the armies of new men which you have to put together to combat at the time, or that you caused to be organized to combat in time, nothing is done without this training, as the Companies are different as in a complete army; for as much discipline is necessary, it must be taught with double the industry and effort to those who do not have it, and be maintained in those who have it, as is seen from the fact that many excellent Captains have tired themselves without any regard to themselves.

COSIMO: And it appears to me that this discussion has somewhat carried you away, for while you have not yet mentioned the means with which Companies are trained, you have discussed engagements and the complete army.

FABRIZIO: You say the truth, and truly the reason is the affection I have for these orders, and the sorrow that I feel seeing that they are not put into action: none the less, have no fear, but I shall return to the subject. As I have told you, of first importance in the training of the Company is to know how to maintain ranks. To do this, it is necessary to exercise them in those orders, which they called Chiocciole (Spiralling). And as I told you that one of these Companies ought to consist of four hundred heavily armed infantry, I will stand on this number. They should, therefore, be arranged into eighty ranks (files), with five per file. Then continuing on either strongly or slowly, grouping them and dispersing them; which, when it is done, can be demonstrated better by deeds than by words: afterwards, it becomes less necessary, for anyone who is practiced in these exercises knows how this order proceeds, which is good for nothing else but to accustom the soldiers to maintain ranks. But let us come and put together one of those Companies.

I say that these can be formed in three ways: the first and most useful is to make it completely massive and give it the form of two squares: the second is to make the square with a homed front: the third is to make it with a space in the center, which they call Piazza (plaza). The method of putting together the first form can be in two steps. The first is to have the files doubled, that is, that the second file enters the first, the fourth into the third, and sixth into the fifth, and so on in succession; so that where there were eighty files and five (men) per file, they become forty files and ten per file. Then make them double another time in the same manner, placing one file within the other, and thus they become twenty files of twenty men per file. This makes almost a square, for although there are so many men on one side (of the square) as the other, none the less, on the side of the front, they come together so that (the side of) one man touches the next; but on the other side (of the square) the men are distant at least two arm lengths from each other, so that the square is longer from the front to the back (shoulders), then from one side (flank) to the other. (So that the rectangle thus formed is called two squares).

And as we have to talk often today of the parts in front, in the rear, and on the side of this Company, and of the complete army, you will understand that when I will say either head or front, I mean to say the part in front; when I say shoulder, the part behind (rear); when I say flanks, the parts on the side.

The fifty ordinary Veliti of the company are not mixed in with the other files, but when the company is formed, they extend along its flanks.

The other method of putting together (forming) the company is this; and because it is better than the first, I want to place in front of your eyes in detail how it ought to be organized. I believe you remember the number of men and the heads which compose it, and with what arms it is armed. The form, therefore, that this company ought to have is ((as I have said)) of twenty files, twenty men per file, five files of pikemen in front, and fifteen files of shield bearers on the shoulders (behind); two centurions are in front and two behind in the shoulders who have the office of those whom the ancients called Tergiduttori (Rear-leaders): The Constable, with the flag and bugler, is in that space which is between the five files of pikemen and the fifteen of shield-bearers: there is one of the Captains of the Ten on every flank, so that each one is alongside his men, those who are on the left side of his right hand, those on the right side on his left hand. The fifty Veliti are on the flanks and shoulders (rear) of the company. If it is desired, now, that regular infantry be employed, this company is put together in this form, and it must organize itself thusly: Have the infantry be brought to eighty files, five per file, as we said a little while ago; leaving the Veliti at the head and on the tail (rear), even though they are outside this arrangement; and it ought to be so arranged that each Centurion has twenty files behind him on the shoulders, and those immediately behind every Centurion are five files of pikemen, and the remaining shield-bearers: the Constable, with his flag and bugler, is in that space that is between the pikemen and the shield-bearers of the second Centurion, and occupies the places of three shield-bearers: twenty of the Heads of Ten are on the Flanks of the first Centurion on the left hand, and twenty are on the flanks of the last Centurion on the right hand. And you have to understand, that the Head of Ten who has to guide (lead) the pikemen ought to have a pike, and those who guide the shield-bearers ought to have similar arms.

The files, therefore, being brought to this arrangement, and if it is desired, by marching, to bring them into the company to form the head (front), you have to cause the first Centurion to stop with the first file of twenty, and the second to continue to march; and turning to the right (hand) he goes along the flanks of the twenty stopped files, so that he comes head-to-head with the other Centurion, where he too stops; and the third Centurion continues to march, also turning to the right (hand), and marches along the flanks of the stopped file so that he comes head-to-head with the other two Centurions; and when he also stops, the other Centurion follows with his file, also going to the right along the flanks of the stopped file, so that he arrives at the head (front) with the others, and then he stops; and the two Centurions who are alone quickly depart from the front and go to the rear of the company, which becomes formed in that manner and with those orders to the point which we showed a little while ago. The Veliti extend themselves along its flanks, according as they were disposed in the first method; which method is called Doubling by the straight line, and this last (method) is called Doubling by the flanks.

The first method is easier, while this latter is better organized, and is more adaptable, and can be better controlled by you, for it must be carried out by the numbers, that from five you make ten, ten twenty, twenty forty: so that by doubling at your direction, you cannot make a front of fifteen, or twenty five or thirty or thirty five, but you must proceed to where the number is less. And yet, every day, it happens in particular situations, that you must make a front with six or eight hundred infantry, so that the doubling by the straight line will disarrange you: yet this (latter) method pleases me more, and what difficulty may exist, can be more easily overcome by the proper exercise and practice of it.

I say to you, therefore, that it is more important than anything to have soldiers who know how to form themselves quickly, and it is necessary in holding them in these Companies, to train them thoroughly, and have them proceed bravely forward or backward, to pass through difficult places without disturbing the order; for the soldiers who know how to do this well, are experienced soldiers, and although they may have never met the enemy face to face, they can be called seasoned soldiers; and, on the contrary, those who do not know how to maintain this order, even if they may have been in a thousand wars, ought always to be considered as new soldiers. This applies in forming them when they are marching in small files: but if they are formed, and then become broken because of some accident that results either from the location or from the enemy, to reorganize themselves immediately is the important and difficult thing, in which much training and practice is needed, and in which the ancients placed much emphasis. It is necessary, therefore, to do two things: first, to have many countersigns in the Company: the other, always to keep this arrangement, that the same infantry always remain in the same file. For instance, if one is commanded to be in the second (file), he will afterwards always stay there, and not only in this same file, but in the same position (in the file); it is to be observed ((as I have said)) how necessary are the great number of countersigns, so that, coming together with other companies, it may be recognized by its own men. Secondly, that the Constable and Centurion have tufts of feathers on their head-dress different and recognizable, and what is more important, to arrange that the Heads of Ten be recognized. To which the ancients paid very much attention, that nothing else would do, but that they wrote numbers on their bucklers, calling then the first, second, third, fourth, etc. And they were not above content with this, but each soldier had to write on his shield the number of his file, and the number of his place assigned him in that file. The men, therefore, being thus countersigned (assigned), and accustomed to stay within these limits, if they should be disorganized, it is easy to reorganize them all quickly, for the flag staying fixed, the Centurions and Heads of Ten can judge their place by eye, and bring the left from the right, or the right from the left, with the usual distances between; the infantry guided by their rules and by the difference in countersigns, can quickly take their proper places, just as, if you were the staves of a barrel which you had first countersigned, I would wager you would put it (the barrel) back together with great ease, but if you had not so countersigned them (the staves), it is impossible to reassemble (the barrel). This system, with diligence and practice, can be taught quickly, and can be quickly learned, and once learned are forgotten with difficulty; for new men are guided by the old, and in time, a province which has such training, would become entirely expert in war. It is also necessary to teach them to turn in step, and do so when he should turn from the flanks and by the soldiers in the front, or from the front to the flanks or shoulders (rear). This is very easy, for it is sufficient only that each man turns his body toward the side he is commanded to, and the direction in which they turned becomes the front. It is true that when they turn by the flank, the ranks which turn go outside their usual area, because there is a small space between the breast to the shoulder, while from one flank to the other there is much space, which is all contrary to the regular formation of the company. Hence, care should be used in employing it. But this is more important and where more practice is needed, is when a company wants to turn entirely, as if it was a solid body. Here, great care and practice must be employed, for if it is desired to turn to the left, for instance, it is necessary that the left wing be halted, and those who are closer to the halted one, march much slower then those who are in the right wing and have to run; otherwise everything would be in confusion.

But as it always happens when an army marches from place to place, that the companies not situated in front, not having to combat at the front, or at the flanks or shoulders (rear), have to move from the flank or shoulder quickly to the front, and when such companies in such cases have the space necessary as we indicated above, it is necessary that the pikemen they have on that flank become the front, and the Heads of the Ten, Centurions, and Constables belonging to it relocate to their proper places. Therefore, in wanting to do this, when forming them it is necessary to arrange the eighty files of five per file, placing all the pikemen in the first twenty files, and placing five of the Heads of Ten (of it) in the front of them and five in the rear: the other sixty files situated behind are all shield-bearers, who total to three hundred. It should therefore be so arranged, that the first and last file of every hundred of Heads of Ten; the Constable with his flag and bugler be in the middle of the first hundred (century) of shield-bearers; and the Centurions at the head of every century. Thus arranged, when you want the pikemen to be on the left flank, you have to double them, century by century, from the right flank: if you want them to be on the right flank, you have to double them from the left. And thus this company turns with the pikemen on the flank, with the Heads of Ten on the front and rear, with the Centurions at the front of them, and the Constable in the middle. Which formation holds when going forward; but when the enemy comes and the time for the (companies) to move from the flanks to the front, it cannot be done unless all the soldiers face toward the flank where the pikemen are, and then the company is turned with its files and heads in that manner that was described above; for the Centurions being on the outside, and all the men in their places, the Centurions quickly enter them (the ranks) without difficulty. But when they are marching frontwards, and have to combat in the rear, they must arrange the files so that, in forming the company, the pikes are situated in the rear; and to do this, no other order has to be maintained except that where, in the formation of the company ordinarily every Century has five files of pikemen in front, it now has them behind, but in all the other parts, observe the order that I have mentioned.

COSIMO: You have said ((if I remember well)) that this method of training is to enable them to form these companies into an army, and that this training serves to enable them to be arranged within it. But if it should occur that these four hundred fifty infantry have to operate as a separate party, how would you arrange them?

FABRIZIO: I will now guide you in judging where he wants to place the pikes, and who should carry them, which is not in any way contrary to the arrangement mentioned above, for although it may be the method that is observed when, together with other companies, it comes to an engagement, none the less, it is a rule that serves for all those methods, in which it should happen that you have to manage it. But in showing you the other two methods for arranging the companies, proposed by me, I will also better satisfy your question; for either they are never used, or they are used when the company is above, and not in the company of others.

And to come to the method of forming it with two horns (wings), I say, that you ought to arrange the eighty files at five per file in this way: place a Centurion in the middle, and behind him twenty five files that have two pikemen (each) on the left side, and three shield-bearers on the right: and after the first five, in the next twenty, twenty Heads of Ten be placed, all between the pikemen and shield-bearers, except that those (Heads) who carry pikes stay with the pikemen. Behind these twenty five files thusly arranged, another Centurion is placed who has fifteen files of shield-bearers behind him. After these, the Constable between the flag and the bugler, who also has behind him another fifteen files of shield-bearers. The third Centurion is placed behind these, and he has twenty five files behind him, in each of which are three shield-bearers on the left left side and two pikemen on the right: and after the first five files are twenty Heads of Ten placed between the pikemen and the shield-bearers. After these files, there is the fourth Centurion. If it is desired, therefore, to arrange these files to form a company with two horns (wings), the first Centurion has to be halted with the twenty five files which are behind him. The second Centurion then has to be moved with the fifteen shield-bearers who are on his rear, and turning to the right, and on the right flank of the twenty five files to proceed so far that he comes to the fifteen files, and here he halts. After, the Constable has to be moved with the fifteen files of shield bearers who are behind, and turning around toward the right, over by the right flank of the fifteen files which were moved first, marches so that he comes to their front, and here he halts. After, move the third Centurion with the twenty five files and with the fourth Centurion who is behind them, and turning to the right, march by the left flank of the last fifteen files of shield-bearers, and he does not halt until he is at the head of them, but continues marching up until the last files of twenty five are in line with the files behind. And, having done this, the Centurion who was Head of the first fifteen files of shield-bearers leaves the place where he was, and goes to the rear of the left angle. And thus he will turn a company of twenty five solid files, of twenty infantry per file, with two wings, on each side of his front, and there will remain a space between then, as much as would (be occupied by) by ten men side by side. The Captain will be between the two wings, and a Centurion in each corner of the wing. There will be two files of pikemen and twenty Heads of Ten on each flank. These two wings (serve to) hold between them that artillery, whenever the company has any with it, and the carriages. The Veliti have to stay along the flanks beneath the pikemen. But, in wanting to bring this winged (formed) company into the form of the piazza (plaza), nothing else need be done than to take eight of the fifteen files of twenty per file and place them between the points of the two horns (wings), which then from wings become the rear (shoulder) of the piazza (plaza). The carriages are kept in this plaza, and the Captain and the flag there, but not the artillery, which is put either in the front or along the flanks. These are the methods which can be used by a company when it has to pass by suspicious places by itself. None the less, the solid company, without wings and without the plaza, is best. But in wanting to make safe the disarmed ones, that winged one is necessary.

The Swiss also have many forms of companies, among which they form one in the manner of a cross, as in the spaces between the arms, they keep their gunners safe from the attacks of the enemy. But since such companies are good in fighting by themselves, and my intention is to show how several companies united together combat with the enemy, I do not belabor myself further in describing it.

COSIMO: And it appears to me I have very well comprehended the method that ought to be employed in training the men in these companies, but ((if I remember well)) you said that in addition to the ten companies in a Battalion, you add a thousand extraordinary pikemen and four hundred extraordinary Veliti. Would you not describe how to train these?

FABRIZIO: I would, and with the greatest diligence: and I would train the pikemen, group by group, at least in the formations of the companies, as the others; for I would serve myself of these more than of the ordinary companies, in all the particular actions, how to escort, to raid, and such things.

But the Veliti I would train at home without bringing them together with the others, for as it is their office to combat brokenly (in the open, separately), it is not as necessary that they come together with the others or to train in common exercises, than to train them well in particular exercises. They ought, therefore, ((as was said in the beginning, and now it appears to me laborious to repeat it)) to train their own men in these companies so that they know how to maintain their ranks, know their places, return there quickly when either the evening or the location disrupts them; for when this is caused to be done, they can easily be taught the place the company has to hold and what its office should be in the armies. And if a Prince or a Republic works hard and puts diligence in these formations and in this training, it will always happen that there will be good soldiers in that country, and they will be superior to their neighbors, and will be those who give, and not receive, laws from other men. But ((as I have told you)) the disorder in which one exists, causes them to disregard and not to esteem these things, and, therefore, our training is not good: and even if there should be some heads or members naturally of virtue, they are unable to demonstrate it.

COSIMO: What carriages would you want each of these companies to have?

FABRIZIO: The first thing I would want is that the Centurions or the Heads of Ten should not go on horseback: and if the Constables want to ride mounted, I would want them to have a mule and not a horse. I would permit them two carriages, and one to each Centurion, and two to every three Heads of Ten, for they would quarter so many in each encampment, as we will narrate in its proper place. So that each company would have thirty six carriages, which I would have (them) to carry the necessary tents, cooking utensils, hatchets, digging bars, sufficient to make the encampment, and after that anything else of convenience.

COSIMO: I believe that Heads assigned by you in each of the companies are necessary: none the less, I would be apprehensive that so many commanders would be confusing.

FABRIZIO: They would be so if I would refer to one, but as I refer to many, they make for order; actually, without those (orders), it would be impossible to control them, for a wall which inclines on every side would need many and frequent supports, even if they are not so strong, but if few, they must be strong, for the virtu of only one, despite its spacing, can remedy any ruin. And so it must be that in the armies and among every ten men there is one of more life, of more heart, or at least of more authority, who with his courage, with words and by example keeps the others firm and disposed to fight. And these things mentioned by me, as the heads, the flags, the buglers, are necessary in an army, and it is seen that we have all these in our (present day) armies, but no one does his duty. First, the Heads of Ten, in desiring that those things be done because they are ordered, it is necessary ((as I have said)) for each of them to have his men separate, lodge with them, go into action with them, stay in the ranks with them, for when they are in their places, they are all of mind and temperament to maintain their ranks straight and firm, and it is impossible for them to become disrupted, or if they become disrupted, do not quickly reform their ranks. But today, they do not serve us for anything other than to give them more pay than the others, and to have them do some particular thing. The same happens with the flags, for they are kept rather to make a beautiful show, than for any military use. But the ancients served themselves of it as a guide and to reorganize themselves, for everyone, when the flag was standing firm, knew the place that he had to be near his flag, and always returned there. He also knew that if it were moving or standing still, he had to move or halt. It is necessary in an army, therefore, that there be many bodies, and that each body have its own flag and its own guide; for if they have this, it needs must be they have much courage and consequently, are livelier. The infantry, therefore, ought to march according to the flag, and the flag move according to the bugle (call), which call, if given well, commands the army, which proceeding in step with those, comes to serve the orders easily. Whence the ancients having whistles (pipes), fifes, and bugles, controlled (modulated) them perfectly; for, as he who dances proceeds in time with the music, and keeping with it does not make a miss-step, so an army obedient in its movement to that call (sound), will not become disorganized. And, therefore, they varied the calls according as they wanted to enkindle or quiet, or firm the spirits of men. And as the sounds were various, so they named them variously. The Doric call (sound) brought on constancy, Frigio, fury (boldness): whence they tell, that Alexander being at table, and someone sounding the Frigio call, it so excited his spirit that he took up arms. It would be necessary to rediscover all these methods, and if this is difficult, it ought not at least to be (totally) put aside by those who teach the soldier to obey; which each one can vary and arrange in his own way, so long as with practice he accustoms the ears of his soldiers to recognize them. But today, no benefit is gotten from these sounds in great part, other than to make noise.

COSIMO: I would desire to learn from you, if you have ever pondered this with yourself, whence such baseness and disorganization arises, and such negligence of this training in our times?

FABRIZIO: I will tell you willingly what I think. You know of the men excellent in war there have been many famed in Europe, few in Africa, and less in Asia. This results from (the fact that) these last two parts of the world have had a Principality or two, and few Republics; but Europe alone has had some Kingdoms and an infinite number of Republics. And men become excellent, and show their virtu, according as they are employed and recognized by their Prince, Republic, or King, whichever it may be. It happens, therefore, that where there is much power, many valiant men spring up, where there is little, few. In Asia, there are found Ninus, Cyrus, Artafersus, Mithradates, and very few others to accompany these. In Africa, there are noted ((omitting those of ancient Egypt)) Maximinius, Jugurtha, and those Captains who were raised by the Carthaginian Republic, and these are very few compared to those of Europe; for in Europe there are excellent men without number, and there would be many more, if there should be named together with them those others who have been forgotten by the malignity of the time, since the world has been more virtuous when there have been many States which have favored virtu, either from necessity or from other human passion. Few men, therefore, spring up in Asia, because, as that province was entirely subject to one Kingdom, in which because of its greatness there was indolence for the most part, it could not give rise to excellent men in business (activity). The same happened in Africa: yet several, with respect to the Carthaginian Republic, did arise. More excellent men come out of Republics than from Kingdoms, because in the former virtu is honored much of the time, in the Kingdom it is feared; whence it results that in the former, men of virtu are raised, in the latter they are extinguished. Whoever, therefore, considers the part of Europe, will find it to have been full of Republics and Principalities, which from the fear one had of the other, were constrained to keep alive their military organizations, and honor those who greatly prevailed in them. For in Greece, in addition to the Kingdom of the Macedonians, there were many Republics, and many most excellent men arose in each of them. In Italy, there were the Romans, the Samnites, the Tuscans, the Cisalpine Gauls. France and Germany were full of Republics and Princes. Spain, the very same. And although in comparison with the Romans, very few others were noted, it resulted from the malignity of the writers, who pursued fortune and to whom it was often enough to honor the victors. For it is not reasonable that among the Samnites and Tuscans, who fought fifty years with the Roman People before they were defeated, many excellent men should not have sprung up. And so likewise in France and Spain. But that virtu which the writers do not commemorate in particular men, they commemorate generally in the peoples, in which they exalt to the stars (skies) the obstinacy which existed in them in defending their liberty. It is true, therefore, that where there are many Empires, more valiant men spring up, and it follows, of necessity, that those being extinguished, little by little, virtu is extinguished, as there is less reason which causes men to become virtuous. And as the Roman Empire afterwards kept growing, and having extinguished all the Republics and Principalities of Europe and Africa, and in greater part those of Asis, no other path to virtu was left, except Rome. Whence it resulted that men of virtu began to be few in Europe as in Asia, which virtu ultimately came to decline; for all the virtu being brought to Rome, and as it was corrupted, so almost the whole world came to be corrupted, and the Scythian people were able to come to plunder that Empire, which had extinguished the virtu of others, but did not know how to maintain its own. And although afterwards that Empire, because of the inundation of those barbarians, became divided into several parts, this virtu was not renewed: first, because a price is paid to recover institutions when they are spoiled; another, because the mode of living today, with regard to the Christian religion, does not impose that necessity to defend it that anciently existed, in which at the time men, defeated in war, were either put to death or remained slaves in perpetuity, where they led lives of misery: the conquered lands were either desolated or the inhabitants driven out, their goods taken away, and they were sent dispersed throughout the world, so that those overcome in war suffered every last misery. Men were terrified from the fear of this, and they kept their military exercises alive, and honored those who were excellent in them. But today, this fear in large part is lost, and few of the defeated are put to death, and no one is kept prisoner long, for they are easily liberated. The Citizens, although they should rebel a thousand times, are not destroyed, goods are left to their people, so that the greatest evil that is feared is a ransom; so that men do not want to subject themselves to dangers which they little fear. Afterwards, these provinces of Europe exist under very few Heads as compared to the past, for all of France obeys a King, all of Spain another, and Italy exists in a few parts; so that weak Cities defend themselves by allying themselves with the victors, and strong States, for the reasons mentioned, do not fear an ultimate ruin.

COSIMO: And in the last twenty five years, many towns have been seen to be pillaged, and lost their Kingdoms; which examples ought to teach others to live and reassume some of the ancient orders.

FABRIZIO: That is what you say, but if you would note which towns are pillaged, you would not find them to be the Heads (Chief ones) of the States, but only members: as is seen in the sacking of Tortona and not Milan, Capua and not Naples, Brescia and not Venice, Ravenna and not Rome. Which examples do not cause the present thinking which governs to change, rather it causes them to remain in that opinion of being able to recover themselves by ransom: and because of this, they do not want to subject themselves to the bother of military training, as it appears to them partly unnecessary, partly a tangle they do not understand. Those others who are slave, to whom such examples ought to cause fear, do not have the power of remedying (their situation), and those Princes who have lost the State, are no longer in time, and those who have (the State) do not have (military training) and those Princes who have lost the State, are no longer in time, and those who have (the State) do not have (military training) or want it; for they want without any hardship to remain (in power) through fortune, not through their own virtu, and who see that, because there is so little virtu, fortune governs everything, and they want it to master them, not they master it. And that that which I have discussed is true, consider Germany, in which, because there are many Principalities and Republics, there is much virtu, and all that is good in our present army, depends on the example of those people, who, being completely jealous of their State ((as they fear servitude, which elsewhere is not feared)) maintain and honor themselves all us Lords. I want this to suffice to have said in showing the reasons for the present business according to my opinion. I do not know if it appears the same to you, or if some other apprehension should have risen from this discussion.

COSIMO: None, rather I am most satisfied with everything. I desire above, returning to our principal subject, to learn from you how you would arrange the cavalry with these companies, and how many, how captained, and how armed.

FABRIZIO: And it, perhaps, appears to you that I have omitted these, at which do not be surprized, for I speak little of them for two reasons: one, because this part of the army is less corrupt than that of the infantry, for it is not stronger than the ancient, it is on a par with it. However, a short while before, the method of training them has been mentioned. And as to arming them, I would arm them as is presently done, both as to the light cavalry as to the men-at-arms. But I would want the light cavalry to be all archers, with some light gunners among them, who, although of little use in other actions of war, are most useful in terrifying the peasants, and place them above a pass that is to be guarded by them, for one gunner causes more fear to them (the enemy) than twenty other armed men. And as to numbers, I say that departing from imitating the Roman army, I would have not less than three hundred effective cavalry for each battalion, of which I would want one hundred fifty to be men-at-arms, and a hundred fifty light cavalry; and I would give a leader to each of these parts, creating among them fifteen Heads of Ten per hand, and give each one a flag and a bugler. I would want that every ten men-at-arms have five carriages and every ten light cavalrymen two, which, like those of the infantry, should carry the tents, (cooking) utensils, hitches, poles, and in addition over the others, their tools. And do not think this is out of place seeing that men-at-arms have four horses at their service, and that such a practice is a corrupting one; for in Germany, it is seen that those men-at-arms are alone with their horses, and only every twenty have a cart which carries the necessary things behind them. The horsemen of the Romans were likewise alone: it is true that the Triari encamped near the cavalry and were obliged to render aid to it in the handling of the horses: this can easily be imitated by us, as will be shown in the distribution of quarters. That, therefore, which the Romans did, and that which the Germans do, we also can do; and in not doing it, we make a mistake. These cavalrymen, enrolled and organized together with a battalion, can often be assembled when the companies are assembled, and caused to make some semblance of attack among them, which should be done more so that they may be recognized among them than for any necessity. But I have said enough on this subject for now, and let us descend to forming an army which is able to offer battle to the enemy, and hope to win it; which is the end for which an army is organized, and so much study put into it.

Libro Secondo

LIBRO SECONDO

Io credo che sia necessario, trovati che sono gli uomini, armargli; e volendo fare questo, credo sia cosa necessaria esaminare che arme usavano gli antichi, e di quelle eleggere le migliori. I Romani dividevano le loro fanterie in gravemente e leggermente armate. Quelle dell'armi leggieri chiamavano con uno vocabolo Veliti. Sotto questo nome s'intendevano tutti quegli che traevano con la fromba, con la balestra, co' dardi; e portavano la maggior parte di loro, per loro difesa, coperto il capo e come una rotella in braccio. Combattevano costoro fuora degli ordini e discosti alla grave armadura; la quale era una celata che veniva infino in sulle spalle, una corazza che con le sue falde perveniva infino alle ginocchia; e avevano le gambe e le braccia coperte dagli stinieri e da' bracciali, con uno scudo imbracciato lungo due braccia e largo uno, il quale aveva un cerchio di ferro di sopra, per potere sostenere il colpo, e un altro di sotto, acciocchè, in terra stropicciandosi, non si consumasse. Per offendere avevano cinta una spada in sul fianco sinistro lunga uno braccio e mezzo, in sul fianco destro uno stiletto. Avevano uno dardo in mano, il quale chiamavono pilo, e nello appiccare la zuffa lo lanciavano al nimico. Questa era la importanza delle armi Romane, con le quali eglino occuparono tutto il mondo. E benchè alcuni di questi antichi scrittori dieno loro, oltre alle predette armi, un'asta in mano in modo che uno spiede, io non so come un'asta grave si possa da chi tiene lo scudo adoperare; perchè, a maneggiarla con due mani, lo scudo lo impedisce, con una, non può fare cosa buona per la gravezza sua. Oltre a questo, combattere nelle frotte e negli ordini con l'arme in asta è inutile, eccetto che nella prima fronte dove si ha lo spazio libero a potere spiegare tutta l'asta; il che negli ordini dentro non si può fare, perchè la natura delle battaglie, come nello ordine di quelle vi dirò, è continuamente ristringersi; perchè si teme meno questo, ancora che sia inconveniente, che il rallargarsi, dove è il pericolo evidentissimo. Talchè tutte le armi che passano di lunghezza due braccia, nelle stretture sono inutili; perchè se voi avete l'asta e vogliate adoperarla a due mani, posto che lo scudo non vi noiasse, non potete offendere con quella uno nimico che vi sia addosso. Se voi la prendete con una mano, per servirvi dello scudo, non la potendo pigliare se non nel mezzo, vi avanza tanta asta dalla parte di dietro, che quelli che vi sono di dietro v'impediscono a maneggiarla. E che sia vero, o che i Romani non avessono queste aste, o che, avendole, se ne valessono poco, leggete tutte le giornate nella sua istoria da Tito Livio celebrate, e vedrete, in quelle radissime volte essere fatta menzione delle aste; anzi sempre dice che, lanciati i pili, ei mettevano mano alla spada. Però io voglio lasciare queste aste, ed attenermi, quanto a' Romani, alla spada per offesa, e per difesa allo scudo con l'altre armi sopradette. I Greci non armavono sì gravemente per difesa come i Romani, ma, per offesa si fondavono più in sull'asta che in sulla spada, e massime le falangi di Macedonia, le quali portavano aste che chiamavono sarisse, lunghe bene dieci braccia, con le quali eglino aprivono le stiere nimiche e tenevano gli ordini nelle loro falangi. E benchè alcuni scrittori dicono ch'egli avevano ancora lo scudo, non so, per le ragioni dette di sopra, come e' potevano stare insieme le sarisse e quegli. Oltre a questo, nella giornata che fece Paulo Emilio con Persa re di Macedonia, non mi ricorda che vi sia fatta menzione di scudi, ma solo delle sarisse e delle difficultà che ebbe lo esercito Romano a vincerle. In modo che io conietturo, che non altrimenti fusse una falange macedonica, che si sia oggi una battaglia di Svizzeri, i quali hanno nelle picche tutto lo sforzo e tutta la potenza loro. Ornavano i Romani oltre alle armi le fanterie con pennacchi; le quali cose fanno l'aspetto d'uno esercito agli amici bello, a' nimici terribile. l'armi degli uomini a cavallo in quella prima antichità Romana erano uno scudo tondo, ed avevano coperto il capo, ed il resto era disarmato. Avevano la spada, ed un'asta con il ferro solamente dinanzi, lunga e sottile, donde venivano a non potere fermare lo scudo; e l'asta nello agitarsi si fiaccava, ed essi, per essere disarmati, erano esposti alle ferite. Dipoi con il tempo si armarono come i fanti; ma avevano lo scudo più breve e quadrato e l'asta più ferma e con due ferri, acciocchè, scollandosi da una parte, si potessero valere dell'altra. Con queste armi, così di piede come di cavallo, occuparono i miei Romani tutto il mondo; ed è credibile, per il frutto che se ne vide, che fussono i meglio armati eserciti che fussero mai. E Tito Livio nelle sue istorie ne fa fede assai volte dove, venendo in comparazione degli eserciti nimici, dice: Ma i Romani per virtù, per generazione di armi e disciplina erano superiori. E però io ho più particolarmente ragionato dell'armi de' vincitori, che de' vinti. Parmi bene solo a ragionare del modo dello armare presente. Hanno i fanti, per loro difesa, uno petto di ferro e, per offesa, una lancia nove braccia lunga, la quale chiamano picca, con una spada al fianco piuttosto tonda nella punta che acuta. Questo è l'armare ordinario delle fanterie d'oggi, perchè pochi ne sono che abbiano armate le stiene e le braccia, niuno il capo; e quelli pochi portano in cambio di picca un'alabarda, l'asta della quale, come sapete, è lunga tre braccia e ha il ferro ritratto come una scure. Hanno tra loro scoppiettieri, i quali, con lo impeto del fuoco, fanno quello ufficio che facevano anticamente i funditori e i balestrieri. Questo modo dello armare fu trovato da' populi Tedeschi e massime dai Svizzeri; i quali, sendo poveri e volendo vivere liberi, erano e sono necessitati combattere con la ambizione de' principi della Magna; i quali, per essere ricchi, potevano nutrire cavalli, il che non potevano fare quelli popoli per la povertà; onde ne nacque che, essendo a piè e volendosi difendere da' nimici che erano a cavallo, convenne loro ricercare degli antichi ordini e trovare arme che dalla furia de' cavalli gli difendesse. Questa necessità ha fatto o mantenere o ritrovare a costoro gli antichi ordini, senza quali, come ciascuno prudente afferma, la fanteria è al tutto inutile. Presono pertanto per arme le picche, arme utilissima non solamente a sostenere i cavalli, ma a vincergli. E hanno per virtù di queste armi e di questi ordini presa i Tedeschi tanta audacia, che quindici o ventimila di loro assalterebbero ogni gran numero di cavalli; e di questo da venticinque anni in qua se ne sono vedute esperienze assai. E sono stati tanto possenti gli esempli della virtù loro fondati in su queste armi e questi ordini, che poi che il re Carlo passò in Italia, ogni nazione gli ha imitati; tantochè gli eserciti Spagnuoli sono divenuti in una grandissima reputazione.

COSIMO: Quale modo di armare lodate voi più, o questo Tedesco o, l'antico Romano?

FABRIZIO: Il Romano senza dubbio; e dirovvi il bene e il male dell'uno e dell'altro. I fanti Tedeschi così armati possono sostenere e vincere i cavalli; sono più espediti al cammino e all'ordinarsi, per non essere carichi d'armi. Dall'altra parte sono esposti a tutti i colpi, e discosto e d'appresso, per essere disarmati; sono inutili alle battaglie delle terre e ad ogni zuffa dove sia gagliarda resistenza. Ma i Romani sostenevano e vincevano i cavalli, come questi; erano sicuri da' colpi da presso e di lontano, per essere coperti d'armi; potevano meglio urtare e meglio sostenere gli urti, avendo gli scudi; potevano più attamente nelle presse valersi con la spada che questi con la picca; e se ancora hanno la spada, per essere senza lo scudo, ella diventa in tale caso inutile. Potevano sicuramente assaltare le terre, avendo il capo coperto e potendoselo meglio coprire con lo scudo. Talmente che ei non avevano altra incommodità che la gravezza dell'armi e la noia dello averle a condurre; le quali cose essi superavano coll'avvezzare il corpo a' disagi e con indurirlo a potere durare fatica. E voi sapete come nelle cose consuete gli uomini non patiscono. E avete ad intendere questo: che le fanterie possono avere a combattere con fanti e con cavalli, e sempre fieno inutili quelle che non potranno o sostenere i cavalli, o, potendoli sostenere, abbiano nondimeno ad avere paura di fanterie che sieno meglio armate e meglio ordinate che loro. Ora se voi considererete la fanteria Tedesca e la Romana, voi troverrete nella Tedesca attitudine, come abbiamo detto, a vincere i cavalli, ma disavvantaggio grande quando combatte con una fanteria ordinata come loro e armata come la Romana. Tale che vi sarà questo vantaggio dall'una all'altra: che i Romani potranno superare i fanti e i cavalli, i Tedeschi solo i cavalli.

COSIMO: Io disidererei che voi venissi a qualche esempio più particolare, acciocchè noi lo intendessimo meglio.

FABRIZIO: Dico così: che voi troverrete, in molti luoghi delle istorie nostre, le fanterie Romane avere vinti innumerabili cavalli, e mai troverrete ch'elle sieno state vinte da uomini a piè, per difetto ch'ell'abbiano avuto nell'armare, o per vantaggio che abbia avuto il nimico nell'armi. Perchè, se il modo del-loro armare avesse avuto difetto, egli era necessario che seguisse l'una delle due cose: o che, trovando chi armasse meglio di loro, ei non andassono più avanti con gli acquisti, o che pigliassero de' modi forestieri e lasciassero i loro. E perchè non seguì nè l'una cosa nè l'altra, ne nasce che si può facilmente conietturare che il modo dell'armare loro fusse migliore che quello di alcuno altro. Non è già così intervenuto alle fanterie Tedesche, perchè si è visto fare loro cattiva pruova qualunque volta quelle hanno avuto a combattere con uomini a piè, ordinati e ostinati come loro; il che è nato dal vantaggio che quelle hanno riscontro nelle armi nimiche. Filippo Visconti, duca di Milano, essendo assaltato da diciottomila Svizzeri, mandò loro incontro il conte Carmignuola, il quale allora era suo capitano. Costui con seimila cavalli e pochi fanti, gli andò a trovare, e, venendo con loro alle mani, fu ributtato con suo danno gravissimo. Donde il Carmignuola, come uomo prudente, subito conobbe la potenza dell'armi nimiche, e quanto contro a' cavalli le prevalevano, e la debolezza de' cavalli contro a quegli a piè così ordinati; e rimesso insieme le sue genti, andò a ritrovare i Svizzeri e, come fu loro propinquo, fece scendere da cavallo le sue genti d'armi; e in tale maniera combattendo con quegli, tutti, fuora che tremila, gli ammazzò; i quali, veggendosi consumare senza avere rimedio, gittate l'armi in terra, si arrenderono.

COSIMO: Donde nasce tanto disavvantaggio?

FABRIZIO: Io ve l'ho poco fa detto; ma poichè voi non l'avete inteso, io ve lo replicherò. Le fanterie Tedesche, come poco fa vi si disse, quasi disarmate per difendersi, hanno, per offendere, la picca e la spada. Vengono con queste armi e con gli loro ordini a trovare il nimico, il quale, se è bene armato per difendersi, come erano gli uomini d'arme del Carmignuola che gli fece scendere a piè, viene con la spada e ne' suoi ordini a trovargli; e non ha altra difficultà che accostarsi a' Svizzeri tantochè gli aggiunga con la spada; perchè, come gli ha aggiunti, li combatte sicuramente, perchè il Tedesco non può dare con la picca al nimico che gli è presso per la lunghezza dell'asta, e gli conviene mettere mano alla spada, la quale è a lui inutile, sendo egli disarmato e avendo all'incontro uno nimico che sia tutto armato. Donde chi considera il vantaggio e il disavvantaggio dell'uno e dell'altro, vedrà come il disarmato non vi arà rimedio veruno; e il vincere la prima punga e passare le prime punte delle picche non è molta difficultà, sendo bene armato chi le combatte; perchè le battaglie vanno, come voi intenderete meglio, quando io vi arò dimostro com'elle si mettono insieme, e, andando, di necessità si accostano in modo l'una all'altra, ch'elle si pigliano per il petto; e se dalle picche ne è alcuno morto o gittato per terra, quegli che rimangono in piè sono tanti che bastano alla vittoria. Di qui nacque che il Carmignuola vinse con tanta strage de' Svizzeri e con poca perdita de' suoi.

COSIMO: Considerate che quegli del Carmignuola furono uomini d'arme, i quali, benchè fussero a piè, erano coperti tutti di ferro, e però poterono fare la pruova che fecero; sì che io mi penso che bisognasse armare una fanteria come loro, volendo fare la medesima pruova.

FABRIZIO: Se voi vi ricordassi come io dissi che i Romani armavano, voi non pensereste a cotesto, perchè uno fante che abbia il capo coperto dal ferro, il petto difeso dalla corazza e dallo scudo, le gambe e le braccia armate, è molto più atto a difendersi dalle picche ed entrare tra loro, che non è uno uomo d'arme a piè. Io ne voglio dare un poco di esemplo moderno. Erano scese di Sicilia nel Regno di Napoli fanterie Spagnuole, per andare a trovare Consalvo, che era assediato in Barletta da' Francesi. Fecesi loro incontro monsignore d'Ubignì con le sue genti d'arme e con circa quattromila fanti Tedeschi. Vennero alle mani i Tedeschi. Con le loro picche basse apersero le fanterie Spagnuole, ma quelle, aiutate da' loro brocchieri e dall'agilità del corpo loro, si mescolarono con i Tedeschi, tantochè gli poterono aggiugnere con la spada; donde ne nacque la morte, quasi, di tutti quegli e la vittoria degli Spagnuoli. Ciascuno sa quanti fanti Tedeschi morirono nella giornata di Ravenna; il che nacque dalle medesime cagioni: perchè le fanterie Spagnuole si accostarono al tiro della spada alle fanterie Tedesche, e le avrebbero consumate tutte, se da' cavalli Francesi non fussero i fanti Tedeschi stati soccorsi; nondimeno gli Spagnuoli, stretti insieme, si ridussero in luogo sicuro. Concludo, adunque, che una buona fanteria dee non solamente potere sostenere i cavalli, ma non avere paura de' fanti; il che, come ho molte volte detto procede dall'armi e dall'ordine.

COSIMO: Dite, pertanto, come voi l'armereste.

FABRIZIO: Prenderei delle armi Romane e delle Tedesche, e vorrei che la metà fussero armati come i Romani e l'altra metà come i Tedeschi. Perchè, se in seimila fanti, come io vi dirò poco dipoi, io avessi tremila fanti con gli scudi alla Romana e dumila picche e mille scoppiettieri alla Tedesca, mi basterebbono; perchè io porrei le picche o nella fronte delle battaglie, o dove io temessi più de' cavalli; e di quelli dello scudo e della spada mi servirei per fare spalle alle picche, e per vincere la giornata, come io vi mostrerò. Tantochè io crederei che una fanteria così ordinata superasse oggi ogni altra fanteria.

COSIMO: Questo che è detto ci basta quanto alle fanterie, ma quanto a' cavalli disideriamo intendere quale vi pare più gagliardo armare, o il nostro o l'antico?

FABRIZIO: Io credo che in questi tempi, rispetto alle selle arcionate e alle staffe non usate dagli antichi, si stia più gagliardamente a cavallo che allora. Credo che si armi anche più sicuro, tale che oggi uno squadrone di uomini d'arme, pesando assai, viene ad essere con più difficultà sostenuto che non erano gli antichi cavalli. Con tutto questo, nondimeno, io giudico che non si debba tenere più conto de' cavalli, che anticamente se ne tenesse; perchè, come di sopra si è detto, molte volte ne' tempi nostri hanno con i fanti ricevuta vergogna, e la riceveranno, sempre che riscontrino una fanteria armata e ordinata come di sopra. Aveva Tigrane, re d'Armenia, contro allo esercito Romano del quale era capitano Lucullo, cento cinquantamila cavalli, tra li quali erano molti armati come gli uomini d'arme nostri, i quali chiamavano catafratti; e dall'altra parte i Romani non aggiugnevano a seimila, con venticinquemila fanti, tantochè Tigrane, veggendo l'esercito de' nimici disse: Questi sono cavalli assai per un'ambasceria; nondimeno, venuto alle mani, fu rotto. E chi scrive quella zuffa vilipende quelli catafratti mostrandogli inutili, perchè dice che, per avere coperto il viso, erano poco atti a vedere e offendere il nimico e, per essere aggravati dall'armi, non potevano, cadendo, rizzarsi nè della persona loro in alcuna maniera valersi. Dico, pertanto, che quegli popoli, o regni, che istimeranno più la cavalleria che la fanteria, sempre fieno deboli ed esposti a ogni rovina, come si è veduta l'Italia ne' tempi nostri; la quale è stata predata, rovinata e corsa da' forestieri, non per altro peccato che per avere tenuta poca cura della milizia di piè, ed essersi ridotti i soldati suoi tutti a cavallo. Debbesi bene avere de' cavalli, ma per secondo e non per primo fondamento dello esercito suo; perchè, a fare scoperte, a correre e guastare il paese nimico, a tenere tribolato e infestato l'esercito di quello e in sull'armi sempre, a impedirgli le vettovaglie, sono necessarj e utilissimi; ma, quanto alle giornate e alle zuffe campali che sono la importanza della guerra e il fine a che si ordinano gli eserciti, sono più utili a seguire il nimico, rotto ch'egli è, che a fare alcuna altra cosa che in quelle si operi, e sono alla virtù del peditato assai inferiori.

COSIMO: E' mi occororno due dubitazioni; l'una, che io so che i Parti non operavano in guerra altro che i cavalli, e pure si divisono il mondo con i Romani; l'altra, che io vorrei che voi mi dicestecome la cavalleria puote essere sostenuta da' fanti, e donde nasca la virtù di questi e la debolezza di quella.

FABRIZIO: O io vi ho detto, o io vi ho voluto dire, come il ragionamento mio delle cose della guerra non ha a passare i termini d'Europa. Quando così sia, io non vi sono obligato a rendere ragione di quello che si è costumato in Asia. Pure io v'ho a dire questo: che la milizia de' Parti era al tutto contraria a quella de' Romani, perchè i Parti militavano tutti a cavallo e, nel combattere, procedevano confusi e rotti ed era uno modo di combattere instabile e pieno di incertitudine. I Romani erano, si può dire, quasi tutti a piè e combattevano stretti insieme e saldi; e vinsono variamente l'uno l'altro secondo il sito largo o stretto; perchè, in questo, i Romani erano superiori, in quello, i Parti; i quali poterono fare gran pruove con quella milizia, rispetto alla regione che loro avevano a difendere; la quale era larghissima, perchè ha le marine lontane mille miglia, i fiumi l'uno dall'altro due o tre giornate, e le terre medesimamente e gli abitatori radi; dimodochè un esercito Romano, grave e tardo per l'armi e per l'ordine, non poteva cavalcarlo senza suo grave danno, per esser chi lo difendeva a cavallo ed espeditissimo, in modochè egli era oggi in uno luogo, e domani discosto cinquanta miglia. Di quì nacque, che i Parti poterono prevalersi con la cavalleria solo, e la rovina dell'esercito di Crasso, e li pericoli di quello di Marcantonio. Ma io come vi ho detto, non intendo in questo mio ragionamento parlare della milizia fuori d'Europa, però voglio star in su quello che ordinarono già i Romani e i Greci, ed oggi fanno i Tedeschi. Ma vegniamo all'altra domanda vostra, dove voi desiderate intendere quale ordine o quale virtù naturale fa che i fanti superano la cavalleria. E vi dico in prima, come i cavalli non possono andare, come i fanti, in ogni luogo. Sono più tardi ad ubbidire, quando occorre variare l'ordine, che i fanti; perchè s'egli è bisogno, o andando avanti tornare indietro, o tornando indietro andare avanti, o muoversi stando fermi, o andando fermarsi, senza dubbio non lo possono così appunto fare i cavalli come i fanti. Non possono i cavalli, sendo da qualche impeto disordinati, ritornare negli ordini, se non con difficoltà, ancorchè quello impeto manchi; il che rarissimo fanno i fanti. Occorre oltre a questo, molte volte, che uno uomo animoso sarà sopra uno cavallo vile e uno vile sopra uno animoso; donde conviene che queste disparità d'animo faccino disordine. Nè alcuno si maravigli, che un nodo di fanti sostenga ogni impeto di cavalli; perchè il cavallo è animale sensato, e conosce i pericoli, e mal volentieri vi entra. E se considererete quali forze lo faccino andar avanti, e quali lo tengano indietro, vedrete senza dubbio esser maggiori quelle che lo ritengono, che quelle che lo spingono; perchè innanzi lo fa andar lo sprone, e dall'altra banda lo ritiene o la spada o la picca. Tale che si è visto per l' antiche e per le moderne esperienze un nodo di fanti essere sicurissimo, anzi insuperabile da' cavalli. E se voi arguissi a questo che la foga con la quale viene, lo fa più furioso a urtare chi lo volesse sostenere, meno stimare la picca che lo sprone, dico che, se il cavallo discosto comincia a vedere di avere a percuotere nelle punte delle picche, o per se stesso egli raffrenerà il corso, di modo che come egli si sentirà pugnere si fermerà affatto, o, giunto a quelle, si volterà a destra o a sinistra. Di che se volete fare esperienza, provate a correre un cavallo contro a un muro; radi ne troverrete che, con quale vi vogliate foga, vi dieno dentro. Cesare, avendo in Francia a combattere con i Svizzeri, scese e fece scendere ciascuno a piè e rimuovere dalla schiera i cavalli, come cosa più atta a fuggire che a combattere. Ma, nonostante questi naturali impedimenti che hanno i cavalli, quello capitano che conduce i fanti, debbe eleggere vie che abbiano per i cavalli più impedimenti si può; e rado occorrerà che l'uomo non possa assicurarsi per la qualità del paese. Perchè, se si cammina per le colline, il sito ti libera da quelle foghe di che voi dubitate; se si va per il piano, radi piani sono che, per le colture o per li boschi, non ti assicurino; perchè ogni macchia, ogni argine, ancora debole, toglie quella foga, e ogni coltura, dove sia vigne e altri arbori, impedisce i cavalli. E se tu vieni a giornata, quello medesimo ti interviene che camminando, perchè ogni poco di impedimento che il cavallo abbia, perde la foga sua. Una cosa nondimeno non voglio scordare di dirvi: come i Romani istimavano tanto i loro ordini e confidavono tanto nelle loro armi, che se gli avessono avuto ad eleggere o un luogo sì aspro per guardarsi dai cavalli, dove ei non avessono potuti spiegare gli ordini loro, o uno dove avessono avuto a temere più de' cavalli, ma vi si fussono potuti distendere, sempre prendevano questo e lasciavano quello. Ma perch'egli è tempo passare allo esercizio, avendo armate queste fanterie secondo l' antico e moderno uso, vedreno quali esercizj facevano loro fare i Romani, avanti che le fanterie si conduchino a fare giornata. Ancora ch'elle sieno bene elette e meglio armate, si deggiono con grandissimo studio esercitare, perchè senza questo esercizio mai soldato alcuno non fu buono. Deggiono essere questi esercizj tripartiti: l'uno, per indurare il corpo e farlo atto a' disagi e più veloce e più destro; l'altro, per imparare ad operare l'armi; il terzo, per imparare ad osservare gli ordini negli eserciti, così nel camminare, come nel combattere e nello alloggiare. Le quali sono le tre principali azioni che faccia uno esercito; perchè, se uno esercito cammina, alloggia e combatte ordinatamente e praticamente, il capitano ne riporta l'onore suo, ancora che la giornata avesse non buono fine. Hanno pertanto a questi esercizj tutte le republiche antiche provvisto in modo, per costume e per legge, che non se ne lasciava indietro alcuna parte. Esercitavano adunque la loro gioventù per fargli veloci nel correre, per fargli destri nel saltare, per fargli forti a trarre il palo o a fare alle braccia. E queste tre qualità sono quasi che necessarie in uno soldato, perchè la velocità lo fa atto a preoccupare i luoghi al nimico, a giugnerlo insperato e inaspettato, a seguitarlo quando egli è rotto. La destrezza lo fa atto a schifare il colpo, a saltare una fossa, a superare uno argine. La fortezza lo fa meglio portare l'armi, urtare il nimico, sostenere uno impeto. E sopratutto, per fare il corpo più atto a' disagi, si avvezzavano a portare gran pesi. La quale consuetudine è necessaria, perchè nelle espedizioni difficili conviene molte volte che il soldato oltre all'armi, porti da vivere per più giorni; e se non fusse assuefatto a questa fatica non potrebbe farlo; e per questo o e' non si potrebbe fuggire uno pericolo o acquistare con fama una vittoria. Quanto ad imparare ad operare l'armi, gli esercitavano in questo modo. Volevano che i giovani si vestissero armi che pesassero più il doppio che le vere, e per spada davano loro un bastone piombato, il quale a comparazione di quella era gravissimo. Facevano a ciascuno di loro ficcare un palo in terra, che rimanesse alto tre braccia, e in modo gagliardo, che i colpi non lo fiaccassero o atterrassono; contro al qual palo il giovane con lo scudo e col bastone, come contro ad un nimico si esercitava, ed ora gli tirava come se gli volesse ferire la testa o la faccia, ora come se lo volesse percuotere per fianco, ora per le gambe, ora si tirava indietro, ora si faceva innanzi. E avevano in questo esercizio questa avvertenza, di farsi atti a coprire se e ferire il nemico; ed avendo l'armi finte gravissime, parevano dipoi loro le vere più leggieri. Volevano i Romani che i loro soldati ferissono di punta e non di taglio, sì per essere il colpo più mortale, ed avere manco difesa, sì per scoprirsi meno chi ferisse, ed esser più atto a raddoppiarsi che il taglio. Non vi maravigliate che quelli antichi pensassero a queste cose minime, perchè dove si ragiona, che gli uomini abbiano a venire alle mani, ogni picciolo vantaggio è di gran momento; ed io vi ricordo quello, che di questo gli scrittori ne dicono, piuttosto ch'io ve l'insegni. Nè istimavano gli antichi cosa più felice in una Repubblica, che essere in quella assai uomini esercitati nell'armi; perchè non lo splendor delle gemme e dell'oro fa che i nemici ti si sottomettono, ma solo il timore dell'armi. Dipoi gli errori che si fanno nelle altre cose, si possono qualche volta correggere; ma quegli che si fanno nella guerra, sopravvenendo subito la pena, non si possono emendare. Oltre a quello il saper combatter fa gli uomini più audaci, perchè niuno teme di fare quelle cose, che gli pare aver imparato a fare. Volevano pertanto gli antichi, che i loro cittadini si esercitassino in ogni bellica azione, e facevano trarre loro contro a quel palo dardi più gravi che i veri; il qual esercizio, oltre al fare gli uomini esperti nel trarre, fa ancora le braccia più snodate e più forti. Insegnavano ancora lor trarre con l'arco e con la fromba, e a tutte queste cose avevano preposti maestri, in modo che poi, quando egli erano eletti per andare alla guerra, egli erano già con l'animo e con la disposizione soldati. Nè restava loro ad imparare altro che andare negli ordini e mantenersi in quegli, o camminando o combattendo, il che facilmente imparavano, mescolandosi con quegli che, per avere più tempo militato, sapevano stare negli ordini.

COSIMO: Quali esercizj fareste voi fare loro al presente?

FABRIZIO: Assai di quegli che si sono detti, come: correre e fare alle braccia, fargli saltare, fargli affaticare sotto armi più gravi che l'ordinarie, fargli trarre con la balestra e con l'arco; a che aggiugnerei lo scoppietto, instrumento nuovo, come voi sapete, e necessario. E a questi esercizj assuefarei tutta la gioventù del mio stato, ma, con maggiore industria e più sollecitudine, quella parte che io avessi descritta per militare; e sempre ne' giorni oziosi si eserciterebbero. Vorrei ancora ch'egl'imparassino a notare; il che è cosa molto utile, perchè non sempre sono i ponti a' fiumi, non sempre sono parati i navigj; tale che, non sapendo il tuo esercito notare, resti privo di molte commodità, e ti si tolgono molte occasioni al bene operare. I Romani non per altro avevano ordinato che i giovani si esercitassero in Campo Marzio, se non perchè, avendo propinquo il Tevere, potessero, affaticati nello esercizio di terra, ristorarsi nella acqua e parte, nel notare, esercitarsi. Farei ancora, come gli antichi, esercitare quegli che militassono a cavallo; il che è necessarissimo, perchè, oltre al sapere cavalcare sappiano a cavallo valersi di loro medesimi. E per questo avevano ordinati cavalli di legno, sopr'alli quali si addestravano, saltandovi sopra armati e disarmati, senza alcuno aiuto e da ogni mano, il che faceva che ad un tratto e ad un cenno d'uno capitano la cavalleria era a piè, e così ad un cenno rimontava a cavallo. E tali esercizi, e di piè e di cavallo, come allora erano facili, così ora non sarebbero difficili a quella Repubblica o a quel principe che volesse farli mettere in pratica alla sua gioventù; come per esperienza si vede in alcune città di Ponente, dove si tengono vivi simili modi con questo ordine. Dividono quelle tutti i loro abitanti in varie parti, e ogni parte nominano da una generazione di quell'armi che egli usano in guerra. E perchè egli usano picche, alabarde, archi e scoppietti, chiamano quelle: picchieri, alabardieri, scoppiettieri e arcieri. Conviene, adunque, a tutti gli abitanti dichiararsi in quale ordine voglia essere descritto. E perchè tutti, o per vecchiezza o per altri impedimenti, non sono atti alla guerra, fanno di ciascuno ordine una scelta, e gli chiamano i Giurati; i quali ne' giorni oziosi sono obligati a esercitarsi in quell'armi dalle quali sono nominati. E ha ciascuno illuogo suo deputato dal publico, dove tale esercizio si debba fare; e quelli che sono di quello ordine, ma non de' Giurati, concorrono con i danari a quelle spese che in tale esercizio sono necessarie. Quello pertanto che fanno loro, potremmo fare noi; ma la nostra poca prudenza non lascia pigliare alcuno buono partito. Da questi esercizj nasceva che gli antichi avevano buone fanterie e che ora quegli di Ponente sono migliori fanti che i nostri; perchè gli antichi gli esercitavano, o a casa, come facevano quelle republiche, o negli eserciti, come facevano quegli imperadori, per le cagioni che di sopra si dissono. Ma noi a casa esercitare non li vogliamo; in campo non possiamo, per non essere nostri suggetti e non gli potere obligare ad altri esercizj che per loro medesimi si vogliono. La quale cagione ha fatto che si sono straccurati prima gli esercizj e poi gli ordini, e che i Regni e le Repubbliche, massime italiane, vivono in tanta debolezza. Ma torniamo all'ordine nostro; e, seguitando questa materia degli esercizi, dico come non basta a far buoni eserciti avere indurati gli uomini, fattigli gagliardi, veloci e destri; che bisogna ancora ch'essi imparino a stare negli ordini, ad ubbidire a' segni a' suoni ed alle voci del capitano; sapere, stando, ritirandosi, andando innanzi, combattendo e camminando, mantenere quelli; perchè senza questa disciplina, con ogni accurata diligenza osservata e praticata, mai esercito non fu buono. E senza dubbio gli uomini feroci e disordinati sono molto più deboli che i timidi e ordinati; perchè l'ordine caccia dagli uomini il timore, il disordine scema la ferocia. E perchè voi intendiate meglio quello che di sotto si dirà, voi avete a intendere come ogni nazione, nell'ordinare gli uomini suoi alla guerra, ha fatto nell'esercito suo, ovvero nella sua milizia uno membro principale; il quale, se l'hanno variato con il nome, l'hanno poco variato con il numero degli uomini, perchè tutti l'hanno composto di sei in ottomila uomini. Questo membro da' Romani fu chiamato Legione, da' Greci Falange, dai Francesi Caterva. Questo medesimo ne' nostri tempi da' Svizzeri, i quali soli dell'antica milizia ritengono alcuna ombra, è chiamato in loro lingua quello che in nostra significa battaglione. Vero è che ciascuno l'ha poi diviso in varie battaglie, ed a suo proposito ordinato. Parmi, adunque, che noi fondiamo il nostro parlare in su questo nome come più noto, e dipoi, secondo gli antichi e moderni ordini, il meglio che è possibile, ordinarlo. E perchè i Romani dividevano la loro legione, che era composta di cinque in seimila uomini, in dieci coorti, io voglio che noi dividiamo il nostro battaglione in dieci battaglie e lo componiamo di seimila uomini di piè; e dareno a ogni battaglia quattrocentocinquanta uomini, de' quali ne sieno quattrocento armati d'armi gravi e cinquanta d'armi leggieri. l'armi gravi sieno trecento scudi con le spade, e chiaminsi scudati; e cento con le picche, e chiaminsi picche ordinarie; l'armi leggieri sieno cinquanta fanti armati di scoppietti, balestra e partigiane e rotelle; e questi da un nome antico si chiamino Veliti ordinarii. Tutte le dieci battaglie pertanto vengono ad avere tremila scudati, mille picche ordinarie e cinquecento Veliti ordinarj; i quali tutti fanno il numero di quattromila e cinquecento fanti. E noi diciamo, che vogliamo fare il battaglione di seimila, però bisogna aggiugnere altri mille cinquecento fanti, de' quali ne farei mille con le picche, le quali chiamerei picche estraordinarie, e cinquecento armati alla leggiera, i quali chiamerei Veliti estraordinarii. E così verrebbero le mie fanterie, secondo che poco fa dissi, a essere composte mezze di scudi e mezze fra picche e altre armi. Preporrei a ogni battaglia uno connestabole, quattro Centurioni e quaranta Capidieci; e di più un capo a' Veliti ordinarj, con cinque Capidieci. Darei alle mille picche estraordinarie tre connestaboli, dieci Centurioni e cento Capidieci; a' Veliti estraordinarj due connestaboli, cinque Centurioni e cinquanta Capidieci. Ordinerei dipoi un capo generale di tutto il battaglione. Vorrei che ciascuno connestabole avesse la bandiera e il suono. Sarebbe pertanto composto uno battaglione di dieci battaglie, di tremila scudati, di mille picche ordinarie, di mille estraordinarie, di cinquecento Veliti ordinarj, di cinquecento estraordinarj; e così verrebbero ad essere seimila fanti, tra quali sarebbero mille cinquecento Capidieci e, di più, quindici connestaboli con quindici suoni e quindici bandiere, cinquantacinque Centurioni, dieci capi de' Veliti ordinarj, e uno capitano di tutto il battaglione con la sua bandiera e con il suo suono. E vi ho volentieri replicato questo ordine più volte, acciocchè poi, quando io vi mostrerò i modi dell'ordinare le battaglie e gli eserciti, voi non vi confondiate. Dico, pertanto, come quel re o quella Repubblica dovrebbe quegli suoi sudditi ch'ella volesse ordinare all'armi, ordinargli con queste armi e con queste parti, e fare nel suo paese tanti battaglioni di quanti fusse capace. E quando gli avesse ordinati, secondo la sopradetta distribuzione, volendogli esercitare negli ordini, basterebbe esercitargli battaglia per battaglia. E benchè il numero degli uomini di ciascuna di esse non possa per se fare forma d'un giusto esercito, nondimeno può ciascuno uomo imparare a fare quello, che s'appartiene a lui particolarmente; perchè negli eserciti si osserva due ordini: l'uno, quello che deggiono fare gli uomini in ciascuna battaglia, e l'altro, quello che dipoi debbe fare la battaglia quando è coll'altre in uno esercito. E quelli uomini che fanno bene il primo, facilmente osservano il secondo; ma, senza sapere quello, non si può mai alla disciplina del secondo pervenire. Possono, adunque, come ho detto, ciascuna di queste battaglie da per se imparare a tenere l'ordine delle file in ogni qualità di moto e di luogo e, dipoi, a sapere mettersi insieme, intendere il suono mediante il quale nelle zuffe si comanda; sapere cognoscere da quello, come i galeotti dal fischio, quanto abbiano a fare, o a stare saldi, o gire avanti, o tornare indietro, o dove rivolgere l'armi e il volto. In modo che, sappiendo tenere bene le file, talmente che nè luogo nè moto le disordinino, intendendo bene i comandamenti del capo mediante il suono e sappiendo di subito ritornare nel suo luogo, possono poi facilmente, come io dissi, queste battaglie, sendone ridotte assai insieme, imparare a fare quello che tutto il corpo loro è obligato, insieme con l'altre battaglie, in un esercito giusto operare. E perchè tale pratica universale ancora non è da istimare poco, si potrebbe una volta o due l'anno, quando fusse pace, ridurre tutto il battaglione insieme e dargli forma d'uno esercito intero, esercitandogli alcuni giorni come se si avesse a fare giornata, ponendo la fronte, i fianchi e i sussidi ne' luoghi loro. E perchè uno capitano ordina il suo esercito alla giornata, o per conto del nimico che vede o per quello del quale senza vederlo dubita, si debbe esercitare il suo esercito nell'uno modo e nell'altro, e istruirlo in modo che possa camminare e, se il bisogno lo ricercasse, combattere, mostrando a' tuoi soldati quando fussero assaltati da questa o da quella banda, come si avessero a governare. E quando lo istruisse da combattere contro al nimico che vedessono, mostrar loro come la zuffa s'appicca, dove si abbiano a ritirare sendo ributtati, chi abbi a succedere in luogo loro, a che segni, a che suoni, a che voci debbano ubbidire e praticarvegli in modo, con le battaglie e con gli assalti finti, ch'egli abbiano a disiderare i veri. Perchè lo esercito animoso non lo fa per essere in quello uomini animosi, ma lo esservi ordini bene ordinati; perchè se io sono de' primi combattitori, e io sappia, sendo superato, dove io m'abbia a ritirare e chi abbia a succedere nelluogo mio, sempre combatterò con animo, veggendomi il soccorso propinquo. Se io sarò de' secondi combattitori, lo essere spinti e ributtati i primi non mi sbigottirà, perchè io mi arò presupposto che possa essere e l'arò disiderato, per essere quello che dia la vittoria al mio padrone, e non sieno quegli. Questi esercizj sono necessarissimi dove si faccia uno esercito di nuovo; e dove sia lo esercito vecchio sono necessarj, perchè si vede come ancora che i Romani sapessero da fanciugli l'ordine degli eserciti loro, nondimeno quegli capitani, avanti che venissero al nimico, continuamente gli esercitavano in quegli. E Iòsafo nella sua Istoria dice che i continui esercizj degli eserciti Romani facevano che tutta quella turba che segue il campo per guadagni, era, nelle giornate, utile; perchè tutti sapevano stare negli ordini e combattere servando quelli. Ma negli eserciti d'uomini nuovi, o che tu abbi messi insieme per combattere allora, o che tu ne faccia ordinanza per combattere con il tempo, senza questi esercizi, così delle battaglie di per se, come di tutto l'esercito, è fatto nulla; perchè, sendo necessarj gli ordini, conviene con doppia industria e fatica mostrargli a chi non gli sa, che mantenergli a chi gli sa, come si vede che per mantenergli e per insegnargli molti capitani eccellenti si sono senza alcuno rispetto affaticati.

COSIMO: E' mi pare che questo ragionamento vi abbia alquanto trasportato, perchè, non avendo voi ancora dichiarati i modi con i quali s'esercitano le battaglie, voi avete ragionato dell'esercito intero e delle giornate.

FABRIZIO: Voi dite la verità; e veramente ne è stata cagione l'affezione che io porto a questi ordini, e il dolore che io sento veggendo che non si mettono in atto, nondimanco non dubitate che io tornerò a segno. Come io v'ho detto la prima importanza che è nell'esercizio, delle battaglie, è sapere tenere bene le file. Per fare questo è necessario esercitargli in quegli ordini che chiamano chiocciole. E perchè io vi dissi che una di queste battaglie debbe essere di quattrocento fanti armati d'armi gravi, io mi fermerò sopra questo numero. Deonsi adunque ridurre in ottanta file a cinque per fila. Di poi, andando o forte o piano, annodargli insieme e sciorli; il che come si faccia, si può dimostrare più con i fatti che con le parole. Di poi è meno necessario, perchè ciascuno che è pratico negli eserciti sa come questo ordine proceda; il quale non è buono ad altro che all'avvezzare i soldati a tenere le file. Ma vegnamo a mettere insieme una di queste battaglie. Dico che si dà loro tre forme principali. La prima, la più utile, è farla tutta massiccia e darle la forma di due quadri; la seconda è fare il quadro con la fronte cornuta; la terza è farla con uno vacuo in mezzo che chiamano piazza. Il modo del mettere insieme la prima forma può essere di due sorti. L'una è fare raddoppiare le file: cioè, che la seconda fila entri nella prima, la quarta nella terza, la sesta nella quinta, e così successive; tanto che, dove ell'erono ottanta file a cinque per fila, diventino quaranta file a dieci per fila. Di poi farle raddoppiare un'altra volta nel medesimo modo, commettendosi l'una fila nell'altra, e così restono venti file a venti uomini per fila. Questo fa due quadri in circa, perchè, ancora che sieno tanti uomini per un verso quanti per l'altro, nondimeno di verso le teste si congiungono insieme, che l'uno fianco tocca l'altro; ma per l'altro verso sono distanti almeno due braccia l'uno dall'altro, di qualità che il quadro è più lungo dalle spalle alla fronte, che dall'uno fianco all'altro. E perchè noi abbiamo oggi a parlare più volte delle parti davanti, di dietro e da lato di queste battaglie e di tutto l'esercito insieme, sappiate che, quando io dirò o testa o fronte, vorrò dire le parti dinanzi; quando dirò spalle, la parte di dietro; quando dirò fianchi, le parti da lato. I cinquanta Veliti ordinarj della battaglia non si mescolano con l'altre file, ma, formata che è la battaglia, si distendono per i fianchi di quella. l'altro modo di mettere insieme la battaglia è questo; e perchè egli è migliore che il primo, io vi voglio mettere davanti agli occhi appunto com'ella si debbe ordinare. Io credo che voi vi ricordiate di che numero d'uomini, di che capi ella è composta e di che armi armata. La forma adunque che debbe avere questa battaglia, è, come io dissi, di venti file a venti uomini per fila: cinque file di picche in fronte e quindici file di scudi a spalle; due Centurioni stieno nella fronte e due dietro alle spalle, i quali facciano l'ufficio di quegli che gli antichi chiamavano tergiduttori; il connestabole con la bandiera e con il suono stia in quello spazio che è tra le cinque file delle picche e le quindici degli scudi; de' Capidieci, ne stia, sopr'ogni fianco di fila, uno, in modo che ciascuno abbia a canto i suoi uomini; quegli che saranno a mano manca, in sulla man destra; quelli che sieno a mano destra, in sulla man manca. Li cinquanta Veliti stieno a' fianchi e a spalle della battaglia. A volere ora che, andando per l'ordinario i fanti, questa battaglia si metta insieme in questa forma, conviene ordinarsi così: fare di avere ridotti i fanti in ottanta file, a cinque per fila, come poco fa dicemmo, lasciando i Veliti o dalla testa o dalla coda, pure ch'egli stieno fuora di quest'ordine; e debbesi ordinare che ogni Centurione abbia dietro alle spalle venti file, e sia dietro a ogni Centurione immediate cinque file di picche, e il resto scudi. Il connestabole stia con il suono e con la bandiera in quello spazio che è tra le picche e gli scudi del secondo Centurione, e occupino i luoghi di tre scudati; degli Capidieci, venti ne stieno ne' fianchi delle file del primo Centurione in sulla man sinistra, e venti ne stieno ne' fianchi delle file dell'ultimo Centurione in sulla man destra. E avete ad intendere che il Capodieci che ha a guidare le picche, debbe avere la picca, e quegli che guidano gli scudi, deggiono avere l'armi simili. Ridotte adunque in questo ordine le file e volendo nel camminare ridurle in battaglia per fare testa, tu hai a fare che si fermi il primo Centurione con le prime venti file, ed il secondo seguiti di camminare e, girandosi in sulla man ritta, ne vada lungo i fianchi delle venti file ferme, tantochè si attesti con l'altro Centurione, dove si fermi ancora egli; e il terzo Centurione seguiti di camminare, pure girando in sulla man destra, e, lungo i fianchi delle file ferme, cammini tanto, che si attesti con gli altri due Centurioni: e, fermandosi ancora egli, l'altro Centurione seguiti con le sue file, pure piegando in sulla destra lungo i fianchi delle file ferme, tanto ch'egli arrivi alla testa degli altri, e allora si fermi; e subito due de' Centurioni soli si partino dalla fronte e vadino a spalle della battaglia, la quale viene fatta in quel modo e con quello ordine appunto che poco fa ve la dimostrammo. I Veliti si distendino per i fianchi di essa, secondo che nel primo modo si dispose, il quale modo si chiama raddoppiargli per retta linea; questo si dice raddoppiargli per fianco. Quel primo modo è più facile, questo più ordinato e vien più appunto e meglio lo puoi a tuo modo correggere; perchè in quello conviene ubbidire al numero, perchè cinque ti fa dieci, dieci venti, venti quaranta; talchè, con il raddoppiare per diritto, tu non puoi fare una testa di quindici nè di venticinque, nè di trenta, nè di trentacinque, ma ti bisogna andare dove quel numero ti mena. Eppure occorre ogni dì, nelle fazioni particolari, che conviene fare testa con secento o ottocento fanti, in modo che il raddoppiare per linea retta ti disordinerebbe. Però mi piace più questo; e quella difficultà che vi è più, conviene con la pratica e con l'esercizio facilitarla.

Dicovi, adunque, com'egli importa più che cosa alcuna avere i soldati che si sappiano mettere negli ordini tosto; ed è necessario tenergli in queste battaglie, esercitarvegli dentro e fargli andare forte o innanzi o indietro, passare per luoghi difficili senza turbare l'ordine; perchè i soldati che sanno fare questo bene, sono soldati pratichi, e, ancora che non avessero mai veduti nimici in viso, si possono chiamare soldati vecchi. E al contrario, quegli che non sanno tenere questi ordini, se si fussero trovati in mille guerre, si deggiono sempre istimare soldati nuovi. Questo è quanto al mettergli insieme, quando sono nelle file piccole, camminando. Ma messi che sono, e poi, essendo rotti per qualche accidente che nasca o dal sito o dal nimico, a fare che in uno subito si riordinino, questa è la importanza e la difficultà e dove bisogna assai esercizio ed assai pratica, e dove gli antichi mettevano assai studio. È necessario pertanto fare due cose: prima, avere questa battaglia piena di contrassegni; l'altra, tenere sempre questo ordine: che quegli medesimi fanti stieno sempre in quelle medesime file. Verbigrazia, se uno ha cominciato a stare nella seconda, ch'egli stia dipoi sempre in quella; e non solamente in quella medesima fila, ma in quello medesimo luogo; a che osservare, come ho detto, sono necessarj gli assai contrassegni. In prima, è necessario che la bandiera sia in modo contrassegnata che, convenendo con l'altre battaglie, ella si conosca da loro. Secondo, che il connestabole e i Centurioni abbiano pennacchi in testa, differenti e conoscibili; e, quello che importa più, ordinare che si conoscano i Capidieci. A che gli antichi avevano tanta cura, che, non ch'altro, avevano scritto nella celata il numero, chiamandoli primo, secondo, terzo, quarto, ecc. E non erano ancora contenti a questo; che de' soldati ciascuno aveva scritto nello scudo il numero della fila e il numero delluogo che in quella fila gli toccava. Sendo dunque gli uomini contrassegnati così e assuefatti a stare tra questi termini, è facil cosa, disordinati che fussono, tutti riordinarli subito; perchè, ferma che è la bandiera, i Centurioni e i Capidieci possono giudicare a occhio illuogo loro, e, ridottisi i sinistri da sinistra, i destri da destra con le distanze loro consuete, i fanti, guidati dalla regola loro e dalle differenze de' contrassegni, possono essere subito ne' luoghi propri; non altrimenti che, se tu scommetti le doghe d'una botte che tu abbi contrassegnata prima, con facilità grandissima la riordini; che non l'avendo contrassegnata, è impossibile a riordinarla. Queste cose con la diligenza e con l'esercizio s'insegnano tosto e tosto s'imparano, e, imparate, con difficultà si scordano, perchè gli uomini nuovi sono guidati da' vecchi, e con il tempo una provincia con questi esercizj diventerebbe tutta pratica nella guerra. È necessario ancora insegnare loro voltarsi in un tempo e fare quando egli accaggia, de' fianchi e delle spalle fronte, e della fronte fianchi e spalle. Il che è facilissimo, perchè basta che ogni uomo volti la sua persona verso quella parte che gli è comandato; e dove voltano il volto, quivi viene ad essere la fronte. Vero è che quando si voltano per fianco, gli ordini tornano fuora della proporzione loro, perchè dal petto alle spalle v'è poca distanza, e dall'un fianco all'altro v'è assai distanza; il che è tutto contro all'ordine ordinario delle battaglie. Però conviene che la pratica e la discrezione gli rassetti. Ma questo è poco disordine, perchè facilmente per loro medesimi vi rimediano. Ma quello che importa più, e dove bisogna più pratica, è quando una battaglia si vuole voltare tutta come s'ella fusse un corpo solido. Qui conviene avere gran pratica e gran discrezione, perchè, volendola girare, verbigrazia, in sulla man manca, bisogna che si fermi il corno manco e, quegli che sono più propinqui a chi sta fermo, camminino tanto adagio, che quegli che sono dritto non abbiano a correre; altrimenti ogni cosa si confonderebbe.

Ma perchè egli occorre sempre, quando uno esercito cammina da luogo a luogo, che le battaglie che non sono poste in fronte, hanno a combattere non per testa, ma o per fianco o a spalle, in modo che una battaglia ha in uno subito a fare del fianco o delle spalle testa, e volendo che simili battaglie in tale caso abbiano la proporzione loro, secondo che di sopra si è dimostro, è necessario che ell'abbiano le picche da quel fianco che abbia ad essere testa e i Capidieci, Centurioni e connestabole, a quello ragguaglio, ne' luoghi loro, però, a volere fare questo, nel metterle insieme vi bisogna ordinare le ottanta file di cinque per fila, così: mettere tutte le picche nelle prime venti file, e, de' Capidieci d'esse, metterne cinque nel primo luogo e cinque nell'ultimo; l'altre sessanta file, che vengono dietro, sono tutte di scudi; che vengono ad essere tre centurie. Vuolsi adunque che la prima e ultima fila d'ogni centuria sieno Capidieci; il connestabole con la bandiera e con il suono stia nel mezzo della prima centuria degli scudi i Centurioni in testa d'ogni centuria ordinati.

Ordinati così, quando volessi che le picche venissono in sul fianco manco, voi gli avete a raddoppiare centuria per centuria dal fianco ritto, se volessi ch'elle venissero dal fianco ritto, voi le avete a raddoppiare dal manco. E così questa battaglia torna con le picche sopr'un fianco, con i Capidieci da testa e da spalle, con i Centurioni per testa e il connestabole nel mezzo. La quale forma tiene andando; ma, venendo il nimico e il tempo ch'ella voglia fare del fianco testa, non si ha se non a fare voltare il viso a tutti i soldati verso quel fianco dove sono le picche; e torna allora la battaglia con le file e con i capi in quel modo si è ordinata di sopra; perchè da' Centurioni in fuora tutti sono ne' luoghi loro, e i Centurioni subito e senza difficultà vi entrano.

Ma quando ell'abbia, camminando per testa, a combattere a spalle, conviene ordinare le file in modo che, mettendole in battaglia, le picche vengano di dietro; e a fare questo non s'ha a tenere altro ordine se non che, dove, nello ordinare la battaglia, per l'ordinario ogni centuria ha cinque file di picche davanti, le abbia di dietro, e in tutte l'altre parti osservare l'ordine che io dissi prima.

COSIMO: Voi avete detto, se bene mi ricorda, che questo modo dello esercizio è per potere poi ridurre queste battaglie insieme in uno esercito, e che questa pratica serve a potere ordinarsi in quello. Ma s'egli occorresse che questi quattrocento cinquanta fanti avessono a fare una fazione separata, come gli ordineresti?

FABRIZIO: Dee, chi gli guida, allora giudicare dove egli vuole collocare le picche, e quivi porle. Il che non repugna in parte alcuna all'ordine soprascritto; perchè, ancora che quello sia il modo che si osserva per fare la giornata insieme con l'altre battaglie, nondimeno non è regola che serve a tutti quegli modi nelli quali ti occorresse averti a maneggiare. Ma nel mostrarvi gli altri due modi, da me preposti, di ordinare le battaglie, sodisfarò ancora più alla domanda vostra; perchè o e' non si usano mai, o e' si usano quando una battaglia è sola e non in compagnia dell'altre. E per venire al modo di ordinarla con due corna, dico che tu dèi ordinare le ottanta file a cinque per fila in questo modo: porre là in mezzo uno Centurione, e, dopo lui, venticinque file che sieno di due picche in sulla sinistra e di tre scudi in sulla destra; e dopo le prime cinque, sieno posti nelle venti sequenti venti Capidieci; tutti tra le picche e gli scudi, eccetto che quelli che portano le picche, i quali possono stare con le picche. Dopo queste venticinque file così ordinate si ponga un altro Centurione: il quale abbia dietro a se quindici file di scudi. Dopo questi il connestabole in mezzo del suono e della bandiera; il quale ancora abbia dietro a se altre quindici file di scudi. Dopo queste si ponga il terzo Centurione; e abbia dietro a se venticinque file, in ognuna delle quali sieno tre scudi in sulla sinistra e due picche in sulla destra; e dopo le cinque prime file sieno venti Capidieci posti tra le picche e gli scudi. Dopo queste file sia il quarto Centurione. Volendo pertanto di queste file così ordinate fare una battaglia con due corna, si ha a fermare il primo Centurione con le venticinque file che gli sono dietro. Di poi si ha a muovere il secondo Centurione con le quindici file scudate che gli sono a spalle, e volgersi a mano ritta e, su per il fianco ritto delle venticinque file, andare tanto ch'egli arrivi alla quintadecima fila, e qui fermarsi. Di poi si ha a muovere il connestabole con le quindici file degli scudati che gli sono dietro, e, girando pure in sulla destra, su per il fianco destro delle quindici file mosse prima, cammini tanto ch'egli arrivi alla testa loro, e quivi si fermi. Di poi muova il terzo Centurione con le venticinque file e con il quarto Centurione che era dietro, e, girando pure in sulla ritta, cammini su per il fianco destro delle quindici file ultime degli scudati, e non si fermi quando è alla testa di quelle, ma seguiti di camminare, tanto che l'ultime file delle venticinque sieno al pari delle file di dietro. E, fatto questo, il Centurione che era capo delle prime quindici file degli scudati, si lievi donde era e ne vadia a spalle nello angulo sinistro. E così tornerà una battaglia di venticinque file ferme, a venti fanti per fila, con due corna, sopr'ogni canto della fronte uno, e ciascuno arà dieci file a cinque per fila, e resterà uno spazio tra le due corna, quanto tengono dieci uomini che volgano i fianchi l'uno all'altro. Sarà tra le due corna il capitano; in ogni punta di corno uno Centurione. Sarà ancora di dietro in ogni canto uno Centurione. Fieno due file di picche e venti Capidieci da ogni fianco. Servono queste due corna a tenere tra quelle l'artiglierie, quando questa battaglia ne avesse con seco, e i carriaggi. I Veliti hanno a stare lungo i fianchi sotto le picche. Ma a volere ridurre questa battaglia cornuta con la piazza, non si dee fare altro che, delle quindici file di venti per fila, prenderne otto e porle in sulla punta delle due corna: le quali allora di corna diventano spalle della piazza. In questa piazza si tengono i carriaggi; stavvi il capitano e la bandiera; ma non già l'artiglierie, le quali si mettono o nella fronte o lungo i fianchi. Questi sono i modi che si possono tenere da una battaglia, quando, sola, dee passare per i luoghi sospetti. Nondimeno la battaglia soda, senza corna e senza piazza è meglio. Pure, volendo assicurare i disarmati, quella cornuta è necessaria. "FORMA DEL CAMMINARE"

Fanno li Svizzeri ancora molte forme di battaglie; tra le quali ne fanno una a modo di croce, perchè, negli spazi che sono tra i rami di quella, tengono sicuri dall'urto de' nimici i loro scoppiettieri. Ma perchè simili battaglie sono buone a combattere da per loro, e la intenzione mia è mostrare come più battaglie unite insieme combattono, non voglio affaticarmi altrimenti in dimostrarle.

COSIMO: E' mi pare avere assai bene compreso il modo che si dee tenere a esercitare gli uomini in queste battaglie; ma, se mi ricorda bene, voi avete detto come, oltre alle dieci battaglie, voi aggiugnevi al battaglione mille picche estraordinarie e cinquecento Veliti estraordinarii. Questi non gli vorreste voi descrivere ed esercitare?

FABRIZIO: Vorrei, e con diligenza grandissima. E le picche eserciterei almeno bandiera per bandiera, negli ordini delle battaglie, come gli altri; perchè di questi io mi servirei più che delle battaglie ordinarie in tutte le fazioni particolari, come è fare scorte, predare, e simili cose. Ma i Veliti gli eserciterei alle case senza ridurli insieme; perchè, sendo l'ufficio loro combattere rotti, non è necessario che convenghino con li altri negli esercizj comuni, perchè assai sarebbe esercitargli bene negli esercizj particolari. Deonsi adunque, come in prima vi dissi nè ora mi pare fatica replicarlo, fare esercitare i suoi uomini in queste battaglie, in modo che sappiano tenere le file, conoscere i luoghi loro, tornarvi subito quando o nimico o sito gli perturbi, perchè, quando si sa fare questo, facilmente s'impara poi illuogo che ha a tenere una battaglia e quale sia l'ufficio suo negli eserciti. E quando uno principe o una Repubblica durerà fatica e metterà diligenza in questi ordini e in queste esercitazioni, sempre avverrà che nel paese suo saranno buoni soldati; ed essi fieno superiori a' loro vicini e saranno quegli che daranno e non riceveranno le leggi dagli altri uomini. Ma come io vi ho detto, il disordine nel quale si vive fa che si straccurano e non si istimano queste cose; e però gli eserciti nostri non son buoni; e se pure ci fusse o capi o membra naturalmente virtuosi, non la possono dimostrare.

COSIMO: Che carriaggi vorreste voi che avesse ciascuna di queste battaglie?

FABRIZIO: La prima cosa, io non vorrei che nè Centurione nè Capodieci avesse da ire a cavallo; e se il connestabole volesse cavalcare vorrei ch'egli avesse mulo e non cavalio. Permettere'gli bene due carriaggi e uno a qualunque Centurione e due ad ogni tre Capidieci, perchè tanti ne alloggiamo per alloggiamento, come nel suo luogo direno; talmente che ogni battaglia verrebbe avere trentasei carriaggi; i quali vorrei portassono di necessità le tende, i vasi da cuocere, scure e pali di ferro in sufficienza per fare gli alloggiamenti e, dipoi, se altro potessono, a commodità loro.

COSIMO: Io credo che i capi da voi ordinati in ciascuna di queste battaglie sieno necessarj; nondimeno io dubiterei che tanti comandatori non si confondessero.

FABRIZIO: Cotesto sarebbe quando non si referissono a uno, ma, referendosi, fanno ordine; anzi senza essi è impossibile reggersi; perchè uno muro il quale da ogni parte inclini, vuole piuttosto assai puntegli e spessi, ancora che non così forti, che pochi, ancora che gagliardi, perchè la virtù d'uno solo non rimedia alla rovina discosto. E però conviene che negli eserciti, e tra ogni dieci uomini, sia uno di più vita, di più cuore o almeno di più autorità, il quale coll'animo, con le parole, con lo esemplo tenga gli altri fermi e disposti al combattere. E che queste cose da me dette sieno necessarie in uno esercito, come i capi, le bandiere, i suoni, si vede che noi l'abbiamo tutte ne' nostri eserciti; ma niuna fa l'ufficio suo. Prima, i Capidieci, a volere che facciano quello per che sono ordinati, è necessario abbia come ho detto, ciascuno distinti i suoi uomini, alloggi con quegli, faccia le fazioni, stia negli ordini con quegli; perchè collocati ne' luoghi loro sono come uno rigo e temperamento a mantenere le file diritte e ferme, ed è impossibile ch'elle disordinino o, disordinando, non si riduchino tosto ne' luoghi loro. Ma noi oggi non ce ne serviamo ad altro che a dare loro più soldo che agli altri e a fare che facciano qualche fazione particolare. Il medesimo ne interviene delle bandiere, perchè si tengono piuttosto per fare bella una mostra, che per altro militare uso. Ma gli antichi se ne servivano per guida e per riordinarsi; perchè ciascuno, ferma che era la bandiera, sapeva illuogo che teneva presso alla sua bandiera e vi ritornava sempre. Sapeva ancora come, movendosi e stando quella, avevano a fermarsi o a muoversi. Però è necessario in uno esercito che vi sia assai corpi, e ogni corpo abbia la sua bandiera e la sua guida; perchè, avendo questo, conviene ch'egli abbia assai anime e, per consequente, assai vita. Deggiono adunque i fanti camminare secondo la bandiera e la bandiera muoversi secondo il suono; il quale suono, bene ordinato, comanda allo esercito; il quale, andando con i passi che rispondano a' tempi di quello, viene a servare facilmente gli ordini. Onde che gli antichi avieno sufoli, pifferi e suoni modulati perfettamente; perchè, come chi balla procede con il tempo della musica e, andando con quella, non erra, così uno esercito, ubbidendo nel muoversi a quel suono, non si disordina. E però variavano il suono, secondo che volevano variare il moto e secondo che volevano accendere o quietare o fermare gli animi degli uomini. E come i suoni erano varj, così variamente gli nominavano. Il suono dorico generava costanzia, il frigio furia, donde che dicono che, essendo Alessandro a mensa e sonando uno il suono frigio, gli accese tanto l'animo, che misse mano all'armi. Tutti questi modi sarebbe necessario ritrovare; e quando questo fosse difficile, non si vorrebbe almeno lasciare indietro quegli che insegnassono ubbidire al soldato; i quali ciascuno può variare e ordinare a suo modo, pure che con la pratica assuefaccia gli orecchi de' suoi soldati a conoscerli. Ma oggi di questo suono non se ne cava altro frutto in maggiore parte, che fare quel rumore.

COSIMO: Io disidererei intendere da voi, se mai con voi medesimo l'avete discorso, donde nasca tanta viltà e tanto disordine e tanta negligenza, in questi tempi, di questo esercizio.

FABRIZIO: Io vi dirò volentieri quello che io ne pensi. Voi sapete come degli uomini eccellenti in guerra ne sono stati nominati assai in Europa, pochi in Affrica e meno in Asia. Questo nasce perchè queste due ultime parti del mondo hanno avuto uno principato o due, e poche republiche; ma l'Europa solamente ha avuto qualche Regno e infinite republiche. Gli uomini diventono eccellenti e mostrano la loro virtù, secondo che sono adoperati e tirati innanzi dal principe loro, o Repubblica o re che si sia. Conviene pertanto che, dove è assai potestadi, vi surga assai valenti uomini; dove ne è poche, pochi. In Asia si truova Nino, Ciro, Artaserse, Mitridate, e pochissimi altri che a questi facciano compagnia. In Affrica si nominano, lasciando stare quella antichità Egizia, Massinissa, Jugurta, e quegli capitani che dalla Repubblica cartaginese furono nutriti; i quali ancora, rispetto a quegli d'Europa, sono pochissimi; perchè in Europa sono gli uomini eccellenti senza numero, e tanti più sarebbero, se insieme con quegli si nominassono gli altri che sono stati dalla malignità del tempo spenti; perchè il mondo è stato più virtuoso dove sono stati più Stati che abbiano favorita la virtù o per necessità o per altra umana passione. Sursero adunque in Asia pochi uomini, perchè quella provincia era tutta sotto uno regno, nel quale, per la grandezza sua, stando esso la maggior parte del tempo ozioso, non poteva nascere uomini nelle faccende eccellenti. All'Affrica intervenne il medesimo; pure vi se ne nutrì più, rispetto alla Repubblica cartaginese. Perchè delle republiche esce più uomini eccellenti che de' regni, perchè in quelle il più delle volte si onora la virtù, ne' Regni si teme; onde ne nasce che nell'una gli uomini virtuosi si nutriscono, nell'altra si spengono. Chi considererà adunque la parte d'Europa, la troverrà essere stata piena di republiche e di principati, i quali, per timore che l'uno aveva dell'altro, erano constretti a tenere vivi gli ordini militari e onorare coloro che in quegli più si prevalevano. Perchè in Grecia, oltre al Regno de' Macedoni, erano assai republiche, e in ciascuna di quelle nacquero uomini eccellentissimi. In Italia erano i Romani, i Sanniti, i Toscani, i Galli Cisalpini. La Francia e la Magna era piena di republiche e di principi; la Ispagna quel medesimo. E benchè a comparazione de' Romani se ne nominino pochi altri, nasce dalla malignità degli scrittori, i quali seguitano la fortuna, e a loro il più delle volte basta onorare i vincitori. Ma egli non è ragionevole che tra i Sanniti e i Toscani, i quali combatterono cento cinquanta anni col popolo Romano prima che fussero vinti, non nascessero moltissimi uomini eccellenti. E così medesimamente in Francia e in Ispagna. Ma quella virtù che gli scrittori non celebrano negli uomini particolari, celebrano generalmente ne' popoli, dove esaltano infino alle stelle l'ostinazione che era in quegli per difendere la libertà loro. Sendo adunque vero che, dove sia più imperj, surga più uomini valenti, seguita di necessità che, spegnendosi quelli, si spenga di mano in mano la virtù, venendo meno la cagione che fa gli uomini virtuosi. Essendo pertanto dipoi cresciuto l'imperio Romano, e avendo spente tutte le republiche e i principati d'Europa e d'Affrica e in maggior parte quelli dell'asia, non lasciò alcuna via alla virtù, se non Roma. Donde ne nacque che cominciarono gli uomini virtuosi ad essere pochi in Europa come in Asia; la quale virtù venne poi in ultima declinazione, perchè, sendo tutta la virtù ridotta in Roma, come quella fu corrotta, venne a essere corrotto quasi tutto il mondo; e poterono i popoli Sciti venire a predare quello Imperio il quale aveva la virtù d'altri spenta e non saputo mantenere la sua. E benchè poi quello Imperio, per la inundazione di quegli barbari, si dividesse in più parti, questa virtù non vi è rinata; l'una, perchè si pena un pezzo a ripigliare gli ordini quando sono guasti; l'altra, perchè il modo del vivere d'oggi, rispetto alla cristiana religione, non impone quella necessità al difendersi, che anticamente era; perchè, allora, gli uomini vinti in guerra o s'ammazzavano o rimanevano in perpetuo schiavi, dove menavano la loro vita miseramente; le terre vinte o si desolavano o ne erano cacciati gli abitatori, tolti loro i beni, mandati dispersi per il mondo; tantochè i superati in guerra pativano ogni ultima miseria. Da questo timore spaventati, gli uomini tenevano gli esercizj militari vivi e onoravano chi era eccellente in quegli. Ma oggi questa paura in maggior parte è perduta; de' vinti, pochi se ne ammazza; niuno se ne tiene lungamente prigione, perchè con facilità si liberano. Le città, ancora ch'elle si sieno mille volte ribellate, non si disfanno; lasciansi gli uomini ne' beni loro, in modo che il maggior male che si tema è una taglia; talmente che gli uomini non vogliono sottomettersi agli ordini militari e stentare tuttavia sotto quegli, per fuggire quegli pericoli de' quali temono poco. Di poi queste provincie d'Europa sono sotto pochissimi capi, rispetto allora; perchè tutta la Francia obedisce a uno re, tutta l'Ispagna a un altro, l'Italia è in poche parti; in modo che le città deboli si difendono coll'accostarsi a chi vince, e gli stati gagliardi, per le cagioni dette, non temono una ultima rovina.

COSIMO: E' si sono pur vedute molte terre andare a sacco, da venticinque anni in qua, e perdere de' regni, il quale esemplo doverrebbe insegnare agli altri vivere e ripigliare alcuno degli ordini antichi.

FABRIZIO: Egli è quello che voi dite; ma se voi noterete quali terre sono ite a sacco, voi non troverrete ch'elle sieno de' capi degli stati, ma delle membra: come si vede che fu saccheggiata Tortona e non Milano, Capova e non Napoli, Brescia e non Vinegia, Ravenna e non Roma. I quali esempli non fanno mutare di proposito chi governa, anzi gli fa stare più nella loro opinione di potersi ricomperare con le taglie; e per questo non vogliono sottoporsi agli affanni degli esercizj della guerra, parendo loro, parte non necessario, parte uno viluppo che non intendono. Quegli altri che sono servi, a chi tali esempli doverrebbero fare paura, non hanno potestà di rimediarvi; e quegli principi, per avere perduto lo stato, non sono più a tempo, e quegli che lo tengono, non sanno e non vogliono; perchè vogliono senza alcuno disagio stare con la fortuna e non con la virtù loro, perchè veggono che, per esserci poca virtù, la fortuna governa ogni cosa, e vogliono che quella gli signoreggi, non essi signoreggiare quella. E che questo che io ho discorso sia vero, considerate la Magna; nella quale, per essere assai principati e republiche, vi è assai virtù, e tutto quello che nella presente milizia è di buono, depende dallo esemplo di quegli popoli; i quali, sendo tutti gelosi de' loro stati, temendo la servitù, il che altrove non si teme, tutti si mantengono signori e onorati. Questo voglio che basti avere detto a mostrare le cagioni della presente viltà, secondo l'opinione mia. Non so se a voi pare il medesimo, o se vi fusse nata, per questo ragionare, alcuna dubitazione.

COSIMO: Niuna; anzi rimango di tutto capacissimo. Solo disidero, tornando alla materia principale nostra, intendere da voi come voi ordineresti i cavalli con queste battaglie, e quanti e come capitanati e come armati.

FABRIZIO: E' vi pare forse che io gli abbia lasciati indietro; di che non vi maravigliate, perchè io sono per due cagioni per parlarne poco: l'una, perchè il nervo e la importanza dello esercito è la fanteria; l'altra, perchè questa parte di milizia è meno corrotta che quella de' fanti; perchè, s'ella non è più forte dell'antica, ell'è al pari. Pure si è detto, poco innanzi, del modo dello esercitargli. E quanto allo armargli, io gli armerei come al presente si fa, così i cavalli leggieri come gli uomini d'arme. Ma i cavalli leggieri vorrei che fussero tutti balestrieri con qualche scoppiettiere tra loro; i quali, benchè negli altri maneggi di guerra sieno poco utili, sono a questo utilissimi: di sbigottire i paesani e levargli di sopra uno passo che fusse guardato da loro, perchè più paura farà loro un scoppiettiere che venti altri armati. Ma, venendo al numero, dico che, avendo tolto a imitare la milizia Romana, io non ordinerei se non trecento cavalli utili per ogni battaglione; de' quali vorrei ne fusse centocinquanta uomini d'arme e centocinquanta cavalli leggieri; e darei a ciascuna di queste parti uno capo, faccendo poi tra loro quindici Capidieci per banda, dando a ciascuna uno suono e una bandiera. Vorrei che ogni dieci uomini d'arme avessero cinque carriaggi e, ogni dieci cavalli leggieri, due; i quali, come quegli de' fanti, portassero le tende, i vasi, e le scure e i pali e, sopravanzando, gli altri arnesi loro. Nè crediate che questo sia disordine, vedendo ora come gli uomini d'arme hanno alloro servizio quattro cavalli, perchè tale cosa è una corruttela; perchè si vede nella Magna quegli uomini d'arme essere soli con illoro cavallo; solo avere, ogni venti, uno carro che porta loro dietro le cose loro necessarie. I cavalli de' Romani erano medesimamente soli; vero è che i triarj alloggiavano propinqui alla cavalleria, i quali erano obligati a somministrare aiuto a quella nel governo de' cavalli; il che si può facilmente imitare da noi, come nel distribuire degli alloggiamenti vi si mostrerà. Quello, adunque, che facevano i Romani, e quello che fanno oggi i Tedeschi, possiamo fare ancora noi, anzi, non lo faccendo, si erra. Questi cavalli ordinati e descritti insieme col battaglione, si potrebbero qualche volta mettere insieme, quando si ragunassono le battaglie, e fare che tra loro facessero qualche vista d'assalto, il quale fussi più per riconoscersi insieme, che per altra necessità. Ma sia per ora detto di questa parte abbastanza; e discendiamo a dare forma a uno esercito per potere presentare la giornata al nimico e sperare di vincerla; la quale cosa è il fine per il quale si ordina la milizia e tanto studio si mette in quella.

Book Three

BOOK THREE

COSIMO: Since we are changing the discussion, I would like the questioner to be changed, so that I may not be held to be presumptuous, which I have always censured in others. I, therefore, resign the speakership, and I surrender it to any of these friends of mine who want it.

ZANOBI: It would be most gracious of you to continue: but since you do not want to, you ought at least to tell us which of us should succeed in your place.

COSIMO: I would like to pass this burden on the Lord Fabrizio.

FABRIZIO: I am content to accept it, and would like to follow the Venetian custom, that the youngest talks first; for this being an exercise for young men, I am persuaded that young men are more adept at reasoning, than they are quick to follow.

COSIMO: It therefore falls to you Luigi: and I am pleased with such a successor, as long as you are satisfied with such a questioner.

FABRIZIO: I am certain that, in wanting to show how an army is well organized for undertaking an engagement, it would be necessary to narrate how the Greeks and the Romans arranged the ranks in their armies. None the less, as you yourselves are able to read and consider these things, through the medium of ancient writers, I shall omit many particulars, and will cite only those things that appear necessary for me to imitate, in the desire in our times to give some (part of) perfection to our army. This will be done, and, in time, I will show how an army is arranged for an engagement, how it faces a real battle, and how it can be trained in mock ones. The greatest mistake that those men make who arrange an army for an engagement, is to give it only one front, and commit it to only one onrush and one attempt (fortune). This results from having lost the method the ancients employed of receiving one rank into the other; for without this method, one cannot help the rank in front, or defend them, or change them by rotation in battle, which was practiced best by the Romans. In explaining this method, therefore, I want to tell how the Romans divided each Legion into three parts, namely, the Astati, the Princeps, and the Triari; of whom the Astati were placed in the first line of the army in solid and deep ranks, (and) behind them were the Princeps, but placed with their ranks more open: and behind these they placed the Triari, and with ranks so sparse, as to be able, if necessary, to receive the Princeps and the Astati between them. In addition to these, they had slingers, bowmen (archers), and other lightly armed, who were not in these ranks, but were situated at the head of the army between the cavalry and the infantry. These light armed men, therefore, enkindled the battle, and if they won ((which rarely happened)), they pursued the victory: if they were repulsed, they retired by way of the flanks of the army, or into the intervals (gaps) provided for such a result, and were led back among those who were not armed: after this proceeding, the Astati came hand to hand with the enemy, and who, if they saw themselves being overcome, retired little by little through the open spaces in the ranks of the Princeps, and, together with them, renewed the fight. If these also were forced back, they all retired into the thin lines of the Triari, and all together, en masse, recommenced the battle; and if these were defeated, there was no other remedy, as there was no way left to reform themselves. The cavalry were on the flanks of the army, placed like two wings on a body, and they some times fought on horseback, and sometimes helped the infantry, according as the need required. This method of reforming themselves three times is almost impossible to surpass, as it is necessary that fortune abandon you three times, and that the enemy has so much virtu that he overcomes you three times. The Greeks, with their Phalanxes, did not have this method of reforming themselves, and although these had many ranks and Leaders within them, none the less, they constituted one body, or rather, one front. So that in order to help one another, they did not retire from one rank into the other, as the Romans, but one man took the place of another, which they did in this way. Their Phalanxes were (made up) of ranks, and supposing they had placed fifty men per rank, when their front came against the enemy, only the first six ranks of all of them were able to fight, because their lances, which they called Sarisse, were so long, that the points of the lances of those in the sixth rank reached past the front rank. When they fought, therefore, if any of the first rank fell, either killed or wounded, whoever was behind him in the second rank immediately entered into his place, and whoever was behind him in the third rank immediately entered into the place in the second rank which had become vacant, and thus successively all at once the ranks behind restored the deficiencies of those in front, so that the ranks were always remained complete, and no position of the combatants was vacant except in the last rank, which became depleted because there was no one in its rear to restore it. So that the injuries which the first rank suffered, depleted the last, and the first rank always remained complete; and thus the Phalanxes, because of their arrangement, were able rather to become depleted than broken, since the large (size of its) body made it more immobile. The Romans, in the beginning, also employed Phalanxes, and instructed their Legions in a way similar to theirs. Afterwards, they were not satisfied with this arrangement, and divided the Legion into several bodies; that is, into Cohorts and Maniples; for they judged ((as was said a little while ago)) that that body should have more life in it (be more active) which should have more spirit, and that it should be composed of several parts, and each regulate itself. The Battalions of the Swiss, in these times, employed all the methods of the Phalanxes, as much in the size and entirety of their organization, as in the method of helping one another, and when coming to an engagement they place the Battalions one on the flank of the other, or they place them one behind the other. They have no way in which the first rank, if it should retire, to be received by the second, but with this arrangement, in order to help one another, they place one Battalion in front and another behind it to the right, so that if the first has need of aid, the latter can go forward and succor it. They put a third Battalion behind these, but distant a gun shot. This they do, because if the other two are repulsed, this (third) one can make its way forward, and the others have room in which to retire, and avoid the onrush of the one which is going forward; for a large multitude cannot be received (in the same way) as a small body, and, therefore, the small and separate bodies that existed in a Roman Legion could be so placed together as to be able to receive one another among themselves, and help each other easily. And that this arrangement of the Swiss is not as good as that of the ancient Romans is demonstrated by the many examples of the Roman Legions when they engaged in battle with the Greek Phalanxes, and the latter were always destroyed by the former, because the kinds of arms ((as I mentioned before)) and this method of reforming themselves, was not able to maintain the solidity of the Phalanx. With these examples, therefore, if I had to organize an army, I would prefer to retain the arms and the methods, partly of the Greek Phalanxes, partly of the Roman Legions; and therefore I have mentioned wanting in a Battalion two thousand pikes, which are the arms of the Macedonian Phalanxes, and three thousand swords and shield, which are the arms of the Romans. I have divided the Battalion into ten Companies, as the Romans (divided) the Legion into ten Cohorts. I have organized the Veliti, that is the light armed, to enkindle the battle, as they (the Romans did). And thus, as the arms are mixed, being shared by both nations and as also the organizations are shared, I have arranged that each company have five ranks of pikes (pikemen) in front, and the remainder shields (swordsmen with shields), in order to be able with this front to resist the cavalry, and easily penetrate the enemy companies on foot, and the enemy at the first encounter would meet the pikes, which I would hope would suffice to resist him, and then the shields (swordsmen) would defeat him. And if you would note the virtu of this arrangement, you will see all these arms will execute their office completely. First, because pikes are useful against cavalry, and when they come against infantry, they do their duty well before the battle closes in, for when they are pressed, they become useless. Whence the Swiss, to avoid this disadvantage, after every three ranks of pikemen place one of halberds, which, while it is not enough, gives the pikemen room (to maneuver). Placing, therefore, our pikes in the front and the shields (swordsmen) behind, they manage to resist the cavalry, and in enkindling the battle, lay open and attack the infantry: but when the battle closes in, and they become useless, the shields and swords take their place, who are able to take care of themselves in every strait.

LUIGI: We now await with desire to learn how you would arrange the army for battle with these arms and with these organizations.

FABRIZIO: I do not now want to show you anything else other than this. You have to understand that in a regular Roman army, which they called a Consular Army, there were not more than two Legions of Roman Citizens, which consist of six hundred cavalry and about eleven thousand infantry. They also had as many more infantry and cavalry which were sent to them by their friends and confederates, which they divided into two parts, and they called one the right wing, and the other the left wing, and they never permitted this (latter) infantry to exceed the number of the infantry of the Legion. They were well content that the cavalry should be greater in number. With this army which consisted of twenty two thousand infantry and about two thousand cavalry effectives, a Consul undertook every action and went on every enterprise. And when it was necessary to face a large force, they brought together two Consuls with two armies. You ought also to note that ordinarily in all three of the principal activities in which armies engage, that is, marching, camping, and fighting, they place the Legion in the middle, because they wanted that virtu in which they should trust most should be greater unity, as the discussion of all these three activities will show you. Those auxiliary infantry, because of the training they had with the infantry of the Legion, were as effective as the latter, as they were disciplined as they were, and therefore they arranged them in a similar way when organizing (for) and engagement. Whoever, therefore, knows how they deployed the entire (army). Therefore, having told you how they divided a Legion into three lines, and how one line would receive the other, I have come to tell you how the entire army was organized for an engagement.

If I would want, therefore, to arrange (an army for) an engagement in imitation of the Romans, just as they had two Legions, I would take two Battalions, and these having been deployed, the disposition of an entire Army would be known: for by adding more people, nothing else is accomplished than to enlarge the organization. I do not believe it is necessary that I remind you how many infantry there are in a Battalion, and that it has ten companies, and what Leaders there are per company, and what arms they have, and who are the ordinary (regular) pikemen and Veliti, and who the extraordinary, because a little while I distinctly told you, and I reminded you to commit it to memory as something necessary if you should want to understand all the other arrangements: and, therefore, I will come to the demonstration of the arrangement, without repeating these again. And it appears to me that ten Companies of a Battalion should be placed on the left flank, and the ten others of the other on the right. Those on the left should be arranged in this way. The five companies should be placed one alongside the other on the front, so that between one and the next there would be a space of four arm lengths which come to occupy an area of one hundred forty one arm lengths long, and forty wide. Behind these five Companies I would place three others, distant in a straight line from the first ones by forty arm lengths, two of which should come behind in a straight line at the ends of the five, and the other should occupy the space in the middle. Thus these three would come to occupy in length and width the same space as the five: but where the five would have a distance of four arm lengths between one another, this one would have thirty three. Behind these I would place the last two companies, also in a straight line behind the three, and distant from those three forty arm lengths, and I would place each of them behind the ends of the three, so that the space between them would be ninety one arm lengths. All of these companies arranged thusly would therefore cover (an area of) one hundred forty one arm lengths long and two hundred wide. The extraordinary pikemen I would extend along the flanks of these companies on the left side, distant twenty arm lengths from it, creating a hundred forty three files of seven per file, so that they should cover the entire length of the ten companies arranged as I have previously described; and there would remain forty files for protecting the wagons and the unarmed people in the tail of the army, (and) assigning the Heads of Ten and the Centurions in their (proper) places: and, of the three Constables, I would put one at the head, another in the middle, and the third in the last file, who should fill the office of Tergiduttore, as the ancients called the one placed in charge of the rear of the Army. But returning to the head (van) of the Army I say, that I would place the extraordinary Veliti alongside the extraordinary pikemen, which, as you know, are five hundred, and would place them at a distance of forty arm lengths. On the side of these, also on the left hand; I would place the men-at-arms, and would assign them a distance of a hundred fifty arm lengths away. Behind these, the light cavalry, to whom I would assign the same space as the men-at-arms. The ordinary Veliti I would leave around their companies, who would occupy those spaces which I placed between one company and another, who would act to minister to those (companies) unless I had already placed them under the extraordinary pikemen; which I would do or not do according as it should benefit my plans. The general Head of all the Battalions I would place in that space that exists between the first and second order of companies, or rather at the head, and in that space with exists between the last of the first five companies and the extraordinary pikemen, according as it should benefit my plans, surrounded by thirty or sixty picked men, (and) who should know how to execute a commission prudently, and stalwartly resist an attack, and should also be in the middle of the buglers and flag carriers. This is the order in which I would deploy a Battalion on the left side, which would be the deployment of half the Army, and would cover an area five hundred and eleven arm lengths long and as much as mentioned above in width, not including the space which that part of the extraordinary pikemen should occupy who act as a shield for the unarmed men, which would be about one hundred arm lengths. The other Battalions I would deploy on the right side exactly in the same way as I deployed those on the left, having a space of thirty arm lengths between our battalions and the other, in the head of which space I would place some artillery pieces, behind which would be the Captain general of the entire Army, who should have around him in addition to the buglers and flag carriers at least two hundred picked men, the greater portion on foot, among whom should be ten or more adept at executing every command, and should be so provided with arms and a horse as to be able to go on horseback or afoot as the needs requires. Ten cannon of the artillery of the Army suffice for the reduction of towns, which should not exceed fifty pounds per charge, of which in the field I would employ more in the defense of the encampment than in waging a battle, and the other artillery should all be rather often than fifteen pounds per charge. This I would place in front of the entire army, unless the country should be such that I could situate it on the flank in a safe place, where it should not be able to be attacked by the enemy.

This formation of the Army thusly arranged, in combat, can maintain the order both of the Phalanxes and of the Roman Legions, because the pikemen are in front and all the infantry so arranged in ranks, that coming to battle with the enemy, and resisting him, they should be able to reform the first ranks from those behind according to the usage of the Phalanxes. On the other hand, if they are attacked so that they are compelled to break ranks and retire, they can enter into the spaces of the second company behind them, and uniting with them, (and) en masse be able to resist and combat the enemy again: and if this should not be enough, they can in the same way retire a second time, and combat a third time, so that in this arrangement, as to combatting, they can reform according to both the Greek method, and the Roman. As to the strength of the Army, it cannot be arranged any stronger, for both wings are amply provided with both leaders and arms, and no part is left weak except that part behind which is unarmed, and even that part has its flanks protected by the extraordinary pikemen. Nor can the enemy assault it in any part where he will not find them organized, and the part in the back cannot be assaulted, because there cannot be an enemy who has so much power that he can assail every side equally, for it there is one, you don't have to take the field with him. But if he should be a third greater than you, and as well organized as you, if he weakens himself by assaulting you in several places, as soon as you defeat one part, all will go badly for him. If his cavalry should be greater than yours, be most assured, for the ranks of pikemen that gird you will defend you from every onrush of theirs, even if your cavalry should be repulsed. In addition to this, the Heads are placed on the side so that they are able easily to command and obey. And the spaces that exist between one company and the next one, and between one rank and the next, not only serve to enable one to receive the other, but also to provide a place for the messengers who go and come by order of the Captain. And as I told you before, as the Romans had about twenty thousand men in an Army, so too ought this one have: and as other soldiers borrowed their mode of fighting and the formation of their Army from the Legions, so too those soldiers that you assembled into your two Battalions would have to borrow their formation and organization. Having given an example of these things, it is an easy matter to initiate it: for if the army is increased either by two Battalions, or by as many men as are contained in them, nothing else has to be done than to double the arrangements, and where ten companies are placed on the left side, twenty are now placed, either by increasing or extending the ranks, according as the place or the enemy should command you.

LUIGI: Truly, (my) Lord, I have so imagined this army, that I see it now, and have a desire to see it facing us, and not for anything in the world would

I desire you to become Fabius Maximus, having thoughts of holding the enemy at bay and delaying the engagement, for I would say worse of you, than the Roman people said of him.

FABRIZIO: Do not be apprehensive. Do you not hear the artillery? Ours has already fired, but harmed the enemy little; and the extraordinary Veliti come forth from their places together with the light cavalry, and spread out, and with as much fury and the loudest shouts of which they are capable, assault the enemy, whose artillery has fired one time, and has passed over the heads of our infantry without doing them an injury. And as it is not able to fire a second time, our Veliti and cavalry have already seized it, and to defend it, the enemy has moved forward, so that neither that of friend or enemy can perform its office. You see with what virtu our men fight, and with what discipline they have become accustomed because of the training they have had, and from the confidence they have in the Army, which you see with their stride, and with the men-at-arms alongside, in marching order, going to rekindle the battle with the adversary. Your see our artillery, which to make place for them, and to leave the space free, has retired to the place from which the Veliti went forth. You see the Captain who encourages them and points out to them certain victory. You see the Veliti and light cavalry have spread out and returned to the flanks of the Army, in order to see if they can cause any injury to the enemy from the flanks. Look, the armies are facing each other: watch with what virtu they have withstood the onrush of the enemy, and with what silence, and how the Captain commands the men-at-arms that they should resist and not attack, and do not detach themselves from the ranks of the infantry. You see how our light cavalry are gone to attack a band of enemy gunners who wanted to attach by the flank, and how the enemy cavalry have succored them, so that, caught between the cavalry of the one and the other, they cannot fire, and retire behind their companies. You see with what fury our pikemen attack them, and how the infantry is already so near each other that they can no longer manage their pikes: so that, according to the discipline taught by us, our pikemen retire little by little among the shields (swordsmen). Watch how in this (encounter), so great an enemy band of men-at-arms has pushed back our men-at-arms on the left side and how ours, according to discipline, have retired under the extraordinary pikemen, and having reformed the front with their aid, have repulsed the adversary, and killed a good part of them. In fact all the ordinary pikemen of the first company have hidden themselves among the ranks of the shields (swordsmen), and having left the battle to the swordsmen, who, look with what virtu, security, and leisure, kill the enemy. Do you not see that, when fighting, the ranks are so straitened, that they can handle the swords only with much effort? Look with what hurry the enemy moves; for, armed with the pike and their swords useless ((the one because it is too long, the other because of finding the enemy too greatly armed)), in part they fall dead or wounded, in part they flee. See them flee on the right side. They also flee on the left. Look, the victory is ours. Have we not won an engagement very happily? But it would have been won with greater felicity if I should have been allowed to put them in action. And see that it was not necessary to avail ourselves of either the second or third ranks, that our first line was sufficient to overcome them. In this part, I have nothing else to tell you, except to dissolve any doubts that should arise in you.

LUIGI: You have won this engagement with so much fury, that I am astonished, and in fact so stupefied, that I do not believe I can well explain if there is any doubt left in my mind. Yet, trusting in your prudence, I will take courage to say that I intend. Tell me first, why did you not let your artillery fire more than one time? and why did you have them quickly retire within the army, nor afterward make any other mention of them? It seems to me also that you pointed the enemy artillery high, and arranged it so that it should be of much benefit to you. Yet, if it should occur ((and I believe it happens often)) that the lines are pierced, what remedy do you provide? And since I have commenced on artillery, I want to bring up all these questions so as not to have to discuss it any more. I have heard many disparage the arms and the organization of the ancient Armies, arguing that today they could do little, or rather how useless they would be against the fury of artillery, for these are superior to their arms and break the ranks, so that it appears to them to be madness to create an arrangement that cannot be held, and to endure hardship in carrying a weapon that cannot defend you.

FABRIZIO: This question of yours has need ((because it has so many items)) of a long answer. It is true that I did not have the artillery fire more than one time, and because of it one remains in doubt. The reason is, that it is more important to one to guard against being shot than shooting the enemy. You must understand that, if you do not want the artillery to injure you, it is necessary to stay where it cannot reach you, or to put yourself behind a wall or embankment. Nothing else will stop it; but it is necessary for them to be very strong. Those Captains who must make an engagement cannot remain behind walls or embankments, nor can they remain where it may reach them. They must, therefore, since they do not have a way of protecting themselves, find one by which they are injured less; nor can they do anything other than to undertake it quickly. The way of doing this is to go find it quickly and directly, not slowly or en masse; for, speed does not allow them to shoot again, and because the men are scattered, they can injure only a few of them. A band of organized men cannot do this, because if they march in a straight line, they become disorganized, and if they scatter, they do not give the enemy the hard work to rout them, for they have routed themselves. And therefore I would organize the Army so that it should be able to do both; for having placed a thousand Veliti in its wings, I would arrange, that after our artillery had fired, they should issue forth together with the light cavalry to seize the enemy artillery. And therefore I did not have my artillery fire again so as not to give the enemy time, for you cannot give me time and take it from others. And for that, the reason I did not have it fired a second time, was not to allow it to be fired first; because, to render the enemy artillery useless, there is no other remedy than to assault it; which, if the enemy abandons it, you seize it; if they want to defend it, it is necessary that they leave it behind, so that in the hands of the enemy or of friends, it cannot be fired. I believe that, even without examples, this discussion should be enough for you, yet, being able to give you some from the ancients, I will do so. Ventidius, coming to battle with the Parthians, the virtu of whom (the latter) in great part consisted in their bows and darts, be allowed them to come almost under his encampments before he led the Army out, which he only did in order to be able to seize them quickly and not give them time to fire. Caesar in Gaul tells, that in coming to battle with the enemy, he was assaulted by them with such fury, that his men did not have time to draw their darts according to the Roman custom. It is seen, therefore, that, being in the field, if you do not want something fired from a distance to injure you, there is no other remedy than to be able to seize it as quickly as possible. Another reason also caused me to do without firing the artillery, at which you may perhaps laugh, yet I do not judge it is to be disparaged. And there is nothing that causes greater confusion in an Army than to obstruct its vision, whence most stalwart Armies have been routed for having their vision obstructed either by dust or by the sun. There is also nothing that impedes the vision than the smoke which the artillery makes when fired: I would think, therefore, that it would be more prudent to let the enemy blind himself, than for you to go blindly to find him. I would, therefore, not fire, or ((as this would not be approved because of the reputation the artillery has)) I would put it in the wings of the Army, so that firing it, its smoke should not blind the front of what is most important of our forces. And that obstructing the vision of the enemy is something useful, can be adduced from the example of Epaminondas, who, to blind the enemy Army which was coming to engage him, had his light cavalry run in front of the enemy so that they raised the dust high, and which obstructed their vision, and gave him the victory in the engagement. As to it appearing to you that I aimed the shots of artillery in my own manner, making it pass over the heads of the infantry, I reply that there are more times, and without comparison, that the heavy artillery does not penetrate the infantry than it does, because the infantry lies so low, and they (the artillery) are so difficult to fire, that any little that you raise them, (causes) them to pass over the heads of the infantry, and if you lower them, they damage the ground, and the shot does not reach them (the infantry). Also, the unevenness of the ground saves them, for every little mound or height which exists between the infantry and it (the artillery), impedes it. And as to cavalry, and especially men-at-arms, because they are taller and can more easily be hit, they can be kept in the rear (tail) of the Army until the time the artillery has fired. It is true that often they injure the smaller artillery and the gunners more that the latter (cavalry), to which the best remedy is to come quickly to grips (hand to hand): and if in the first assault some are killed ((as some always do die)) a good Captain and a good Army do not have to fear an injury that is confined, but a general one; and to imitate the Swiss, who never shun an engagement even if terrified by artillery, but rather they punish with the capital penalty those who because of fear of it either break ranks or by their person give the sign of fear. I made them ((once it had been fired)) to retire into the Army because it left the passage free to the companies. No other mention of it was made, as something useless, once the battle was started.

You have also said in regard to the fury of this instrument that many judge the arms and the systems of the ancients to be useless, and it appears from your talk that the modems have found arms and systems which are useful against the artillery. If you know this, I would be pleased for you to show it to me, for up to now I do not know of any that have been observed, nor do I believe any can be found. So that I would like to learn from those men for what reasons the soldiers on foot of our times wear the breastplate or the corselet of iron, and those on horseback go completely covered with armor, since, condemning the ancient armor as useless with respect to artillery, they ought also to shun these. I would also like to learn for what reason the Swiss, in imitation of the ancient systems, for a close (pressed) company of six or eight thousand infantry, and for what reason all the others have imitated them, bringing the same dangers to this system because of the artillery as the others brought which had been imitated from antiquity. I believe that they would not know what to answer; but if you asked the soldiers who should have some experience, they would answer, first that they go armed because, even if that armor does not protect them from the artillery, it does every other injury inflicted by an enemy, and they would also answer that they go closely together as the Swiss in order to be better able to attack the infantry, resist the cavalry, and give the enemy more difficulty in routing them. So that it is observed that soldiers have to fear many other things besides the artillery, from which they defend themselves with armor and organization. From which it follows that as much as an Army is better armed, and as much as its ranks are more serrated and more powerful, so much more is it secure. So that whoever is of the opinion you mentioned must be either of little prudence, or has thought very little on this matter; for if we see the least part of the ancient way of arming in use today, which is the pike, and the least part of those systems, which are the battalions of the Swiss, which do us so much good, and lend so much power to our Armies, why shouldn't we believe that the other arms and other systems that they left us are also useful? Moreover, if we do not have any regard for the artillery when we place ourselves close together, like the Swiss, what other system than that can make us afraid? inasmuch as there is no other arrangement that can make us afraid than that of being pressed together. In addition to this, if the enemy artillery does not frighten me when I lay siege to a town, where he may injure me with great safety to himself, and where I am unable to capture it as it is defended from the walls, but can stop him only with time with my artillery, so that he is able to redouble his shots as he wishes, why do I have to be afraid of him in the field where I am able to seize him quickly? So that I conclude this, that the artillery, according to my opinion, does not impede anyone who is able to use the methods of the ancients, and demonstrate the ancient virtu. And if I had not talked another time with you concerning this instrument, I would extend myself further, but I want to return to what I have now said.

LUIGI: We are able to have a very good understanding since you have so much discoursed about artillery, and in sum, it seems to me you have shown that the best remedy that one has against it when he is in the field and having an Army in an encounter, is to capture it quickly. Upon which, a doubt rises in me, for it seems to me the enemy can so locate it on a side of his army from which he can injure you, and would be so protected by the other sides, that it cannot be captured. You have ((if you will remember)) in your army's order for battle, created intervals of four arm lengths between one company and the next, and placed twenty of the extraordinary pikemen of the company there. If the enemy should organize his army similarly to yours, and place his artillery well within those intervals, I believe that from here he would be able to injure you with the greatest safety to himself, for it would not be possible to enter among the enemy forces to capture it.

FABRIZIO: You doubt very prudently, and I will endeavor either to resolve the doubt, or to give you a remedy. I have told you that these companies either when going out or when fighting are continually in motion, and by nature always end up close together, so that if you make the intervals small, in which you would place the artillery, in a short time, they would be so closed up that the artillery can no longer perform its function: if you make them large to avoid this danger, you incur a greater, so that, because of those intervals, you not only give the enemy the opportunity to capture your artillery, but to rout you. But you have to know that it is impossible to keep the artillery between the ranks, especially those that are mounted on carriages, for the artillery travel in one direction, and are fired in the other, so that if they are desired to be fired while travelling, it is necessary before they are fired that they be turned, and when they are being turned they need so much space, that fifty carriages of artillery would disrupt every Army. It is necessary, therefore, to keep them outside the ranks where they can be operated in the manner which we showed you a short time ago. But let us suppose they can be kept there, and that a middle way can be found, and of a kind which, when closed together, should not impede the artillery, yet not be so open as to provide a path for the enemy, I say that this is easily remedied at the time of the encounter by creating intervals in your army which give a free path for its shots, and thus its fury will be useless. Which can be easily done, because the enemy, if it wants its artillery to be safe, must place it in the end portions of the intervals, so that its shots, if they should not harm its own men, must pass in a straight line, and always in the same line, and, therefore, by giving them room, can be easily avoided. Because this is a general rule, that you must give way to those things which cannot be resisted, as the ancients did to the elephants and chariots with sickles. I believe, rather I am more than certain, that it must appear to you that I prepared and won an engagement in my own manner; none the less, I will repeat this, if what I have said up to now is now enough, that it would be impossible for an Army thus organized and armed not to overcome, at the first encounter, every other Army organized as modern Armies are organized, which often, unless they have shields (swordsmen), do not form a front, and are of an unarmed kind, which cannot defend themselves from a near-by enemy; and so organized that, that if they place their companies on the flanks next to each other, not having a way of receiving one another, they cause it to be confused, and apt to be easily disturbed. And although they give their Armies three names, and divide them into three ranks, the Vanguard, the Company (main body) and the Rearguard, none the less, they do not serve for anything else than to distinguish them in marching and in their quarters: but in an engagement, they are all pledged to the first attack and fortune.

LUIGI: I have also noted that in making your engagement, your cavalry was repulsed by the enemy cavalry, and that it retired among the extraordinary pikemen, whence it happened that with their aid, they withstood and repulsed the enemy in the rear. I believe the pikemen can withstand the cavalry, as you said, but not a large and strong Battalion, as the Swiss do, which, in your Army, have five ranks of pikemen at the head, and seven on the flank, so that I do not know how they are able to withstand them.

FABRIZIO: Although I have told you that six ranks were employed in the Phalanxes of Macedonia at one time, none the less, you have to know that a Swiss Battalion, if it were composed of ten thousand tanks could not employ but four, or at most five, because the pikes are nine arm lengths long and an arm length and a half is occupied by the hands; whence only seven and a half arm lengths of the pike remain to the first rank. The second rank, in addition to what the hand occupies, uses up an arm's length of the space that exists between one rank and the next; so that not even six arm lengths of pike remain of use. For the same reasons, these remain four and one half arm lengths to the third rank, three to the fourth, and one and a half to the fifth. The other ranks are useless to inflict injury; but they serve to replace the first ranks, as we have said, and serve as reinforcements for those (first) five ranks. If, therefore, five of their ranks can control cavalry, why cannot five of ours control them, to whom five ranks behind them are also not lacking to sustain them, and give the same support, even though they do not have pikes as the others do? And if the ranks of extraordinary pikemen which are placed along the flanks seem thin to you, they can be formed into a square and placed by the flank of the two companies which I place in the last ranks of the army, from which place they would all together be able easily to help the van and the rear of the army, and lend aid to the cavalry according as their need may require.

LUIGI: Would you always use this form of organization, when you would want to engage in battle?

FABRIZIO: Not in every case, for you have to vary the formation of the army according to the fitness of the site, the kind and numbers of the enemy, which will be shown before this discussion is furnished with an example. But this formation that is given here, not so much because it is stronger than others, which is in truth very strong, as much because from it is obtained a rule and a system, to know how to recognize the manner of organization of the others; for every science has its generations, upon which, in good part, it is based. One thing only, I would remind you, that you never organize an army so that whoever fights in the van cannot be helped by those situated behind, because whoever makes this error renders useless the great part of the army, and if any virtu is eliminated, he cannot win.

LUIGI: And on this part, some doubt has arisen in me. I have seen that in the disposition of the companies you form the front with five on each side the center with three, and the rear with two; and I would believe that it should be better to arrange them oppositely, because I think that an army can be routed with more difficulty, for whoever should attack it, the more he should penetrate into it, so much harder would he find it: but the arrangement made by you appears to me results, that the more one enters into it, the more he finds it weak.

FABRIZIO: If you would remember that the Triari, who were the third rank of the Roman Legions, were not assigned more than six hundred men, you would have less doubt, when you leave that they were placed in the last ranks, because you will see that I (motivated by this example) have placed two companies in the last ranks, which comprise nine-hundred infantry; so that I come to err rather with the Roman people in having taken away too many, than few. And although this example should suffice, I want to tell you the reasons, which is this. The first front (line) of the army is made solid and dense because it has to withstand the attack of the enemy, and does not have to receive any friends into it, and because of this, it must abound in men, for few men would make it weak both from their sparseness and their numbers. But the second line, because it has to relieve the friends from the first who have withstood the enemy, must have large intervals, and therefore must have a smaller number than the first; for if it should be of a greater or equal number, it would result in not leaving any intervals, which would cause disorder, or if some should be left, it would extend beyond the ends of those in front, which would make the formation of the army incomplete (imperfect). And what you say is not true, that the more the enemy enters into the

Battalions, the weaker he will find them; for the enemy can never fight with the second line, if the first one is not joined up with it: so that he will come to find the center of the Battalion stronger and not weaker, having to fight with the first and second (lines) together. The same thing happens if the enemy should reach the third line, because here, he will not only have to fight with two fresh companies, but with the entire Battalion. And as this last part has to receive more men, its spaces must be larger, and those who receive them lesser in number.

LUIGI: And I like what you have said; but also answer me this. If the five companies retire among the second three, and afterwards, the eight among the third two, does it not seem possible that the eight come together then the ten together, are able to crowd together, whether they are eight or ten, into the same space which the five occupied.

FABRIZIO: The first thing that I answer is, that it is not the same space; for the five have four spaces between them, which they occupy when retiring between one Battalion and the next, and that which exists between the three or the two: there also remains that space which exists between the companies and the extraordinary pikemen, which spaces are all made large. There is added to this whatever other space the companies have when they are in the lines without being changed, for, when they are changed, the ranks are either compressed or enlarged. They become enlarged when they are so very much afraid, that they put themselves in flight: they become compressed when they become so afraid, that they seek to save themselves, not by flight, but by defense; so that in this case, they would compress themselves, and not spread out. There is added to this, that the five ranks of pikemen who are in front, once they have started the battle, have to retire among their companies in the rear (tail) of the army to make place for the shield-bearers (swordsmen) who are able to fight: and when they go into the tail of the army they can serve whoever the captain should judge should employ them well, whereas in the front, once the fight becomes mixed, they would be completely useless. And therefore, the arranged spaces come to be very capacious for the remaining forces. But even if these spaces should not suffice, the flanks on the side consist of men and not walls, who, when they give way and spread out, are able to create a space of such capacity, which should be sufficient to receive them.

LUIGI: The ranks of the extraordinary pikemen, which you place on the flank of the army when the first company retires into the second, do you want them to remain firm, and become as two wings of the army or do you also want them to retire with the company. Which, if they have to do this, I do not see how they can, as they do not have companies behind them with wide intervals which would receive them.

FABRIZIO: If the enemy does not fight them when he faces the companies to retire, they are able to remain firm in their ranks, and inflict injury on the enemy on the flank since the first companies had retired: but if they should also fight them, as seems reasonable, being so powerful as to be able to force the others to retire, they should cause them also to retire. Which they are very well able to do, even though they have no one behind who should receive them, for from the middle forward they are able to double on the right, one file entering into the other in the manner we discussed when we talked of the arrangement for doubling themselves. It is true, that when doubling, they should want to retire behind, other means must be found than that which I have shown you, since I told you that the second rank had to enter among the first, the fourth among the third, and so on little by little, and in this case, it would not be begun from the front, but from the rear, so that doubling the ranks, they should come to retire to the rear, and not to turn in front. But to reply to all of that, which (you have asked) concerning this engagement as shown by me, it should be repeated, (and) I again say that I have so organized this army, and will (again) explain this engagement to you for two reasons: one, to show you how it (the army) is organized: the other, to show you how it is trained. As to the systems, I believe you all most knowledgeable. As to the army, I tell you that it may often be put together in this form, for the Heads are taught to keep their companies in this order: and because it is the duty of each individual soldier to keep (well) the arrangement of each company, and it is the duty of each Head to keep (well) those in each part of the Army, and to know well how to obey the commands of the general Captain. They must know, therefore, how to join one company with another, and how to take their places instantly: and therefore, the banner of each company must have its number displayed openly, so that they may be commanded, and the Captain and the soldiers will more readily recognize that number. The Battalions ought also to be numbered, and have their number on their principal banner. One must know, therefore, what the number is of the Battalion placed on the left or right wing, the number of those placed in the front and the center, and so on for the others. I would want also that these numbers reflect the grades of positions in the Army. For instance, the first grade is the Head of Ten, the second is the head of fifty ordinary Veliti, the third the Centurion, the fourth the head of the first company, the fifth that of the second (company), the sixth of the third, and so on up to the tenth Company, which should be in the second place next to the general Captain of the Battalion; nor should anyone arrive to that Leadership, unless he had (first) risen through all these grades. And, as in addition to these Heads, there are the three Constables (in command) of the extraordinary pikemen, and the two of the extraordinary Veliti, I would want them to be of the grade of Constable of the first company, nor would I care if they were men of equal grade, as long as each of them should vie to be promoted to the second company. Each one of these Captains, therefore, knowing where his Company should be located, of necessity it will follow that, at the sound of the trumpet, once the Captain's flag was raised, all of the Army would be in its proper places. And this is the first exercise to which an Army ought to become accustomed, that is, to assemble itself quickly: and to do this, you must frequently each day arrange them and disarrange them.

LUIGI: What signs would you want the flags of the Army to have, in addition to the number?

FABRIZIO: I would want the one of the general Captain to have the emblem of the Army: all the others should also have the same emblem, but varying with the fields, or with the sign, as it should seem best to the Lord of the Army, but this matters little, so long as their effect results in their recognizing one another.

But let us pass on to another exercise in which an army ought to be trained, which is, to set it in motion, to march with a convenient step, and to see that, while in motion, it maintains order. The third exercise is, that they be taught to conduct themselves as they would afterwards in an engagement; to fire the artillery, and retire it; to have the extraordinary Veliti issue forth, and after a mock assault, have them retire; have the first company, as if they were being pressed, retire within the intervals of the second (company), and then both into the third, and from here each one return to its place; and so to accustom them in this exercise, that it become understood and familiar to everyone, which with practice and familiarity, will readily be learned. The fourth exercise is that they be taught to recognize commands of the Captain by virtue of his (bugle) calls and flags, as they will understand, without other command, the pronouncements made by voice. And as the importance of the commands depends on the (bugle) calls, I will tell you what sounds (calls) the ancients used. According as Thucydides affirms, whistles were used in the army of the Lacedemonians, for they judged that its pitch was more apt to make their Army proceed with seriousness and not with fury. Motivated by the same reason, the Carthaginians, in their first assault, used the zither. Alliatus, King of the Lydians, used the zither and whistles in war; but Alexander the Great and the Romans used horns and trumpets, like those who thought the courage of the soldiers could be increased by virtue of such instruments, and cause them to combat more bravely. But just as we have borrowed from the Greek and Roman methods in equipping our Army, so also in choosing sounds should we serve ourselves of the customs of both those nations. I would, therefore, place the trumpets next to the general Captain, as their sound is apt not only to inflame the Army, but to be heard over every noise more than any other sound. I would want that the other sounds existing around the Constables and Heads of companies to be (made by) small drums and whistles, sounded not as they are presently, but as they are customarily sounded at banquets. I would want, therefore, for the Captain to use the trumpets in indicating when they should stop or go forward or turn back, when they should fire the artillery, when to move the extraordinary Veliti, and by changes in these sounds (calls) point out to the Army all those moves that generally are pointed out; and those trumpets afterwards followed by drums. And, as training in these matters are of great importance, I would follow them very much in training your Army. As to the cavalry, I would want to use the same trumpets, but of lower volume and different pitch of sounds from those of the Captain. This is all that occurs to me concerning the organization and training of the Army.

LUIGI: I beg you not to be so serious in clearing up another matter for me: why did you have the light cavalry and the extraordinary Veliti move with shouts and noise and fury when they attacked, but they in rejoining the Army you indicated the matter was accomplished with great silence: and as I do not understand the reason for this fact, I would desire you to clarify it for me.

FABRIZIO: When coming to battle, there have been various opinions held by the ancient Captains, whether they ought either to accelerate the step (of the soldiers) by sounds, or have them go slowly in silence. This last manner serves to keep the ranks firmer and have them understand the commands of the Captain better: the first serves to encourage the men more. And, as I believe consideration ought to be given to both these methods, I made the former move with sound, and the latter in silence. And it does not seem to me that in any case the sounds are planned to be continuous, for they would impede the commands, which is a pernicious thing. Nor is it reasonable that the Romans, after the first assault, should follow with such sounds, for it is frequently seen in their histories that soldiers who were fleeing were stopped by the words and advice of the Captains, and changed the orders in various ways by his command: which would not have occurred if the sounds had overcome his voice.

Libro Terzo

LIBRO TERZO

COSIMO: Pichè noi mutiamo ragionamento, io voglio che si muti domandatore, perchè io non vorrei essere tenuto presuntuoso; il che sempre ho biasimato negli altri. Però io depongo la dittatura, e do questa autorità a chi la vuole di questi altri miei amici.

ZANOBI: E' ci era gratissimo che voi seguitassi; pure, poichè voi non volete, dite almeno quale di noi dee succedere nel luogo vostro.

COSIMO: Io voglio dare questo carico al signore.

FABRIZIO: Io sono contento prenderlo, e voglio che noi seguitiamo il costume viniziano: che il più giovane parli prima, perchè, sendo questo esercizio da giovani, mi persuado che i giovani sieno più atti a ragionarne, come essi sono più pronti a esseguirlo.

COSIMO: Adunque tocca a voi, Luigi. E come io ho piacere di tale successore, così voi vi sodisfarete di tale domandatore. Però vi priego torniamo alla materia e non perdiamo più tempo.

FABRIZIO: Io son certo che, a volere dimostrare bene come si ordina uno esercito per far la giornata, sarebbe necessario narrare come i Greci e i Romani ordinavano le schiere negli loro eserciti. Nondimeno, potendo voi medesimi leggiere e considerare queste cose mediante gli scrittori antichi, lascerò molti particolari indietro, e solo ne addurrò quelle cose che di loro mi pare necessario imitare, a volere ne' nostri tempi dare alla milizia nostra qualche parte di perfezione. Il che farà che in uno tempo io mostrerò come uno esercito si ordini alla giornata, e come si affronti nelle vere zuffe, e come si possa esercitarlo nelle finte. Il maggiore disordine che facciano coloro che ordinano uno esercito alla giornata, è dargli solo una fronte e obligarlo a uno impeto e una fortuna. Il che nasce dallo avere perduto il modo che tenevano gli antichi a ricevere l'una schiera nell'altra; perchè, senza questo modo, non si può nè sovvenire a' primi, nè difendergli, nè succedere nella zuffa in loro scambio; il che da' Romani era ottimamente osservato. Per volere adunque mostrare questo modo, dico come i Romani avevano tripartita ciascuna Legione in Astati, Principi e Triarj; de' quali, gli Astati erano messi nella prima fronte dell'esercito con gli ordini spessi e fermi; dietro a' quali erano i Principi, ma posti con gli loro ordini più radi: dopo questi mettevano i Triarj, e con tanta radità di ordini che potessono, bisognando, ricevere tra loro i Principi e gli Astati. Avevano, oltre a questi, i funditori e i balestrieri e gli altri armati alla leggiera; i quali non stavano in questi ordini, ma li collocavano nella testa dell'esercito tra li cavalli e i fanti. Questi, adunque, leggiermente armati appiccavano la zuffa, e se vincevano, il che occorreva rade volte, essi seguivano la vittoria; se erano ributtati, si ritiravano per i fianchi dell'esercito o per gli intervalli a tale effetto ordinati, e si riducevano tra' disarmati. Dopo la partita de' quali venivano alle mani con il nemico gli Astati; i quali, se si vedevano superare, si ritiravano a poco a poco per la radità degli ordini tra' Principi e, insieme con quegli, rinnovavano la zuffa. Se questi ancora erano sforzati, si ritiravano tutti nella radità degli ordini de' Triarj e, tutti insieme, fatto uno mucchio, ricominciavano la zuffa; e se questi la perdevano, non vi era più rimedio, perchè non vi restava più modo a rifarsi. I cavalli stavano sopra alli canti dell'esercito, posti a similitudine di due ali e a uno corpo; e or combattevano con i cavalli, or sovvenivano i fanti, secondo che il bisogno lo ricercava. Questo modo di rifarsi tre volte è quasi impossibile a superare, perchè bisogna che tre volte la fortuna ti abbandoni e che il nemico abbia tanta virtù che tre volte ti vinca. I Greci non avevano con le loro Falangi questo modo di rifarsi; e benchè in quelle fussero assai capi e di molti ordini, nondimeno ne facevano un corpo o vero una testa. Il modo ch'essi tenevano in sovvenire l'uno l'altro era, non di ritirarsi l'uno ordine nell'altro, come i Romani, ma di entrare l'uno uomo nel luogo dell'altro. Il che facevano in questo modo: la loro Falange era ridotta in file; e pognamo che mettessono per fila cinquanta uomini, venendo poi con la testa sua contro al nemico; di tutte le file, le prime sei potevano combattere perchè le loro lance, le quali chiamavano Sarisse, erano sì lunghe che la sesta fila passava con la punta della sua lancia fuora della prima fila. Combattendo, adunque, se alcuno della prima o per morte o per ferite cadeva, subito entrava nel luogo suo quello che era di dietro nella seconda fila, e, nel luogo che rimaneva vòto della seconda, entrava quello che gli era dietro nella terza; e così successive in uno subito le file di dietro instauravano i difetti di quegli davanti; in modo che le file sempre restavano intere e niuno luogo era di combattitori vacuo, eccetto che la fila ultima, la quale si veniva consumando per non avere dietro alle spalle chi la instaurasse, in modo che i danni che pativano le prime file consumavano le ultime, e le prime restavano sempre intere; e così queste Falangi, per l'ordine loro, si potevano piuttosto consumare che rompere, perchè il corpo grosso le faceva più immobili. Usarono i Romani, nel principio, le Falangi, e instruirono le loro Legioni a similitudine di quelle. Dipoi non piacque loro questo ordine, e divisero le Legioni in più corpi, cioè in coorti e in manipuli; perchè giudicarono, come poco fa dissi, che quel corpo avesse più vita, che avesse più anime, e che fusse composto di più parti, in modo che ciascheduna per se stessa si reggesse. I battaglioni de' Svizzeri usano in questi tempi tutti i modi della Falange, così nello ordinarsi grossi e interi, come nel sovvenire l'uno l'altro; e nel fare la giornata pongono i battaglioni l'uno a' fianchi dell'altro; e, se li mettono dietro l'uno all'altro, non hanno modo che il primo, ritirandosi, possa essere ricevuto dal secondo; ma tengono, per potere sovvenire l'uno l'altro, quest'ordine: che mettono uno battaglione innanzi e un altro dietro a quello in sulla man ritta, tale che, se il primo ha bisogno d'aiuto, quello si può fare innanzi e soccorrerlo. Il terzo battaglione mettono dietro a questi, ma discosto un tratto di scoppietto. Questo fanno perchè, sendo quegli due ributtati, questo si possa fare innanzi, e abbiano spazio, e i ributtati e quel che si fa innanzi, a evitare l'urto l'uno dell'altro; perchè una moltitudine grossa non può essere ricevuta come un corpo piccolo, e però i corpi piccoli e distinti che erano in una Legione Romana si potevano collocare in modo che si potessono tra loro ricevere e l'uno l'altro con facilità sovvenire. E che questo ordine de' Svizzeri non sia buono quanto lo antico Romano, lo dimostrano molti esempj delle Legioni Romane quando si azzuffarono con le Falangi Greche; e sempre queste furono consumate da quelle, perchè la generazione dell'armi, come io dissi dianzi, e questo modo di rifarsi, potè più che la solidità delle Falangi. Avendo, adunque, con questi esempj a ordinare uno esercito, mi è parso ritenere l'armi e i modi, parte delle Falangi Greche, parte delle Legioni Romane; e però io ho detto di volere in uno battaglione duemila picche, che sono l'armi delle Falangi Macedoniche, e tremila scudi con la spada, che sono l'armi de' Romani. Ho diviso il battaglione in dieci battaglie, come i Romani; la Legione in dieci coorti. Ho ordinato i Veliti, cioè l'armi leggieri, per appiccare la zuffa come loro. E perchè così, come l'armi sono mescolate e participano dell'una e dell'altra nazione, ne participino ancora gli ordini, ho ordinato che ogni battaglia abbia cinque file di picche in fronte e il restante di scudi, per potere, con la fronte, sostenere i cavalli e entrare facilmente nelle battaglie de' nemici a piè, avendo nel primo scontro le picche, come il nemico, le quali voglio mi bastino a sostenerlo, gli scudi, poi, a vincerlo. E se voi noterete la virtù di questo ordine, voi vedrete queste armi tutte fare interamente l'ufficio loro; perchè le picche sono utili contro a' cavalli, e, quando vengono contro a' fanti, fanno bene l'ufficio loro prima che la zuffa si ristringa; perchè, ristretta ch'ella è, diventano inutili. Donde che i Svizzeri, per fuggire questo inconveniente, pongono dopo ogni tre file di picche una fila d'alabarde; il che fanno per dare spazio alle picche, il quale non è tanto che basti. Ponendo adunque le nostre picche davanti e gli scudi di dietro, vengono a sostenere i cavalli e, nello appiccare la zuffa, aprono e molestano i fanti; ma poi che la zuffa è ristretta, e ch'elle diventerebbono inutili, succedono gli scudi e le spade; i quali possono in ogni strettura maneggiarsi.

LUIGI: Noi aspettiamo ora con desiderio di intendere come voi ordinereste l'esercito a giornata con queste armi e con questi ordini.

FABRIZIO: E io non voglio ora dimostrarvi altro che questo. Voi avete a intendere come in uno esercito Romano ordinario, il quale chiamavano esercito Consolare, non erano più che due Legioni di cittadini Romani, che erano secento cavalli e circa undicimila fanti. Avevano dipoi altrettanti fanti e cavalli, che erano loro mandati dagli amici e confederati loro; i quali dividevano in due parti e chiamavano, l'una, corno destro e, l'altra, corno sinistro; nè mai permettevano che questi fanti ausiliari passassero il numero de' fanti delle Legioni loro; erano bene contenti che fusse più numero quello de' cavalli. Con questo esercito, che era di ventiduemila fanti e circa duemila cavalli utili, faceva uno Consolo ogni fazione e andava a ogni impresa. Pure, quando bisognava opporsi a maggiori forze, raccozzavano due Consoli con due eserciti. Dovete ancora notare come, per l'ordinario, in tutte le tre azioni principali che fanno gli eserciti, cioè camminare, alloggiare e combattere, mettevano le Legioni in mezzo; perchè volevano che quella virtù in la quale più confidavano, fusse più unita, come nel ragionare di tutte queste azioni vi si mostrerà. Quelli fanti ausiliarj, per la pratica che avevano con i fanti Legionari, erano utili quanto quelli; perchè erano disciplinati come loro e però, nel simile modo, nello ordinare la giornata gli ordinavano. Chi adunque sa come i Romani disponevano una Legione nell'esercito a giornata, sa come lo disponevano tutto. Però, avendovi io detto come essi dividevano una Legione in tre schiere, e come l'una schiera riceveva l'altra, vi vengo ad avere detto come tutto lo esercito in una giornata si ordinava.

Volendo io pertanto ordinare una giornata a similitudine de' Romani come quegli avevano due Legioni, io prenderò due battaglioni, e, disposti questi, si intenderà la disposizione di tutto un esercito; perchè nello aggiungere più genti non si arà a fare altro che ingrossare gli ordini. Io non credo che bisogni che io vi ricordi quanti fanti abbia uno battaglione, e come egli ha dieci battaglie, e che capi sieno per battaglia, e quali armi abbiano, e quali sieno le picche e i Veliti ordinarj e quali gli estraordinarj; perchè poco fa ve lo dissi distintamente, e vi ricordai lo mandassi alla memoria come cosa necessaria a volere intendere tutti gli altri ordini; e però io verrò alla dimostrazione dell'ordine senza replicare altro. E' mi pare che le dieci battaglie d'uno battaglione si pongano nel sinistro fianco e, le dieci altre dell'altro, nel destro.

Ordininsi quelle del sinistro in questo modo: ponghansi cinque battaglie l'una allato all'altra nella fronte, in modo che tra l'una e l'altra rimanga uno spazio di quattro braccia che vengano a occupare, per larghezza, centoquarantuno braccio di terreno e, per la lunghezza, quaranta. Dietro a queste cinque battaglie ne porrei tre altre, discosto per linea retta dalle prime quaranta braccia; due delle quali venissero dietro per linea retta alle estreme delle cinque, e l'altra tenesse lo spazio di mezzo. E così verrebbero queste tre ad occupare per larghezza e per lunghezza il medesimo spazio che le cinque; ma, dove le cinque hanno tra l'una e l'altra una distanza di quattro braccia, queste l'arebbero di trentatrè. Dopo queste porrei le due ultime battaglie pure dietro alle tre, per linea retta e distanti, da quelle tre, quaranta braccia; e porrei ciascuna d'esse dietro alle estreme delle tre, tale che lo spazio che restasse tra l'una e l'altra sarebbe novantuno braccio. Terrebbero adunque tutte queste battaglie così ordinate, per larghezza, centoquarantuno braccio e, per lunghezza, dugento. Le picche estraordinarie distenderei lungo i fianchi di queste battaglie dal lato sinistro, discosto venti braccia da quelle, faccendone centoquarantatrè file a sette per fila; in modo ch'elle fasciassono con la loro lunghezza tutto il lato sinistro delle dieci battaglie, nel modo da me detto, ordinate; e ne avanzerebbe quaranta file per guardare i carriaggi e i disarmati che rimanessono nella coda dell'esercito, distribuendo i Capidieci e i Centurioni ne' luoghi loro; e degli tre Connestabili ne metterei uno nella testa, l'altro nel mezzo, il terzo nell'ultima fila, il quale facesse l'ufficio del tergiduttore; chè così chiamavano gli antichi quello che era proposto alle spalle dell'esercito. Ma, ritornando alla testa dell'esercito, dico come io collocherei appresso alle picche estraordinarie i Veliti estraordinarj, che sapete che sono cinquecento, e darei loro uno spazio di quaranta braccia. A lato a questi, pure in sulla man manca, metterei gli uomini d'arme, e vorrei avessero uno spazio di centocinquanta braccia. Dopo questi, i cavalli leggieri, a' quali darei il medesimo spazio che alle genti d'arme. I Veliti ordinarj lascerei intorno alle loro battaglie, i quali stessono in quegli spazi che io pongo tra l'una battaglia e l'altra, che sarebbero come ministri di quelle, se già egli non mi paresse da metterli sotto le picche estraordinarie; il che farei, o no, secondo che più a proposito mi tornasse. Il capo generale di tutto il battaglione metterei in quello spazio che fusse tra il primo e il secondo ordine delle battaglie, ovvero nella testa e in quello spazio che è tra l'ultima battaglia delle prime cinque e le picche estraordinarie, secondo che più a proposito mi tornasse, con trenta o quaranta uomini intorno, scelti e che sapessono per prudenza esseguire una commissione e per fortezza sostenere uno impeto; e fusse ancora esso in mezzo del suono e della bandiera. Questo è l'ordine col quale io disporrei uno battaglione nella parte sinistra, che sarebbe la disposizione della metà dell'esercito; e terrebbe, per larghezza, cinquecento undici braccia e, per lunghezza, quanto di sopra si dice, non computando lo spazio che terrebbe quella parte delle picche estraordinarie che facessono scudo a' disarmati, che sarebbe circa cento braccia. L'altro battaglione disporrei sopra il destro canto, in quel modo appunto che io ho disposto quello del sinistro, lasciando dall'uno battaglione all'altro uno spazio di trenta braccia, nella testa del quale spazio porrei qualche carretta di artiglieria, dietro alle quali stesse il capitano generale di tutto l'esercito e avesse intorno, con il suono e con la bandiera capitana, dugento uomini almeno, eletti, a piè la maggior parte, tra' quali ne fusse dieci, o più, atti a esseguire ogni comandamento; e fusse in modo a cavallo e armato, che potesse essere e a cavallo e a piè, secondo che il bisogno ricercasse. L'artiglierie dell'esercito, bastano dieci cannoni per la espugnazione delle terre, che non passassero cinquanta libbre di portata; de' quali in campagna mi servirei più per la difesa degli alloggiamenti che per fare giornata; l'altra artiglieria tutta fusse piuttosto di dieci che di quindici libbre di portata. Questa porrei innanzi alla fronte di tutto l'esercito, se già il paese non stesse in modo che io la potessi collocare per fianco in luogo sicuro, dov'ella non potesse dal nemico essere urtata.

Questa forma d'esercito così ordinato può tenere nel combattere l'ordine delle Falangi e l'ordine delle Legioni Romane; perchè nella fronte sono picche, sono tutti i fanti ordinati nelle file, in modo che, appiccandosi col nemico e sostenendolo, possono ad uso delle Falangi ristorare le prime file con quelli di dietro. Dall'altra parte, se sono urtati in modo che fieno necessitati rompere gli ordini e ritirarsi, possono entrare negli intervalli delle seconde battaglie che hanno dietro, e unirsi con quelle, e di nuovo, fatto uno mucchio, sostenere il nemico e combatterlo. E quando questo non basti, possono nel medesimo modo ritirarsi la seconda volta, e la terza combattere; sì che in questo ordine, quanto al combattere, ci è da rifarsi e secondo il modo Greco e secondo il Romano. Quanto alla fortezza dell'esercito, non si può ordinare più forte; perchè l'uno e l'altro corno è munitissimo e di capi e di armi, nè gli resta debole altro che la parte di dietro de' disarmati; e quella ha ancora fasciati i fianchi dalle picche estraordinarie. Nè può il nemico da alcuna parte assaltarlo che non lo truovi ordinato; e la parte di dietro non può essere assaltata, perchè non può essere nemico che abbia tante forze che equalmente ti possa assalire da ogni banda; perchè, avendole, tu non ti hai a mettere in campagna seco. Ma quando fusse il terzo più di te e bene ordinato come te, se si indebolisce per assaltarti in più luoghi, una parte che tu ne rompa, tutto va male. Da' cavalli, quando fussono più che i tuoi, sei sicurissimo; perchè gli ordini delle picche che ti fasciano, ti difendano da ogni impeto di quegli, quando bene i tuoi cavalli fussero ributtati. I capi, oltre a questo, sono disposti in lato che facilmente possono comandare e ubbidire. Gli spazi che sono tra l'una battaglia e l'altra e tra l'uno ordine e l'altro, non solamente servono a potere ricevere l'uno l'altro, ma ancora a dare luogo a' mandati che andassono e venissono per ordine del capitano. E com'io vi dissi prima, i Romani avevano per esercito circa ventiquattromila uomini, così debbe essere questo; e come il modo del combattere e la forma dell'esercito gli altri soldati lo prendevano dalle Legioni, così quelli soldati che voi aggiugneste agli due battaglioni vostri avrebbero a prendere la forma e ordine da quelli. Delle quali cose avendone posto uno esemplo, è facil cosa imitarlo; perchè, accrescendo o due altri battaglioni all'esercito, o tanti soldati degli altri quanti sono quegli, egli non si ha a fare altro che duplicare gli ordini e, dove si pose dieci battaglie nella sinistra parte, porvene venti, o ingrossando o distendendo gli ordini secondo che il luogo o il nemico ti comandasse.

LUIGI: Veramente, signore, io mi immagino in modo questo esercito, che già lo veggo, e ardo d'uno desiderio di vederlo affrontare. E non vorrei, per cosa del mondo, che voi diventassi Fabio Massimo, faccendo pensiero di tenere a bada il nemico e differire la giornata, perchè io direi peggio di voi che il popolo Romano non diceva di quello.

FABRIZIO: Non dubitate. Non sentite voi l'artiglierie? Le nostre hanno già tratto, ma poco offeso il nemico; e i Veliti estraordinarj escono de' luoghi loro insieme con la cavalleria leggiere, e più sparsi e con maggiore furia e maggior grida che possono, assaltano il nemico; l'artiglieria del quale ha scarico una volta e ha passato sopra la testa de' nostri fanti senza fare loro offensione alcuna. E perch'ella non possa trarre la seconda volta, vedete i Veliti e i cavalli nostri che l'hanno già occupata, e che i nemici, per difenderla, si sono fatti innanzi; talchè quella degli amici e nemici non può più fare l'ufficio suo. Vedete con quanta virtù combattono i nostri, e con quanta disciplina, per lo esercizio che ne ha fatto loro fare abito e per la confidenza ch'egli hanno nell'esercito; il quale vedete che, col suo passo, e con le genti d'arme allato, cammina ordinato per appiccarsi con l'avversario. Vedete l'artiglierie nostre che, per dargli luogo e lasciargli lo spazio libero, si sono ritirate per quello spazio donde erano usciti i Veliti. Vedete il capitano che gli inanimisce e mostra loro la vittoria certa. Vedete che i Veliti ed i cavalli leggieri si sono allargati e ritornati ne' fianchi dell'esercito, per vedere se possono per fianco fare alcuna ingiuria alli avversarj. Ecco che si sono affrontati gli eserciti. Guardate con quanta virtù egli hanno sostenuto lo impeto de nemici, e con quanto silenzio, e come il capitano comanda agli uomini d'arme che sostengano e non urtino e dall'ordine delle fanterie non si spicchino. Vedete come i nostri cavalli leggieri sono iti a urtare una banda di scoppettieri nemici che volevano ferire per fianco, e come i cavalli nemici gli hanno soccorsi: talchè, rinvolti tra l'una e l'altra cavalleria, non possono trarre e ritiransi dietro alle loro battaglie. Vedete con che furia le picche nostre si affrontano, e come i fanti sono già sì propinqui l'uno all'altro, che le picche non si possono più maneggiare; dimodochè, secondo la disciplina imparata da noi, le nostre picche si ritirano a poco a poco tra gli scudi. Guardate come, in questo tanto, una grossa banda d'uomini d'arme, nemici, hanno spinti gli uomini d'arme nostri dalla parte sinistra, e come i nostri, secondo la disciplina, si sono ritirati sotto le picche estraordinarie, e, con lo aiuto di quelle avendo rifatto testa, hanno ributtati gli avversari e morti buona parte di loro. Intanto tutte le picche ordinarie delle prime battaglie si sono nascose tra gli ordini degli scudi, e lasciata la zuffa agli scudati; i quali guardate con quanta virtù, sicurtà e ozio ammazzano il nemico. Non vedete voi quanto, combattendo, gli ordini sono ristretti, che a fatica possono menare le spade? Guardate con quanta furia i nemici muoiono. Perchè, armati con la picca e con la loro spada, inutile l'una per essere troppo lunga, l'altra per trovare il nemico troppo armato, in parte cascano feriti o morti, in parte fuggono. Vedetegli fuggire dal destro canto; fuggono ancora dal sinistro, ecco che la vittoria è nostra. Non abbiamo noi vinto una giornata felicissimamente? Ma con maggiore felicità si vincerebbe, se mi fusse concesso il metterla in atto. E vedete che non è bisognato valersi nè del secondo nè del terzo ordine; che gli è bastata la nostra prima fronte a superargli. In questa parte io non ho che dirvi altro, se non risolvere se alcuna dubitazione vi nasce.

LUIGI: Voi avete con tanta furia vinta questa giornata, che io ne resto tutto ammirato e in tanto stupefatto, che io non credo potere bene esplicare se alcuno dubbio mi resta nell'animo. Pure, confidandomi nella vostra prudenza, piglierò animo a dire quello che io intendo. Ditemi prima: perchè non facesti voi trarre le vostre artiglierie più che una volta? E perchè subito le facesti ritirare dentro all'esercito, nè poi ne facesti menzione? Parvemi ancora che voi poneste l'artiglierie del nemico alte e ordinassile a vostro modo; il che può molto bene essere. Pure, quando egli occorresse, che credo ch'egli occorrà spesso, che percuotano le schiere, che rimedio ne date? E poichè io mi sono cominciato dalle artiglierie, io voglio fornire tutta questa domanda, per non ne avere a ragionare più. Io ho sentito a molti spregiare l'armi e gli ordini degli eserciti antichi, arguendo come oggi potrebbono poco, anzi tutti quanti sarebbero inutili, rispetto al furore delle artiglierie; perchè queste rompono gli ordini e passono l'armi in modo, che pare loro pazzia fare uno ordine che non si possa tenere, e durare fatica a portare an'arme che non ti possa difendere.

FABRIZIO: Questa domanda vostra ha bisogno, perch'ella ha assai capi, d'una lunga risposta. Egli è vero che io non feci tirare l'artiglieria più che una volta, e ancora di quella una stetti in dubbio. La cagione è, perchè egli importa più a uno guardare di non essere percosso, che non importa percuotere il nemico. Voi avete a intendere che, a volere che an'artiglieria non ti offenda, è necessario o stare dov'ella non ti aggiunga, o mettersi dietro a uno muro o dietro a uno argine. Altra cosa non è che la ritenga, ma bisogna ancora che l'uno e l'altro sia fortissimo. Quelli capitani che si riducono a fare giornata, non possono stare dietro a' muri o agli argini, nè dove essi non sieno aggiunti. Conviene adunque loro, poichè non possono trovare uno modo che gli difenda, trovarne uno per il quale essi sieno meno offesi; nè possono trovare altro modo che preoccuparla subito. Il modo del preoccuparla è andare a trovarla tosto e rotto, non adagio e in mucchio; perchè, con la prestezza, non se le lascia raddoppiare il colpo e, per la radità, può meno numero d'uomini offendere. Questo non può fare una banda di gente ordinata, perchè, s'ella cammina ratta, ella si disordina; s'ella va sparsa, non dà quella fatica al nemico di romperla, perchè si rompe per se stessa. E però io ordinai l'esercito in modo che potesse fare l'una cosa e l'altra; perchè, avendo messo nelle sue corna mille Veliti, ordinai che, dopo che le nostre artiglierie avessono tratto, uscissero insieme con la cavalleria leggiere a occupare l'artiglierie nemiche. E però non feci ritrarre l'artiglieria mia, per non dare tempo alla nemica; perchè e' non si poteva dare spazio a me e torlo ad altri. E per quella cagione che io non la feci trarre la seconda volta, fu per non lasciare trarre la prima, acciocchè, anche la prima volta, la nemica non potesse trarre. Perchè, a volere che l'artiglieria nemica sia inutile, non è altro rimedio che assaltarla; perchè, se i nemici l'abbandonano, tu la occupi; se la vogliono difendere, bisogna se la lascino dietro; in modo che, occupata da' nemici e dagli amici, non può trarre. Io crederrei che senza esempj queste ragioni vi bastassero; pure, potendone dare degli antichi, lo voglio fare. Ventidio venendo a giornata con li Parti, la virtù de' quali in maggior parte consisteva negli archi e nelle saette, gli lasciò quasi venire sotto i suoi alloggiamenti, avanti che traesse fuora l'esercito; il che solamente fece per poterli tosto occupare e non dare loro spazio a trarre. Cesare in Francia referisce che, nel fare una giornata con gli nemici, fu con tanta furia assaltato da loro, che i suoi non ebbero tempo a trarre i dardi secondo la consuetudine Romana. Pertanto si vede che, a volere che una cosa che tira discosto, sendo alla campagna, non ti offenda, non ci è altro rimedio che, con quanta più celerità si può, occuparla. Un'altra cagione ancora mi moveva a fare senza trarre l'artiglieria, della quale forse voi vi riderete; pure io non giudico ch'ella sia da spregiarla. E' non è cosa che facci maggiore confusione in uno esercito che impedirgli la vista; onde che molti gagliardissimi eserciti sono stati rotti, per essere loro stato impedito il vedere o dalla polvere o dal sole. Non è ancora cosa che più impedisca la vista che il fumo che fa l'artiglieria nel trarla; però io crederrei che fusse più prudenza lasciare accecarsi il nemico da se stesso, che volere tu, cieco, andarlo a trovare. Però o io non la trarrei, o, perchè questo non sarebbe approvato, rispetto alla riputazione che ha l'artiglieria, io la metterei in su' corni dell'esercito, acciocchè, traendola, con il fumo ella non accecasse la fronte di quello; che è la 'mportanza delle mie genti. E che lo impedire la vista al nemico sia cosa utile, se ne può addurre per esemplo Epaminonda; il quale, per accecare l'esercito nemico che veniva a fare seco giornata, fece correre i suoi cavalli leggieri innanzi alla fronte de' nemici, perchè levassono alta la polvere e gli impedissono la vista; il che gli dette vinta la giornata. Quanto al parervi che io abbia guidati i colpi delle artiglierie a mio modo, faccendogli passare sopra la testa de' fanti, vi rispondo che sono molte più le volte, e senza comparazione, che l'artiglierie grosse non percuotono le fanterie, che quelle ch'elle percuotono; perchè la fanteria è tanto bassa e quelle sono sì difficili a trattare, che, ogni poco che tu l'alzi, elle passano sopra la testa de' fanti; e se l'abbassi, danno in terra, e il colpo non perviene a quegli. Salvagli ancora la inequalità del terreno, perchè ogni poco di macchia o di rialto che sia tra' fanti e quelle, le impedisce. E quanto a' cavalli, e massime quegli degli uomini d'arme, perchè hanno a stare più stretti che i leggieri, e per essere più alti possono essere meglio percossi, si può, infino che l'artiglierie abbiano tratto, tenergli nella coda dell'esercito. Vero è che assai più nuocono gli scoppietti e l'artiglierie minute, che quelle; alle quali è il maggiore rimedio venire alle mani tosto; e se nel primo assalto ne muore alcuno, sempre ne morì; e uno buono capitano e uno buono esercito non ha a temere uno danno che sia particolare, ma uno generale; ed imitare i Svizzeri, i quali non schifarono mai giornata sbigottiti dalle artiglierie; anzi puniscono di pena capitale quegli che per paura di quelle o si uscissero della fila o facessero con la persona alcuno segno di timore. Io le feci, tratto ch'elle ebbero, ritirare nell'esercito, perch'elle lasciassero il passo libero alle battaglie. Non ne feci più menzione, come di cosa inutile, appiccata che è la zuffa. Voi avete ancora detto che, rispetto alla furia di questo instrumento, molti giudicano l'armi e gli ordini antichi essere inutili; e pare, per questo vostro parlare, che i moderni abbiano trovati ordini e armi che contro all'artiglieria sieno utili. Se voi sapete questo, io arò caro che voi me lo insegniate, perchè infino a quì non ce ne so io vedere alcuno, nè credo se ne possa trovare. In modo che io vorrei intendere da cotestoro, per quali cagioni i soldati a piè de' nostri tempi portano il petto o il corsaletto di ferro e quegli a cavallo vanno tutti coperti d'arme; perchè, poi che dannano l'armare antico come inutile rispetto alle artiglierie, doverrebbero fuggire ancora queste. Vorrei intendere anche per che cagione i Svizzeri, a similitudine degli antichi ordini, fanno una battaglia stretta di sei o ottomila fanti, e per quale cagione tutti gli hanno imitati, portando questo ordine quel medesimo pericolo, per conto dell'artiglierie, che si porterebbono quegli altri che dell'antichità si imitassero. Credo che non saprebbero che si rispondere; ma se voi ne dimandassi i soldati che avessero qualche giudicio, risponderebbero, prima, che vanno armati, perchè, sebbene quelle armi non gli difendono dalle artiglierie, gli difendono dalle balestre, dalle picche, dalle spade, da' sassi e da ogni altra offesa che viene da' nemici. Risponderebbero ancora che vanno stretti insieme come i Svizzeri, per potere più facilmente urtare i fanti, per potere sostenere meglio i cavalli e per dare più difficultà al nemico a rompergli. In modo che si vede che i soldati hanno a temere molte altre cose oltre alle artiglierie, dalle quali cose con l'armi e con gli ordini si difendono. Di che ne seguita che, quanto meglio armato è uno esercito e quanto ha gli ordini suoi più serrati e più forti, tanto è più sicuro. Tale che, chi è di quella opinione che voi dite, conviene o che sia di poca prudenza, o che a queste cose abbia pensato molto poco; perchè, se noi veggiamo che una minima parte del modo dello armare antico che si usa oggi, che è la picca, è una minima parte di quegli ordini, che sono i battaglioni de' Svizzeri, ci fanno tanto bene e porgono agli eserciti nostri tanta fortezza, perchè non abbiamo noi a credere che l'altre armi e gli altri ordini che si sono lasciati, sieno utili? dipoi, se noi non abbiamo riguardo all'artiglieria nel metterci stretti insieme come i Svizzeri, quali altri ordini ci possono fare più temere di quella? Con ciò sia cosa che niuno ordine può fare che noi temiamo tanto quella, quanto quegli che stringono gli uomini insieme. Oltre a questo, se non mi sbigottisce l'artiglieria de' nemici nel pormi col campo a una terra dov'ella mi offende con più sua sicurtà, non la potendo io occupare per essere difesa dalle mura, ma solo col tempo con la mia artiglieria impedire di modo ch'ella può raddoppiare i colpi a suo modo, , perchè la ho io a temere in campagna dove io la posso tosto occupare? Tanto che io vi conchiudo questo: che l'artiglierie, secondo l'opinione mia, non impediscono che non si possano usare gli antichi modi e mostrare l'antica virtù. E se io non avessi parlato altra volta con voi di questo instrumento, mi vi distenderei più; ma io mi voglio rimettere a quello che allora ne dissi.

LUIGI: Noi possiamo avere inteso benissimo quanto voi ne avete circa l'artiglierie discorso; e, in somma, mi pare abbiate mostro che lo occuparle prestamente sia il maggiore rimedio si abbia con quelle, sendo in campagna e avendo uno esercito allo incontro. Sopra che mi nasce una dubitazione: perchè mi pare che il nemico potrebbe collocarle in lato, nel suo esercito, ch'elle vi offenderebbero, e sarebbono in modo guardate da' fanti, ch'elle non si potrebbero occupare. Voi avete, se bene mi ricordo, nello ordinare lo esercito vostro a giornata, fatto intervalli di quattro braccia dall'una battaglia all'altra; fatto di venti quegli che sono dalle battaglie alle picche estraordinarie. Se il nemico ordinasse l'esercito a similitudine del vostro, e mettesse l'artiglierie bene dentro in quegli intervalli, io credo che di quivi elle vi offenderebbero con grandissima sicurtà loro, perchè non si potrebbe entrare nelle forze de' nemici a occuparle.

FABRIZIO: Voi dubitate prudentissimamente, e io mi ingegnerò o di risolvervi il dubbio o di porvi il rimedio. Io vi ho detto che continuamente queste battaglie, o per lo andare o per il combattere, sono in moto e sempre, per natura, si vengono a ristringere; in modo che, se voi fate gli intervalli di poca larghezza dove voi mettete l'artiglierie, in poco tempo son ristretti in modo che l'artiglieria non potrà più fare l'ufficio suo; se voi gli fate larghi per fuggire questo pericolo, voi incorrerete in uno maggiore; che voi per quegli intervalli non solamente date commodità al nemico di occuparvi l'artiglieria, ma di rompervi. Ma voi avete a sapere ch'egli è impossibile tenere l'artiglierie tra le schiere, massime quelle che vanno in sulle carrette, perchè l'artiglierie camminano per uno verso e traggono per l'altro; dimodochè, avendo a camminare e trarre, è necessario, innanzi al trarre, si voltino e, per voltarsi, vogliono tanto spazio che cinquanta carri d'artiglieria disordinerebbono ogni esercito. Però è necessario tenerle fuora delle schiere, dov'elle possono essere combattute nel modo che poco fa dimostrammo. Ma poniamo ch'elle vi si potessono tenere e che si potesse trovare una via di mezzo, e di qualità che, ristringendosi, non impedisse l'artiglieria e non fusse sì aperta ch'ella desse la via al nemico; dico che ci si rimedia facilmente col fare all'incontro intervalli nell'esercito tuo che dieno la via libera a' colpi di quella; e così verrà la furia sua ad essere vana. Il che si può fare facilissimamente, perchè, volendo il nemico che l'artiglieria sua stia sicura, conviene ch'egli la ponga dietro nell'ultima parte degli intervalli; in modo che i colpi di quella, a volere che non offendano i suoi proprj, conviene passino per una linea retta e per quella medesima, sempre; e però col dare loro luogo, facilmente si possono fuggire; perchè questa è una regola generale: che a quelle cose le quali non si possono sostenere, si ha a dare la via, come facevano gli antichi a' liofanti e a' carri falcati. Io credo, anzi sono più che certo, che vi pare che io abbia acconcia e vinta una giornata a mio modo; nondimeno io vi replico questo, quando non basti quanto ho detto infino a quì, che sarebbe impossibile che uno esercito, così ordinato e armato, non superasse nel primo scontro ogni altro esercito che si ordinasse come si ordinano gli eserciti moderni. I quali il più delle volte non fanno se non una fronte, non hanno scudi e sono di qualità disarmati, che non possono difendersi dal nemico propinquo; ed ordinansi in modo che, se mettono le loro battaglie per fianco l'una all'altra, fanno l'esercito sottile; se le mettono dietro l'una all'altra, non avendo modo a ricevere l'una l'altra, lo fanno confuso e atto ad essere facilmente perturbato. E benchè essi pongano tre nomi agli loro eserciti e li dividano in tre schiere, antiguardo, battaglia e retroguardo, nondimeno non se ne servono ad altro che a camminare e a distinguere gli alloggiamenti; ma nelle giornate tutti gli obligano a uno primo impeto e a una prima fortuna.

LUIGI: Io ho notato ancora, nel fare la vostra giornata, come la vostra cavalleria fu ributtata da' cavalli nemici, donde ch'ella si ritirò dalle picche estraordinarie; donde nacque che, con l'aiuto di quelle, sostenne e ripinse i nemici indietro. Io credo che le picche possano sostenere i cavalli, come voi dite, ma in uno battaglione grosso e sodo, come fanno i Svizzeri; ma voi nel vostro esercito avete per testa cinque ordini di picche e, per fianco, sette, in modo che io non so come si possano sostenergli.

FABRIZIO: Ancora che io v'abbia detto come sei file si adoperavano nelle Falangi di Macedonia ad un tratto, nondimeno voi avete a intendere che uno battaglione de' Svizzeri, se fusse composto di mille file, non ne può adoperare se non quattro o, al più, cinque; perchè le picche sono lunghe nove braccia; uno braccio e mezzo è occupato dalle mani; donde alla prima fila resta libero sette braccia e mezzo di picca. La seconda fila, oltre a quello ch'ella occupa con mano, ne consuma uno braccio e mezzo nello spazio che resta tra l'una fila e l'altra; di modo che non resta di picca utile se non sei braccia. Alla terza fila, per queste medesime ragioni, ne resta quattro e mezzo; alla quarta tre, alla quinta uno braccio e mezzo. L'altre file, per ferire, sono inutili, ma servono a instaurare queste prime file, come avemo detto, e a fare come uno barbacane a quelle cinque. Se adunque cinque delle loro file possono reggere i cavalli, perchè non gli possono reggere cinque delle nostre, alle quali ancora non manca file dietro che le sostengano e facciano loro quel medesimo appoggio, benchè non abbiano picche come quelle? E quando le file delle picche estraordinarie che sono poste ne' fianchi, vi paressono sottili, si potrebbe ridurle in uno quadro e porle per fianco alle due battaglie che io pongo nell'ultima schiera dell'esercito; dal quale luogo potrebbono facilmente tutte insieme favorire la fronte e le spalle dell'esercito e prestare aiuto a' cavalli, secondo che il bisogno lo ricercasse.

LUIGI: Useresti voi sempre questa forma di ordine, quando voi voleste fare giornata?

FABRIZIO: No, in alcun modo: perchè voi avete a variare la forma dell'esercito secondo la qualità del sito e la qualità e quantità del nemico; come se ne mostrerà, avanti che si fornisca questo ragionamento, qualche esemplo. Ma questa forma vi si è data, non tanto come più gagliarda che l'altre, che è in vero gagliardissima, quanto perchè da quella prendiate una regola e uno ordine a sapere conoscere i modi d'ordinare l'altre; perchè ogni scienza ha le sue generalità, sopra le quali in buona parte si fonda. Una cosa solo vi ricordo: che mai voi non ordiniate esercito in modo che, chi combatte dinanzi, non possa essere sovvenuto da quegli che sono posti di dietro; perchè, chi fa questo errore, rende la maggior parte del suo esercito inutile, e, se riscontra alcuna virtù, non può vincere.

LUIGI: E' mi è nato sopra questa parte uno dubbio. Io ho visto che nella disposizione delle battaglie voi fate la fronte di cinque per lato, il mezzo di tre e l'ultime parti di due; ed io crederrei che fusse meglio ordinarle al contrario, perchè io penso che uno esercito si potesse con più difficultà rompere, quando chi l'urtasse, quanto più penetrasse in quello, tanto più lo trovasse duro, e l'ordine fatto da voi mi pare che faccia che, quanto più s'entri in quello, tanto più si truovi debole.

FABRIZIO: Se voi vi ricordassi come a' Triarj, i quali erano il terzo ordine delle Legioni Romane, non erano assegnati più che secento uomini, voi dubiteresti meno, avendo inteso come quegli erano posti nell'ultima schiera; perchè voi vedresti come io, mosso da questo esemplo, ho posto nella ultima schiera due battaglie, che sono novecento fanti; in modo che io vengo piuttosto, andando con l'ordine Romano, a errare per averne tolti troppi che pochi. E benchè questo esemplo bastasse, io ve ne voglio dire la ragione. La quale è questa: la prima fronte dell'esercito si fa solida e spessa, perch'ella ha a sostenere l'impeto de' nemici e non ha a ricevere in se alcuno degli amici, e per questo conviene ch'ell'abbondi di uomini, perchè i pochi uomini la farebbero debole o per radità o per numero. Ma la seconda schiera, perchè ha prima a ricevere gli amici che a sostenere il nemico, conviene che abbia gli intervalli grandi; e per questo conviene che sia di minore numero che la prima, perchè, s'ella fusse di numero maggiore o equale, converrebbe o non vi lasciare gli intervalli, il che sarebbe disordine, o lasciandovegli, passare il termine di quelle dinanzi; il che farebbe la forma dell'esercito imperfetta. E non è vero quel che voi dite: che il nemico, quanto più entra dentro al battaglione, tanto più lo truovi debole; perchè il nemico non può combattere mai col secondo ordine se il primo non è congiunto con quello; in modo che viene a trovare il mezzo del battaglione più gagliardo e non più debole, avendo a combattere col primo e col secondo ordine insieme. Quel medesimo interviene, quando il nemico pervenisse alla schiera terza, perchè quivi, non con due battaglie che vi truova fresche, ma con tutto il battaglione avrebbe a combattere. E perchè questa ultima parte ha a ricevere più uomini, conviene che gli spazi sieno maggiori e, chi li riceve, sia minore numero.

LUIGI: E' mi piace quello che voi avete detto; ma rispondetemi ancora a questo: se le cinque prime battaglie si ritirano tra le tre seconde e, dipoi, le otto tra le due terze, non pare possibile che, ridotte le otto insieme e dipoi le dieci insieme, cappiano, o quando sono otto o quando sono dieci, in quel medesimo spazio che capevano le cinque.

FABRIZIO: La prima cosa che io vi rispondo, è ch'egli non è quel medesimo spazio; perchè le cinque hanno quattro spazi in mezzo, che ritirandosi tra le tre o tra le due, gli occupano: restavi poi quello spazio che è tra uno battaglione e l'altro e quello che è tra le battaglie e le picche estraordinarie; i quali spazi tutti fanno larghezza. Aggiugnesi a questo, che altro spazio tengono le battaglie quando sono negli ordini senza essere alterate, che quando le sono alterate; perchè, nell'alterazione, o elle stringono o elle allargano gli ordini. Allargangli, quando temono tanto ch'elle si mettono in fuga; stringongli, quando temono in modo ch'elle cercono assicurarsi non con la fuga, ma con la difesa, tale che in questo caso elle verrebbero a ristringersi e non a rallargarsi. Aggiugnesi a questo, che le cinque file delle picche che sono davanti, appiccata ch'elle hanno la zuffa, si hanno tra le loro battaglie a ritirare nella coda dell'esercito, per dare luogo agli scudati che possano combattere, e quelle, andando nella coda dell'esercito, possono servire a quello che il capitano giudicasse fusse bene operarle; dove dinanzi, mescolata che è la zuffa, sarebbono al tutto inutili. E per questo gli spazi ordinati vengono ad essere del rimanente delle genti capacissimi. Pure, quando questi spazi non bastassero, i fianchi dal lato sono uomini e non mura, i quali, cedendo e rallargandosi, possono fare lo spazio di tanta capacità che sia sufficiente a ricevergli.

LUIGI: Le file delle picche estraordinarie che voi ponete nell'esercito per fianco, quando le battaglie prime si ritirano nelle seconde, volete voi ch'elle stieno salde e rimangano come due corna allo esercito, o volete che ancora loro insieme con le battaglie si ritirino? Il che, quando abbiano a fare, non veggo come si possano, per non avere dietro battaglie con intervalli radi che le ricevano.

FABRIZIO: Se il nemico non le combatte quando egli sforza le battaglie a ritirarsi, possono star salde nell'ordine loro e ferire il nemico per fianco, poi che le battaglie prime si fussero ritirate; ma se combattesse ancora loro, come pare ragionevole, sendo sì possente che possa sforzare l'altre, si deggiono ancora esse ritirare. Il che possono fare ottimamente, ancora ch'elle non abbiano dietro chi le riceva; perchè dal mezzo innanzi si possono raddoppiare per dritto, entrando l'una fila nell'altra, nel modo che ragionammo quando si parlò dell'ordine del raddoppiarsi. Vero è che a volere, raddoppiando, ritirarsi indietro, conviene tenere altro modo che quello che io vi mostrai; perchè io vi dissi che la seconda fila aveva a entrare nella prima, la quarta nella terza, e così di mano in mano; in questo caso non s'arebbe a cominciare davanti, ma di dietro, acciocchè, raddoppiandosi le file, si venissero a ritirare indietro, non a gire innanzi. Ma per rispondere a tutto quello che da voi, sopra questa giornata da me dimostrata, si potesse replicare, io di nuovo vi dico che io vi ho ordinato questo esercito e dimostro questa giornata per due cagioni: l'una, per mostrarvi come si ordina, l'altra, per mostrarvi come si esercita. Dell'ordine io credo che voi restiate capacissimi; e quanto allo esercizio, vi dico che si dee, più volte che si può, mettergli insieme in queste forme, perchè i capi imparino a tenere le loro battaglie in questi ordini. Perchè a' soldati particolari s'appartiene tenere bene gli ordini di ciascuna battaglia, a' capi delle battaglie s'appartiene tenere bene quelle in ciascuno ordine di esercito e che sappiano ubbidire al comandamento del capitano generale. Conviene pertanto che sappiano congiugnere l'una battaglia con l'altra, sappiano pigliare il luogo loro in un tratto; e perciò conviene che la bandiera di ciascuna battaglia abbia descritto, in parte evidente, il numero suo, sì per poterle comandare, sì perchè il capitano e i soldati a quel numero più facilmente le riconoscano. deggiono ancora i battaglioni essere numerati e avere il numero nella loro bandiera principale. Conviene, adunque, sapere di qual numero sia il battaglione posto nel sinistro o nel destro corno, di quale numero sieno le battaglie poste nella fronte e nel mezzo, e così l'altre di mano in mano.

Vuolsi ancora che questi numeri sieno scala a' gradi degli onori degli eserciti; verbigrazia: il primo grado sia il Capodieci, il secondo il capo de' cinquanta Veliti ordinarj, il terzo il Centurione, il quarto il capo della prima battaglia, il quinto della seconda, il sesto della terza; e, di mano in mano, infino alla decima battaglia, il quale fusse onorato in secondo luogo dopo al capo generale d'uno battaglione, nè potesse venire a quel capo alcuno se non vi fusse salito per tutti questi gradi. E perchè, fuora di questi capi, ci sono gli tre Connestabili delle picche estraordinarie e gli due dei Veliti estraordinarj vorrei che fussono in quel grado del connestabole della prima battaglia; nè mi curerei che fussero sei uomini di pari grado, acciocchè ciascuno di loro facesse a gara per essere promosso alla seconda battaglia. Sappiendo adunque ciascheduno di questi capi in quale luogo avesse a essere collocata la sua battaglia, di necessità ne seguirebbe che, ad un suono di tromba, ritta che fusse la bandiera capitana, tutto l'esercito sarebbe ai luoghi suoi. E questo è il primo esercizio a che si debbe assuefare uno esercito, cioè a mettersi prestamente insieme; e per fare questo conviene ogni giorno, e in uno giorno più volte, ordinarlo e disordinarlo.

LUIGI: Che segno vorresti voi che avessono le bandiere di tutto l'esercito, oltre al numero?

FABRIZIO: Quella del capitano generale avesse il segno del principe dell'esercito, l'altre tutte potrebbero avere il medesimo segno e variare con i campi, o variare con i segni, come paresse meglio al signore dell'esercito; perchè questo importa poco, pure che ne nasca l'effetto ch'elle si conoscano l'una dall'altra. Ma passiamo all'altro esercizio in che si debba esercitare uno esercito, il quale è farlo muovere e con il passo conveniente andare, e vedere che, andando, mantenga gli ordini. Il terzo esercizio è ch'egli impari a maneggiarsi in quel modo che si ha dipoi a maneggiare nella giornata; far trarre l'artiglierie e ritirarle; fare uscire fuora i Veliti estraordinari; e dopo uno sembiante di assalto, ritirargli; fare che le prime battaglie, come s'elle fussono spinte, si ritirino nella radità delle seconde, e dipoi tutte nelle terze, e di quivi ciascuna ritorni al suo luogo; e in modo assuefargli in questo esercizio, che a ciascuno ogni cosa fosse nota e familiare; il che con la pratica e con la familiarità si conduce prestissimamente. Il quarto esercizio è ch'egli imparino a conoscere, per virtù del suono e delle bandiere, il comandamento del loro capitano; perchè quello che sarà loro pronunziato in voce, essi senza altro comandamento lo intenderanno. E, perchè l'importanza di questo comandamento dee nascere dal suono, io vi dirò quali suoni usavano gli antichi. Da'

Lacedemonj, secondo che afferma Tucidide, ne' loro eserciti erano usati zufoli; perchè giudicavano che questa armonia fusse più atta a fare procedere il loro esercito con gravità e non con furia. Da questa medesima ragione mossi i Cartaginesi, nel primo assalto, usavano la citera. Aliatte, Re de' Lidj, usava nella guerra la citera e i zufoli; ma Alessandro Magno e i Romani usavano i corni e le trombe, come quelli che pensavano per virtù di tali istrumenti, potere più accendere gli animi de' soldati e farli combattere più gagliardamente. Ma come noi abbiamo, nello armare lo esercito preso del modo Greco e del Romano, così nel distribuire i suoni servereno i costumi dell'una e dell'altra nazione. Però farei presso al capitano generale stare i trombetti, come suono non solamente atto a infiammare l'esercito, ma atto a sentirsi in ogni romore più che alcuno altro suono. Tutti gli altri suoni che fussero intorno a' Connestabili e a' capi de' battaglioni, vorrei che fussono tamburi piccoli e zufoli sonati, non come si suonano ora, ma come è consuetudine sonargli ne' conviti. Il capitano, adunque, con le trombe mostrasse quando si avesse a fermare o ire innanzi o tornare indietro, quando avessono a trarre l'artiglierie, quando muovere gli Veliti estraordinarj, e, con la variazione di tali suoni, mostrare all'esercito tutti quegli moti che generalmente si possono mostrare; le quali trombe fussero dipoi seguitate da' tamburi. E in questo esercizio, perch'egli importa assai, converrebbe assai esercitare il suo esercito. Quanto alla cavalleria, si vorrebbe usare medesimamente trombe, ma di minore suono e di diversa voce da quelle del capitano. Questo è quanto mi è occorso circa l'ordine dell'esercito e dell'esercizio di quello.

LUIGI: Io vi priego che non vi sia grave dichiararmi un'altra cosa: per che cagione voi facesti muovere con grida e romore e furia i cavalli leggieri e i Veliti estraordinarj, quando assaltarono, e dipoi, nello appiccare il resto dell'esercito, mostrasti che la cosa seguiva con uno silenzio grandissimo? E perchè io non intendo la cagione di questa varietà, desidererei me la dichiarasse.

FABRIZIO: E' sono state varie l'opinioni de' capitani antichi circa al venire alle mani: se si dee o con romore accelerare il passo o con silenzio andare adagio. Questo ultimo modo serve a tenere l'ordine più fermo e a intendere meglio i comandamenti del capitano. Quel primo serve ad accendere più gli animi degli uomini. E perchè io credo che si dee avere rispetto all'una e all'altra di queste due cose, io feci muovere quegli con romore e quegli altri con silenzio. Nè mi pare in alcun modo che i romori continui sieno a proposito, perch'egli impediscono i comandamenti; il che è cosa perniciosissima. Nè è ragionevole che i Romani, fuora del primo assalto, seguissero di romoreggiare, perchè si vede, nelle loro istorie, essere molte volte intervenuto, per le parole e conforti del capitano, i soldati che fuggivano essersi fermi e in varj modi per suo comandamenti avere variati gli ordini; il che non sarebbe seguito, se i romori avessero la sua voce superato.

BOOK FOUR

BOOK FOUR

LUIGI: Since an engagement has been won so honorably under my Rule, I think it is well if I do not tempt fortune further, knowing how changeable and unstable it is. And, therefore, I desire to resign my speakership, and that, wanting to follow the order that belongs to the youngest, Zanobi now assume this office of questioning. And I know he will not refuse this honor, or we would rather say, this hard work, as much in order to (give) pleasure, as also because he is naturally more courageous than I: nor should he be afraid to enter into these labors, where he can thus be overcome, as he can overcome.

ZANOBI: I intend to stay where you put me, even though I would more willingly stay to listen, because up to now I am more satisfied with your questions than those which occurred to me in listening to your discussions pleased me. But I believe it is well, Lords, that since you have time left, and have patience, we do not annoy you with these ceremonies of ours.

FABRIZIO: Rather you give me pleasure, because this change of questioners makes me know the various geniuses, and your various desires. Is there anything remaining of the matter discussed which you think should be added?

ZANOBI: There are two things I desire before we pass on to another part: the one is, that you would show me if there is another form of organizing the Army which may occur to you: the other, what considerations ought a Captain have before going to battle, and if some accident should arise concerning it, what remedies can be made.

FABRIZIO: I will make an effort to satisfy you, I will not reply to your questions in detail; for, when I answer one, often it will also answer another. I have told you that I proposed a form for the Army which should fill all the requirements according to the (nature of) the enemy and the site, because in this case, one proceeds according to the site and the enemy. But note this, that there is no greater peril than to over extend the front of your army, unless you have a very large and very brave Army: otherwise you have to make it rather wide and of short length, than of long length and very narrow. For when you have a small force compared to the enemy, you ought to seek other remedies; for example, arrange your army so that you are girded on a side by rivers or swamps, so that you cannot be surrounded or gird yourself on the flanks with ditches, as Caesar did in Gaul. In this case, you have to take the flexibility of being able to enlarge or compress your front, according to the numbers of the enemy: and if the enemy is of a lesser number, you ought to seek wide places, especially if you have your forces so disciplined, that you are able not only to surround the enemy, but extend your ranks, because in rough and difficult places, you do not have the advantage of being able to avail yourself of (all) your ranks. Hence it happened that the Romans almost always sought open fields, and avoided the difficult ones. On the other hand ((as I have said)) you ought to, if you have either a small force or a poorly disciplined one, for you have to seek places where a small number can defend you, or where inexperience may not cause you injury. Also, higher places ought to be sought so as to be able more easily to attack (the enemy). None the less, one ought to be aware not to arrange your Army on a beach and in a place near the adjoining hills, where the enemy Army can come; because in this case, with respect to the artillery, the higher place would be disadvantageous to you, because you could continuously and conveniently be harmed by the enemy artillery, without being able to undertake any remedy, and similarly, impeded by your own men, you cannot conveniently injure him. Whoever organizes an Army for battle, ought also to have regard for both the sun and the wind, that the one and the other do not strike the front, because both impede your vision, the one with its rays, the other with dust. And in addition, the wind does not aid the arms that are thrown at the enemy, and makes their blows more feeble. And as to the sun, it is not enough that you take care that it is not in your face at the time, but you must think about it not harming you when it comes up. And because of this, in arranging the army, I would have it (the sun) behind them, so that much time should pass before it should come in front of you. This method was observed by Hannibal at Cannae and by Marius against the Cimbrians. If you should be greatly inferior in cavalry, arrange your army between vines and trees, and such impediments, as the Spaniards did in our times when they routed the French in the Kingdom (of Naples) on the Cirignuola. And it has been frequently seen that the same soldiers, when they changed only their arrangement and the location, from being overcome became victorious, as happened to the Carthaginians, who, after having been often defeated by Marius Regulus, were afterwards victorious, through the counsel of Xantippe, the Lacedemonian, who had them descend to the plain, where, by the virtu of their cavalry and Elephants, they were able to overcome the Romans. And it appears to me, according to the examples of the ancients, that almost all the excellent Captains, when they learned that the enemy had strengthened one side of the company, did not attack the stronger side, but the weaker, and the other stronger side they oppose to the weaker: then, when starting a battle, they cornered the stronger part that it only resist the enemy, and not push it back, and the weaker part that it allow itself to be overcome, and retire into the rear ranks of the Army. This causes two great disorders to the enemy: the first, that he finds his strongest part surrounded: the second is, that as it appears to them they will obtain the victory quickly, it rarely happens that he will not become disorganized, whence his defeat quickly results. Cornelius Scipio, when he was in Spain, (fighting) against Hasdrubal, the Carthaginian, and knowing that Hasdrubal was noted, that in arranging the Army, placed his legions in the center, which constituted the strongest part of his Army, and therefore, when Hasdrubal was to proceed in this manner, afterwards, when he came to the engagement, changed the arrangement, and put his Legions in the wings of the Army, and placed his weakest forces in the center. Then when they came hand to hand, he quickly had those forces in the center to walk slowly, and the wings to move forward swiftly: so that only the wings of both armies fought, and the ranks in the center, being distant from each other, did not join (in battle), and thus the strongest part of (the army of) Scipio came to fight the weakest part of (that of) Hasdrubal, and defeated it. This method at that time was useful, but today, because of the artillery, could not be employed, because that space that existed between one and the other army, gives them time to fire, which is most pernicious, as we said above. This method, therefore, must be set aside, and be used, as was said a short time ago, when all the Army is engaged, and the weaker part made to yield. When a Captain finds himself to have an army larger than that of the enemy, and not wanting to be prevented from surrounding him, arranges his Army with fronts equal to those of the enemy: then when the battle is started, has his front retire and the flanks extend little by little, and it will always happen that the enemy will find himself surrounded without being aware of it. When a Captain wants to fight almost secure in not being routed, he arranges his army in a place where he has a safe refuge nearby, either amid swamps or mountains or in a powerful city; for, in this manner, he cannot be pursued by the enemy, but the enemy cannot be pursued by him. This means was employed by Hannibal when fortune began to become adverse for him, and he was apprehensive of the valor of Marcus Marcellus. Several, in order to disorganize the ranks of the enemy, have commanded those who are lightly armed, that they begin the fight, and having begun it, retire among the ranks; and when the Armies afterwards have joined fronts together, and each front is occupied in fighting, they have allowed them to issue forth from the flanks of the companies, and disorganized and routed them. If anyone finds himself inferior in cavalry, he can, in addition to the methods mentioned, place a company of pikemen behind his cavalry, and in the fighting, arrange for them to give way for the pikemen, and he will always remain superior. Many have accustomed some of the lightly armed infantry to get used to combat amidst the cavalry, and this has been a very great help to the cavalry. Of all those who have organized Armies for battle, the most praiseworthy have been Hannibal and Scipio when they were fighting in Africa: and as Hannibal had his Army composed of Carthaginians and auxiliaries of various kinds, he placed eighty Elephants in the first van, then placed the auxiliaries, after these he placed his Carthaginians, and in the rear, he placed the Italians, whom he trusted little. He arranged matters thusly, because the auxiliaries, having the enemy in front and their rear closed by his men, they could not flee: so that being compelled to fight, they should overcome or tire out the Romans, thinking afterwards with his forces of virtu, fresh, he could easily overcome the already tired Romans. In the encounter with this arrangement, Scipio placed the Astati, the Principi, and the Triari, in the accustomed fashion for one to be able to receive the other, and one to help the other. He made the vans of the army full of intervals; and so that they should not be seen through, but rather appear united, he filled them with Veliti, whom he commanded that, as soon as the Elephants arrived, they should give way, and enter through the regular spaces among the legions, and leave the way open to the Elephants: and thus come to render their attack vain, so that coming hand to hand with them, he was superior.

ZANOBI: You have made me remember in telling me of this engagement, that Scipio, during the fight, did not have the Astati retire into the ranks of the Principi, but divided them and had them retire into the wings of the army, so as to make room for the Principi, if he wanted to push them forward. I would desire, therefore, that you tell me what reason motivated him not to observe the accustomed arrangement.

FABRIZIO: I will tell you. Hannibal had placed all the virtu of his army in the second line; whence Scipio, in order to oppose a similar virtu to it, assembled the Principi and the Triari; so that the intervals of the Principi being occupied by the Triari, there was no place to receive the Astati, and therefore, he caused the Astati to be divided and enter the wings of the army, and did not bring them among the Principi. But take note that this method of opening up the first lines to make a place for the second, cannot be employed except when the other are superior, because then the convenience exists to be able to do it, as Scipio was able to. But being inferior and repulsed, it cannot be done except with your manifest ruin: and, therefore, you must have ranks in the rear which will receive you. But let us return to our discussion. The ancient Asiatics ((among other things thought up by them to injure the enemy)) used chariots which had scythes on their sides, so that they not only served to open up the lines with their attack, but also kill the adversary with the scythes. Provisions against these attacks were made in three ways. It was resisted by the density of the ranks, or they were received within the lines as were the Elephants, or a stalwart resistance was made with some stratagems, as did Sulla, the Roman, against Archelaus, who had many of those chariots which they called Falcati; he (Sulla), in order to resist them, fixed many poles in the ground behind the first ranks, by which the chariots, being resisted, lost their impetus. And note is to be taken of the new method which Sulla used against this man in arranging the army, since he put the Veliti and the cavalry in the rear, and all the heavily armed in front, leaving many intervals in order to be able to send those in the rear forward if necessity should require it; whence when the battle was started, with the aid of the cavalry, to whom he gave the way, he obtained the victory. To want to worry the enemy during the battle, something must be made to happen which dismays him, either by announcing new help which is arriving, or by showing things which look like it, so that the enemy, being deceived by that sight, becomes frightened; and when he is frightened, can be easily overcome. These methods were used by the Roman Consuls Minucius Rufus and Accilius Glabrius, Caius Sulpicius also placed many soldier-packs on mules and other animals useless in war, but in a manner that they looked like men-at-arms, and commanded that they appear on a hill while they were (in) hand to hand (combat) with the Gauls: whence his victory resulted. Marius did the same when he was fighting against the Germans. Feigned assaults, therefore, being of great value while the battle lasts, it happens that many are benefited by the real (assaults), especially if, improvised in the middle of the battle, it is able to attack the enemy from behind or on the sides. Which can be done only with difficulty, unless the (nature of the) country helps you; for if it is open, part of your forces cannot be speeded, as must be done in such enterprises: but in wooded or mountainous places, and hence capable of ambush, part of your forces can be well hidden, so that the enemy may be assaulted, suddenly and without his expecting it, which will always be the cause of giving you the victory. And sometimes it has been very important, while the battle goes on, to plant voices which announce the killed of the enemy Captain, or to have defeated some other part of the army; and this often has given the victory to whoever used it. The enemy cavalry may be easily disturbed by unusual forms (sights) or noises; as did Croesus, who opposed camels to the cavalry of his adversaries, and Pyrrhus who opposed elephants to the Roman cavalry, the sight of which disturbed and disorganized it. In our times, the Turk routed the Shah in Persia and the Soldan in Syria with nothing else than the noise of guns, which so affected their cavalry by their unaccustomed noises, that the Turk was able easily to defeat it. The Spaniards, to overcome the army of Hamilcar, placed in their first lines chariots full of tow drawn by oxen, and when they had come to battle, set fire to them, whence the oxen, wanting to flee the fire, hurled themselves on the army of Hamilcar and dispersed it. As we mentioned, where the country is suitable, it is usual to deceive the enemy when in combat by drawing him into ambushes: but when it is open and spacious, many have employed the making (digging) of ditches, and then covering them lightly with earth and branches, but leaving several places (spaces) solid in order to be able to retire between them; then when the battle is started, retire through them, and the enemy pursuing, comes to ruin in them. If, during the battle, some accident befalls you which dismays your soldiers, it is a most prudent thing to know how to dissimulate and divert them to (something) good, as did Lucius Sulla, who, while the fighting was going on, seeing that a great part of his forces had gone over to the side of the enemy, and that this had dismayed his men, quickly caused it to be understood throughout the entire army that everything was happening by his order, and this not only did not disturb the army, but so increased its courage that it was victorious. It also happened to Sulla, that having sent certain soldiers to undertake certain business, and they having been killed, in order that his army would not be dismayed said, that because he had found them unfaithful, he had cunningly sent them into the hands of the enemy. Sertorious, when undertaking an engagement in Spain, killed one who had pointed out to him the slaying of one of his Heads, for fear that by telling the same to the others, he should dismay them. It is a difficult matter to stop an army already in flight, and return it to battle. And you have to make this distinction: either they are entirely in flight (motion), and here it is impossible to return them: or only a part are in flight, and here there is some remedy. Many Roman Captains, by getting in front of those fleeing, have stopped them, by making them ashamed of their flight, as did Lucius Sulla, who, when a part of his Legions had already turned, driven by the forces of Mithradates, with his sword in hand he got in front of them and shouted, "if anyone asks you where you have left your Captain, tell them, we have left him in Boetia fighting." The Consul Attilius opposed those who fled with those who did not flee, and made them understand that if they did not turn about, they would be killed by both friends and enemies. Phillip of Macedonia, when he learned that his men were afraid of the Scythian soldiers, put some of his most trusted cavalry behind his army, and commissioned them to kill anyone who fled; whence his men, preferring to die fighting rather than in flight, won. Many Romans, not so much in order to stop a flight, as to give his men an occasion to exhibit greater prowess, while they were fighting, have taken a banner out of their hands, and tossing it amid the enemy, offered rewards to whoever would recover it.

I do not believe it is out of order to add to this discussion those things that happen after a battle, especially as they are brief, and not to be omitted, and conform greatly to this discussion. I will tell you, therefore, how engagements are lost, or are won. When one wins, he ought to follow up the victory with all speed, and imitate Caesar in this case, and not Hannibal, who, because he had stopped after he had defeated the Romans at Cannae, lost the Empire of Rome. The other (Caesar) never rested after a victory, but pursued the routed enemy with great impetus and fury, until he had completely assaulted it. But when one loses, a Captain ought to see if something useful to him can result from this loss, especially if some residue of the army remains to him. An opportunity can arise from the unawareness of the enemy, which frequently becomes obscured after a victory, and gives you the occasion to attack him; as Martius, the Roman, attacked the Carthaginian army, which, having killed the two Scipios and defeated their armies, thought little of that remnant of the forces who, with Martius, remained alive; and was (in turn) attacked and routed by him. It is seen, therefore, that there is nothing so capable of success as that which the enemy believes you cannot attempt, because men are often injured more when they are less apprehensive. A Captain ought, therefore, when he cannot do this, at least endeavor with industry to restrict the injury caused by the defeat. And to do this, it is necessary for you to take steps that the enemy is not able to follow you easily, or give him cause for delay. In the first case some, after they realize they are losing, order their Leaders to flee in several parts by different paths, having (first) given an order where they should afterward reassemble, so that the enemy, fearing to divide his forces, would leave all or a greater part of them safe. In the second case, many have thrown down their most precious possessions in front of the enemy, so that being retarded by plundering, he gave them more time for flight. Titus Dimius used not a little astuteness in hiding the injury received in battle; for, after he had fought until nightfall with a loss of many of his men, caused a good many of them to be buried during the night; whence in the morning, the enemy seeing so many of their dead and so few Romans, believing they had had the disadvantage, fled. I believe I have thus confused you, as I said, (but) satisfied your question in good part: it is true, that concerning the shape of the army, there remains for me to tell you how sometimes it is customary for some Captains to make the front in the form of a wedge, judging in that way to be able more readily to open (penetrate) the Army of the enemy. In opposition to this shape they customarily would use a form of a scissor, so as to be able to receive that wedge into that space, and surround and fight it from every side. On this, I would like you to have this general rule, that the greatest remedy used against the design of the enemy, is to do that willingly which he designs for you to do by force, because doing it willingly you do it with order and to your advantage, but to his disadvantage: if you should do it by force, it would be to your ruin. As to the fortifying of this, I would not care to repeat anything already said. Does the adversary make a wedge in order to open your ranks? if you proceed with yours open, you disorganize him, and he does not disorganize you. Hannibal placed Elephants in front of his Army to open that of the Army of Scipio; Scipio went with his open and was the cause of his own victory and the ruin of the former (Hannibal). Hasdrubal placed his most stalwart forces in the center of the van of his Army to push back the forces of Scipio: Scipio commanded in like fashion that they should retire, and defeated him. So that such plans, when they are put forward, are the cause for the victory of him against whom they were organized. It remains for me yet, if I remember well, to tell you what considerations a Captain ought to take into account before going into battle: upon which I have to tell you first that a Captain never has to make an engagement, if he does not have the advantage, or if he is not compelled to. Advantages arise from the location, from the organization, and from having either greater or better forces. Necessity, (compulsion) arises when you see that, by not fighting, you must lose in an event; for example, when you see you are about to lack money, and therefore your Army has to be dissolved in any case; when hunger is about to assail you, or when you expect the enemy to be reinforced again by new forces. In these cases, one ought always to fight, even at your disadvantage; for it is much better to try your fortune when it can favor you, than by not trying, see your ruin sure: and in such a case, it is as serious an error for a Captain not to fight, as it is to pass up an opportunity to win, either from ignorance, or from cowardice. The enemy sometimes gives you the advantage, and sometimes (it derives from) your prudence. Many have been routed while crossing a river by an alert enemy of theirs, who waited until they were in the middle of the stream, and then assaulted them on every side; as Caesar did to the Swiss, where he destroyed a fourth part of them, after they had been split by the river. Some time you may find your enemy tired from having pursued you too inconsiderately, so that, finding yourself fresh, and rested, you ought not to lose such an opportunity. In addition to this, if an enemy offers you battle at a good hour of the morning, you can delay going out of your encampment for many hours: and if he has been under arms for a long time, and has lost that first ardor with which he started, you can then fight with him. Scipio and Metellus employed this method in Spain, the first against Hasdrubal, and the other against Sertorius. If the enemy has diminished in strength, either from having divided the Armies, as the Scipios (did) in Spain, or from some other cause, you ought to try (your) fortune. The greater part of prudent Captains would rather receive the onrush of the enemy, who impetuously go to assault them, for their fury is easily withstood by firm and resolute men, and that fury which was withstood, easily converts itself into cowardice. Fabius acted thusly against the Samnites and against the Gauls, and was victorious, but his colleague, Decius was killed. Some who feared the virtu of their enemy, have begun the battle at an hour near nightfall, so that if their men were defeated, they might be able to be protected by its darkness and save themselves. Some, having known that the enemy Army, because of certain superstitions, does not want to undertake fighting at such a time, selected that time for battle, and won: which Caesar did in Gaul against Ariovistus, and Vespatianus in Syria against the Jews. The greater and more important awareness that a Captain ought to have, is (to see) that he has about him, men loyal and most expert in war, and prudent, with whom he counsels continually, and discusses his forces and those of the enemy with them: which are the greater in number, which are better armed or better trained, which are more apt to suffer deprivation, which to confide in more, the infantry or the cavalry. Also, they consider the location in which they are, and if it is more suitable for the enemy than for themselves; which of them has the better convenience of supply; whether it is better to delay the engagement or undertake it, and what benefit the weather might give you or take away from them; for often when the soldiers see the war becoming long, they become irritable, and weary from hard work and tedium, will abandon you. Above all, it is important for the Captain to know the enemy, and who he has around him: if he is foolhardy or cautious: if timid or audacious. See whether you can trust the auxiliary soldiers. And above all, you ought to guard against leading an army into battle which is afraid, or distrustful in any way of victory, for the best indication of defeat is when one believes he cannot win. And, therefore, in this case, you ought to avoid an engagement, either by doing as Fabius Maximus did, who, by encamping in strong places, did not give Hannibal courage to go and meet him, or by believing that the enemy, also in strong places, should come to meet you, you should depart from the field, and divide your forces among your towns, so that the tedium of capturing them will tire him.

ZANOBI: Can he not avoid the engagement in other ways than by dividing it (the army) into several parts, and putting them in towns?

FABRIZIO: I believe at another time I have discussed with some of you that whoever is in the field, cannot avoid an engagement if he has an enemy who wants to fight in any case; and he has but one remedy, and that is to place himself with his Army at least fifty miles distant from his adversary, so as to be in time to get out of his way if he should come to meet him. And Fabius Maximus never avoided an engagement with Hannibal, but wanted it at his advantage; and Hannibal did not presume to be able to overcome him by going to meet him in the places where he was encamped. But if he supposed he could defeat him, it was necessary for Fabius to undertake an engagement with him in any case, or to flee. Phillip, King of Macedonia, he who was the father of Perseus, coming to war with the Romans, placed his encampment on a very high mountain so as not to have an engagement with them; but the Romans went to meet him on that mountain, and routed him. Vercingetorix, a Captain of the Gauls, in order to avoid an engagement with Caesar, who unexpectedly had crossed the river, placed himself miles distant with his forces. The Venetians in our times, if they did not want to come to an engagement with the King of France, ought not to have waited until the French Army had crossed the Adda, but should have placed themselves distant from him, as did Vercingetorix: whence, having waited for him, they did not know how to take the opportunity of undertaking an engagement during the crossing, nor how to avoid it; for the French being near to them, as the Venetians decamped, assaulted and routed them. And so it is, that an engagement cannot be avoided if the enemy at all events wants to undertake it. Nor does anyone cite Fabius, for he avoided an engagement in cases like that, just as much as did Hannibal. It often happens that your soldiers are not willing to fight, and you know that because of their number or the location, or from some other cause, you have a disadvantage, and would like them to change their minds. It also happens that necessity or opportunity constrains you to (come to) an engagement, and that your soldiers are discontent and little disposed to fight, whence it is necessary for you in one case to frighten them, and in the other to excite them. In the first instance, if persuasion is not enough, there is no better way to have both those who fight and those who would not believe you, than to give some of them over to the enemy as plunder. It may also be well to do with cunning that which happened to Fabius Maximus at home. The Army of Fabius desired ((as you know)) to fight with the Army of Hannibal: his Master of cavalry had the same desire. It did not seem proper to Fabius to attempt the battle, so that in order to dispel such (desires), he had to divide the Army. Fabius kept his men in the encampments: and the other (the Master of cavalry) going forth, and coming into great danger, would have been routed, if Fabius had not succored him. By this example, the Master of the cavalry, together with the entire army, realized it was a wise course to obey Fabius. As to exciting them to fight, it is well to make them angry at the enemy, by pointing out that (the enemy) say slanderous things of them, and showing them to have with their intelligence (in the enemy camp) and having corrupted some part, to encamp on the side where they see they enemy, and undertake some light skirmishes with them; because things that are seen daily are more easily disparaged. By showing yourself indignant, and by making an oration in which you reproach them for their laziness, you make them so ashamed by saying you want to fight only if they do not accompany you. And above every thing, to have this awareness, if you want to make the soldiers obstinate in battle, not to permit them to send home any of their possessions, or settle in any place, until the war ends, so that they understand that if flight saves them their lives, it will not save them their possessions, the love of the latter, not less than the former, renders men obstinate in defense.

ZANOBI: You have told how soldiers can be made to turn and fight, by talking to them. Do you mean by this that he has to talk to the entire Army, or to its Heads?

FABRIZIO: To persuade or dissuade a few from something, is very easy; for if words are not enough, you can use authority and force: but the difficulty is to take away a sinister idea from a multitude, whether it may be in agreement or contrary to your own opinion, where only words can be used, which, if you want to persuade everyone, must be heard by everyone. Captains, therefore, must be excellent Orators, for without knowing how to talk to the entire Army, good things can only be done with difficulty. Which, in these times of ours, is completely done away with. Read the life (biography) of Alexander the Great, and see how many times it was necessary to harangue and speak publicly to the Army; otherwise he could never have them led them ((having become rich and full of plunder)) through the deserts of Arabia and into India with so much hardship and trouble; for infinite numbers of things arose by which an Army is ruined if a Captain does not know how or is not accustomed to talking to it; for this speaking takes away fear, incites courage, increases obstinacy, and sweeps away deceptions, promises rewards, points out dangers and the ways to avoid them, reprimands, begs, threatens, fills with hope, praises, slanders, and does all those things by which human passion are extinguished or enkindled. Whence that Prince or Republic planning to raise a new army, and to give this army reputation, ought to accustom the soldiers to listen to the talk of the Captain, and the Captain to know how to talk to them. Religion was (also) of much value in keeping the ancient soldiers well disposed and an oath was given to (taken by) them when they came into the army; for whenever they made a mistake, they were threatened not only by those evils that can be feared by men, but also by those that can be expected from the Deity. This practice, mixed with other religious means, often made an entire enterprise easy for the ancient Captains, and would always be so whenever religion was feared and observed. Sertorius availed himself of this when he told of talking with a Hind (female stag), which promised him victory on the part of the Deity. Sulla was said to talk with a Statue which he had taken from the Temple of Apollo. Many have told of God appearing to them in their sleep, and admonishing them to fight. In the times of our fathers, Charles the seventh, King of France, in the war he waged against the English, was said to counsel with a young girl sent by God, who is called the Maid of France, and who was the cause for victory. You can also take means to make your (soldiers) value the enemy little, as Agesilaus the Spartan did, who showed his soldiers some Persians in the nude, so that seeing their delicate members, they should have no cause for being afraid of them. Some have constrained them to fight from necessity, by removing from their paths all hope of saving themselves, except through victory. This is the strongest and the best provision that can be made when you want to make your soldiers obstinate. Which obstinacy is increased by the confidence and the love either of the Captain or of the Country. Confidence is instilled by arms organization, fresh victories, and the knowledge of the Captain. Love of Country springs from nature: that of the Captain from (his) virtu more than any other good event. Necessities can be many, but that is the strongest, which constrains you either to win or to die.

Libro Quarto

LUIGI: Poichè sotto l'imperio mio si è vinta una giornata sì onorevolmente, io penso che sia bene che io non tenti più la fortuna, sapendo quanto quella è varia e instabile. E però io desidero deporre la dittatura e che Zanobi faccia ora questo uffizio del domandare, volendo seguire l'ordine che tocchi al più giovane. E io so che non ricuserà questo onore o, vogliamo dire, questa fatica, sì per compiacermi, sì ancora per essere naturalmente più animoso di me; nè gli recherà paura avere a entrare in questi travagli, dove egli potesse così essere vinto, come vincere.

ZANOBI: Io sono per stare dove voi mi metterete, ancora che io stessi più volentieri ad ascoltare; perchè, infino a quì, mi sono più soddisfatte le domande vostre che non mi sarieno piaciute quelle che a me, nello ascoltare i vostri ragionamenti, occorrevano. Ma io credo che sia bene, signore, che voi avanziate tempo e abbiate pazienza, se con queste nostre cerimonie vi infastidissimo.

FABRIZIO: Anzi mi date piacere, perchè questa variazione de' domandatori mi fa conoscere i varj ingegni e i varj appetiti vostri. Ma restavi cosa alcuna che vi paia da aggiugnere alla materia ragionata?

ZANOBI: Due cose desidero, avanti che si passi ad un'altra parte: l'una, è che voi ne mostriate se altra forma di ordinare eserciti vi occorre; l'altra, quali rispetti debbe avere uno capitano prima che si conduca alla zuffa, e, nascendo alcuno accidente in essa, quali rimedj vi si possa fare.

FABRIZIO: Io mi sforzerò soddisfarvi. Non risponderò già distintamente alle domande vostre, perchè, mentre che io risponderò a una, molte volte si verrà a rispondere all'altra. Io vi ho detto come io vi proposi una forma di esercito, acciocchè, secondo quella, gli potesse dare tutte quelle forme che il nemico e il sito ricerca; perchè, in questo caso, e secondo il sito e secondo il nemico si procede. Ma notate questo: che non ci è la più pericolosa forma che distendere assai la fronte dell'esercito tuo, se già tu non hai un gagliardissimo e un grandissimo esercito; altrimenti tu l'hai a fare piuttosto grosso e poco largo, che assai largo e sottile. Perchè, quando tu hai poche genti a comparazione del nemico, tu dei cercare degli altri rimedj, come sono: ordinare l'esercito tuo in lato che tu sia fasciato o da fiume o da palude, in modo che tu non possa essere circondato; o fasciarti da' fianchi con le fosse, come fece

Cesare in Francia. E avete a prendere in questo caso questa generalità: di allargarvi o ristrignervi con la fronte, secondo il numero vostro e quello del nemico; ed essendo il nemico di minore numero, dei cercare di luoghi larghi, avendo tu massimamente le genti tue disciplinate, acciocchè tu possa non solamente circondare il nemico, ma distendervi i tuoi ordini; perchè ne' luoghi aspri e difficili, non potendo valerti degli ordini tuoi, non vieni ad avere alcuno vantaggio. Quinci nasceva che i Romani quasi sempre cercavano i campi aperti e fuggivano i difficili. Al contrario, come ho detto, dei fare se hai o poche genti o male disciplinate; perchè tu hai a cercare luoghi, o dove il poco numero si salvi, o dove la poca esperienza non ti offenda. Debbesi ancora eleggere il luogo superiore, per potere più facilmente urtarlo. Nondimanco si debbe avere questa avvertenza: di non ordinare l'esercito tuo in una spiaggia e in luogo propinquo alle radici di quella, dove possa venire l'esercito nemico; perchè in questo caso, rispetto alle artiglierie, il luogo superiore ti arrecherebbe disavvantaggio; perchè sempre e commodamente potresti dalle artiglierie nemiche essere offeso senza potervi fare alcuno rimedio, e tu non potresti commodamente offendere quello, impedito da' tuoi medesimi. Debbe ancora, chi ordina uno esercito a giornata, avere rispetto al sole e al vento, che l'uno e l'altro non ti ferisca la fronte; perchè l'uno e l'altro ti impediscono la vista, l'uno con i razzi, l'altro con la polvere. E di più il vento disfavorisce l'armi che si traggono al nemico e fa più deboli i colpi loro. E quanto al sole, non basta avere cura che allora non ti dia nel viso, ma conviene pensare che, crescendo il dì, non ti offenda. E per questo converrebbe, nello ordinare le genti, averlo tutto alle spalle, acciocch'egli avesse a passare assai tempo nello arrivarti in fronte. Questo modo fu osservato da Annibale a Canne e da Mario contro a' Cimbri. Se tu fossi assai inferiore di cavalli, ordina l'esercito tuo tra vigne e arbori e simili impedimenti, come fecero ne' nostri tempi gli Spagnuoli, quando ruppono i Francesi nel Reame alla Cirignuola. E si è veduto molte volte come con i medesimi soldati, variando solo l'ordine e il luogo, si diventa di perdente vittorioso, come intervenne a' Cartaginesi, i quali, sendo stati vinti da Marco Regolo più volte, furono dipoi, per il consiglio di Santippo lacedemonio, vittoriosi, il quale gli fece scendere nel piano, dove, per virtù de' cavalli e degli liofanti, poterono superare i Romani. E mi pare, secondo gli antichi esempj, che quasi tutti i capitani eccellenti, quando eglino hanno conosciuto che il nemico ha fatto forte uno lato della battaglia, non gli hanno opposta la parte più forte, ma la più debole; e l'altra più forte hanno opposta alla più debole; poi, nello appiccare la zuffa, hanno comandato alla loro parte più gagliarda, che solamente sostenga il nemico e non lo spinga, e alla più debole, che si lasci vincere e ritirisi nell'ultima schiera dell'esercito. Questo genera due grandi disordini al nemico: il primo, ch'egli si truova la sua parte più gagliarda circondata; il secondo è che, parendogli avere la vittoria subito, rade volte è che non si disordini; donde ne nasce la sua subita perdita. Cornelio Scipione, sendo in Ispagna contro ad Asdrubale cartaginese, e sapendo come ad Asdrubale era noto ch'egli nell'ordinare l'esercito poneva le sue Legioni in mezzo, la quale era la più forte parte del suo esercito, e, per questo, come Asdrubale con simile ordine doveva procedere; quando dipoi venne alla giornata, mutò ordine, e le sue Legioni messe ne' corni dell'esercito, e nel mezzo pose tutte le sue genti più deboli. Dipoi, venendo alle mani, in un subito quelle genti poste nel mezzo fece camminare adagio ed i corni dell'esercito con celerità farsi innanzi; dimodochè solo i corni dell'uno e dell'altro esercito combattevano, e le schiere di mezzo, per essere distante l'una dall'altra, non si aggiugnevano; e così veniva a combattere la parte di Scipione più gagliarda con la più debole d'Asdrubale; e vinselo. Il quale modo fu allora utile; ma oggi, rispetto alle artiglierie, non si potrebbe usare; perchè quello spazio che rimarrebbe nel mezzo, tra l'uno esercito e l'altro, darebbe tempo a quelle di potere trarre; il che è perniciosissimo, come di sopra dicevo. Però conviene lasciare questo modo da parte, e usarlo, come poco fa dissi, faccendo appiccare tutto lo esercito e la parte più debole cedere. Quando uno capitano si truova avere più esercito di quello del nemico, a volerlo circondare che non lo prevegga, ordini lo esercito suo di equale fronte a quello dello avversario; dipoi, appiccata la zuffa, faccia che a poco a poco la fronte si ritiri e i fianchi si distendano; e sempre occorrerà che il nemico si troverrà, senza accorgersene, circondato. Quando uno capitano voglia combattere quasi che sicuro di non potere essere rotto, ordini l'esercito suo in luogo dove egli abbia il refugio propinquo e sicuro, o tra paludi o tra monti o in una città potente; perchè, in questo caso, egli non può essere seguito dal nemico e il nemico può essere seguitato da lui. Questo termine fu usato da Annibale, quando la fortuna cominciò a diventargli avversa e che dubitava del valore di Marco Marcello. Alcuni, per turbare gli ordini del nemico, hanno comandato a quegli che sono leggiermente armati, che appicchino la zuffa, e, appiccata, si ritirino tra gli ordini; e quando dipoi gli eserciti si sono attestati insieme e che la fronte di ciascuno è occupata al combattere, gli hanno fatti uscire per li fianchi delle battaglie, e quello turbato e rotto. Se alcuno si truova inferiore di cavalli, può, oltre a' modi detti, porre dietro a' suoi cavalli una battaglia di picche, e, nel combattere, ordinare che dieno la via alle picche; e rimarrà sempre superiore. Molti hanno consueto di avvezzare alcuni fanti leggiermente armati a combattere tra' cavalli; il che è stato alla cavalleria di aiuto grandissimo. Di tutti coloro che hanno ordinati eserciti alla giornata, sono i più lodati Annibale e Scipione quando combatterono in Affrica, e perchè Annibale aveva l'esercito suo composto di Cartaginesi e di ausiliarj di varie generazioni, pose nella prima fronte ottanta liofanti; dipoi collocò gli ausiliarj, dopo a' quali pose i suoi Cartaginesi; nell'ultimo luogo messe gli Italiani, ne' quali confidava poco. Le quali cose ordinò così, perchè gli ausiliarj, avendo innanzi il nemico e di dietro sendo chiusi da' suoi, non potessono fuggire; dimodochè, sendo necessitati al combattere, vincessero o straccassero i Romani, pensando poi, con la sua gente fresca e virtuosa facilmente i Romani già stracchi superare. All'incontro di questo ordine, Scipione collocò gli Astati, i Principi e i Triarj nel modo consueto da potere ricevere l'uno l'altro e sovvenire l'uno all'altro. Fece la fronte dell'esercito piena di intervalli; e perch'ella non transparesse, anzi paresse unita, li riempiè di Veliti; a' quali comandò che, tosto ch'e' liofanti venivano, cedessero, e, per li spazi ordinarj, entrassono tra le Legioni e lasciassero la via aperta a' liofanti; e così venne a rendere vano l'impeto di quegli, tanto che, venuto alle mani, ei fu superiore.

ZANOBI: Voi mi avete fatto ricordare, nello allegarmi cotesta giornata, come Scipione nel combattere non fece ritirare gli Astati negli ordini de' Principi, ma gli divise e fecegli ritirare nelle corna dell'esercito, acciocchè dessono luogo a' Principi, quando gli volle spingere innanzi. Però vorrei mi diceste quale cagione lo mosse a non osservare l'ordine consueto.

FABRIZIO: Dirovvelo. Aveva Annibale posta tutta la virtù del suo esercito nella seconda schiera; donde che Scipione, per opporre, a quella, simile virtù, raccozzò i Principi e i Triarj insieme: tale che essendo gli intervalli de' Principi occupati da' Triarj, non vi era luogo a potere ricevere gli Astati; e però fece dividere gli Astati e andare ne' corni dell'esercito, e non gli ritirò tra' Principi. Ma notate che questo modo dello aprire la prima schiera per dare luogo alla seconda, non si può usare se non quando altri è superiore; perchè allora si ha commodità a poterlo fare, come potette Scipione. Ma essendo al disotto e ributtato, non lo puoi fare se non con tua manifesta rovina; e però conviene avere, dietro, ordini che ti ricevino. Ma torniamo al ragionamento nostro. Usavano gli antichi Asiatici, tra l'altre cose pensate da loro per offendere i nemici, carri i quali avevano da' fianchi alcune falce; tale che, non solamente servivano ad aprire con il loro impeto le schiere, ma ancora ad ammazzare con le falci gli avversarj. Contro a questi impeti in tre modi si provvedeva: o si sostenevano con la densità degli ordini, o si ricevevano dentro nelle schiere come i liofanti, o e' si faceva con arte alcuna resistenza gagliarda; come fece Silla Romano contro ad Archelao, il quale aveva assai di questi carri che chiamavano falcati, che, per sostenergli, ficcò assai pali in terra dopo le prime schiere, da' quali i carri sostenuti perdevano l'impeto loro. Ed è da notare il nuovo modo che tenne Silla contro a costui in ordinare lo esercito; perchè misse i Veliti e i cavalli dietro e tutti gli armati gravi davanti, lasciando assai intervalli da potere mandare innanzi quegli di dietro quando la necessità lo richiedesse; donde, appiccata la zuffa, con lo aiuto de' cavalli a' quali dette la via, ebbe la vittoria. A volere turbare nella zuffa l'esercito nemico, conviene fare nascere qualche cosa che lo sbigottisca, o con annunziare nuovi aiuti che vengano, o col dimostrare cose che gli rappresentino; talmente che i nemici, ingannati da quello aspetto, sbigottiscono e, sbigottiti, si possano facilmente vincere. I quali modi tennono Minuzio Ruffo e Acilio Glabrione Consoli Romani. Caio Sulpizio ancora misse assai saccomanni sopra muli e altri animali alla guerra inutili, ma in modo ordinati che rappresentavano gente d'arme, e comandò ch'eglino apparissono sopra uno con le, mentre ch'egli era alle mani con i Francesi; donde ne nacque la sua vittoria. Il medesimo fece Mario quando combattè contro a' Tedeschi. Valendo, adunque, assai gli assalti finti mentre che la zuffa dura, conviene che molto più giovino i veri, massimamente se allo improvviso nel mezzo della zuffa si potesse di dietro o da lato assaltare il nemico. Il che difficilmente si può fare se il paese non ti aiuta; perchè, quando egli è aperto, non si può celare parte delle tue genti come conviene fare in simili imprese; ma ne' luoghi silvosi o montuosi, e per questo atti agli agguati, si può bene nascondere parte delle tue genti, per potere, in uno subito e fuora di sua opinione assaltare il nemico; la quale cosa sempre sarà cagione di darti la vittoria. È stato qualche volta di grande momento, mentre che la zuffa dura, seminare voci che pronuncino il capitano de' nemici essere morto, o avere vinto dall'altra parte dell'esercito; il che molte volte a chi l'ha usato ha dato la vittoria. Turbasi facilmente la cavalleria nemica o con forme o con romori inusitati; come fece Creso, che oppose i cammegli agli cavalli degli avversarj; e Pirro oppose alla cavalleria Romana i liofanti, lo aspetto de' quali la turbò e la disordinò. Ne' nostri tempi il Turco ruppe il Sofì in Persia e il Soldano in Sorìa, non con altro se non con i romori degli scoppietti; i quali in modo alterarono con gli loro inusitati romori la cavalleria di quegli, che il Turco potèo facilmente vincerla. Gli Spagnuoli, per vincere l'esercito d'Amilcare missero nella prima fronte carri pieni di stipa tirati da buoi, e, venendo alle mani, appiccarono fuoco a quella; donde che i buoi, volendo fuggire il fuoco, urtarono nell'esercito di Amilcare e lo apersero. Soglionsi, come abbiamo detto, ingannare i nemici nel combattere, tirandogli negli agguati, dove il paese è accomodato; ma, quando fusse aperto e largo, hanno molti usato di fare fosse, e dipoi ricopertole leggiermente di frasche e terra e lasciato alcuni spazi solidi da potersi tra quelle ritirare; dipoi, appiccata la zuffa, ritiratosi per quelli, e il nemico seguendogli, è rovinato in esse. Se nella zuffa ti occorre alcuno accidente da sbigottire i tuoi soldati, è cosa prudentissima il saperlo dissimulare e pervertirlo in bene, come fece Tullo Ostilio e Lucio Silla; il quale, veggendo come, mentre che si combatteva, una parte delle sue genti se ne era ita dalla parte nemica, e come quella cosa aveva assai sbigottiti i suoi, fece subito intendere per tutto lo esercito come ogni cosa seguiva per ordine suo; il che non solo non turbò lo esercito, ma gli accrebbe in tanto lo animo, che rimase vittorioso. Occorse ancora a Silla che, avendo mandati certi soldati a fare alcuna faccenda, ed essendo stati morti, disse, perchè l'esercito suo non si sbigottisse, avergli con arte mandati nelle mani de' nemici perchè gli aveva trovati poco fedeli. Sertorio, faccendo una giornata in Ispagna, ammazzò uno che gli significò la morte d'uno de' suoi capi, per paura che, dicendo il medesimo agli altri, non gli sbigottisse. È cosa difficilissima, uno esercito già mosso a fuggire, fermarlo e renderlo alla zuffa. E avete a fare questa distinzione: o egli è mosso tutto, e quì è impossibile restituirlo; o ne è mossa una parte, e quì è qualche rimedio. Molti capitani Romani con il farsi innanzi a quegli che fuggivano, gli hanno fermi, faccendoli vergognare della fuga; come fece Lucio Silla, che, sendo già parte delle sue Legioni in volta cacciate dalle genti di Mitridate, si fece innanzi con una spada in mano, gridando: Se alcuno vi domanda dove voi avete lasciato il capitano vostro, dite: Noi lo abbiamo lasciato in Beozia che combatteva. Attilio Consolo a quegli che fuggivano oppose quegli che non fuggivano, e fece loro intendere che, se non voltavano, sarebbero morti dagli amici e da' nemici. Filippo di Macedonia, intendendo come i suoi temevano de' soldati sciti, pose dietro al suo esercito alcuni de' suoi cavalli fidatissimi, e commisse loro ammazzassono qualunque fuggiva; onde che i suoi, volendo più tosto morire combattendo che fuggendo, vinsero. Molti Romani, non tanto per fermare una fuga, quanto per dare occasione a' suoi di fare maggiore forza, hanno, mentre che si combatte tolta una bandiera di mani a' suoi e gittatala tra i nimici e proposto premj a chi la riguadagnava. Io non credo che sia fuora di proposito aggiugnere a questo ragionamento quelle cose che intervengono dopo la zuffa, massime sendo cose brevi e da non le lasciare indietro e a questo ragionamento assai conformi. Dico, adunque, come le giornate si perdono o si vincono. Quando si vince, si dee con ogni celerità seguire la vittoria e imitare in questo caso Cesare e non Annibale; il quale, per essersi fermo da poi ch'egli ebbe rotti i Romani a Canne, ne perdè lo imperio di Roma. Quello altro mai dopo la vittoria non si posava, ma con maggiore impeto e furia seguiva el nemico rotto, che non l'aveva assaltato intero. Ma quando si perde, dee un capitano vedere se dalla perdita ne può nascere alcuna sua utilità, massimamente se gli è rimaso alcuno residuo di esercito. La commodità può nascere dalla poca avvertenza del nemico, il quale, il più delle volte, dopo la vittoria diventa trascurato e ti dà occasione di opprimerlo; come Marzio Romano oppresse gli eserciti cartaginesi, i quali, avendo morti i duoi Scipioni e rotti i loro eserciti, non stimando quello rimanente delle genti che con Marzio erano rimase vive, furono da lui assaltati e rotti. Per che si vede che non è cosa tanto riuscibile quanto quella che il nemico crede che tu non possa tentare, perchè il più delle volte gli uomini sono offesi più dove dubitano meno. Debbe un capitano pertanto, quando egli non possa fare questo, ingegnarsi almeno con la industria che la perdita sia meno dannosa. A fare questo ti è necessario tenere modi che il nemico non ti possa con facilità seguire, o dargli cagione ch'egli abbia a ritardare. Nel primo caso, alcuni, poi ch'egli hanno conosciuto di perdere, ordinarono agli loro capi che in diverse parti e per diverse vie si fuggissono, avendo dato ordine dove si avevano dipoi a raccozzare; il che faceva che il nemico, temendo di dividere l'esercito, ne lasciava ire salvi o tutti o la maggior parte di essi. Nel secondo caso, molti hanno gittato innanzi al nemico le loro cose più care, acciocchè quello, ritardato dalla preda, dia loro più spazio alla fuga. Tito Dimio usò non poca astuzia per nascondere il danno ch'egli aveva ricevuto nella zuffa; perchè, avendo combattuto infino a notte con perdita di assai de' suoi, fece la notte sotterrare la maggior parte di quegli; donde che la mattina, vedendo i nemici tanti morti de' loro e si pochi de' Romani, credendo avere disavvantaggio, si fuggirono. Io credo di avere così confusamente, come io dissi, soddisfatto in buona parte alla domanda vostra. Vero è che, circa la forma degli eserciti, mi resta a dirvi come alcuna volta per alcun capitano si è costumato fargli con la fronte a uso d'uno conio, giudicando potere per tale via più facilmente aprire l'esercito nemico. Contro a questa forma hanno usato fare una forma a uso di forbici, per potere tra quello vacuo ricevere quello conio e circondarlo e combatterlo da ogni parte. Sopra che voglio che voi prendiate questa regola generale: che il maggiore rimedio che si usi contro a uno disegno del nemico, è fare volontario quello ch'egli disegna che tu faccia per forza; perchè, faccendolo volontario, tu lo fai con ordine e con vantaggio tuo e disavvantaggio suo; se lo facessi forzato, vi sarebbe la tua rovina. A fortificazione di questo non mi curerò di replicarvi alcuna cosa già detta. Fa il conio lo avversario per aprire le tue schiere? Se tu vai con esse aperte, tu disordini lui ed esso non disordina te. Pose i liofanti in fronte del suo esercito Annibale per aprire con quegli l'esercito di Scipione; andò Scipione con esso aperto e fu cagione e della sua vittoria e della rovina di quello. Pose Asdrubale le sue genti più gagliarde nel mezzo della fronte del suo esercito, per spingere le genti di Scipione; comandò Scipione che per loro medesime si ritirassono, e ruppelo. In modo che simili disegni, quando si presentano, sono cagione della vittoria di colui contro a chi essi sono ordinati. Restami ancora, se bene mi ricorda, dirvi quali rispetti debbe avere uno capitano prima che si conduca alla zuffa. Sopra che io vi ho a dire, in prima, come uno capitano non ha mai a fare giornata se non ha vantaggio, o se non è necessitato. Il vantaggio nasce dal sito, dall'ordine, dall'avere o più o migliore gente, La necessità nasce quando tu vegga, non combattendo, dovere in ogni modo perdere; come è: che sia per mancarti danari e, per questo, lo esercito tuo si abbia in ogni modo a risolvere; che sia per assaltarti la fame; che il nemico aspetti di ingrossare di nuova gente. In questi casi sempre si dee combattere, ancora con tuo disavvantaggio, perch'egli è assai meglio tentare la fortuna dov'ella ti possa favorire, che, non la tentando, vedere la tua certa rovina. Ed è così grave peccato, in questo caso, in uno capitano il non combattere, come è d'avere avuta occasione di vincere e non la avere o conosciuta per ignoranza o lasciata per viltà. I vantaggi qualche volta te gli dà il nemico e qualche volta la tua prudenza. Molti, nel passare i fiumi, sono stati rotti da uno loro nemico accorto, il quale ha aspettato che sieno mezzi da ogni banda e, dipoi, gli ha assaltati; come fece Cesare a' Svizzeri, che consumò la quarta parte di loro, per essere tramezzati da uno fiume. Trovasi alcuna volta il tuo nemico stracco per averti seguito troppo inconsideratamente, dimodochè, trovandoti tu fresco e riposato, non dei lasciare passare tale occasione. Oltre a questo, se il nemico ti presenta, la mattina di buona ora, la giornata, tu puoi differire di uscir de' tuoi alloggiamenti per molte ore; e quando egli è stato assai sotto l'armi e ch'egli ha perso quel primo ardore con il quale venne, puoi allora combattere seco. Questo modo tenne Scipione e Metello in Ispagna, l'uno contro ad Asdrubale, l'altro contro a Sertorio. Se il nemico è diminuito di forze, o per avere diviso gli eserciti, come gli Scipioni in Ispagna, o per qualche altra cagione, dei tentare la sorte. La maggior parte de' capitani prudenti piuttosto ricevano l'impeto de' nemici, che vadano con impeto ad assaltare quelli: perchè il furore è facilmente sostenuto dagli uomini fermi e saldi, e il furore sostenuto facilmente si convertisce in viltà. Così fece Fabio contro a' Sanniti e contro a' Galli, e fu vittorioso; e Decio suo collega vi rimase morto. Alcuni che hanno temuto della virtù del loro nemico, hanno cominciato la zuffa nell'ora propinqua alla notte, acciocchè i suoi, sendo vinti, potessero, difesi dalla oscurità di quella, salvarsi. Alcuni, avendo conosciuto come l'esercito nemico è preso da certa superstizione di non combattere in tale tempo, hanno quel tempo eletto alla zuffa, e vinto. Il che osservò Cesare in Francia contro ad Ariovisto, e Vespasiano in Sorìa contro a' Giudei. La maggiore e più importante avvertenza che debba avere uno capitano, è di avere appresso di se uomini fedeli, peritissimi della guerra e prudenti, con gli quali continuamente si consigli e con loro ragioni delle sue genti e di quelle del nemico: quale sia maggiore numero, quale meglio armato, o meglio a cavallo, o meglio esercitato; quali sieno più atti a patire la necessità; in quali confidi più, o ne' fanti o ne' cavalli. Dipoi considerino il luogo dove sono, e s'egli è più a proposito per il nemico che per lui; chi abbia di loro più commodamente la vettovaglia; s'egli è bene differire la giornata o farla; che di bene gli potesse dare o torre il tempo; perchè molte volte i soldati, veduta allungare la guerra, infastidiscono e, stracchi nella fatica e nel tedio, ti abbandonano. Importa sopra tutto conoscere il capitano de' nemici e chi egli ha intorno: s'egli è temerario o cauto, se timido o audace. Vedere come tu ti puoi fidare de' soldati ausiliarj. E sopra tutto ti debbi guardare di non condurre l'esercito ad azzuffarsi che tema o che in alcuno modo diffidi della vittoria; perchè il maggiore segno di perdere è quando non si crede potere vincere. E però in questo caso dei fuggire la giornata, o col fare come Fabio Massimo che, accampandosi ne' luoghi forti, non dava animo ad Annibale d'andarlo a trovare; o, quando tu credessi che il nemico ancora ne' luoghi forti ti venisse a trovare, partirsi della campagna e dividere le genti per le tue terre, acciocchè il tedio della espugnazione di quelle lo stracchi.

ZANOBI: Non si può egli fuggire altrimenti la giornata, che dividersi in più parti e mettersi nelle terre?

FABRIZIO: Io credo, altra volta, con alcuno di voi avere ragionato come quello che sta alla campagna non può fuggire la giornata, quando egli ha uno nemico che lo vogli combattere in ogni modo; e non ha se non uno rimedio: porsi con l'esercito suo discosto cinquanta miglia almeno dall'avversario suo, per essere a tempo a levarsegli dinanzi quando lo andasse a trovare. E Fabio Massimo non fuggì mai la giornata con Annibale, ma la voleva fare a suo vantaggio; e Annibale non presumeva poterlo vincere andando a trovarlo ne' luoghi dove quello alloggiava; chè s'egli avesse presupposto poterlo vincere, a Fabio conveniva fare giornata seco in ogni modo, o fuggirsi. Filippo, Re di Macedonia, quello che fu padre di Perse, venendo a guerra con i Romani, pose gli alloggiamenti suoi sopra uno monte altissimo per non fare giornata con quegli; ma i Romani lo andarono a trovare in su quello monte e lo ruppono. Cingentorige, capitano de' Franciosi, per non avere a fare giornata con Cesare, il quale fuora della sua opinione aveva passato un fiume, si discostò molte miglia con le sue genti. I Viniziani, ne' tempi nostri, se non volevano venire a giornata con il Re di Francia, non dovevano aspettare che l'esercito francioso passasse l'Adda, ma discostarsi da quello, come Cingentorige. Donde che quegli, avendo aspettato, non seppono pigliare nel passare delle genti la occasione del fare la giornata, nè fuggirla; perchè i Franciosi, sendo loro pripinqui, come i Viniziani disalloggiarono, gli assaltarono e ruppero. Tanto è che la giornata non si può fuggire quando il nemico la vuole in ogni modo fare. Nè alcuno alleghi Fabio, perchè tanto in quel caso fuggì la giornata egli, quanto Annibale. Egli occorre molte volte che i tuoi soldati sono volonterosi di combattere, e tu cognosci, per il numero e per il sito o per qualche altra cagione, avere disavvantaggio, e desideri fargli rimuovere da questo desiderio. Occorre ancora che la necessità o l'occasione ti costringe alla giornata, e che i tuoi soldati sono male confidenti e poco disposti a combattere; donde che ti è necessario nell'uno caso sbigottirgli e nell'altro accendergli. Nel primo caso, quando le persuasioni non bastano, non è il migliore modo che darne in preda una parte di loro al nemico, acciocchè quegli che hanno e quegli che non hanno combattuto, ti credano. E puossi molto bene fare con arte quello che a Fabio Massimo intervenne a caso. desiderava, come voi sapete, l'esercito di Fabio combattere con l'esercito d'Annibale; il medesimo desiderio aveva il suo maestro de' cavalli; a Fabio non pareva di tentare la zuffa; tantochè, per tale disparere, egli ebbero a dividere l'esercito. Fabio ritenne i suoi negli alloggiamenti; quell'altro combattè, e, venuto in pericolo grande, sarebbe stato rotto, se Fabio non lo avesse soccorso. Per il quale esemplo il maestro de' cavalli, insieme con tutto lo esercito, cognobbe come egli era partito savio ubbidire a Fabio. Quanto allo accendergli al combattere, è bene fargli sdegnare contro a' nemici, mostrando che dicono parole ignominiose di loro; mostrare di avere con loro intelligenza e averne corrotti parte; alloggiare in lato che veggano i nemici e che facciano qualche zuffa leggiere con quegli, perchè le cose che giornalmente si veggono, con più facilità si dispregiano; mostrarsi indegnato e, con una orazione a proposito, riprendergli della loro pigrizia e, per fargli vergognare dire di ogni giorno al fare del dì, quando si moveva, lo assaltavano e, per tutto il cammino, lo infestavano; dimodochè prese per partito di non partire prima che a mezzogiorno. Tale che i Parti, credendo che per quel giorno egli non volesse disalloggiare, se ne tornarono alle loro stanze; e Marco Antonio potèo dipoi tutto il rimanente dì camminare senza alcuna molestia. Questo medesimo, per fuggire il saettume de' Parti, comandò alle sue genti che quando i Parti venivano verso di loro, s'inginocchiassero, e la seconda fila delle battaglie ponesse gli scudi in capo alla prima, la terza alla seconda, la quarta alla terza, e così successive; tanto che tutto l'esercito veniva ad essere come sotto uno tetto e difeso dal saettume nemico. Questo è tanto quanto mi occorre dirvi che possa a uno esercito, camminando, intervenire; però quando a voi non occorra altro, io passerò ad un'altra parte.

Volere combattere solo, quando non gli vogliano fare compagnia. E dei, sopra ogni cosa, avere questa avvertenza, volendo fare il soldato ostinato alla zuffa: di non permettere che ne mandino a casa alcuna loro facultà, o depongano in alcuno luogo, infino ch'egli è terminata la guerra, acciocchè intendano che, se il fuggire salva loro la vita, egli non salva loro la roba; l'amore della quale non suole meno di quella rendere ostinati gli uomini alla difesa.

ZANOBI: Voi avete detto come egli si può fare i soldati volti a combattere parlando loro. Intendete voi, per questo, che si abbia a parlare a tutto l'esercito, o a' capi di quello?

FABRIZIO: A persuadere o a dissuadere a' pochi una cosa è molto facile perchè, se non bastano le parole, tu vi puoi usare l'autorità e la forza; ma la difficultà è rimuovere da una moltitudine una sinistra opinione e che sia contraria o al bene comune o all'opinione tua; dove non si può usare se non le parole le quali conviene che sieno udite da tutti, volendo persuadergli tutti. Per questo gli eccellenti capitani conveniva che fussono oratori, perchè, senza sapere parlare a tutto l'esercito, con difficultà si può operare cosa buona; il che al tutto in questi nostri tempi è dismesso. Leggete la vita d'Alessandro Magno, e vedete quante volte gli fu necessario concionare e parlare pubblicamente all'esercito; altrimenti non l'arebbe mai condotto, sendo diventato ricco e pieno di preda, per i deserti d'Arabia e nell'India con tanto suo disagio e noia; perchè infinite volte nascono cose mediante le quali uno esercito rovina, quando il capitano o non sappia o non usi di parlare a quello; perchè questo parlare lieva il timore, accende gli animi, cresce l'ostinazione, scuopre gl'inganni, promette premj, mostra i pericoli e la via di fuggirli, riprende, priega, minaccia, riempie di speranza, loda, vitupera, e fa tutte quelle cose per le quali le umane passioni si spengono o si accendono. Donde quel principe o Repubblica che disegnasse fare una nuova milizia e rendere riputazione a questo esercizio, debbe assuefare i suoi soldati a udire parlare il capitano, e il capitano a sapere parlare a quegli. Valeva assai, nel tenere disposti gli soldati antichi, la religione e il giuramento che si dava loro quando si conducevano a militare; perchè in ogni loro errore si minacciavano non solamente di quelli mali che potessono temere dagli uomini, ma di quegli che da Dio potessono aspettare. La quale cosa, mescolata con altri modi religiosi, fece molte volte facile a' capitani antichi ogni impresa, e farebbe sempre, dove la religione si temesse e osservasse. Sertorio si valse di questa, mostrando di parlare con una cervia la quale, da parte d'Iddio, gli prometteva la vittoria. Silla diceva di parlare con una immagine ch'egli aveva tratta dal tempio di Apolline. Molti hanno detto essere loro apparso in sogno Iddio, che gli ha ammoniti al combattere. Ne' tempi de' padri nostri, Carlo VII Re di Francia, nella guerra che fece contro agli Inghilesi, diceva consigliarsi con una fanciulla mandata da Iddio, la quale si chiamò per tutto la Pulzella di Francia; il che gli fu cagione della vittoria. Puossi ancora tenere modi che facciano che i tuoi apprezzino poco il nemico; come tenne Agesilao spartano, il quale mostrò a' suoi soldati alcuni Persiani ignudi, acciocchè, vedute le loro membra dilicate, non avessero cagione di temergli. Alcuni gli hanno costretti a combattere per necessità, levando loro via ogni speranza di salvarsi, fuora che nel vincere; la quale è la più gagliarda e la migliore provvisione che si faccia, a volere fare il suo soldato ostinato. La quale ostinazione è accresciuta dalla confidenza e dall' amore del capitano o della patria. La confidenza, la causa l'armi; l'ordine, le vittorie fresche e l'opinione del capitano. L'amore della patria è causato dalla natura; quello del capitano, dalla virtù più che da niuno altro beneficio. Le necessitadi possono essere molte, ma quella è più forte, che ti costringe o vincere o morire.

BOOK FIVE

BOOK FIVE

FABRIZIO: I have shown you how to organize an army to battle another army which is seen posted against you, and I have told you how it is overcome, and also of the many circumstances which can occur because of the various incidents surrounding it, so that it appears to me now to be the time to show you how to organize an army against an enemy which is unseen, but which you are continually afraid will assault you. This happens when marching through country which is hostile, or suspected (of being so). And first you have to understand that a Roman Army ordinarily always sent ahead some groups of cavalry as observers for the march. Afterwards the right wing followed. After this came all the wagons which pertained to it. After those, another Legion, and next its wagons. After these come the left wing with its wagon in the rear, and the remainder of the cavalry followed in the last part. This was in effect the manner in which one ordinarily marched. And if it happened that the Army should be assaulted on the march in front or from the rear, they quickly caused all the wagons to be withdrawn either on the right, or on the left, according as it happened, or rather as best they could depending on the location, and all the forces together, free from their baggage, set up a front on that side from which the enemy was coming. If they were assaulted on the flank, they would withdraw the wagons to the side which was secure, and set up a front on the other. This method being good, and prudently conducted, appears to me ought to be imitated, sending cavalry ahead to observe the country, then having four battalions, having them march in line, and each with its wagons in the rear. And as the wagons are of two kinds, that is, those pertaining to individual soldiers, and the public ones for use by the whole camp, I would divide the public wagons into four parts, and assign a part to each Battalion, also dividing the artillery and all the unarmed men, so that each one of those armed should have its equal share of impedimenta. But as it sometimes happens that one marches in a country not only suspect, but hostile in fact, that you are afraid of being attacked hourly, in order to go on more securely, you are compelled to change the formation of the march, and go on in the regular way, so that in some unforeseen place, neither the inhabitants nor the Army can injure you. In such a case, the ancient Captains usually went on with the Army in squares, for such they called these formations, not because it was entirely square, but because it was capable of fighting on four sides, and they said that they were going prepared either for marching or for battle. I do not want to stray far from this method, and want to arrange my two Battalions, which I have taken as a rule for an Army, in this manner. If you want, therefore, to walk securely through the enemy country, and be able to respond from every side, if you had been assaulted by surprise, and wanting, in accordance with the ancients, to bring it into a square, I would plan to make a square whose hollow was two hundred arm lengths on every side in this manner. I would first place the flanks, each distant from the other by two hundred twelve arm lengths, and would place five companies in each flank in a file along its length, and distant from each other three arm lengths; these would occupy their own space, each company occupying (a space) forty arm lengths by two hundred twelve arm lengths. Between the front and rear of these two flanks, I would place another ten companies, five on each side, arranging them in such a way that four should be next to the front of the right flank, and five at the rear of the left flank, leaving between each one an interval (gap) of four arm lengths: one of which should be next to the front of the left flank, and one at the rear of the right flank. And as the space existing between the one flank and the other is two hundred twelve arm lengths, and these companies placed alongside each other by their width and not length, they would come to occupy, with the intervals, one hundred thirty four arm lengths, (and) there would be between the four companies placed on the front of the right flank, and one placed on the left, a remaining space of seventy eight arm lengths, and a similar space be left among the companies placed in the rear parts; and there would be no other difference, except that one space would be on the rear side toward the right wing, the other would be on the front side toward the left wing. In the space of seventy eight arm lengths in front, I would place all the ordinary Veliti, and in that in the rear the extraordinary Veliti, who would come to be a thousand per space. And if you want that the space taken up by the Army should be two hundred twelve arm lengths on every side, I would see that five companies are placed in front, and those that are placed in the rear, should not occupy any space already occupied by the flanks, and therefore I would see that the five companies in the rear should have their front touch the rear of their flanks, and those in front should have their rear touch the front (of their flanks), so that on every side of that army, space would remain to receive another company. And as there are four spaces, I would take four banners away from the extraordinary pikemen and would put one on every corner: and the two banners of the aforementioned pikemen left to me, I would place in the middle of the hollow of their army (formed) in a square of companies, at the heads of which the general Captain would remain with his men around him. And as these companies so arranged all march in one direction, but not all fight in one, in putting them together, one has to arrange which sides are not guarded by other companies during the battle. And, therefore, it ought to be considered that the five companies in front protect all the other sides, except the front; and therefore these have to be assembled in an orderly manner (and) with the pikemen in front. The five companies behind protect all the sides, except the side in the back; and therefore ought to be assembled so that the pikemen are in the rear, as we will demonstrate in its place. The five companies on the right flank protect all the sides, from the right flank outward. The five on the left, engird all the sides, from the left flank outward: and therefore in arranging the companies, the pikemen ought to be placed so that they turn by that flank which in uncovered. And as the Heads of Ten are placed in the front and rear, so that when they have to fight, all the army and its members are in their proper places, the manner of accomplishing this was told when we discussed the methods of arranging the companies. I would divide the artillery, and one part I would place outside the right flank, and the other at the left. I would send the light cavalry ahead to reconnoiter the country. Of the men-at-arms, I would place part in the rear on the right wing, and part on the left, distant forty arms lengths from the companies. And no matter how you arrange your Army, you have to take up ((as the cavalry)) this general (rule), that you have to place them always either in the rear or on the flanks. Whoever places them ahead in front of the Army must do one of two things: either he places them so far ahead, that if they are repulsed they have so much room to give them time to be able to obtain shelter for themselves from your infantry and not collide with them; or to arrange them (the infantry) with so many intervals, that by means of them the cavalry can enter among them without disorganizing them. Let not anyone think little of this instruction, because many, not being aware of this, have been ruined, and have been disorganized and routed by themselves. The wagons and the unarmed men are placed in the plaza that exists within the Army, and so compartmented, that they easily make way for whoever wants to go from one side to the other, or from one front of the Army to the other. These companies, without artillery and cavalry, occupy two hundred eighty two arm lengths of space on the outside in every direction. And as this square is composed of two Battalions, it must be devised as to which part one Battalion makes up, and which part the other. And since the Battalions are called by number, and each of them has ((as you know)) ten companies and a general Head, I would have the first Battalion place its first five companies in the front, the other five on the left flank, and the Head should be in the left angle of the front. The first five companies of the second Battalion then should be placed on the right flank, and the other five in the rear, and the Head should be in the right angle, who would undertake the office of the Tergiduttore.

The Army organized in this manner is ready to move, and in its movement should completely observe this arrangement: and without doubt it is secure from all the tumults of the inhabitants. Nor ought the Captain make other provisions against these tumultuous assaults, than sometime to give a commission to some cavalry or band of Veliti to put them in their place. Nor will it ever happen that these tumultuous people will come to meet you within the drawing of a sword or pike, because disorderly people are afraid of order; and it will always be seen that they make a great assault with shouts and noises without otherwise approaching you in the way of yelping dogs around a mastiff. Hannibal, when he came to harm from the Romans in Italy, passed through all of France, and always took little account of the tumults of the French. When you want to march, you must have levellers and men with pick axes ahead who clear the road for you, and who are well protected by that cavalry sent ahead to reconnoiter. An Army will march in this order ten miles a day, and enough Sun (light will remain for them to dine and camp, since ordinarily an Army marches twenty miles. If it happens that it is assaulted by an organized Army, this assault cannot arise suddenly, because an organized Army travels at its own rate (step), so that you are always in time to reorganize for the engagement, and quickly bring yourself to that formation, or similar to that formation of the Army, which I showed you above. For if you are assaulted on the front side, you do nothing except (to have) the artillery in the flanks and the cavalry behind come forward and take those places and with those distances mentioned above. The thousand Veliti who are forward, come forth from their positions, and dividing into groups of a hundred, enter into their places between the cavalry and the wings of the Army. Then, into the voids left by them, enter the two bands of extraordinary pikemen which I had placed in the plaza of the Army. The thousand Veliti that I had placed in the rear depart from there, and distribute themselves among the flanks of the companies to strengthen them: and from the open space they leave all the wagons and unarmed men issue forth and place themselves at the rear of the companies. The plaza, therefore, remains vacant as everyone has gone to their places, and the five companies that I placed in the rear of the Army come forward through the open void that exists between the one and the other flank, and march toward the company in the front, and the three approach them at forty arm lengths with equal intervals between one another, and two remain behind distant another forty arm lengths. This formation can be organized quickly, and comes to be almost the same as the first disposition of the Army which we described before: and if it becomes more straitened in the front, it becomes larger in the flanks, which does not weaken it. But as the five companies in the back have their pikemen in the rear for the reasons mentioned above, it is necessary to have them come from the forward part, if you want them to get behind the front of the Army; and, therefore, one must either make them turn company by company, as a solid body, or make them enter quickly between the ranks of the shield-bearers (swordsmen), and bring them forward; which method is more swift and less disorderly than to make them turn. And thus you ought to do with all those who are in the rear in every kind of assault, as I will show you. If it should happen that the enemy comes from the rear, the first thing that ought to be done is to have everyone turn to face the enemy, so that at once the front of the army becomes the rear, and the rear the front. Then all those methods of organizing the front should be followed, which I mentioned above. If the enemy attacks on the right flank, the entire army ought to be made to face in that direction, and then those things ought to be done to strengthen that (new) front which were mentioned above, so that the cavalry, the Veliti, and the artillery are in the position assigned in this front. There is only this difference, that in the changing of fronts, of those who move about, some have to go further, and some less. It is indeed true that when a front is made of the right flank, the Veliti would have to enter the intervals (gaps) that exist between the wings of the Army, and the cavalry would be those nearer to the left flank, in the position of those who would have to enter into the two bands of extraordinary pikemen placed in the center. But before they enter, the wagons and unarmed men stationed at the openings, should clear the plaza and retire behind the left flank, which then becomes the rear of the army. And the other Veliti who should be placed in the rear according to the original arrangement, in this case should not be changed, as that place should not remain open, which, from being the rear, would become a flank. All the other things ought to be done as was said concerning the first front.

What has been said concerning making a front from the right flank, is intended also in making one from the left flank, since the same arrangements ought to be observed. If the enemy should happen to be large and organized to assault you on two sides, the two sides on which he assaults you ought to be strengthened from the two that are not assaulted, doubling the ranks in each one, and distributing the artillery, Veliti, and cavalry among each side. If he comes from three or four sides, it needs must be either you or he lacks prudence, for if you were wise, you would never put yourself on the side where the enemy could assault you from three or four sides with large and organized forces, and if he wanted to attach you in safety he must be so large and assault you on each side with a force almost as large as you have in your entire Army. And if you are so little prudent that you put yourself in the midst of the territory and forces of an enemy, who has three times the organized forces that you have, you cannot complain if evil happens to you, except of yourself. If it happens, not by your fault, but by some misadventure, the injury will be without shame, and it will happen to you as it did to the Scipios in Spain, and the Hasdrubal in Italy. But if the enemy has a much larger force than you, and in order to disorganize you wants to assault you on several sides, it will be his foolishness and his gamble; for to do this, he must go (spread) himself thin, that you can always attack on one side and resist on another, and in a brief time ruin him. This method of organizing an Army which is not seen, but who is feared, is necessary, and it is a most useful thing to accustom your soldiers to assemble, and march in such order, and in marching arrange themselves to fight according to the first front (planned), and then return to marching formation, from that make a front from the rear, and then from the flank, and from that return to the original formation. These exercises and accustomization are necessary matters if you want a disciplined and trained Army. Captains and Princes have to work hard at these things: nor is military discipline anything else, than to know how to command and how to execute these things, nor is a disciplined Army anything else, than an army which is well trained in these arrangements; nor would it be possible for anyone in these times who should well employ such discipline ever to be routed. And if this square formation which I have described is somewhat difficult, such difficulty is necessary, if you take it up as exercise; since knowing how to organize and maintain oneself well in this, one would afterwards know how to manage more easily those which not be as difficult.

ZANOBI: I believe as you say, that these arrangements are very necessary, and by myself, I would not know what to add or leave out. It is true that I desire to know two things from you: the one, when you want to make a front from the rear or from a flank, and you want them to turn, whether the command is given by voice or by sound (bugle call): the other, whether those you sent ahead to clear the roads in order to make a path for the Army, ought to be soldiers of your companies, or other lowly people assigned to such practices.

FABRIZIO: Your first question is very important, for often the commands of the Captain are not very well understood or poorly interpreted, have disorganized their Army; hence the voices with which they command in (times of) danger, ought to be loud and clear. And if you command with sounds (bugle calls), it ought to be done so that they are so different from each other that one cannot be mistaken for another; and if you command by voice, you ought to be alert to avoid general words, and use particular ones, and of the particular ones avoid those which might be able to be interpreted in an incorrect manner. Many times saying "go back, go back", has caused an Army to be ruined: therefore this expression ought to be avoided, and in its place use "Retreat". If you want them to turn so as to change the front, either from the rear or from the flank, never use "Turn around", but say, "To the left", "To the right", "To the rear", "To the front". So too, all the other words have to be simple and clear, as "Hurry", "Hold still", "Forward", "Return". And all those things which can be done by words are done, the others are done by sounds (calls). As to the (road) clearers, which is your second question, I would have this job done by my own soldiers, as much because the ancient military did so, as also because there would be fewer unarmed men and less impediments in the army: and I would draw the number needed from every company, and I would have them take up the tools suitable for clearing, and leave their arms in those ranks that are closest to them, which would carry them so that if the enemy should come, they would have nothing to do but take them up again and return to their ranks.

ZANOBI: Who would carry the clearing equipment?

FABRIZIO: The wagons assigned to carry such equipment.

ZANOBI: I'm afraid you have never led these soldiers of ours to dig.

FABRIZIO: Everything will be discussed in its place. For now I want to leave these parts alone, and discuss the manner of living of the Army, for it appears to me that having worked them so hard, it is time to refresh and restore it with food. You have to understand that a Prince ought to organize his army as expeditiously as possible, and take away from it all those things that add burdens to it and make the enterprise difficult. Among those that cause more difficulty, are to have to keep the army provided with wine and baked bread. The ancients did not think of wine, for lacking it, they drank water tinted with a little vinegar, and not wine. They did not cook bread in ovens, as is customary throughout the cities; but they provided flour, and every soldier satisfied himself of that in his own way, having lard and grease for condiment, which gave flavor to the bread they made, and which kept them strong. So that the provisions of living (eating) for the army were Flour, Vinegar, Lard (Bacon) and Grease (Lard), and Barley for the horses. Ordinarily, they had herds of large and small beasts that followed the Army, which ((as they did not need to be carried)) did not impede them much. This arrangement permitted an ancient Army to march, sometimes for many days, through solitary and difficult places without suffering hardship of (lack of) provisions, for it lived from things which could be drawn behind. The contrary happens in modern Armies, which, as they do not want to lack wine and eat baked bread in the manner that those at home do, and of which they cannot make provision for long, often are hungry; or even if they are provided, it is done with hardship and at very great expense. I would therefore return my Army to this form of living, and I would not have them eat other bread than that which they should cook for themselves. As to wine, I would not prohibit its drinking, or that it should come into the army, but I would not use either industry or any hard work to obtain it, and as to other provisions, I would govern myself entirely as the ancients. If you would consider this matter well, you will see how much difficulty is removed, and how many troubles and hardships an army and a Captain avoid, and what great advantage it will give any enterprise which you may want to undertake.

ZANOBI: We have overcome the enemy in the field, and then marched on his country: reason wants that there be no booty, ransoming of towns, prisoners taken. Yet I would like to know how the ancients governed themselves in these matters.

FABRIZIO: Here, I will satisfy you. I believe you have considered ((since I have at another time discussed this with some of you)) that modern wars impoverish as much those Lords who win, as those who lose; for if one loses the State, the other loses his money and (movable) possessions. Which anciently did not happen, as the winner of a war (then) was enriched. This arises from not keeping track in these times of the booty (acquired), as was done anciently, but everything is left to the direction of the soldiers. This method makes for two very great disorders: the one, that of which I have spoken: the other, that a soldier becomes more desirous of booty and less an observer of orders: and it has often been said that the cupidity for booty has made him lose who had been victorious. The Romans, however, who were Princes in this matter, provided for both these inconveniences, ordering that all the booty belong to the public, and that hence the public should dispense it as it pleased. And so they had Quaestors in the Army, who were, as we would say, chamberlains, to whom all the ransoms and booty was given to hold: from which the Consul served himself to give the soldiers their regular pay, to help the wounded and infirm, and to provide for the other needs of the army. The Consul could indeed, and often did, concede a booty to the soldiers, but this concession did not cause disorders; for when the (enemy) army was routed, all the booty was placed in the middle and was distributed to each person, according to the merits of each. This method made for the soldiers attending to winning and not robbing, and the Roman legions defeating the enemy but not pursuing him: for they never departed from their orders: only the cavalry and lightly armed men pursued him, unless there were other soldiers than legionnaires, which, if the booty would have been kept by whoever acquired it, it was neither possible nor reasonable to (expect to) hold the Legion firm, and would bring on many dangers. From this it resulted, therefore that the public was enriched, and every Consul brought, with his triumphs, much treasure into the Treasury, which (consisted) entirely of ransoms and booty. Another thing well considered by the ancients, was the pay they gave to each soldier: they wanted a third part to be placed next to him who carried the flag of the company, who never was given any except that furnished by the war. They did this for two reasons: The first so that the soldier would make capital (save) of his pay: for the greater part of them being young and irresponsible, the more they had, the more they spent without need to. The other part because, knowing that their movable possessions were next to the flag, they would be forced to have greater care, and defend it with greater obstinacy: and thus this method made them savers, and strong. All of these things are necessary to observe if you want to bring the military up to your standards.

ZANOBI: I believe it is not possible for an army while marching from place to place not to encounter dangerous incidents, (and) where the industry of the Captain and the virtu of the soldier is needed if they are to be avoided; therefore, if you should have something that occurs to you, I would take care to listen.

FABRIZIO: I will willingly content you, especially as it is necessary, if I want to give you complete knowledge of the practice. The Captains, while they march with the Army, ought, above everything else, to guard against ambushes, which may happen in two ways: either you enter into them while marching, or the enemy cunningly draws you into them without your being aware of it. In the first case, if you want to avoid them, it is necessary to send ahead double the guard, who reconnoiter the country. And the more the country is suitable for ambush, as are wooded and mountainous countries, the more diligence ought to be used, for the enemy always place themselves either in woods or behind a hill. And, just as by not foreseeing an ambush you will be ruined, so by foreseeing it you will not be harmed. Birds or dust have often discovered the enemy, for where the enemy comes to meet you, he will always raise a great dust which will point out his coming to you. Thus often a Captain when he sees in a place whence he ought to pass, pigeons taking off and other birds flying about freely, circling and not setting, has recognized this to be the place of any enemy ambush, and knowing this has sent his forces forward, saving himself and injuring the enemy. As to the second case, being drawn into it ((which our men call being drawn into a trap)) you ought to look out not to believe readily those things that appear to be less reasonable than they should be: as would be (the case) if an enemy places some booty before you, you would believe that it to be (an act of) love, but would conceal deceit inside it. If many enemies are driven out by few of your man: if only a few of the enemy assault you: if the enemy takes to sudden and unreasonable flight: in such cases, you ought always to be afraid of deceit; and you should never believe that the enemy does not know his business, rather, if you want to deceive yourself less and bring on less danger, the more he appears weak, the more enemy appears more cautious, so much the more ought you to esteem (be wary) of him. And in this you have to use two different means, since you have to fear him with your thoughts and arrangements, but by words and other external demonstrations show him how much you disparage him; for this latter method causes your soldiers to have more hope in obtaining the victory, the former makes you more cautious and less apt to be deceived. And you have to understand that when you march through enemy country, you face more and greater dangers than in undertaking an engagement. And therefore, when marching, a Captain ought to double his diligence, and the first thing he ought to do, is to have all the country through which he marches described and depicted, so that he will know the places, the numbers, the distances, the roads, the mountains, the rivers, the marshes, and all their characteristics. And in getting to know this, in diverse ways one must have around him different people who know the places, and question them with diligence, and contrast their information, and make notes according as it checks out. He ought to send cavalry ahead, and with them prudent Heads, not so much to discover the enemy as to reconnoiter the country, to see whether it checks with the places and with the information received from them. He ought also to send out guides, guarded (kept loyal) by hopes of reward and fear of punishment. And above all, he ought to see to it that the Army does not know to which sides he guides them, since there is nothing more useful in war, than to keep silent (about) the things that have to be done. And so that a sudden assault does not disturb your soldiers, you ought to advise them to be prepared with their arms, since things that are foreseen cause less harm. Many have ((in order to avoid the confusion of the march)) placed the wagons and the unarmed men under the banners, and commanded them to follow them, so that having to stop or retire during the march, they are able to do so more easily: which I approve very much as something useful. He ought also to have an awareness during the march, that one part of the Army does not detach itself from another, or that one (part) going faster and the other more slowly, the Army does not become compacted (jumbled), which things cause disorganization. It is necessary, therefore, to place the Heads along the sides, who should maintain the steps uniform, restraining those which are too fast, and hastening the slow; which step cannot be better regulated than by sound (music). The roads ought to be widened, so that at least one company can always move in order. The customs and characteristics of the enemy ought to be considered, and if he wants to assault you in the morning, noon, or night, and if he is more powerful in infantry or cavalry, from what you have learned, you may organize and prepare yourself. But let us come to some incident in particular. It sometimes happens that as you are taking yourself away from in front of the enemy because you judge yourself to be inferior (to him), and therefore do not want to come to an engagement with him, he comes upon your rear as you arrive at the banks of a river, which causes you to lose times in its crossing, so that the enemy is about to join up and combat with you. There have been some who have found themselves in such a peril, their army girded on the rear side by a ditch, and filling it with tow, have set it afire, then have passed on with the army without being able to be impeded by the enemy, he being stopped by that fire which was in between.

ZANOBI: And it is hard for me to believe that this fire can check him, especially as I remember to have heard that Hanno, the Carthaginian, when he was besieged by the enemy, girded himself on that side from which he wanted to make an eruption with wood, and set fire to it. Whence the enemy not being intent to guard that side, had his army pass over the flames, having each (soldier) protect his face from the fire and smoke with his shield.

FABRIZIO: You say well; but consider what I have said and what Hanno did: for I said that he dug a ditch and filled it with tow, so that whoever wanted to pass had to contend with the ditch and the fire. Hanno made the fire without a ditch, and as he wanted to pass through it did not make it very large (strong), since it would have impeded him even without the ditch. Do you not know that Nabidus, the Spartan, when he was besieged in Sparta by the Romans, set fire to part of his own town in order to stop the passage of the Romans, who had already entered inside? and by those flames not only stopped their passage, but pushed them out. But let us return to our subject. Quintus Luttatius, the Roman, having the Cimbri at his rear, and arriving at a river, so that the enemy should give him time to cross, made as if to give him time to combat him, and therefore feigned to make camp there, and had ditches dug, and some pavilions raised, and sent some horses to the camps to be shod: so that the Cimbri believing he was encamping, they also encamped, and divided themselves into several parts to provide themselves with food: of which Luttatius becoming aware, he crossed the river without being able to be impeded by them. Some, in order to cross a river, not having a bridge, have diverted it, and having drawn a part of it in their rear, the other then became so low that they crossed it easily. If the rivers are rapid, (and) desiring that the infantry should cross more safely, the more capable horses are placed on the side above which holds back the water, and another part below which succor the infantry if any, in crossing, should be overcome by the river. Rivers that are not forded, are crossed by bridges, boats, and rafts: and it is therefore well to have skills in your Armies capable of doing all these things. It sometimes happens that in crossing a river, the enemy on the opposite bank impedes you. If you want to overcome this difficulty there is no better example known than that of Caesar, who, having his army on the bank of a river in Gaul, and his crossing being impeded by Vercingetorix, the Gaul, who had his forces on the other side of the river, marched for several days along the river, and the enemy did the same. And Caesar having made an encampment in a woody place (and) suitable to conceal his forces, withdrew three cohorts from every Legion, and had them stop in that place, commanding then that as soon as he should depart, they should throw a bridge across and fortify it, and he with the rest of his forces continued the march: Whence Vercingetorix seeing the number of Legions, and believing that no part had remained behind, also continued the march: but Caesar, as soon as he thought the bridge had been completed, turned back, and finding everything in order, crossed the river without difficulty.

ZANOBI: Do you have any rule for recognizing the fords?

FABRIZIO: Yes, we have. The river, in that part between the stagnant water and the current, always looks like a line to whoever looks at it, is shallower, and is a place more suitable for fording than elsewhere, for the river always places more material, and in a pack, which it draws (with it) from the bottom. Which thing, as it has been experienced many times, is very true.

ZANOBI: If it happens that the river has washed away the bottom of the ford, so that horses sink, what remedy do you have?

FABRIZIO: Make grids of wood, and place them on the bottom of the river, and cross over those. But let us pursue our discussion. If it happens that a Captain with his army is led (caught) between two mountains, and has but two ways of saving himself, either that in front, or the one in the rear, and both being occupied by the enemy, has, as a remedy, to do what some have done in the past, which is to dig a large ditch, difficult to cross, and show the enemy that by it you want to be able to hold him with all his forces, without having to fear those forces in the rear for which the road in front remains open. The enemy believing this, fortifies himself on the side open, and abandons the (side) closed, and he then throws a wooden bridge, planned for such a result, over the ditch, and without any impediment, passes on that side and freed himself from the hands of the enemy. Lucius Minutius, the Roman Consul, was in Liguria with the Armies, and had been enclosed between certain mountains by the enemy, from which he could not go out. He therefore sent some soldiers of Numidia, whom he had in his army, who were badly armed, and mounted on small and scrawny horses, toward those places which were guarded by the enemy, and the first sight of whom caused the enemy to assemble to defend the pass: but then when they saw those forces poorly organized, and also poorly mounted, they esteemed them little and loosened their guard. As soon as the Numidians saw this, giving spurs to their horses and attacking them, they passed by without the enemy being able to take any remedy; and having passed, they wasted and plundered the country, constraining the enemy to leave the pass free to the army of Lucius. Some Captain, who has found himself assaulted by a great multitude of the enemy, has tightened his ranks, and given the enemy the faculty of completely surrounding him, and then has applied force to that part which he has recognized as being weaker, and has made a path in that way, and saved himself. Marcantonio, while retiring before the army of the Parthians, became aware that every day at daybreak as he moved, the enemy assaulted him, and infested him throughout the march: so that he took the course of not departing before midday. So that the Parthians, believing he should not want to decamp that day returned to their quarters, and Marcantonio was able then for the remainder of the day to march without being molested. This same man, to escape the darts of the Parthians, commanded that, when the Parthians came toward them, they should kneel, and the second rank of the company should place their shields on the heads of (those in the) first, the third on (those of the) second, the fourth on the third, and so on successively: so that the entire Army came to be as under a roof, and protected from the darts of the enemy. This is as much as occurs to me to tell you of what can happen to an army when marching: therefore, if nothing else occurs to you, I will pass on to another part.

Libro Quinto

LIBRO QUINTO

FABRIZIO: Io vi ho mostro come si ordina uno esercito per fare giornata con un altro esercito che si vegga posto all'incontro di se, e narratovi come quella si vince e, dipoi, molte circustanze per li varj accidenti che possono occorrere intorno a quella; tanto che mi pare tempo da mostrarvi ora come si ordina uno esercito contro a quel nemico che altri non vede, ma che continuamente si teme non ti assalti. Questo interviene quando si cammina per il paese nemico o sospetto. E prima avete a intendere come uno esercito Romano, per l'ordinario, sempre mandava innanzi alcune torme di cavalli come speculatori del cammino. Dipoi seguitava il corno destro. Dopo questo ne venivano tutti i carriaggi che a quello appartenevano. Dopo questi veniva una Legione. Dopo lei i suoi carriaggi. Dopo quelli un'altra Legione, ed appresso a quella, i suoi carriaggi. Dopo i quali ne veniva il corno sinistro co' suoi carriaggi a spalle e, nell'ultima parte, seguiva il rimanente della cavalleria. Questo era in effetto il modo col quale ordinariamente si camminava. E se avveniva che l'esercito fusse assaltato a cammino da fronte o da spalle, essi facevano a un tratto ritirare tutti i carriaggi o in sulla destra o in sulla sinistra, secondo che occorreva o che meglio, rispetto al sito, si poteva e tutte le genti insieme, libere dagli impedimenti loro, facevano testa da quella parte donde il nemico veniva. Se erano assaltate per fianco, si ritiravano i carriaggi verso quella parte che era sicura, e dell'altra facevano testa. Questo modo, sendo buono e prudentemente governato, mi parrebbe da imitare, mandando innanzi i cavalli leggieri come speculatori del paese, dipoi, avendo quattro battaglioni, fare che camminassero alla fila, e ciascuno con i suoi carriaggi a spalle. E perchè sono di due ragioni carriaggi, cioè pertinenti a' particolari soldati e pertinenti al pubblico uso di tutto il campo, dividerei i carriaggi pubblici in quattro parti e, ad ogni battaglione, ne concederei la sua parte, dividendo ancora in quarto le artiglierie e tutti i disarmati, acciocchè ogni numero di armati avesse equalmente gli impedimenti suoi. Ma perchè egli occorre alcuna volta che si cammina per il paese, non solamente sospetto, ma in tanto nemico che tu temi a ogni ora di essere assalito, sei necessitato, per andare più sicuro, mutare forma di cammino e andare in modo ordinato, che nè i paesani nè l'esercito ti possa offendere, trovandoti in alcuna parte improvvisto. Solevano in tale caso gli antichi capitani andare con l'esercito quadrato, chè così chiamavano questa forma, non perch'ella fusse al tutto quadra, ma per essere atta a combattere da quattro parti, e dicevano che andavano parati e al cammino e alla zuffa; dal quale modo io non mi voglio discostare, e voglio ordinare i miei due battaglioni, i quali ho preso per regola d'uno esercito, a questo effetto. Volendo pertanto camminare sicuro per il paese nemico e potere rispondere da ogni parte quando fusse all'improvviso assaltato, e volendo, secondo gli antichi, ridurlo in quadro, disegnerei fare uno quadro, che il vacuo suo fusse di spazio da ogni parte dugentododici braccia, in questo modo: io porrei prima i fianchi, discosto l'uno fianco dall'altro dugentododici braccia, e metterei cinque battaglie per fianco in filo per lunghezza, e discosto l'una dall'altra tre braccia; le quali occuperebbero con gli loro spazj, occupando ogni battaglia quaranta braccia, dugentododici braccia. Tra le teste poi e tra le code di questi due fianchi porrei l'altre dieci battaglie, in ogni parte cinque, ordinandole in modo che quattro se ne accostassono alla testa del fianco destro, e quattro alla coda del fianco sinistro, lasciando tra ciascuna uno intervallo di tre braccia; una poi se ne accostasse alla testa del fianco sinistro e una alla coda del fianco destro. E perchè il vano che è dall'uno fianco all'altro è dugentododici braccia, e queste battaglie, che sono poste allato l'una all'altra per larghezza e non per lunghezza, verrebbero a occupare con gli intervalli centotrentaquattro braccia, verrebbe, tra le quattro battaglie poste in sulla fronte del fianco destro e l'una posta in su quella del sinistro, a restare uno spazio di settantotto braccia; e quello medesimo spazio verrebbe a rimanere nelle battaglie poste nella parte posteriore; nè vi sarebbe altra differenza se non che l'uno spazio verrebbe dalla parte di dietro verso il corno destro, l'altro verrebbe dalla parte davanti verso il corno sinistro. Nello spazio delle settantotto braccia davanti porrei tutti i Veliti ordinarj: in quello di dietro gli straordinarj, che ne verrebbe ad essere mille per spazio. E volendo che lo spazio che avesse di dentro l'esercito fusse per ogni verso dugentododici braccia, converrebbe che le cinque battaglie che si pongono nella testa, e quelle che si pongono nella coda, non occupassono alcuna parte dello spazio che tengono i fianchi; e però converrebbe che le cinque battaglie di dietro toccassero, con la fronte, la coda de' loro fianchi, e quelle davanti, con la coda, toccassero le teste, in modo che sopra ogni canto di questo esercito resterebbe uno spazio da ricevere un'altra battaglia. E perchè sono quattro spazi, io torrei quattro bandiere delle picche estraordinarie e, in ogni canto, ne metterei una; e le due bandiere di dette picche che mi avanzassero, porrei nel mezzo del vano di questo esercito in uno quadro in battaglia, alla testa delle quali stesse il capitano generale co' suoi uomini intorno. E perchè queste battaglie, ordinate così, camminano tutte per uno verso, ma non tutte per uno verso combattono, si ha, nel porle insieme, a ordinare quegli lati a combattere che non sono guardati dall'altre battaglie. E però si dee considerare che le cinque battaglie che sono in fronte, hanno guardate tutte l'altre parti eccetto che la fronte; e però queste s'hanno a mettere insieme ordinariamente e con le picche davanti. Le cinque battaglie che sono dietro, hanno guardate tutte le bande fuora che la parte di dietro; e però si dee mettere insieme queste in modo che le picche vengano dietro, come nel suo luogo dimostrammo. Le cinque battaglie che sono nel fianco destro hanno guardati tutti i lati, dal fianco destro in fuora. Le cinque che sono in sul sinistro, hanno fasciate tutte le parti, dal fianco sinistro in fuora; e però nell'ordinare le battaglie si debbe fare che le picche tornino da quel fianco che resta scoperto. E perchè i Capidieci vengano per testa e per coda, acciocchè, avendo a combattere, tutte l'armi e le membra sieno ne' luoghi loro, il modo a fare questo si disse quando ragionammo de' modi dell'ordinare le battaglie. L'artiglierie dividerei; e una parte ne metterei di fuora nel fianco destro e l'altra nel sinistro. I cavalli leggieri manderei innanzi a scoprire il paese. Degli uomini d'arme, ne porrei parte dietro in sul corno destro, e parte in sul sinistro, distanti un quaranta braccia dalle battaglie. E avete a pigliare, in ogni modo che voi ordinate uno esercito, quanto a' cavalli, questa generalità: che sempre si hanno a porre o dietro o da' fianchi. Chi li pone davanti, nel dirimpetto dell'esercito, conviene faccia una delle due cose: o che gli metta tanto innanzi che, sendo ributtati, eglino abbiano tanto spazio che dia loro tempo a potere cansarsi dalle fanterie tue e non le urtare; o ordinare in modo quelle con tanti intervalli, che i cavalli, per quegli, possano entrare tra loro senza disordinarle. Nè sia alcuno che stimi poco questo ricordo, perchè molti, per non ci avere avvertito, ne sono rovinati e, per loro medesimi, si sono disordinati e rotti. I carriaggi e gli uomini disarmati si mettono nella piazza che resta dentro all'esercito, e in modo compartiti che dieno la via facilmente a chi volesse andare o dall'uno canto all'altro o dall'una testa all'altra dell'esercito. Occupano queste battaglie, senza l'artiglierie e i cavalli, per ogni verso dal lato di fuora, dugentottantadue braccia di spazio. E perchè questo quadro è composto di due battaglioni, conviene divisare quale parte ne faccia uno battaglione e quale l'altro. E perchè i battaglioni si chiamano dal numero e ciascuno di loro ha, come sapete, dieci battaglie e uno capo generale, farei che il primo battaglione ponesse le sue prime cinque battaglie nella fronte, l'altre cinque nel fianco sinistro, e il capo stesse nell'angulo sinistro della fronte. Il secondo battaglione dipoi mettesse le prime cinque sue battaglie nel fianco destro, e le altre cinque nella coda, e il capo stesse nell'angulo destro; il quale verrebbe a fare l'ufficio del Tergiduttore.

Ordinato in questo modo l'esercito, si ha a fare muovere e, nello andare, osservare tutto questo ordine; e senza dubbio egli è sicuro da tutti i tumulti de' paesani. Nè dee fare il capitano altra provvisione agli assalti tumultuarj, che dare qualche volta commissione, a qualche cavallo o bandiera de' Veliti, che gli rimettano. Nè mai occorrerà che queste genti tumultuarie vengano a trovarti al tiro della spada o della picca, perchè la gente inordinata ha paura della ordinata; e sempre si vedrà che, con le grida e con i romori, faranno uno grande assalto senza appressartisi altrimenti, a guisa di cani botoli intorno a uno maschino. Annibale, quando venne a' danni de' Romani in Italia passò per tutta la Francia e, sempre, de' tumulti Francesi tenne poco conto. Conviene, a volere camminare, avere spianatori e marraiuoli innanzi che ti facciano la via; i quali saranno guardati da quegli cavalli che si mandono avanti a scoprire. Camminerà uno esercito in questo ordine dieci miglia il giorno, e avanzeragli tanto di sole, che egli alloggerà e cenerà; perchè per l'ordinario uno esercito cammina venti miglia. Se viene che sia assaltato da uno esercito ordinato, questo assalto non può nascere subito, perchè uno esercito ordinato viene col passo tuo; tanto che tu sei a tempo a riordinarti alla giornata e ridurti tosto in quella forma, o simile a quella forma di esercito che di sopra ti si mostrò. Perchè, se tu sei assaltato dalla parte dinanzi, tu non hai se non a fare che l'artiglierie che sono ne' fianchi e i cavalli che sono di dietro vengano dinanzi e pongansi in quegli luoghi e con quelle distanze che di sopra si dice. I mille Veliti che sono davanti escano del luogo suo, e dividansi in cinquecento per parte, ed entrino nel luogo loro tra' cavalli e le corna dell'esercito. Dipoi nel vuoto che lasceranno, entrino le due bandiere delle picche estraordinarie che io posi nel mezzo della piazza dell'esercito. I mille Veliti che io posi di dietro, si partano di quel luogo e dividansi per i fianchi delle battaglie a fortificazione di quelle; e, per la apertura che loro lasceranno, escano tutti i carriaggi e i disarmati, e mettansi alle spalle delle battaglie. Rimasa adunque la piazza vota e andato ciascuno a' luoghi suoi, le cinque battaglie che io posi dietro all'esercito si facciano innanzi per il vòto che è tra l'uno e l'altro fianco, e camminino verso le battaglie di testa; e le tre si accostino a quelle a quaranta braccia con uguali intervalli intra l'una e l'altra; e le due rimangano addietro, discosto altre quaranta braccia. La quale forma si può ordinare in uno subito; e viene ad essere quasi simile alla prima disposizione che dell'esercito dianzi dimostrammo; e se viene più stretto in fronte, viene più grosso ne' fianchi; che non gli dà meno fortezza. Ma perchè le cinque battaglie che sono nella coda hanno le picche dalla parte di dietro, per le cagioni che dianzi dicemmo, è necessario farle venire dalla parte davanti, volendo ch'elle facciano spalle alla fronte dell'esercito; e però conviene: o fare voltare battaglia per battaglia come uno corpo solido, o farle subito entrare tra gli ordini degli scudi e condurle davanti; il quale modo è più ratto e di minore disordine che farle voltare. E così dèi fare di tutte quelle che restono di dietro, in ogni qualità di assalto, come io vi mostrerò. Se si presenta che il nemico venga dalla parte di dietro, la prima cosa, si ha a fare che ciascuno volti il viso dov'egli aveva le schiene; e subito l'esercito viene ad avere fatto del capo coda e della coda capo. Dipoi si dee tenere tutti quegli modi in ordinare quella fronte che io dico di sopra. Se il nemico viene ad affrontare il fianco destro, si debbe, verso quella banda, fare voltare il viso a tutto l'esercito; dipoi fare tutte quelle cose, in fortificazione di quella testa, che di sopra si dicono; tale che i cavalli, i Veliti, l'artiglierie sieno ne' luoghi conformi a questa testa. Solo vi è questa differenza: che nel variare le teste di quelli che si tramutano, chi ha ad ire meno e chi più. Bene è vero che faccendo testa del fianco destro, i Veliti che avessono ad entrare negli intervalli che sono tra le corna dell'esercito e i cavalli, sarebbono quegli che fussono più propinqui al fianco sinistro; nel luogo de' quali avrebbero ad entrare le due bandiere delle picche estraordinarie, poste nel mezzo. Ma, innanzi vi entrassero, i carriaggi e i disarmati per l'apertura sgomberassono la piazza e ritirassonsi dietro al fianco sinistro; il che verrebbe ad essere allora coda dell'esercito. E gli altri Veliti che fussono posti nella coda secondo l'ordinazione principale, in questo caso non si mutassero, perchè quello luogo non rimanesse aperto, il quale di coda verrebbe ad essere fianco. Tutte l'altre cose si deggiono fare come nella prima testa si disse.

Questo che si è detto circa il far testa del fianco destro, s'intende detto avendola a fare del fianco sinistro; perchè si dee osservare il medesimo ordine. Se il nemico venisse grosso ed ordinato per assaltarti da due bande, si deggiono fare quelle due bande, ch'egli viene ad assaltare, forti con quelle due che non sono assaltate, duplicando gli ordini in ciascheduna e dividendo, per ciascuna parte, l'artiglieria, i Veliti e i cavalli. Se viene da tre o da quattro bande, è necessario o che tu o esso manchi di prudenza; perchè, se tu sarai savio, tu non ti metterai mai in lato che il nemico da tre o da quattro bande con gente grossa e ordinata ti possa assaltare; perchè, a volere che sicuramente ti offenda, conviene che sia sì grosso, che da ogni banda egli ti assalti con tanta gente quanta abbia quasi tutto il tuo esercito. E se tu se' si poco prudente, che tu ti metta nelle terre e forze d'uno nemico che abbia tre volte gente ordinata più di te, non ti puoi dolere, se tu capiti male, se non di te. Se viene, non per tua colpa, ma per qualche sventura, sarà il danno senza la vergogna, e ti interverrà come agli Scipioni in Ispagna e ad Asdrubale in Italia. Ma se il nemico non ha molta più gente di te, e voglia, per disordinarti, assaltarti da più bande, sarà stoltizia sua e ventura tua; perchè conviene che a fare questo egli s'assottigli in modo che tu puoi facilmente urtarne una banda e sostenerne un'altra, e in brieve tempo rovinarlo. Questo modo dell'ordinare un esercito contro a uno nemico che non si vede ma che si teme, è necessario, ed è cosa utilissima assuefare i tuoi soldati a mettersi insieme e camminare con tale ordine e, nel camminare, ordinarsi per combattere secondo la prima testa e, dipoi, ritornare nella forma che si cammina; da quella, fare testa della coda, poi del fianco; da queste, ritornare nella prima forma. I quali esercizj e assuefazioni sono necessarj, volendo avere uno esercito disciplinato e pratico. Nelle quali cose si hanno ad affaticare i capitani ed i principi; nè è altro la disciplina militare, che sapere bene comandare ed eseguire queste cose; nè è altro uno esercito disciplinato, che uno esercito che sia bene pratico in su questi ordini; nè sarebbe possibile che chi in questi tempi usasse bene simile disciplina, fusse mai rotto. E se questa forma quadrata che io vi ho dimostra, è alquanto difficile, tale difficultà è necessaria, pigliandola per esercizio; perchè, sapendo bene ordinarsi e mantenersi in quella, si saprà dipoi più facilmente stare in quelle che non avessono tanta difficultà.

ZANOBI: Io credo, come voi dite che questi ordini sieno molto necessarj; e io per me non saprei che mi vi aggiungere o levare. Vero è che io desidero sapere da voi due cose: l'una, se, quando voi volete fare della coda o del fianco, testa, e voi gli volete fare voltare, se questo si comanda con la voce o con il suono; l'altra, se quegli che voi mettete davanti a spianare le strade per fare la via all'esercito, deggiono essere de' medesimi soldati delle vostre battaglie, oppure altra gente vile, deputata a simile esercizio.

FABRIZIO: La prima vostra domanda importa assai; perchè molte volte lo essere i comandamenti de' capitani non bene intesi, o male interpretati, ha disordinato il loro esercito; però le voci con le quali si comanda ne' pericoli deggiono essere chiare e nette. E se tu comandi con il suono, conviene fare che dall'uno modo all'altro sia tanta differenza, che non si possa scambiare l'uno dall'altro; e, se comandi con le voci, dèi avere avvertenza di fuggire le voci generali e usare le particolari, e delle particulari fuggire quelle che si potessono interpretare sinistramente. Molte volte il dire, addietro, addietro, ha fatto rovesciare un esercito; però questa voce si dee fuggire, ed in suo luogo usare: ritiratevi. Se voi gli volete fare rimutare testa o per fianco o a spalle, non usate mai, voltatevi, ma dite: a sinistra, a destra, a spalle, A fronte. Così tutte le altre voci hanno ad essere semplici e nette, come: Premete! State forti! Innanzi! Tornate!. E tutte quelle cose che si possono fare con la voce, si facciano; l'altre si facciano con il suono. Quanto agli spianatori, che è la seconda domanda vostra, io fare' fare questo uffizio a' miei soldati proprj, sì perchè così si faceva nella antica milizia, sì ancora, perchè fusse nell'esercito meno gente disarmata e meno impedimenti, e ne trarrei d'ogni battaglia quel numero bisognasse, e farei loro pigliare gli istrumenti atti a spianare, e l'armi lasciare a quelle file che fussero loro più presso, le quali le porterebbero loro, e, venendo il nemico non avrebbono a fare altro che ripigliarle e ritornare negli ordini loro.

ZANOBI: Gli istrumenti da spianare chi gli porterebbe?

FABRIZIO: I carri, a portare simili istrumenti, deputati.

ZANOBI: Io dubito che voi non condurresti mai questi vostri soldati a zappare.

FABRIZIO: Di tutto si ragionerà nel luogo suo. Per ora io voglio lasciare stare questa parte e ragionare del modo del vivere dell'esercito; perchè mi pare, avendolo tanto affaticato, che sia tempo da rinfrescarlo e ristorarlo con il cibo. Voi avete ad intendere che uno principe debbe ordinare l'esercito suo più espedito che sia possibile e torgli tutte quelle cose che gli aggiugnessero carico e gli facessero difficili le imprese. Tra quelle che arrecono più difficultà, sono avere a tenere provvisto l'esercito di vino e di pane cotto. Gli antichi al vino non pensavano, perchè, mancandone, beevano acqua tinta con un poco d'aceto per darle sapore; donde che tra le munizioni de' viveri dell'esercito era l'aceto e non il vino. Non cocevano il pane ne' forni, come si usa per le cittadi, ma provvedevano le farine; e di quelle ogni soldato a suo modo si soddisfaceva, avendo per condimento lardo e sugna; il che dava, al pane che facevano, sapore e gli manteneva gagliardi. In modo che le provvisioni di vivere per l'esercito erano farine, aceto, lardo e sugna e, per i cavalli, orzo. Avevano, per l'ordinario, branchi di bestiame grosso e minuto che seguiva l'esercito; il quale, per non avere bisogno di essere portato, non dava molto impedimento. Da questo ordine nasceva che uno esercito antico camminava alcuna volta molti giorni per luoghi solitarj e difficili senza patire disagi di vettovaglie, perchè viveva di cose che facilmente se le poteva tirare dietro. Al contrario interviene ne' moderni eserciti; i quali, volendo non mancare del vino e mangiare pane cotto in quegli modi che quando sono a casa, di che non possono fare provvisione a lungo, rimangono spesso affamati, o, se pure ne sono provvisti, si fa con uno disagio e con una spesa grandissima. Pertanto io ritirerei l'esercito mio a questa forma del vivere, nè vorrei mangiassono altro pane che quello che per loro medesimi si cocessero. Quanto al vino non proibirei il berne, nè che nell'esercito ne venisse, ma non userei nè industria nè fatica alcuna per averne, e nell'altre provvisioni mi governerei al tutto come gli antichi. La quale cosa se considererete bene, vedrete quanta difficultà si lieva via, e di quanti affanni e disagi si priva uno esercito e uno capitano, e quanta commodità si darà a qualunque impresa si volesse fare.

ZANOBI: Noi abbiamo vinto il nemico alla campagna, camminato dipoi sopra il paese suo; la ragione vuole che si sia fatto prede, taglieggiato terre, preso prigioni; però io vorrei sapere come gli antichi in queste cose si governavano.

FABRIZIO: Ecco che io vi soddisfarò. Io credo che voi abbiate considerato, perchè altra volta con alcuni di voi ne ho ragionato, come le presenti guerre impoveriscono così quegli signori che vincono, come quegli che perdono; perchè se l'uno perde lo stato, l'altro perde i danari e il mobile suo; il che anticamente non era, perchè il vincitore delle guerre arricchiva. Questo nasce da non tenere conto in questi tempi delle prede, come anticamente si faceva, ma si lasciano tutte alla discrezione de' soldati. Questo modo fa due disordini grandissimi: l'uno, quello che io ho detto; l'altro, che il soldato diventa più cupido del predare e meno osservante degli ordini; e molte volte si è veduto come la cupidità della preda ha fatto perdere chi era vittorioso. I Romani pertanto, che furno Principi di questo esercizio, provvidero all'uno e all'altro di questi inconvenienti, ordinando che tutta la preda appartenesse al pubblico, e che il pubblico poi la dispensasse come gli paresse. E però avevano negli eserciti i questori, che erano, come diremmo noi, i camarlinghi; appresso a' quali tutte le taglie e le prede si collocavano; di che il Consolo si serviva a dar la paga ordinaria a' soldati, a sovvenire i feriti e gl'infermi, e agli altri bisogni dell'esercito. Poteva bene il Consolo, e usavalo spesso, concedere una preda a' soldati; ma questa concessione non faceva disordine, perchè, rotto l'esercito, tutta la preda si metteva in mezzo e distribuivasi per testa secondo le qualità di ciascuno. Il quale modo faceva che i soldati attendevano a vincere e non a rubare; e le Legioni Romane vincevano il nemico e non lo seguitavano, perchè mai non si partivano degli ordini loro; solamente lo seguivano i cavalli con quegli armati leggiermente e, se vi erano, altri soldati che Legionari. Che se le prede fussero state di chi le guadagnava, non era possibile nè ragionevole tenere le Legioni ferme, e portavasi molti pericoli. Di quì nasceva pertanto che il pubblico arricchiva, e ogni Consolo portava con gli suoi trionfi nello erario assai tesoro, il quale era tutto di taglie e di prede. Un'altra cosa facevano gli antichi bene considerata; che del soldo che davano a ciascuno soldato, la terza parte volevano che deponesse appresso quello che della sua battaglia portava la bandiera; il quale mai non gliene riconsegnava se non fornita la guerra. Questo facevano mossi da due ragioni: la prima, perchè il soldato facesse del suo soldo capitale; perchè, essendo la maggior parte giovani e straccurati, quanto più hanno, tanto più senza necessità spendono; l'altra, perchè sapendo che il mobile loro era appresso alla bandiera, fussero forzati averne più cura e con più ostinazione difenderla; e così questo modo gli faceva massai e gagliardi. Le quali cose tutte è necessario osservare, a volere ridurre la milizia ne' termini suoi.

ZANOBI: Io credo che non sia possibile che ad uno esercito, mentre che cammina da luogo a luogo, non scaggia accidenti pericolosi dove bisogni la industria del capitano e la virtù de' soldati, volendogli evitare; però io arei caro che voi, occorrendone alcuno, lo narrassi.

FABRIZIO: Io vi contenterò volentieri, essendo massimamente necessario, volendo dare di questo esercizio perfetta scienza. deggiono i capitani, sopra ogni altra cosa, mentre che camminano con l'esercito, guardarsi dagli agguati; ne' quali si incorre in due modi: o camminando tu entri in quegli, o con arte del nemico vi se' tirato dentro, senza che tu gli presenta. Al primo caso volendo obviare, è necessario mandare innanzi doppie guardie le quali scuoprano il paese; e tanto maggiore diligenza vi si debba usare, quanto più il paese fusse atto agli agguati, come sono i paesi selvosi e montuosi, perchè sempre si mettono o in una selva o dietro a uno con le. E come lo agguato, non lo prevedendo, ti rovina, così, prevedendolo, non ti offende. Hanno gli uccegli o la polvere molte volte scoperto il nemico, perchè, sempre che il nemico ti venga a trovare, farà polverio grande che ti significherà la sua venuta. Così molte volte uno capitano veggendo, ne' luoghi donde egli debbe passare, levare colombi o altri di quegli uccelli che volono in schiera, e aggirarsi e non si porre, ha conosciuto essere quivi lo agguato de' nemici e mandato innanzi sue genti; e, conosciuto quello ha salvato se e offeso il nemico suo. Quanto al secondo caso di esservi tirato dentro, che questi nostri chiamono essere tirato alla tratta, dèi stare accorto di non credere facilmente a quelle cose che sono poco ragionevoli ch'elle sieno, come sarebbe: se il nemico ti mettesse innanzi una preda, dèi credere che in quella sia l'amo e che vi sia dentro nascoso lo inganno. Se gli assai nemici sono cacciati da' tuoi pochi; se pochi nemici assaltono i tuoi assai; se i nemici fanno una subita fuga e non ragionevole; sempre dèi in tali casi temere di inganno. E non hai a credere mai che il nemico non sappia fare i fatti suoi; anzi, a volerti ingannare meno e a volere portare meno pericolo, quanto è più debole, quanto è meno cauto il nemico, tanto più dèi stimarlo. E hai in questo ad usare due termini diversi, perchè tu hai a temerlo con il pensiero e con l'ordine; ma con le parole e con l'altre estrinseche dimostrazioni mostrare di spregiarlo, perchè questo ultimo modo fa che i tuoi soldati sperano più di avere vittoria, quell'altro ti fa più cauto e meno atto ad essere ingannato. E hai ad intendere che, quando si cammina per il paese nemico, si porta più e maggiori pericoli che nel fare la giornata.

E però il capitano, camminando, dee raddoppiare la diligenza; e la prima cosa che dee fare, è di avere descritto e dipinto tutto il paese per il quale egli cammina, in modo che sappia i luoghi, il numero, le distanze, le vie, i monti, i fiumi, i paludi e tutte le qualità loro: e a fare di sapere questo, conviene abbia a se, diversamente e in diversi modi, quegli che sanno i luoghi, e dimandargli con diligenza, e riscontrare il loro parlare e, secondo i riscontri, notare. Deve mandare innanzi cavalli e, con loro, capi prudenti, non tanto a scoprire il nemico, quanto a speculare il paese, per vedere se riscontra col disegno e con la notizia ch'egli ha avuta di quello. Deve ancora mandare guardate le guide con speranza di premio, e timore di pena e, sopra tutto, deve fare che l'esercito non sappia a che fazione egli lo guida; perchè non è cosa nella guerra più utile che tacere le cose che si hanno a fare. E perchè uno subito assalto non turbi i tuoi soldati, li dèi avvertire ch'egli stieno parati con l'armi; perchè le cose previse offendono meno. Molti hanno, per fuggire le confusioni del cammino, messo sotto le bandiere i carriaggi e i disarmati, e comandato loro che seguino quelle, acciocchè, avendosi, camminando, a fermare o a ritirare, lo possano fare più facilmente, la quale cosa, come utile, io appruovo assai. Debbesi avere ancora quella avvertenza nel camminare, che l'una parte dell'esercito non si spicchi dall'altra, o che, per andare l'uno tosto e l'altro adagio, l'esercito non si assottigli, le quali cose sono cagione di disordine. Però bisogna collocare i capi in lato che mantengano il passo uniforme, ritenendo i troppo solleciti e sollecitando i tardi; il quale passo non si può meglio regolare che col suono. Debbonsi fare rallargare le vie, acciocchè sempre una battaglia almeno possa ire in ordinanza. Debbesi considerare il costume e le qualità del nemico, e se ti suole assaltare o da mattino o da mezzo dì o da sera, e s'egli è più potente co' fanti o co' cavalli; e, secondo intendi, ordinarti e provvederti. Ma vegnamo a qualche particolare accidente. Egli occorre qualche volta che, levandoti dinanzi al nemico per giudicarti inferiore, e per questo, non volere fare giornata seco, e venendoti quello a spalle, arrivi alla ripa d'un fiume il quale ti toglie tempo nel passare, in modo che il nemico è per raggiungerti e per combatterti. Hanno alcuni, che si sono trovati in tale pericolo, cinto l'esercito loro dalla parte di dietro con una fossa, e quella ripiena di stipa e messovi fuoco; dipoi passato con l'esercito senza potere essere impediti dal nemico, essendo quello da quel fuoco che era di mezzo ritenuto.

ZANOBI: E mi è duro a credere che cotesto fuoco li possa ritenere, massime perchè mi ricorda avere udito come Annone cartaginese, essendo assediato da' nemici, si cinse, da quella parte che voleva fare eruzione, di legname e messevi fuoco; donde che, i nemici non essendo intenti da quella parte a guardarlo, fece sopra quelle fiamme passare il suo esercito, faccendo tenere a ciascuno gli scudi al viso per difendersi dal fuoco e dal fumo.

FABRIZIO: Voi dite bene; ma considerate come io ho detto e come fece Annone; perchè io dissi che fecero una fossa e la riempierono di stipa; in modo che, chi voleva passare, aveva a contendere con la fossa e col fuoco. Annone fece il fuoco senza la fossa; e perchè lo voleva passare, non lo dovette fare gagliardo, perchè, ancora senza la fossa l'arebbe impedito. Non sapete voi che Nabide spartano, sendo assediato in Sparta da' Romani, messe fuoco in parte della sua terra per impedire il passo a' Romani, i quali erano di già entrati dentro? E mediante quelle fiamme, non solamente impedì loro il passo, ma gli ributtò fuora. Ma torniamo alla materia nostra. Quinto Lutazio Romano, avendo alle spalle i Cimbri e arrivato ad uno fiume, perchè il nemico gli desse tempo a passare, mostrò di dare tempo a lui al combatterlo; e però finse di volere alloggiare quivi, e fece fare fosse e rizzare alcuno padiglione e mandò alcuni cavalli per i campi a saccomanno; tanto che, credendo i Cimbri ch'egli alloggiasse, ancora essi alloggiarono e si divisero in più parti per provvedere a' viveri; di che essendosi Lutazio accorto, passò il fiume senza potere essere impedito da loro. Alcuni, per passare uno fiume non avendo ponte, lo hanno derivato e una parte tiratasi dietro alle spalle; e l'altra dipoi, divenuta più bassa, con facilità passata. Quando i fiumi sono rapidi, a volere che le fanterie passino più sicuramente, si mettono i cavalli più possenti dalla parte di sopra, che sostengano l'acqua, e un'altra parte di sotto, che soccorra i fanti, se alcuno dal fiume nel passare ne fusse vinto. Passansi ancora i fiumi che non si guadano, con ponti, con barche, con otri; e però è bene avere ne' suoi eserciti attitudine a potere fare tutte queste cose. Occorre alcuna volta che, nel passare uno fiume, il nemico opposto dall'altra ripa t'impedisce. A volere vincere questa difficultà non ci conosco esemplo da imitare migliore che quello di Cesare; il quale, avendo l'esercito suo alla riva d'un fiume in Francia, ed essendogli impedito il passare da Vergingetorige Francese il quale dall'altra parte del fiume aveva le sue genti, camminò più giornate lungo il fiume, e il simile faceva il nemico. E avendo Cesare fatto uno alloggiamento in uno luogo selvoso e atto a nascondere gente, trasse da ogni Legione tre coorti e fecele fermare in quello luogo, comandando loro che, subito che fusse partito, gittassero uno ponte e lo fortificassero, ed egli con l'altre sue genti seguitò il cammino. Donde che Vergingetorige vedendo il numero delle Legioni, credendo che non ne fusse rimasa parte a dietro, seguì ancora egli il camminare; ma Cesare, quando credette che il ponte fusse fatto, se ne tornò indietro e, trovato ogni cosa ad ordine, passò il fiume senza difficultà.

ZANOBI: Avete voi regola alcuna a conoscere i guadi?

FABRIZIO: Sì, abbiamo. Sempre il fiume in quella parte la quale è tra l'acqua che stagna e la corrente, che fa a chi vi riguarda come una riga, ha meno fondo ed è luogo più atto a essere guadato che altrove; perchè sempre in quello luogo il fiume ha posto più, e ha tenuto più in collo di quella materia che per il fondo trae seco. La quale cosa, perchè è stata esperimentata assai volte, è verissima.

ZANOBI: Se egli avviene che il fiume abbia sfondato il guado, tale che i cavalli vi si affondino, che rimedio ne date?

FABRIZIO: Fare graticci di legname e porgli nel fondo del fiume e, sopra quegli, passare. Ma seguitiamo il ragionamento nostro. S'egli accade che uno capitano si conduca col suo esercito tra due monti e che non abbia se non due vie a salvarsi, o quella davanti o quella di dietro, e quelle sieno da' nemici occupate, ha, per rimedio, di far quello che alcuno ha per l'addietro fatto; il che è: fare dalla parte di dietro una fossa grande e difficile a passare, e mostrare al nemico di volere con quella ritenerlo, per potere con tutte le forze senza avere a temere di dietro, fare forza per quella via che davanti resta aperta. Il che credendo i nemici, si fecero forti di verso la parte aperta e abbandonarono la chiusa, e quello allora gittò uno ponte di legname a tale effetto ordinato sopra la fossa, e da quella parte senza alcuno impedimento passò e liberossi dalle mani del nemico. Lucio Minuzio, Consolo Romano, era in Liguria con gli eserciti, ed era stato da' nemici rinchiuso tra certi monti donde non poteva uscire. Pertanto mandò quello alcuni soldati di Numidia a cavallo, ch'egli aveva nel suo esercito, i quali erano male armati e sopra cavalli piccoli e magri, verso i luoghi che erano guardati da' nemici, i quali, nel primo aspetto, fecero che i nemici si missero insieme a difendere il passo; ma, poi che viddero quelle genti male in ordine e, secondo loro, male a cavallo, stimandogli poco, allargarono gli ordini della guardia. Di che come i Numidi si avviddero, dato di sproni a' cavalli e fatto impeto sopra di loro, passarono senza che quegli vi potessero fare alcuno rimedio; i quali passati, guastando e predando il paese, costrinsero i nemici a lasciare il passo libero all'esercito di Lucio. Alcuno capitano che si è trovato assaltato da gran moltitudine di nemici, si è ristretto insieme e dato al nemico facultà di circondarlo tutto, e dipoi, da quella parte ch'egli l'ha conosciuto più debole, ha fatto forza e, per quella via, si ha fatto fare luogo, e salvatosi. Marco Antonio andando ritirandosi dinanzi all'esercito de' Parti, s'accorse come i nemici

ogni giorno al fare del dì, quando si moveva, lo assaltavano e, per tutto il cammino, lo infestavano; dimodochè prese per partito di non partire prima che a mezzogiorno. Tale che i Parti, credendo che per quel giorno egli non volesse disalloggiare, se ne tornarono alle loro stanze; e Marco Antonio potèo dipoi tutto il rimanente dì camminare senza alcuna molestia. Questo medesimo, per fuggire il saettume de' Parti, comandò alle sue genti che quando i Parti venivano verso di loro, s'inginocchiassero, e la seconda fila delle battaglie ponesse gli scudi in capo alla prima, la terza alla seconda, la quarta alla terza, e così successive; tanto che tutto l'esercito veniva ad essere come sotto uno tetto e difeso dal saettume nemico. Questo è tanto quanto mi occorre dirvi che possa a uno esercito, camminando, intervenire; però quando a voi non occorra altro, io passerò ad un'altra parte.

Book Six

ZANOBI: I believe it is well, since the discussion ought to be changed, that Battista take up his office, and I resign mine; and in this case we would come to imitate the good Captains, according as I have already learned here from the Lord, who place the best soldiers in the front and in the rear of the Army, as it appears necessary to them to have those who bravely enkindle the battle, and those in the rear who bravely sustain it. Cosimo, therefore, begun this discussion prudently, and Battista will prudently finish it. Luigi and I have come in between these. And as each one of us has taken up his part willingly, so too I believe Battista is about to close it.

BATTISTA: I have allowed myself to be governed up to now, so too I will allow myself (to be governed) in the future. Be content, therefore, (my) Lords, to continue your discussions, and if we interrupt you with these questions (practices), you have to excuse us.

FABRIZIO: You do me, as I have already told you, a very great favor, since these interruptions of yours do not take away my imagination, rather they refresh it. But if we want to pursue our subject I say, that it is now time that we quarter this Army of ours, since you know that everything desires repose, and safety; since to repose oneself, and not to repose safely, is not complete (perfect) repose. I am afraid, indeed, that you should not desire that I should first quarter them, then had them march, and lastly to fight, and we have done the contrary. Necessity has led us to this, for in wanting to show when marching, how an army turns from a marching formation to that of battle, it was necessary first to show how they were organized for battle. But returning to our subject I say, that if you want the encampment to be safe, it must be Strong and Organized. The industry of the Captain makes it organized: Arts or the site make it Strong. The Greeks sought strong locations, and never took positions where there was neither grottoes (caves), or banks of rivers, or a multitude of trees, or other natural cover which should protect them. But the Romans did not encamp safely so much from the location as by arts, nor ever made an encampment in places where they should not have been able to spread out all their forces, according to their discipline. From this resulted that the Romans were always able to have one form of encampment, for they wanted the site to obey them, and not they the site. The Greeks were not able to observe this, for as they obeyed the site, and the sites changing the formation, it behooved them that they too should change the mode of encamping and the form of their encampment. The Romans, therefore, where the site lacked strength, supplied it with (their) art and industry. And since in this narration of mine, I have wanted that the Romans be imitated, I will not depart from their mode of encamping, not, however, observing all their arrangements: but taking (only) that part which at the present time seems appropriate to me. I have often told you that the Romans had two Legions of Roman men in their consular armies, which comprised some eleven thousand infantry of forces sent by friends (allies) to aid them; but they never had more foreign soldiers in their armies than Romans, except for cavalry, which they did not care if they exceeded the number in their Legions; and that in every action of theirs, they place the Legions in the center, and the Auxiliaries on the sides. Which method they observed even when they encamped, as you yourselves have been able to read in those who write of their affairs; and therefore I am not about to narrate in detail how they encamped, but will tell you only how I would at present arrange to encamp my army, and then you will know what part of the Roman methods I have treated. You know that at the encounter of two Roman Legions I have taken two Battalions of six thousand infantry and three hundred cavalry effective for each Battalion, and I have divided them by companies, by arms, and names. You know that in organizing the army for marching and fighting, I have not made mention of other forces, but have only shown that in doubling the forces, nothing else had to be done but to double the orders (arrangements).

Since at present I want to show you the manner of encamping, it appears proper to me not to stay only with two Battalions, but to assemble a fair army, and composed like the Roman of two Battalions and as many auxiliary forces. I know that the form of an encampment is more perfect, when a complete army is quartered: which matter did not appear necessary to me in the previous demonstration. If I want, therefore, to quarter a fair (sized) army of twenty four thousand infantry and two thousand cavalry effectives, being divided into four companies, two of your own forces and two of foreigners, I would employ this method. When I had found the site where I should want to encamp, I would raise the Captain's flag, and around it I would draw a square which would have each face distant from it fifty arm lengths, of which each should look out on one of the four regions of the sky, that is, east, west, south and north, in which space I would put the quarters of the Captain. And as I believe it prudent, and because thus the Romans did in good part, I would divide the armed men from the unarmed, and separate the men who carry burdens from the unburdened ones. I would quarter all or a greater part of the armed men on the east side, and the unarmed and burdened ones on the west side, making the east the front and the west the rear of the encampment, and the south and north would be the flanks. And to distinguish the quarters of the armed men, I would employ this method. I would run a line from the Captain's flag, and would lead it easterly for a distance of six hundred eighty (680) arm lengths. I would also run two other lines which I would place in the middle of it, and be of the same length as the former, but distant from each of them by fifteen arm lengths, at the extremity of which, I would want the east gate to be (placed): and the space which exists between the two extreme (end) lines, I would make a road that would go from the gate to the quarters of the Captain, which would be thirty arm lengths in width and six hundred thirty (630) long ((since the Captain's quarters would occupy fifty arm lengths)) and call this the Captain's Way. I would then make another road from the south gate up to the north gate, and cross by the head of the Captain's Way, and along the east side of the Captain's quarters which would be one thousand two hundred fifty (1250) arm lengths long ((since it would occupy the entire width of the encampment)) and also be thirty arm lengths wide and be called the Cross Way. The quarters of the Captain and these two roads having been designed, therefore the quarters of the two battalions of your own men should begin to be designed; and I would quarter one on the right hand (side) of the Captain's Way, and one on the left. And hence beyond the space which is occupied by the width of the Cross Way, I would place thirty two quarters on the left side of the Captain's Way, and thirty two on the right side, leaving a space of thirty arm lengths between the sixteenth and seventeenth quarters which should serve as a transverse road which should cross through all of the quarters of the battalions, as will be seen in their partitioning. Of these two arrangements of quarters, in the first tents that would be adjacent to the Cross Way, I would quarter the heads of men-at-arms, and since each company has one hundred and fifty men-at-arms, there would be assigned ten men-at-arms to each of the quarters. The area (space) of the quarters of the Heads should be forty arm lengths wide and ten arm lengths long. And it is to be noted that whenever I say width, I mean from south to north, and when I say length, that from west to east. Those of the men-at-arms should be fifteen arm lengths long and thirty wide. In the next fifteen quarters which in all cases are next ((which should have their beginning across the transverse road, and which would have the same space as those of the men-at-arms)) I would quarter the light cavalry, which, since they are one hundred fifty, ten cavalrymen would be assigned to each quarter, and in the sixteenth which would be left, I would quarter their Head, giving him the same space which is given to the Head of men-at-arms. And thus the quarters of the cavalry of the two battalions would come to place the Captain's Way in the center and give a rule for the quarters of the infantry, as I will narrate. You have noted that I have quartered the three hundred cavalry of each battalion with their heads in thirty two quarters situated on the Captain's Way, and beginning with the Cross Way, and that from the sixteenth to the seventeenth there is a space of thirty arm lengths to make a transverse road. If I want, therefore, to quarter the twenty companies which constitute the two regular Battalions, I would place the quarters of every two companies behind the quarters of the cavalry, each of which should be fifteen arm lengths long and thirty wide, as those of the cavalry, and should be joined on the rear where they touch one another. And in every first quarter of each band that fronts on the Cross Way, I would quarter the Constable of one company, which would come to correspond with the quartering of the Head of the men-at-arms: and their quarters alone would have a space twenty arm lengths in width and ten in length. And in the other fifteen quarters in each group which follow after this up the Transverse Way, I would quarter a company of infantry on each side, which, as they are four hundred fifty, thirty would be assigned to each quarter. I would place the other fifteen quarters contiguous in each group to those of the cavalry with the same space, in which I would quarter a company of infantry from each group. In the last quarter of each group I would place the Constable of the company, who would come to be adjacent to the Head of the light cavalry, with a space of ten arm lengths long and twenty wide. And thus these first two rows of quarters would be half of cavalry and half of infantry.

And as I want ((as I told you in its place)) these cavalry to be all effective, and hence without retainers who help taking care of the horses or other necessary things, I would want these infantry quartered behind the cavalry should be obligated to help the owners (of the horses) in providing and taking care of them, and because of this should be exempt from other activities of the camp, which was the manner observed by the Romans. I would also leave behind these quarters on all sides a space of thirty arm lengths to make a road, and I would call one of the First Road on the right hand (side) and the other the First Road on the left, and in each area I would place another row of thirty two double quarters which should face one another on the rear, with the same spaces as those which I have mentioned, and also divided at the sixteenth in the same manner to create a Transverse Road, in which I would quarter in each area four companies of infantry with the Constables in the front at the head and foot (of each row). I would also leave on each side another space of thirty arm lengths to create a road which should be called the Second Road on the right hand (side) and on the other side the Second Road to the left; I would place another row in each area of thirty two double quarters, with the same distances and divisions, in which I would quarter on every side four companies (of infantry) with their Constables. And thus there would come to be quartered in three rows of quarters per area the cavalry and the companies (of infantry) of the two regular battalions, in the center of which I would place the Captain's Way. The two battalions of auxiliaries ((since I had them composed of the same men)) I would quarter on each side of these two regular battalions with the same arrangement of double quarters, placing first a row of quarters in which I should quarter half with cavalry and half infantry, distant thirty arm lengths from each other, to create two roads which I should call, one the Third Road on the right hand (side), the other the Third on the left hand. And then I would place on each side two other rows of quarters, separate but arranged in the same way, which are those of the regular battalions, which would create two other roads, and all of these would be called by the number and the band (side) where they should be situated. So that all this part of the Army would come to be quartered in twelve rows of double quarters, and on thirteen roads, counting the Captain's Way and the Cross Way.

I would want a space of one hundred arm lengths all around left between the quarters and the ditch (moat). And if you count all those spaces, you will see, that from the middle of the quarters of the Captain to the east gate, there are seven hundred arm lengths. There remains to us now two spaces, of which one is from the quarters of the Captain to the south gate, the other from there to the north gate, each of which comes to be, measuring from the center point, six hundred thirty five (635) arm lengths. I then subtract from each of these spaces fifty arm lengths which the quarters of the Captain occupies, and forty five arm lengths of plaza which I want to give to each side, and thirty arm lengths of road, which divides each of the mentioned spaces in the middle, and a hundred arm lengths which are left on each side between the quarters and the ditch, and there remains in each area a space left for quarters four hundred arm lengths wide and a hundred long, measuring the length to include the space occupied by the Captain's quarters. Dividing the said length in the middle, therefore, there would be on each side of the Captain forty quarters fifty arm lengths long and twenty wide, which would total eighty quarters, in which would be quartered the general Heads of the battalions, the Chamberlains, the Masters of the camps, and all those who should have an office (duty) in the army, leaving some vacant for some foreigners who might arrive, and for those who should fight through the courtesy of the Captain. On the rear side of the Captain's quarters, I would create a road thirty arm lengths wide from north to south, and call it the Front Road, which would come to be located along the eighty quarters mentioned, since this road and the Cross Way would have between them the Captain's quarters and the eighty quarters on their flanks. From this Front road and opposite to the Captain's quarters, I would create another road which should go from there to the west gate, also thirty arm lengths wide, and corresponding in location and length to the Captain's Way, and I should call it the Way of the Plaza. These two roads being located, I would arrange the plaza where the market should be made, which I would place at the head of the Way of the Plaza, opposite to the Captain's quarters, and next to the Front Road, and would want it to be square, and would allow it a hundred twenty one arm lengths per side. And from the right hand and left hand of the said plaza, I would make two rows of quarters, and each row have eight double quarters, which would take up twelve arm lengths in length and thirty in width so that they should be on each side of the plaza, in which there would be sixteen quarters, and total thirty two all together, in which I would quarter that cavalry left over from the auxiliary battalions, and if this should not be enough, I would assign them some of the quarters about the Captain, and especially those which face the ditch.

It remains for us now to quarter the extraordinary pikemen and Veliti, which every battalion has; which you know, according to our arrangement, in addition to the ten companies (of infantry), each has a thousand extraordinary pikemen, and five hundred Veliti; so that each of the two regular battalions have two thousand extraordinary pikemen, and a thousand extraordinary pikemen, and five hundred Veliti; so that each of the two regular battalions have two thousand extraordinary pikemen, and a thousand extraordinary Veliti, and the auxiliary as many as they; so that one also comes to have to quarter six thousand infantry, all of whom I would quarter on the west side along the ditches. From the point, therefore, of the Front Road, and northward, leaving the space of a hundred arm lengths from those (quarters) to the ditch, I would place a row of five double quarters which would be seventy five arm lengths long and sixty in width: so that with the width divided, each quarters would be allowed fifteen arm lengths for length and thirty for width. And as there would be ten quarters, I would quarter three hundred infantry, assigning thirty infantry to each quarters. Leaving then a space of thirty one arm lengths, I would place another row of five double quarters in a similar manner and with similar spaces, and then another, so that there would be five rows of five double quarters, which would come to be fifty quarters placed in a straight line on the north side, each distant one hundred arm lengths from the ditches, which would quarter one thousand five hundred infantry. Turning then on the left hand side toward the west gate, I would want in all that tract between them and the said gate, five other rows of double quarters, in a similar manner and with the same spaces, ((it is true that from one row to the other there would not be more than fifteen arm lengths of space)) in which there would also be quartered a thousand five hundred infantry: and thus from the north gate to that on the west, following the ditches, in a hundred quarters, divided into ten rows of five double quarters per row, the extraordinary pikemen and Veliti of the regular battalions would be quartered. And so, too, from the west gate to that on the south, following the ditches, in exactly the same manner, in another ten rows of ten quarters per row, the extraordinary pikemen and Veliti of the auxiliary battalions would be quartered. Their Heads, or rather their Constables, could take those quarters on the side toward the ditches which appeared most convenient for themselves.

I would dispose the artillery all along the embankments of the ditches: and in all the other space remaining toward the west, I would quarter all the unarmed men and all the baggage (impedimenta) of the Camp. And it has to be understood that under this name of impedimenta ((as you know)) the ancients intended all those carriages (wagons) and all those things which are necessary to an Army, except the soldiers; as are carpenters (wood workers), smiths, blacksmiths, shoe makers, engineers, and bombardiers, and others which should be placed among the number of the armed: herdsmen with their herds of castrated sheep and oxen, which are used for feeding the Army: and in addition, masters of every art (trade), together with public wagons for the public provisions of food and arms. And I would not particularly distinguish their quarters: I would only designate the roads that should not be occupied by them. Then the other spaces remaining between the roads, which would be four, I would assign in general to all the impedimenta mentioned, that is, one to the herdsmen, another to Artificers and workmen, another to the public wagons for provisions, and the fourth to the armorers. The roads which I would want left unoccupied would be the Way of the Plaza, the Front Road, and in addition, a road that should be called the Center Road, which should take off at the north and proceed toward the south, and pass through the center of the Way of the Plaza, which, on the west side, should have the same effect as has the Transverse Road on the east side. And in addition to this a Road that should go around the rear along the quarters of the extraordinary pikemen and Veliti. And all these roads should be thirty arm lengths wide. And I would dispose the artillery along the ditches on the rear of the camp.

BATTISTA: I confess I do not understand, and I also do not believe that to say so makes me ashamed, as this is not my profession. None the less, I like this organization very much: I would want only that you should resolve these doubts for me. The one, why you make the roads and the spaces around the quarters so wide. The other, which annoys me more, is this, how are these spaces that you designate for quarters to be used.

FABRIZIO: You know that I made all the roads thirty arm lengths wide, so that a company of infantry is able to go through them in order (formation): which, if you remember well, I told you that each of these (formations) were twenty five to thirty arm lengths wide. The space between the ditch and the quarters, which is a hundred arm lengths wide, is necessary, since the companies and the artillery can be handled here, through which booty is taken, (and) when space is needed into which to retire, new ditches and embankments are made. The quarters very distant from the ditches are better, for they are more distant from the fires and other things that might be able to draw the enemy to attack them. As to the second question, my intention is not that every space designated by me is covered by only one pavilion, but is to be used as an all-round convenience for those who are quartered, with several or few tents, so long as they do not go outside its limits. And in designing these quarters, the men must be most experienced and excellent architects, who, as soon as the Captain has selected the site, know how to give it form, and divide it, and distinguishing the roads, dividing the quarters with cords and hatchets in such a practical manner, that they might be divided and arranged quickly. And if confusion is not to arise, the camp must always face the same way, so that everyone will know on which Road and in which space he has to find his quarters. And this ought to be observed at all times, in every place, and in a manner that it appears to be a movable City, which, wherever it goes, brings with it the same roads, the same houses, and the same appearance: which cannot be observed by those men who, seeking strong locations, have to change the form according to the variations in the sites. But the Romans made the places strong with ditches, ramparts, and embankments, for they placed a space around the camp, and in front of it they dug a ditch and ordinarily six arm lengths wide and three deep, which spaces they increased according to the (length of) time they resided in the one place, and according as they feared the enemy. For myself, I would not at present erect a stockade (rampart), unless I should want to winter in a place. I would, however, dig the ditch and embankment, not less than that mentioned, but greater according to the necessity. With respect to the artillery, on every side of the encampment, I would have a half circle ditch, from which the artillery should be able to batter on the flanks whoever should come to attack the moats (ditches). The soldiers ought also to be trained in this practice of knowing how to arrange an encampment, and work with them so they may aid him in designing it, and the soldiers quick in knowing their places. And none of these is difficult, as will be told in its proper place. For now I want to pass on to the protection of the camp, which, without the distribution (assignment) of guards, all the other efforts would be useless.

BATTISTA: Before you pass on to the guards, I would want you to tell me, what methods are employed when others want to place the camp near the enemy, for I do not know whether there is time to be able to organize it without danger.

FABRIZIO: You have to know this, that no Captain encamps near the enemy, unless he is disposed to come to an engagement whenever the enemy wants; and if the others are so disposed, there is no danger except the ordinary, since two parts of the army are organized to make an engagement, while the other part makes the encampment. In cases like this, the Romans assigned this method of fortifying the quarters to the Triari, while the Principi and the Astati remained under arms. They did this, because the Triari, being the last to combat, were in time to leave the work if the enemy came, and take up their arms and take their places. If you want to imitate the Romans, you have to assign the making of the encampment to that company which you would want to put in the place of the Triari in the last part of the army.

But let us return to the discussion of the guards. I do not seem to find in connection with the ancients guarding the camp at night, that they had guards outside, distant from the ditches, as is the custom today, which they call the watch. I believe I should do this, when I think how the army could be easily deceived, because of the difficulty which exists in checking (reviewing) them, for they may be corrupted or attacked by the enemy, so that they judged it dangerous to trust them entirely or in part. And therefore all the power of their protection was within the ditches, which they dug with very great diligence and order, punishing capitally anyone who deviated from such an order. How this was arranged by them, I will not talk to you further in order not to tire you, since you are able to see it by yourselves, if you have not seen it up to now. I will say only briefly what would be done by me. I would regularly have a third of the army remain armed every night, and a fourth of them always on foot, who would be distributed throughout the embankments and all the places of the army, with double guards posted at each of its squares, where a part should remain, and a part continually go from one side of the encampment to the other. And this arrangement I describe, I would also observe by day if I had the enemy near. As to giving it a name, and renewing it every night, and doing the other things that are done in such guarding, since they are things (already) known, I will not talk further of them. I would only remind you of a most important matter, and by observing it do much good, by not observing it do much evil; which is, that great diligence be used as to who does not lodge within the camp at night, and who arrives there anew. And this is an easy matter, to review who is quartered there, with those arrangements we have designated, since every quarter having a predetermined number of men, it is an easy thing to see if there are any men missing or if any are left over; and when they are missing without permission, to punish them as fugitives, and if they are left over, to learn who they are, what they know, and what are their conditions. Such diligence results in the enemy not being able to have correspondence with your Heads, and not to have co-knowledge of your counsels. If this had not been observed with diligence by the Romans, Claudius Nero could not, when he had Hannibal near to him, have departed from the encampment he had in Lucania, and go and return from the Marches, without Hannibal having been aware of it. But it is not enough to make these good arrangements, unless they are made to be observed by great security, for there is nothing that wants so much observance as any required in the army. Therefore, the laws for their enforcement should be harsh and hard, and the executor very hard. The Roman punished with the capital penalty whoever was missing from the guard, whoever abandoned the place given him in combat, whoever brought anything concealed from outside the encampment; if anyone should tell of having performed some great act in battle, and should not have done it; if anyone should have fought except at the command of the Captain, if anyone from fear had thrown aside his arms. And if it occurred that an entire Cohort or an entire Legion had made a similar error, in order that they not all be put to death, they put their names in a purse, and drew the tenth part, and those they put to death. Which penalty was so carried out, that if everyone did not hear of it, they at least feared it. And because where there are severe punishments, there also ought to be rewards, so that men should fear and hope at the same time, they proposed rewards for every great deed; such as to him who, during the fighting, saved the life of one of its citizens, to whoever first climbed the walls of enemy towns, to whoever first entered the encampment of the enemy, to whoever in battle wounded or killed an enemy, to whoever had thrown him from his horse. And thus any act of virtu was recognized and rewarded by the Consuls, and publicly praised by everyone: and those who received gifts for any of these things, in addition to the glory and fame they acquired among the soldiers, when they returned to their country, exhibited them with solemn pomp and with great demonstrations among their friends and relatives. It is not to marvel therefore, if that people acquired so much empire, when they had so great an observance of punishment and reward toward them, which operated either for their good or evil, should merit either praise or censure; it behooves us to observe the greater part of these things. And it does not appear proper for me to be silent on a method of punishment observed by them, which was, that as the miscreant was convicted before the Tribune or the Consul, he was struck lightly by him with a rod: after which striking of the criminal, he was allowed to flee, and all the soldiers allowed to kill him, so that immediately each of them threw stones or darts, or hit him with other arms, of a kind from which he went little alive, and rarely returned to camp; and to such that did return to camp, he was not allowed to return home except with so much inconvenience and ignominy, that it was much better for him to die. You see this method almost observed by the Swiss, who have the condemned publicly put to death by the other soldiers. Which is well considered and done for the best, for if it is desired that one be not a defender of a criminal, the better remedy that is found, is to make him the punisher of him (the criminal); for in some respects he favors him while from other desires he longs for his punishment, if he himself is the executioner, than if the execution is carried out by another. If you want, therefore, that one is not to be favored in his mistakes by a people, a good remedy is to see to it that the public judged him. In support of this, the example of Manlius Capitol that can be cited, who, when he was accused by the Senate, was defended so much by the public up to the point where it no longer became the judge: but having become arbiter of his cause, condemned him to death. It is, therefore, a method of punishing this, of doing away with tumults, and of having justice observed. And since in restraining armed men, the fear of laws, or of men, is not enough, the ancients added the authority of God: and, therefore, with very great ceremony, they made their soldiers swear to observe the military discipline, so that if they did the contrary, they not only had to fear the laws and men, but God; and they used every industry to fill them with Religion.

BATTISTA: Did the Romans permit women to be in their armies, or that they indulge in indolent games that are used to day?

FABRIZIO: They prohibited both of them, and this prohibition was not very difficult, because the exercises which they gave each day to the soldiers were so many, sometimes being occupied all together, sometimes individually, that no time was left to them to think either of Venery, or of games, or of other things which make soldiers seditious and useless.

BATTISTA: I like that. But tell me, when the army had to take off, what arrangements did they have?

FABRIZIO: The captain's trumpet was sounded three times: at the first sound the tents were taken down and piled into heaps, at the second they loaded the burdens, and at the third they moved in the manner mentioned above, with the impedimenta behind, the armed men on every side, placing the Legions in the center. And, therefore, you would have to have a battalion of auxiliaries move, and behind it its particular impedimenta, and with those the fourth part of the public impedimenta, which would be all those who should be quartered in one of those (sections of the camp) which we showed a short while back. And, therefore, it would be well to have each one of them assigned to a battalion, so that when the army moved, everyone would know where his place was in marching. And every battalion ought to proceed on its way in this fashion with its own impedimenta, and with a quarter of the public (impedimenta) at its rear, as we showed the Roman army marched.

BATTISTA: In placing the encampment, did they have other considerations than those you mentioned?

FABRIZIO: I tell you again, that in their encampments, the Romans wanted to be able to employ the usual form of their method, in the observance of which, they took no other consideration. But as to other considerations, they had two principal ones: the one, to locate themselves in a healthy place: to locate themselves where the enemy should be unable to besiege them, and cut off their supply of water and provisions. To avoid this weakness, therefore, they avoided marshy places, or exposure to noxious winds. They recognized these, not so much from the characteristics of the site, but from the looks of the inhabitants: and if they saw them with poor color, or short winded, or full of other infections, they did not encamp there. As to the other part of not being besieged, the nature of the place must be considered, where the friends are, and where the enemy, and from these make a conjecture whether or not you can be besieged. And, therefore, the Captain must be very expert concerning sites of the countries, and have around him many others who have the same expertness. They also avoided sickness and hunger so as not to disorganize the army; for if you want to keep it healthy, you must see to it that the soldiers sleep under tents, that they are quartered, where there are trees to create shade, where there is wood to cook the food, and not to march in the heat. You need, therefore, to consider the encampment the day before you arrive there, and in winter guard against marching in the snow and through ice without the convenience of making a fire, and not lack necessary clothing, and not to drink bad water. Those who get sick in the house, have them taken care of by doctors; for a captain has no remedy when he has to fight both sickness and the enemy. But nothing is more useful in maintaining an army healthy than exercise: and therefore the ancients made them exercise every day. Whence it is seen how much exercise is of value, for in the quarters it keeps you healthy, and in battle it makes you victorious. As to hunger, not only is it necessary to see that the enemy does not impede your provisions, but to provide whence you are to obtain them, and to see that those you have are not lost. And, therefore, you must always have provisions (on hand) for the army for a month, and beyond that to tax the neighboring friends that they provide you daily, keep the provisions in a strong place, and, above all, dispense it with diligence, giving each one a reasonable measure each day, and so observe this part that they do not become disorganized; for every other thing in war can be overcome with time, this only with time overcomes you. Never make anyone your enemy, who, while seeking to overcome you with the sword (iron), can overcome you by hunger, because if such a victory is not as honorable, it is more secure and more certain. That army, therefore, cannot escape hunger which does not observe justice, and licentiously consume whatever it please, for one evil causes the provisions not to arrive, and the other that when they arrive, they are uselessly consumed: therefore the ancients arranged that what was given was eaten, and in the time they assigned, so that no soldier ate except when the Captain did. Which, as to being observed by the modern armies, everyone does (the contrary), and deservedly they cannot be called orderly and sober as the ancients, but licentious and drunkards.

BATTISTA: You have said in the beginning of arranging the encampment, that you did not want to stay only with two battalions, but took up four, to show how a fair (sized) army was quartered. Therefore I would want you to tell me two things: the one, if I have more or less men, how should I quarter them: the other, what number of soldiers would be enough to fight against any enemy?

FABRIZIO: To the first question, I reply, that if the army has four or six thousand soldiers more or less, rows of quarters are taken away or added as are needed, and in this way it is possible to accommodate more or fewer infinitely. None the less, when the Romans joined together two consular armies, they made two encampments and had the parts of the disarmed men face each other. As to the second question, I reply, that the regular Roman army had about twenty four thousand soldiers: but when a great force pressed them, the most they assembled were fifty thousand. With this number they opposed two hundred thousand Gauls whom they assaulted after the first war which they had with the Carthaginians. With the same number, they opposed Hannibal. And you have to note that the Romans and Greeks had made war with few (soldiers), strengthened by order and by art; the westerners and easterners had made it with a multitude: but one of these nations serves itself of natural fury, as are the westerners; the other of the great obedience which its men show to their King. But in Greece and Italy, as there is not this natural fury, nor the natural reverence toward their King, it has been necessary to turn to discipline; which is so powerful, that it made the few able to overcome the fury and natural obstinacy of the many. I tell you, therefore, if you want to imitate the Romans and Greeks, the number of fifty thousand soldiers ought not to be exceeded, rather they should actually be less; for the many cause confusion, and do not allow discipline to be observed nor the orders learned. And Pyrrhus used to say that with fifteen thousand men he would assail the world.

But let us pass on to another part. We have made our army win an engagement, and I showed the troubles that can occur in battle; we have made it march, and I have narrated with what impedimenta it can be surrounded while marching: and lastly we have quartered it: where not only a little repose from past hardship ought to be taken, but also to think about how the war ought to be concluded; for in the quarters, many things are discussed, especially if there remain enemies in the field, towns under suspicion, of which it is well to reassure oneself, and to capture those which are hostile. It is necessary, therefore, to come to these demonstrations, and to pass over this difficulty with that (same) glory with which we have fought up to the present. Coming down to particulars, therefore, that if it should happen to you that many men or many peoples should do something, which might be useful to you and very harmful to them, as would be the destruction of the walls of their City, or the sending of many of themselves into exile, it is necessary that you either deceive them in a way that everyone should believe he is affected, so that one not helping the other, all find themselves oppressed without a remedy, or rather, to command everyone what they ought to do on the same day, so that each one believing himself to be alone to whom the command is given, thinks of obeying it, and not of a remedy; and thus, without tumult, your command is executed by everyone. If you should have suspicion of the loyalty of any people, and should want to assure yourself and occupy them without notice, in order to disguise your design more easily, you cannot do better than to communicate to him some of your design, requesting his aid, and indicate to him you want to undertake another enterprise, and to have a mind alien to every thought of his: which will cause him not to think of his defense, as he does not believe you are thinking of attacking him, and he will give you the opportunity which will enable you to satisfy your desire easily. If you should have present in your army someone who keeps the enemy advised of your designs, you cannot do better if you want to avail yourself of his evil intentions, than to communicate to him those things you do not want to do, and keep silent those things you want to do, and tell him you are apprehensive of the things of which you are not apprehensive, and conceal those things of which you are apprehensive: which will cause the enemy to undertake some enterprise, in the belief that he knows your designs, in which you can deceive him and defeat him. If you should design ((as did Claudius Nero)) to decrease your army, sending aid to some friend, and they should not be aware of it, it is necessary that the encampment be not decreased, but to maintain entire all the signs and arrangements, making the same fires and posting the same guards as for the entire army. Likewise, if you should attach a new force to your army, and do not want the enemy to know you have enlarged it, it is necessary that the encampment be not increased, for it is always most useful to keep your designs secret. Whence Metellus, when he was with the armies in Spain, to one who asked him what he was going to do the next day, answered that if his shirt knew it, he would bum it. Marcus Crassus, to one who asked him when he was going to move his army, said: "do you believe you are alone in not hearing the trumpets?" If you should desire to learn the secrets of your enemy and know his arrangement, some used to send ambassadors, and with them men expert in war disguised in the clothing of the family, who, taking the opportunity to observe the enemy army, and consideration of his strengths and weaknesses, have given them the occasion to defeat him. Some have sent a close friend of theirs into exile, and through him have learned the designs of their adversary. You may also learn similar secrets from the enemy if you should take prisoners for this purpose. Marius, in the war he waged against Cimbri, in order to learn the loyalty of those Gauls who lived in Lombardy and were leagued with the Roman people, sent them letters, open and sealed: and in the open ones he wrote them that they should not open the sealed ones except at such a time: and before that time, he called for them to be returned, and finding them opened, knew their loyalty was not complete. Some Captains, when they were assaulted have not wanted to go to meet the enemy, but have gone to assail his country, and constrain him to return to defend his home. This often has turned out well, because your soldiers begin to win and fill themselves with booty and confidence, while those of the enemy become dismayed, it appearing to them that from being winners, they have become losers. So that to whoever has made this diversion, it has turned out well. But this can only be done by that man who has his country stronger than that of the enemy, for if it were otherwise, he would go on to lose. It has often been a useful thing for a Captain who finds himself besieged in the quarters of the enemy, to set in motion proceedings for an accord, and to make a truce with him for several days; which only any enemy negligent in every way will do, so that availing yourself of his negligence, you can easily obtain the opportunity to get out of his hands. Sulla twice freed himself from his enemies in this manner, and with this same deceit, Hannibal in Spain got away from the forces of Claudius Nero, who had besieged him.

It also helps one in freeing himself from the enemy to do something in addition to those mentioned, which keeps him at bay. This is done in two ways: either by assaulting him with part of your forces, so that intent on the battle, he gives the rest of your forces the opportunity to be able to save themselves, or to have some new incident spring up, which, by the novelty of the thing, makes him wonder, and for this reason to become apprehensive and stand still, as you know Hannibal did, who, being trapped by Fabius Maximus, at night placed some torches between the horns of many oxen, so that Fabius is suspense over this novelty, did not think further of impeding his passage. A Captain ought, among all the other actions of his, endeavor with every art to divide the forces of the enemy, either by making him suspicious of his men in whom he trusted, or by giving him cause that he has to separate his forces, and, because of this, become weaker. The first method is accomplished by watching the things of some of those whom he has next to him, as exists in war, to save his possessions, maintaining his children or other of his necessities without charge. You know how Hannibal, having burned all the fields around Rome, caused only those of Fabius Maximus to remain safe.

You know how Coriolanus, when he came with the army to Rome, saved the possessions of the Nobles, and burned and sacked those of the Plebs. When Metellus led the army against Jugurtha, all me ambassadors, sent to him by Jugurtha, were requested by him to give up Jugurtha as a prisoner; afterwards, writing letters to these same people on the same subject, wrote in such a way that in a little while Jugurtha became suspicious of all his counsellors, and in different ways, dismissed them. Hannibal, having taken refuge with Antiochus, the Roman ambassadors frequented him so much at home, that Antiochus becoming suspicious of him, did not afterwards have any faith in his counsels. As to dividing the enemy forces, there is no more certain way than to have one country assaulted by part of them (your forces), so that being constrained to go to defend it, they (of that country) abandon the war. This is the method employed by Fabius when his Army had encountered the forces of the Gauls, the Tuscans, Umbrians, and Samnites. Titus Didius, having a small force in comparison with those of the enemy, and awaiting a Legion from Rome, the enemy wanted to go out to meet it; so that in order that it should not do so, he gave out by voice throughout his army that he wanted to undertake an engagement with the enemy on the next day; then he took steps that some of the prisoners he had were given the opportunity to escape, who carried back the order of the Consul to fight on the next day, (and) caused the enemy, in order not to diminish his forces, not to go out to meet that Legion: and in this way, kept himself safe. Which method did not serve to divide the forces of the enemy, but to double his own. Some, in order to divide his (the enemy) forces, have employed allowing him to enter their country, and (in proof) allowed him to take many towns so that by placing guards in them, he diminished his forces, and in this manner having made him weak, assaulted and defeated him. Some others, when they wanted to go into one province, feigned making an assault on another, and used so much industry, that as soon as they extended toward that one where there was no fear they would enter, have overcome it before the enemy had time to succor it. For the enemy, as he is not certain whether you are to return back to the place first threatened by you, is constrained not to abandon the one place and succor the other, and thus often he does not defend either. In addition to the matters mentioned, it is important to a Captain when sedition or discord arises among the soldiers, to know how to extinguish it with art. The better way is to castigate the heads of this folly (error); but to do it in a way that you are able to punish them before they are able to become aware of it. The method is, if they are far from you, not to call only the guilty ones, but all the others together with them, so that as they do not believe there is any cause to punish them, they are not disobedient, but provide the opportunity for punishment. When they are present, one ought to strengthen himself with the guiltless, and by their aid, punish them. If there should be discord among them, the best way is to expose them to danger, which fear will always make them united. But, above all, what keeps the Army united, is the reputation of its Captain, which only results from his virtu, for neither blood (birth) or authority attain it without virtu. And the first thing a Captain is expected to do, is to see to it that the soldiers are paid and punished; for any time payment is missed, punishment must also be dispensed with, because you cannot castigate a soldier you rob, unless you pay him; and as he wants to live, he can abstain from being robbed. But if you pay him but do not punish him, he becomes insolent in every way, because you become of little esteem, and to whomever it happens, he cannot maintain the dignity of his position; and if he does not maintain it, of necessity, tumults and discords follow, which are the ruin of an Army. The Ancient Captains had a molestation from which the present ones are almost free, which was the interpretation of sinister omen to their undertakings; for if an arrow fell in an army, if the Sun or the Moon was obscured, if an earthquake occurred, if the Captain fell while either mounting or dismounting from his horse, it was interpreted in a sinister fashion by the soldiers, and instilled so much fear in them, that when they came to an engagement, they were easily defeated. And, therefore, as soon as such an incident occurred, the ancient Captains either demonstrated the cause of it or reduced it to its natural causes, or interpreted it to (favor) their own purposes. When Caesar went to Africa, and having fallen while he was putting out to sea, said, "Africa, I have taken you": and many have profited from an eclipse of the Moon and from earthquakes: these things cannot happen in our time, as much because our men are not as superstitious, as because our Religion, by itself, entirely takes away such ideas. Yet if it should occur, the orders of the ancients should be imitated. When, either from hunger, or other natural necessity, or human passion, your enemy is brought to extreme desperation, and, driven by it, comes to fight with you, you ought to remain within your quarters, and avoid battle as much as you can. Thus the Lacedemonians did against the Messinians: thus Caesar did against Afranius and Petreius. When Fulvius was Consul against the Cimbri, he had the cavalry assault the enemy continually for many days, and considered how they would issue forth from their quarters in order to pursue them; whence he placed an ambush behind the quarters of the Cimbri, and had them assaulted by the cavalry, and when the Cimbri came out of their quarters to pursue them, Fulvius seized them and plundered them. It has been very effective for a Captain, when his army is in the vicinity of the enemy army, to send his forces with the insignia of the enemy, to rob and burn his own country: whence the enemy, believing they were forces coming to their aid, also ran out to help them plunder, and, because of this, have become disorganized and given the adversary the faculty of overcoming them. Alexander of Epirus used these means fighting against the Illirici, and Leptenus the Syracusan against the Carthaginians, and the design succeeded happily for both. Many have overcome the enemy by giving him the faculty of eating and drinking beyond his means, feigning being afraid, and leaving his quarters full of wine and herds, and when the enemy had filled himself beyond every natural limit, they assaulted him and overcome him with injury to him. Thus Tamirus did against Cyrus, and Tiberius Gracchus against the Spaniards. Some have poisoned the wine and other things to eat in order to be able to overcome them more easily. A little while ago, I said I did not find the ancients had kept a night Watch outside, and I thought they did it to avoid the evils that could happen, for it has been found that sometimes, the sentries posted in the daytime to keep watch for the enemy, have been the ruin of him who posted them; for it has happened often that when they had been taken, and by force had been made to give the signal by which they called their own men, who, coming at the signal, have been either killed or taken. Sometimes it helps to deceive the enemy by changing one of your habits, relying on which, he is ruined: as a Captain had already done, who, when he wanted to have a signal made to his men indicating the coming of the enemy, at night with fire and in the daytime with smoke, commanded that both smoke and flame be made without any intermission; so that when the enemy came, he should remain in the belief that he came without being seen, as he did not see the signals (usually) made to indicate his discovery, made ((because of his going disorganized)) the victory of his adversary easier. Menno Rodius, when he wanted to draw the enemy from the strong places, sent one in the disguise of a fugitive, who affirmed that his army was full of discord, and that the greater part were deserting, and to give proof of the matter, had certain tumults started among the quarters: whence to the enemy, thinking he was able to break him, assaulted him and was routed.

In addition to the things mentioned, one ought to take care not to bring the enemy to extreme desperation; which Caesar did when he fought the Germans, who, having blocked the way to them, seeing that they were unable to flee, and necessity having made them brave, desired rather to undergo the hardship of pursuing them if they defended themselves. Lucullus, when he saw that some Macedonian cavalry who were with him, had gone over to the side of the enemy, quickly sounded the call to battle, and commanded the other forces to pursue it: whence the enemy, believing that Lucullus did not want to start the battle, went to attack the Macedonians with such fury, that they were constrained to defend themselves, and thus, against their will, they became fighters of the fugitives. Knowing how to make yourself secure of a town when you have doubts of its loyalty once you have conquered it, or before, is also important; which some examples of the ancients teach you. Pompey, when he had doubts of the Catanians, begged them to accept some infirm people he had in his army, and having sent some very robust men in the disguise of infirm ones, occupied the town. Publius Valerius, fearful of the loyalty of the Epidaurians, announced an amnesty to be held, as we will tell you, at a Church outside the town, and when all the public had gone there for the amnesty, he locked the doors, and then let no one out from inside except those whom he trusted. Alexander the Great, when he wanted to go into Asia and secure Thrace for himself, took with him all the chiefs of this province, giving them provisions, and placed lowborn men in charge of the common people of Thrace; and thus he kept the chiefs content by paying them, and the common people quiet by not having Heads who should disquiet them. But among all the things by which Captains gain the people over to themselves, are the examples of chastity and justice, as was that of Scipio in Spain when he returned that girl, beautiful in body, to her husband and father, which did more than arms in gaining over Spain. Caesar, when he paid for the lumber that he used to make the stockades around his army in Gaul, gained such a name for himself of being just, that he facilitated the acquisition of that province for himself. I do not know what else remains for me to talk about regarding such events, and there does not remain any part of this matter that has not been discussed by us. The only thing lacking is to tell of the methods of capturing and defending towns, which I am about to do willingly, if it is not painful for you now.

BATTISTA: Your humaneness is so great, that it makes us pursue our desires without being afraid of being held presumptuous, since you have offered it willingly, that we would be ashamed to ask you. Therefore we say only this to you, that you cannot do a greater or more thankful benefit to us than to furnish us this discussion. But before you pass on to that other matter, resolve a doubt for us: whether it is better to continue the war even in winter, as is done today, or wage it only in the summer, and go into quarters in the winter, as the ancients did.

FABRIZIO: Here, if there had not been the prudence of the questioner, some part that merits consideration would have been omitted. I tell you again that the ancients did everything better and with more prudence than we; and if some error is made in other things, all are made in matters of war. There is nothing more imprudent or more perilous to a Captain than to wage war in winter, and more dangerous to him who brings it, than to him who awaits it. The reason is this: all the industry used in military discipline, is used in order to be organized to undertake an engagement with your enemy, as this is the end toward which a Captain must aim, for the engagement makes you win or lose a war. Therefore, whoever know how to organize it better, and who has his army better disciplined, has the greater advantage in this, and can hope more to win it. On the other hand, there is nothing more inimical to organization than the rough sites, or cold and wet seasons; for the rough side does not allow you to use the plentitude (of your forces) according to discipline, and the cold and wet seasons do not allow you to keep your forces together, and you cannot have them face the enemy united, but of necessity, you must quarter them separately, and without order, having to take into account the castles, hamlets, and farm houses that receive you; so that all the hard work employed by you in disciplining your army is in vain. And do not marvel if they war in winter time today, for as the armies are without discipline, and do not know the harm that is done to them by not being quartered together, for their annoyance does not enable those arrangements to be made and to observe that discipline which they do not have. Yet, the injury caused by campaigning in the field in the winter ought to be observed, remembering that the French in the year one thousand five hundred three (1503) were routed on the Garigliano by the winter, and not by the Spaniards. For, as I have told you, whoever assaults has even greater disadvantage, because weather harms him more when he is in the territory of others, and wants to make war. Whence he is compelled either to withstand the inconveniences of water and cold in order to keep together, or to divide his forces to escape them. But whoever waits, can select the place to his liking, and await him (the enemy) with fresh forces, and can unite them in a moment, and go out to find the enemy forces who cannot withstand their fury. Thus were the French routed, and thus are those always routed who assault an enemy in winter time, who in itself has prudence. Whoever, therefore, does not want the forces, organization, discipline, and virtu, in some part, to be of value, makes war in the field in the winter time. And because the Romans wanted to avail themselves of all of these things, into which they put so much industry, avoided not only the winter time, but rough mountains and difficult places, and anything else which could impede their ability to demonstrate their skill and virtu. So this suffices to (answer) your question; and now let us come to treat of the attacking and defending of towns, and of the sites, and of their edifices.

Libro Sesto

LIBRO SESTO

ZANOBI: Io credo che sia bene, poichè si debbe mutare ragionamento, che Batista pigli l'ufficio suo e io deponga il mio; e verreno in questo caso ad imitare i buoni capitani, secondo che io intesi già quì dal signore; i quali pongono i migliori soldati dinanzi e di dietro all'esercito, parendo loro necessario avere davanti chi gagliardamente appicchi la zuffa e chi, di dietro, gagliardamente la sostenga. Cosimo, pertanto, cominciò questo ragionamento prudentemente, e Batista prudentemente lo finirà. Luigi ed io l'abbiamo in questi mezzi intrattenuto. E come ciascuno di noi ha presa la parte sua volentieri, così non credo che Batista sia per ricusarla.

BATISTA: Io mi sono lasciato governare infino a quì; così sono per lasciarmi per lo avvenire. Pertanto, signore, siate contento di seguitare i ragionamenti vostri e, se noi v'interrompiamo con queste pratiche, abbiateci per iscusati.

FABRIZIO: Voi mi fate, come già vi dissi, cosa gratissima; perchè questo vostro interrompermi non mi toglie fantasia, anzi me la rinfresca. Ma, volendo seguitare la materia nostra, dico come ormai è tempo che noi alloggiamo questo nostro esercito; perchè voi sapete che ogni cosa desidera il riposo, e sicuro, perchè riposarsi, e non si riposare sicuramente, non è riposo perfetto. Dubito bene che da voi non si fusse desiderato che io l'avessi prima alloggiato, dipoi fatto camminare e, in ultimo, combattere; e noi abbiamo fatto al contrario. A che ci ha indotto la necessità, perchè, volendo mostrare, camminando, come uno esercito si riduceva dalla forma del camminare a quella dell'azzuffarsi, era necessario avere prima mostro come si ordinava alla zuffa. Ma, tornando alla materia nostra, dico che, a volere che lo alloggiamento sia sicuro, conviene che sia forte e ordinato. Ordinato lo fa la industria del capitano, forte lo fa o il sito o l'arte. I Greci cercavano de' siti forti, e non si sarebbero mai posti dove non fusse stata o grotta o ripa di fiume o moltitudine di arbori, o altro naturale riparo che gli difendesse. Ma i Romani non tanto alloggiavano sicuri dal sito quanto dall'arte; nè mai sarebbero alloggiati ne' luoghi dove eglino non avessero potuto, secondo la disciplina loro, distendere tutte le loro genti. Di quì nasceva che i Romani potevano tenere una forma d'alloggiamento, perchè volevano che il sito ubbidisse a loro, non loro al sito. Il che non potevano osservare i Greci, perchè, ubbidendo al sito e variando i siti di forma, conveniva che ancora eglino variassero il modo dello alloggiare e la forma degli loro alloggiamenti. I Romani adunque, dove il sito mancava di fortezza, supplivano con l'arte e con la industria. E perchè io, in questa mia narrazione, ho voluto che si imitino i Romani, non

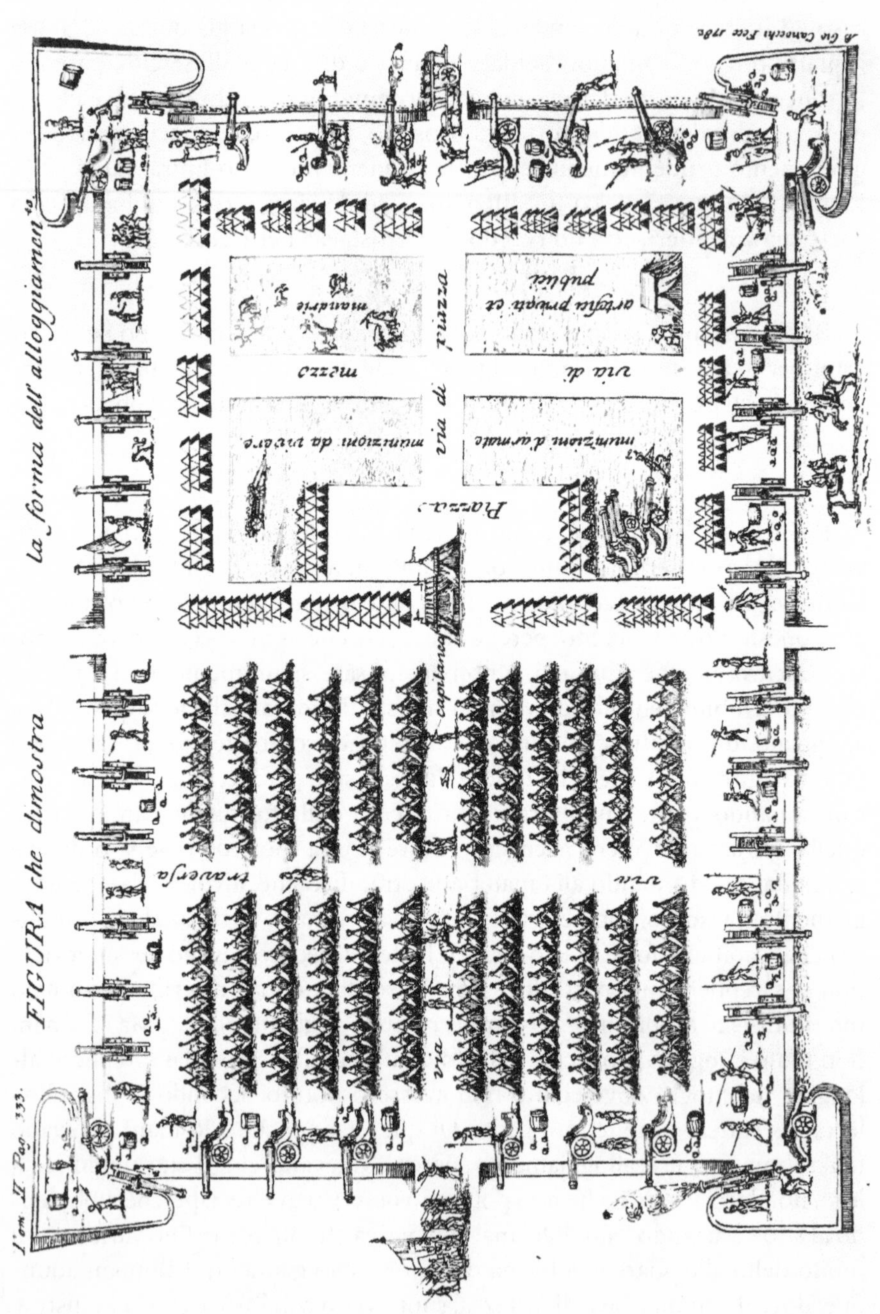
FIGURA che dimostra
la forma dell' alloggiamento
Piazza
via di mezzo
via di piazza
munizioni da vivere
munizioni d'armate
mandrie
artefici privati et publici
capitano
via traversa
via

mi partirò nel modo dello alloggiare da quegli, non osservando però al tutto gli ordini loro, ma prendendone quella parte quale mi pare che a' presenti tempi si confaccia. Io vi ho detto più volte come i Romani avevano, negli loro eserciti Consolari, due Legioni d'uomini Romani, i quali erano circa undicimila fanti e seicento cavalli; e di più avevano altri undicimila fanti di gente mandata dagli amici in loro aiuto: nè mai negli loro eserciti avevano più soldati forestieri che Romani, eccetto che di cavalli, i quali non si curavano passassero il numero delle Legioni loro; e, come in tutte l'azioni loro, mettevano le Legioni in mezzo e, gli ausiliari da lato. Il quale modo osservavano ancora nello alloggiarsi, come per voi medesimi avete potuto leggiere in quegli che scrivono le cose loro; e però io non sono per narrarvi appunto come quegli alloggiassero, ma per dirvi solo con quale ordine io al presente alloggerei il mio esercito, e voi allora conoscerete quale parte io abbia tratta da' modi Romani. Voi sapete che, all'incontro di due Legioni Romane, io ho preso due battaglioni di fanti, di semila fanti e trecento cavalli utili per battaglione, e in che battaglie, in che arme, in che nomi io li ho divisi. Sapete come nell'ordinare l'esercito a camminare e a combattere, io non ho fatto menzione d'altre genti, ma solo ho mostro come, raddoppiando le genti, non si aveva se non a raddoppiare gli ordini. Ma volendo, al presente, mostrarvi il modo dello alloggiare, mi pare da non stare solamente con due battaglioni, ma da ridurre insieme uno esercito giusto, composto, a similitudine del Romano, di due battaglioni e di altrettante genti ausiliarie. Il che fo, perchè la forma dello alloggiamento sia più perfetta, alloggiando uno esercito perfetto; la quale cosa nelle altre dimostrazioni non mi è paruta necessaria. Volendo adunque alloggiare uno esercito giusto di ventiquattro mila fanti e di duemila cavalli utili, essendo diviso in quattro battaglioni, due di gente propria e due di forestieri, terrei questo modo. Trovato il sito dove io volessi alloggiare, rizzerei la bandiera capitana e, intorno, le disegnerei uno quadro che avesse ogni faccia discoste da lei cinquanta braccia; delle quali qualunque, l'una guardasse l'una delle quattro regioni del cielo, come è levante, ponente, mezzodì e tramontana; tra il quale spazio vorrei che fusse lo alloggiamento del capitano. E perchè io credo che sia prudenza, e perchè così in buona parte facevano i Romani, dividerei gli armati da' disarmati e separerei gli uomini impediti dagli espediti. Io alloggerei tutti, o la maggior parte degli armati, dalla parte di levante, e i disarmati e gli impediti dalla parte di ponente, faccendo levante la testa e ponente le spalle dello alloggiamento e mezzodì e tramontana fussero i fianchi. E per distinguere gli alloggiamenti degli armati, terrei questo modo: io moverei una linea dalla bandiera capitana e la guiderei verso levante per uno spazio di secentottanta braccia. Farei dipoi due altre linee che mettessero in mezzo quella e fussero di lunghezza quanto quella, ma distante ciascuna da lei quindici braccia; nella estremità delle quali vorrei fusse la porta di levante, e lo spazio, che è tra le due estreme linee, facesse una via che andasse dalla porta allo alloggiamento del capitano; la quale verrebbe ad essere larga trenta braccia e lunga secento trenta, perchè cinquanta braccia ne occuperebbe lo alloggiamento del capitano, e chiamassesi questa la via capitana; movessesi dipoi un'altra via dalla porta di mezzodì infino alla porta di tramontana, e passasse per la testa della via capitana e rasente lo alloggiamento del capitano di verso levante, la quale fusse lunga mille dugento cinquanta braccia, perchè occuperebbe tutta la larghezza dello alloggiamento, e fusse larga pure trenta braccia e si chiamasse la via di croce. Disegnato adunque che fusse lo alloggiamento del capitano e queste due vie, si cominciassero a disegnare gli alloggiamenti de' due battaglioni proprj; e uno ne alloggerei da mano destra della via capitana, e uno da sinistra. E però, passato lo spazio che tiene la larghezza della via di croce, porrei trentadue alloggiamenti dalla parte sinistra della via capitana, e trentadue dalla parte destra, lasciando, tra il sedicesimo e diciassettesimo alloggiamento, uno spazio di trenta braccia; il che servisse a una via traversa che attraversasse per tutti gli alloggiamenti de' battaglioni, come nella distribuzione d'essi si vedrà. Di questi due ordini di alloggiamenti, ne' primi delle teste, che verrebbero ad essere appiccati alla via di croce, alloggerei i capi degli uomini d'arme; ne' quindici alloggiamenti che da ogni banda seguissono appresso, le loro genti d'arme, che, avendo ciascuno battaglione centocinquanta uomini d'arme, toccherebbe dieci uomini d'arme per alloggiamento. Gli spazi degli alloggiamenti de' capi fussero, per larghezza, quaranta e, per lunghezza, dieci braccia. E notisi che, qualunque volta io dico larghezza, significo lo spazio da mezzodì a tramontana, e, dicendo lunghezza, quello da ponente a levante. Quelli degli uomini d'arme fussero quindici braccia per lunghezza e trenta per larghezza. Negli altri quindici alloggiamenti che da ogni parte seguissono, i quali avrebbero il principio loro passata la via traversa e che avrebbero il medesimo spazio che quegli degli uomini d'arme, alloggerei i cavalli leggieri; de' quali, per essere centocinquanta, ne toccherebbe dieci cavalli per alloggiamento; e nel sedecimo che ne restasse, alloggerei il capo loro, dandogli quel medesimo spazio che si dà al capo degli uomini d'arme. E così gli alloggiamenti de' cavalli de' due battaglioni verrebbero a mettere in mezzo la via capitana e dare regola agli alloggiamenti delle fanterie, come io narrerò. Voi avete notato come io ho alloggiato i trecento cavalli d'ogni battaglione, con gli loro capi, in trentadue alloggiamenti posti in sulla via capitana e cominciati dalla via di Croce; come dal sedici al diciassette resta uno spazio di trenta braccia per fare una via traversa. Volendo pertanto alloggiare le venti battaglie che hanno i due battaglioni ordinarj, porrei gli alloggiamenti d'ogni due battaglie dietro gli alloggiamenti de' cavalli, che avessero ciascuno, di lunghezza, quindici braccia e, di larghezza, trenta come quegli de' cavalli, e fussero congiunti dalla parte di dietro, che toccassero l'uno l'altro. E in ogni primo alloggiamento, da ogni banda, che viene appiccato con la via di croce, alloggerei il connestabole d'una battaglia, che verrebbe a rispondere allo alloggiamento del capo degli uomini d'arme; ed avrebbe questo alloggiamento solo di spazio, per lunghezza, venti braccia e, per lunghezza, dieci. Negli altri quindici alloggiamenti, che da ogni banda seguissono dopo questo infino alla via traversa, alloggerei da ogni parte una battaglia di fanti, che, essendo quattrocentocinquanta, ne toccherebbe per alloggiamento trenta. Gli altri quindici alloggiamenti porrei continui, da ogni banda, a quegli de' cavalli leggieri, con gli medesimi spazi, dove alloggerei da ogni parte un'altra battaglia di fanti. E nell'ultimo alloggiamento porrei da ogni parte il connestabole della battaglia, che verrebbe ad essere appiccato con quello del capo de' cavalli leggieri, con lo spazio di dieci braccia per lunghezza e di venti per larghezza. E così questi due primi ordini di alloggiamenti sarebbero mezzi di cavalli e mezzi di fanti. E perchè io voglio, come nel suo luogo vi dissi, che questi cavalli sieno tutti utili, e per questo non avendo famigli che, nel governare i cavalli o nell'altre cose necessarie, gli sovvenissono, vorrei che questi fanti che alloggiassero dietro a' cavalli, fussero obligati ad aiutargli provvedere e governare a' padroni, e per questo fussero esenti dall'altre fazioni del campo; il quale modo era osservato da' Romani. Lasciato dipoi, dopo questi alloggiamenti, da ogni parte, uno spazio di trenta braccia che facesse via e chiamassesi l'una, prima via a mano destra, e l'altra, prima via a sinistra, porrei da ogni banda un altro ordine di trentadue alloggiamenti doppi, che voltassero la parte di dietro l'uno all'altro, con gli medesimi spazi che quegli ho detti, e divisi dopo i sedecimi nel medesimo modo, per fare la via traversa; dove alloggerei da ogni lato quattro battaglie di fanti con i Connestabili nelle teste da piè e da capo. Lasciato dipoi, da ogni lato, un altro spazio di trenta braccia che facesse via, che si chiamasse da una parte, la seconda via a man destra, e dall'altra parte, la seconda via a sinistra, metterei un altro ordine da ogni banda di trentadue alloggiamenti doppi, con le medesime distanze e divisioni; dove alloggerei da ogni lato altre quattro battaglie con gli loro Connestabili. E così verrebbero ad essere alloggiati, in tre ordini d'alloggiamenti per banda, i cavalli e le battaglie degli due battaglioni ordinarj, e metterebbero in mezzo la via capitana. I due battaglioni ausiliarj, perchè io gli fo composti de' medesimi uomini, alloggerei da ogni parte di questi due battaglioni ordinarj, con gli medesimi ordini di alloggiamenti, ponendo prima uno ordine di alloggiamenti doppi dove alloggiassono mezz'i cavalli e mezz'i fanti, discosto trenta braccia dagli altri, per fare una via che si chiamasse, l'una, terza via a man destra, e l'altra, terza via a sinistra. E dipoi farei da ogni lato due altri ordini di alloggiamenti, nel medesimo modo distinti e ordinati che sono quegli de' battaglioni ordinarj, che farebbero due altre vie; e tutte quante si chiamassono dal numero e dalla mano dov'elle fussero collocate. In modo che tutta quanta questa banda di esercito verrebbe ad essere alloggiata in dodici ordini d'alloggiamenti doppi, e in tredici vie, computando la via capitana e quella di croce. Vorrei restasse uno spazio, dagli alloggiamenti al fosso, di cento braccia intorno intorno. E se voi computerete tutti questi spazi, vedrete che dal mezzo dello alloggiamento del capitano alla porta di levante, sono seicento ottanta braccia. Restaci ora due spazi, de' quali, uno è dallo alloggiamento del capitano alla porta di mezzodì, l'altro è da quello alla porta di tramontana; che viene ad essere ciascuno, misurandolo dal punto del mezzo, secentoventicinque braccia. Tratto dipoi da ciascuno di questi spazi cinquanta braccia, che occupa l'alloggiamento del capitano, e quarantacinque braccia di piazza, che io gli voglio dare da ogni lato, e trenta braccia di via, che divida ciascuno di detti spazi nel mezzo, e cento braccia che si lasciano da ogni parte tra gli alloggiamenti e il fosso, resta da ogni banda uno spazio per alloggiamenti largo quattrocento braccia e lungo cento, misurando la lunghezza con lo spazio che tiene l'alloggiamento del capitano. Dividendo adunque per il mezzo dette lunghezze, si farebbe da ciascuna mano del capitano quaranta alloggiamenti lunghi cinquanta braccia e larghi venti, che verrebbero ad essere in tutto ottanta alloggiamenti; ne' quali si alloggerebbe i capi generali de' battaglioni, i camarlinghi, i maestri di campi e tutti quegli che avessono uffizio nell'esercito, lasciandone alcuno voto per gli forestieri che venissono e per quegli che militassero per grazia del capitano. Dalla parte di dietro dello alloggiamento del capitano moverei una via da mezzodì a tramontana, larga trenta braccia, e chiamassesi la via di testa, la quale verrebbe ad essere posta lungo gli ottanta alloggiamenti detti, perchè questa via e la via di croce metterebbero in mezzo l'alloggiamento del capitano e gli ottanta alloggiamenti che gli fussero da' fianchi. Da questa via di testa, e di rincontro allo alloggiamento del capitano, moverei un'altra via che andasse da quella alla porta di ponente, larga pure trenta braccia, e rispondesse per sito e per lunghezza alla via capitana e si chiamasse la via di piazza. Poste queste due vie ordinerei la piazza dove si facesse il mercato; la quale porrei nella testa della via di piazza, all'incontro allo alloggiamento del capitano, ed appiccata con la via di testa; e vorrei ch'ella fusse quadra, e le consegnerei novantasei braccia per quadro. E da man destra e man sinistra di detta piazza farei due ordini d'alloggiamenti, che ogni ordine avesse otto alloggiamenti doppi, i quali occupassero per lunghezza dodici braccia e per larghezza trenta; sì che verrebbero ad essere da ogni mano della piazza che la mettessono in mezzo,

sedici alloggiamenti che sarebbero in tutto trentadue; ne' quali alloggerei quegli cavalli che avanzassero a' battaglioni ausiliarj; e quando questi non bastassero, consegnerei loro alcuni di quegli alloggiamenti che mettono in mezzo il capitano, e massime di quegli che guardano verso i fossi. Restanci ora ad alloggiare le picche e i Veliti estraordinarj che ha ogni battaglione; che sapete, secondo l'ordine nostro, come ciascuno ha, oltre alle dieci battaglie, mille picche estraordinarie e cinquecento Veliti; talmente che i due battaglioni proprj hanno duemila picche estraordinarie e mille Veliti estraordinarj e gli ausiliarj quanto quegli; dimodochè si viene ancora avere ad alloggiare semila fanti, i quali tutti alloggerei nella parte di verso ponente e lungo i fossi. Dalla punta adunque della via di testa e di verso tramontana lasciando lo spazio delle cento braccia da quegli al fosso, porrei uno ordine di cinque alloggiamenti doppi, che tenessero tutti settantacinque braccia per lunghezza e sessanta per larghezza; tale che, divisa la larghezza, toccherebbe a ciascuno alloggiamento quindici braccia per lunghezza e trenta per larghezza. E perchè sarebbero dieci alloggiamenti, alloggerebbero trecento fanti, toccando ad ogni alloggiamento trenta fanti. Lasciando dipoi uno spazio di trentun braccio, porrei in simile modo e con simili spazi un altro ordine di cinque alloggiamenti doppi, e dipoi un altro, tanto che fossero cinque ordini di cinque alloggiamenti doppi; che verrebbero ad essere cinquanta alloggiamenti posti per linea retta dalla parte di tramontana, distanti tutti da' fossi cento braccia, che alloggerebbero mille cinquecento fanti. Voltando dipoi in sulla mano sinistra verso la porta di ponente, porrei in tutto quel tratto che fusse da loro a detta porta, cinque altri ordini d'alloggiamenti doppi, co' medesimi spazi e co' medesimi modi; vero è che dall'uno ordine all'altro non sarebbe più che quindici braccia di spazio, ne' quali si alloggerebbero ancora mille cinquecento fanti; e così dalla porta di tramontana a quella di ponente, come girano i fossi in cento alloggiamenti, compartiti in dieci ordini di cinque alloggiamenti doppi per ordine, si alloggerebbero tutte le picche e i Veliti estraordinarj de' battaglioni proprj. E così dalla porta di ponente a quella di mezzodì, come girano i fossi nel medesimo modo appunto in altri dieci ordini di dieci alloggiamenti per ordine, si alloggerebbero le picche e i Veliti estraordinarj de' battaglioni ausiliarii. I capi ovvero i Connestabili loro, potrebbero pigliarsi quegli alloggiamenti paressono loro più commo
fossi. L'artiglierie disporrei per tutto lungo gli argini
tro spazio che restasse di verso ponente, alloggerei t
impedimenti del campo. E hassi ad intendere che, s
pedimenti, come voi sapete, gli antichi intendevano
quelle cose che sono necessarie a uno esercito, fuor
legnaiuoli, fabbri, maniscalchi, scarpellini, ingegne

che quegli si potessero mettere nel numero degli armati, mandriani con le loro mandrie di castroni e buoi che per vivere dell'esercito bisognano e, di più, maestri d'ogni arte, insieme co' carriaggi pubblici delle munizioni pubbliche, pertinenti al vivere e allo armare. Nè distinguerei particolarmente questi alloggiamenti; solo disegnerei le vie che non avessero ad essere occupate da loro; dipoi gli altri spazi che tra le vie restassero, che sarebbero quattro, consegnerei in genere a tutti i detti impedimenti, cioè l'uno a' mandriani, l'altro agli artefici e maestranze, l'altro a carriaggi pubblici de' viveri, il quarto a quegli dell'armare. Le vie, le quali io vorrei si lasciassero senza occuparle, sarebbero la via di piazza, la via di testa e, di più, una via che si chiamasse la via di mezzo; la quale si partisse da tramontana e andasse verso mezzodì e passasse per il mezzo della via di piazza, la quale dalla parte di ponente facesse quello effetto che fa la via traversa dalla parte di levante. E, oltre a questo, una via che girasse dalla parte di dentro, lungo gli alloggiamenti delle picche e de' Veliti estraordinarj. E tutte queste vie fussero larghe trenta braccia. E l'artiglierie disporrei lungo i fossi del campo dalla parte di drento.

BATISTA: Io confesso non me ne intendere; nè credo anche che a dire così mi sia vergogna, non sendo questo mio esercizio. Nondimanco, questo ordine mi piace assai; solo vorrei che voi mi solveste questi dubbi: l'uno, perchè voi fate le vie e gli spazi d'intorno sì larghi; l'altro, che mi dà più noia, è, questi spazi che voi disegnate per gli alloggiamenti, come eglino hanno a essere usati.

FABRIZIO: Sappiate che io fo le vie tutte larghe trenta braccia, acciocchè per quelle possa andare una battaglia di fanti in ordinanza, che, se bene vi ricorda, vi dissi come per larghezza tiene ciascuna dalle venticinque alle trenta braccia. Che lo spazio il quale è tra il fosso e gli alloggiamenti sia cento braccia, è necessario, perchè vi si possano maneggiare le battaglie e l'artiglierie, condurre per quello le prede e, bisognando, avere spazio da ritirarsi con nuovi fossi e nuovi argini. Stanno meglio ancora gli alloggiamenti discosto assai da' fossi, per essere più discosto a' fuochi e alle altre cose che potesse trarre il nemico per offesa di quegli. Quanto alla seconda domanda, la intenzione mia non è che ogni spazio da me disegnato sia coperto da uno padiglione solo, ma sia usato come torna commodità a quegli che vi alloggiano, o con più o con manco tende, pure che non si esca de' termini di quello. E a disegre questi alloggiamenti, conviene sieno uomini pratichissimi e architettori nti; i quali, subito che il capitano ha eletto il luogo, gli sappiano dare e distribuirlo, distinguendo le vie, dividendo gli alloggiamenti con corde e con aste in modo, praticamente, che subito sieno ordinati e divisi. E a volere che non nasca confusione conviene voltare sempre il campo in uno medesimo modo, acciocchè ciascuno sappia in quale via, in quale spazio egli ha a trovare il suo alloggiamento. E questo si dee osservare in ogni tempo, in ogni luogo, e in maniera che paia una città mobile, la quale, dovunque va, porti seco le medesime vie, le medesime case e il medesimo aspetto; la quale cosa non possono osservare coloro i quali, cercando di siti forti, hanno a mutare forma secondo la variazione del sito. Ma i Romani facevano forte il luogo co' fossi, col vallo e con gli argini, perchè facevano uno steccato intorno al campo e, innanzi a quello, la fossa, per l'ordinario larga sei braccia e fonda tre; i quali spazi accrescevano, secondo che volevano dimorare in uno luogo e secondo che temevano il nemico. Io per me al presente non farei lo steccato, se già io non volessi vernare in uno luogo. Farei bene la fossa e l'argine non minore che la detta, ma maggiore secondo la necessità, farei ancora, rispetto all'artiglierie, sopra ogni canto dello alloggiamento un mezzo circulo di fosso, dal quale le artiglierie potessero battere per fianco chi venisse a combattere i fossi. In questo esercizio di sapere ordinare uno alloggiamento si deggiono ancora esercitare i soldati e fare, con quello, i ministri pronti a disegnarlo e i soldati presti a cognoscere i luoghi loro. Nè cosa alcuna è difficile, come nel luogo suo più largamente si dirà. Perchè io voglio passare per ora alle guardie del campo, perchè, senza la distribuzione delle guardie, tutte l'altre fatiche sarebbero vane.

BATISTA: Avanti che voi passiate alle guardie, vorrei mi dicessi: quando altri vuole porre gli alloggiamenti propinqui al nemico, che modi si tengono? perchè io non so come vi sia tempo a potergli ordinare senza pericolo.

FABRIZIO: Voi avete a sapere questo: che niuno capitano alloggia propinquo al nemico, se non quello che è disposto fare la giornata qualunque volta il nemico voglia; e quando altri è così disposto, non ci è pericolo se non ordinario; perchè si ordinano le due parti dell'esercito a fare la giornata, e l'altra parte fa gli alloggiamenti. I Romani in questo caso davano questa via di fortificare gli alloggiamenti a' Triari, ed i Principi e gli Astati stavano in arme. Questo facevano perchè, essendo i Triari gli ultimi a combattere, erano a tempo, se il nemico veniva, a lasciare l'opera e pigliare l'armi e entrare ne' luoghi loro. Voi, a imitazione de' Romani, avresti a far fare gli alloggiamenti a quelle battaglie che voi voleste mettere nella ultima parte dell'esercito in luogo de' Triarj. Ma torniamo a ragionare delle guardie. E' non mi pare avere trovato, appresso agli antichi, che per guardare il campo la notte tenessero guardie fuora de' fossi discosto, come si usa oggi, le quali chiamano ascolte. Il che credo facessero, pensando che facilmente l'esercito ne potesse restare ingannato per la difficultà che è nel rivederle, e per potere essere quelle o corrotte o oppresse dal nemico; in modo che fidarsi o in parte o in tutto di loro giudicavano pericoloso. E però tutta la forza della guardia era dentro a' fossi; la quale facevano con una diligenza e con uno ordine grandissimo, punendo capitalmente qualunque da tale ordine deviava. Il quale, come era da loro ordinato non vi dirò altrimenti, per non vi tediare, potendo per voi medesimi vederlo quando, infino a ora, non l'aveste veduto. Dirò solo brevemente quello che per me si farebbe. Io farei stare per l'ordinario ogni notte il terzo dell'esercito armato, e di quello la quarta parte sempre in piè; la quale sarebbe distribuita per tutti gli argini e per tutti i luoghi dell'esercito con guardie doppie poste da ogni quadro di quello; delle quali, parte stessono saldi, parte continuamente andassero dall'uno canto dello alloggiamento all'altro. E questo ordine che io dico, osserverei ancora di giorno quando io avessi il nemico propinquo. Quanto a dare il nome, e quello rinnovare ogni sera e fare l'altre cose che in simili guardie si usano, per essere cose note, non ne parlerò altrimenti. Solo ricorderò una cosa, per essere importantissima e che genera molto bene osservandola, e, non la osservando, molto male; la quale è, che si usi gran diligenza di chi la sera non alloggia dentro al campo e di chi vi viene di nuovo. E questo è facile cosa rivedere a chi alloggia con quello ordine che noi abbiamo disegnato; perchè, avendo ogni alloggiamento il numero degli uomini determinato, è facile cosa vedere se vi manca o se vi avanza uomini, e, quando ve ne manca senza licenza, punirgli come fuggitivi, e, se ve ne avanza, intendere chi sono, quello che fanno e dell'altre condizioni loro. Questa diligenza fa che il nemico non può, se non con difficultà, tenere pratica co' tuoi capi ed essere consapevole de' tuoi consigli. La quale cosa se da' Romani non fusse stata osservata con diligenza, non poteva Claudio Nerone, avendo Annibale appresso, partirsi da' suoi alloggiamenti ch'egli aveva in Lucania, e andare e tornare dalla Marca, senza che Annibale ne avesse presentito alcuna cosa. Ma egli non basta fare questi ordini buoni, se non si fanno con una gran severità osservare; perchè non è cosa che voglia tanta osservanza, quanta si ricerca in uno esercito. Però le leggi a fortificazione di quello deggiono essere aspre e dure, e lo esecutore durissimo. I Romani punivano di pena capitale chi mancava nelle guardie, chi abbandonava il luogo che gli era dato a combattere, chi portava cosa alcuna di nascosto fuora degli alloggiamenti, se alcuno dicesse avere fatta qualche cosa egregia nella zuffa e non l'avesse fatta, se alcuno avesse combattuto fuora del comandamento del capitano, se alcuno avesse per timore gittato via l'armi. E quando egli occorreva che una coorte o una Legione intera avesse fatto simile errore, per non gli fare morire tutti, gl'imborsavano tutti e ne traevano la decima parte, e quegli morivano. La quale pena era in modo fatta che, se ciascuno non la sentiva, ciascuno nondimeno la temeva. E perchè dove sono le punizioni grandi, vi deggiono essere ancora i premi, a volere che gli uomini ad un tratto temano o sperino, egli avevano proposti premj a ogni egregio fatto: come a colui che, combattendo, salvava la vita ad uno suo cittadino, a chi prima saliva sopra il muro delle terre nemiche, a chi prima entrava negli alloggiamenti de' nemici, a chi avesse, combattendo, ferito o morto il nemico, a chi lo avesse gittato da cavallo. E così qualunque atto virtuoso era da' Consoli riconosciuto e premiato e, pubblicamente, da ciascuno lodato; e quegli che conseguitavano doni per alcuna di queste cose, oltre alla gloria e alla fama che ne acquistavano tra' soldati, poi ch'egli erano tornati nella patria, con solenni pompe e con gran dimostrazioni tra gli amici e parenti le dimostravano. Non è adunque maraviglia se quel popolo acquistò tanto imperio, avendo tanta osservanza di pena e di merito verso di quegli che, o per loro bene o per loro male operare, meritassono o lode o biasimo; delle quali cose converrebbe osservare la maggior parte. Nè mi pare da tacere un modo di pena da loro osservato; il quale era che, come il reo era, innanzi al tribuno o il Consolo, convinto, era da quello leggiermente con una verga percosso; dopo la quale percossa, al reo era lecito fuggire e a tutti i soldati ammazzarlo; in modo che subito ciascuno gli traeva o sassi o dardi, o con altre armi lo percoteva; di qualità ch'egli andava poco vivo e radissimi ne campavano; e a quegli tali campati non era lecito tornare a casa, se non con tanti incommodi e ignominie, ch'egli era molto meglio morire. Vedesi questo modo essere quasi osservato da' Svizzeri, i quali fanno i condannati ammazzare popularmente dagli altri soldati. Il che è bene considerato e ottimamente fatto; perchè, a volere che uno non sia defensore d'uno reo, il maggiore rimedio che si truovi è farlo punitore di quello; perchè con altro rispetto lo favorisce e con altro desiderio brama la punizione sua, quando egli proprio ne è esecutore, che quando la esecuzione perviene ad uno altro. Volendo adunque che uno non sia negli errori sua favorito da uno popolo, gran rimedio è fare che il popolo l'abbia egli a giudicare. A fortificazione di questo si può addurre lo esemplo di Manlio Capitolino; il quale, essendo accusato dal senato, fu difeso dal popolo infino a tanto che non ne diventò giudice; ma, diventato arbitro nella causa sua, lo condannò a morte. È adunque un modo di punire questo da levare i tumulti e da fare osservare la giustizia. E perchè a frenare gli uomini armati non bastono nè il timore delle leggi, nè quello degli uomini, vi aggiugnevano gli antichi l'autorità di Iddio; e però con cerimonie grandissime facevano a' loro soldati giurare l'osservanza della disciplina militare, acciocchè contrafaccendo, non solamente avessero a temere le leggi e gli uomini, ma Iddio; e usavano ogni industria per empiergli di religione.

BATISTA: Permettevano i Romani che negli loro eserciti fussero femmine, o vi si usasse di questi giuochi oziosi che si usano oggi?

FABRIZIO: Proibivano l'uno e l'altro. E non era questa proibizione molto difficile, perchè egli erano tanti gli esercizj ne' quali tenevano ogni dì i soldati, ora particolarmente, ora generalmente occupati, che non restava loro tempo a pensare o a Venere o a' giuochi, nè ad altre cose che facciano i soldati sediziosi e inutili.

BATISTA: Piacemi. Ma ditemi: quando l'esercito si aveva a levare, che ordine tenevano?

FABRIZIO: Sonava la tromba capitana tre volte. Al primo suono si levavano le tende e facevano le balle; al secondo caricavano le some; al terzo movevano in quel modo dissi di sopra, con gli impedimenti dopo, ogni parte di armati, mettendo le Legioni in mezzo. E però voi avresti a fare muovere uno battaglione ausiliare e, dopo quello, i suoi particolari impedimenti e, con quegli la quarta parte degli impedimenti pubblici; che sarebbero tutti quegli che fussero alloggiati in uno di quegli quadri che poco fa dimostrammo. E però converrebbe avere ciascuno di este consegnato ad uno battaglione, acciocchè, movendosi l'esercito, ciascuno sapesse quale luogo fusse il suo nel camminare. E così debbe andare via ogni battaglione co' suoi impedimenti proprj, e con la quarta parte de' pubblici a spalle, in quel modo dimostrammo che camminava l'esercito Romano.

BATISTA: Nel porre lo alloggiamento avevano eglino altri rispetti che quegli avete detti?

FABRIZIO: Io vi dico di nuovo che i Romani volevano, nello alloggiare, potere tenere la consueta forma del modo loro; il che per osservare, non avevano alcuno rispetto. Ma quanto all'altre considerazioni, ne avevano due principali: l'una, di porsi in luogo sano; l'altra, di porsi dove il nemico non lo potesse assediare e torgli la via dell'acqua o delle vettovaglie. Per fuggire adunque le infermità, ei fuggivano i luoghi paludosi o esposti a' venti nocivi. Il che conoscevano non tanto dalle qualità del sito quanto dal viso degli abitatori, e quando gli vedevano male colorati o bolsi, o di altra infezione ripieni, non vi alloggiavano. Quanto all'altra parte di non essere assediato, conviene considerare la natura del luogo, dove sono posti gli amici e dove i nemici, e da questo fare tua coniettura se tu puoi essere assediato o no. E però conviene che il capitano sia peritissimo de' siti de' paesi, e abbia intorno assai che ne abbiano la medesima perizia. Fuggesi ancora le malattie e la fame, col non fare disordinare l'esercito; perchè, a volerlo mantenere sano, conviene operare che i soldati dormano sotto le tende, che si alloggi dove sieno arbori che facciano ombra, dove sia legname da potere cuocere il cibo, che non cammini per il caldo. E però bisogna trarlo dello alloggiamento innanzi dì, la state, e di verno guardarsi che non cammini per le nevi e per i ghiacci senza avere commodità di fare fuoco, e non manchi del vestito necessario e non bea acque malvage. Quelli che ammalano a caso, farli curare da' medici; perchè uno capitano non ha rimedio quando egli ha a combattere con le malattie e col nemico. Ma niuna cosa è tanto utile a mantenere l'esercito sano quanto è l'esercizio; e però gli antichi ciascuno dì gli facevano esercitare. Donde si vede quanto questo esercizio vale; perchè, negli alloggiamenti, ti fa sano e, nelle zuffe, vittorioso. Quanto alla fame, non solamente è necessario vedere che il nemico non t'impedisca la vettovaglia, ma provvedere donde tu abbia a averla, e vedere che quella che tu hai, non si sperda. E però ti conviene averne sempre in munizione coll'esercito per uno mese, e dipoi tassare i vicini amici che giornalmente te ne provveggano; farne munizioni in qualche luogo forte e, sopra tutto, dispensarla con diligenza, dandone ogni giorno a ciascuno una ragionevole misura; e osservare in modo questa parte ch'ella non ti disordini, perchè ogni altra cosa nella guerra si può col tempo vincere, questa sola col tempo vince te. Nè sarà mai alcuno tuo nemico, il quale ti possa superare con la fame, che cerchi vincerti col ferro; perchè, se la vittoria non è sì onorevole, ella è più sicura e più certa. Non può adunque fuggire la fame quell'esercito che non è osservante di giustizia e che licenziosamente consuma quello che gli pare; perchè l'uno disordine fa che la vettovaglia non vi viene, l'altro, che la venuta inutilmente si consuma. Però ordinavano gli antichi che si consumasse quella che davano e in quel tempo che volevano; perchè niuno soldato mangiava se non quando il capitano. Il che quanto sia osservato da' moderni eserciti lo sa ciascuno, e meritamente non si possono chiamare ordinati e sobrj come gli antichi, ma licenziosi ed ebbriachi.

BATISTA: Voi dicesti nel principio dello ordinare lo alloggiamento, che non volevi stare solamente in su due battaglioni, ma che ne volevi torre quattro, per mostrare come uno esercito giusto si alloggiava. Però vorrei mi dicessi due cose: l'una, quando io avessi più o meno gente, come io avessi ad alloggiare: l'altra, che numero di soldati vi basterebbe a combattere contro a qualunque nemico?

FABRIZIO: Alla prima domanda vi rispondo che, se l'esercito è più o meno quattro o semila fanti si lieva od aggiugne ordini di alloggiamenti tanto che basti; e con questo modo si può ire nel più e nel meno in infinito. Nondimeno i Romani, quando congiugnevano insieme due eserciti Consolari, facevano due alloggiamenti e voltavano la parte de' disarmati l'una all'altra. Quanto alla seconda domanda, vi replico come l'esercito ordinario Romano era intorno a ventiquattromila soldati; ma quando maggiore forza gli premeva, i più che ne mettevano insieme erano cinquantamila. Con questo numero si opposono a dugentomila Francesi, che gli assaltarono dopo la guerra prima ch'egli ebbero co' Cartaginesi. Con questo medesimo si opposono ad Annibale; e avete a notare che i Romani e i Greci hanno fatto la guerra co' pochi, affortificati dall'ordine e dall'arte; gli occidentali o gli orientali l'hanno fatta con la moltitudine, ma l'una di queste nazioni si serve del furore naturale, come sono gli occidentali, l'altra della grande ubbidienza che quegli uomini hanno agli loro re. Ma in Grecia e in Italia, non essendo il furore naturale nè la naturale reverenza verso i loro re, è stato necessario voltarsi alla disciplina; la quale è di tanta forza, ch'ella ha fatto che i pochi hanno potuto vincere il furore e la naturale ostinazione degli assai. Però vi dico che, volendo imitare i Romani e i Greci, non si debbe passare il numero di cinquantamila soldati, anzi piuttosto torne meno; perchè i più fanno confusione, nè lasciano osservare la disciplina e gli ordini imparati. E Pirro usava dire che con quindicimila uomini voleva assalire il mondo. Ma passiamo ad un'altra parte. Noi abbiamo a questo nostro esercito fatta vincere una giornata, e mostro i travagli che in essa zuffa possono occorrere; abbiànlo fatto camminare, e narrato da quali impedimenti, camminando, egli possa essere circumvenuto; e in fine lo abbiamo alloggiato dove, non solamente si dee pigliare un poco di requie delle passate fatiche, ma ancora pensare come si dee finire la guerra perchè negli alloggiamenti si maneggia di molte cose, massime restandoti ancora de' nemici alla campagna e delle terre sospette, delle quali è bene assicurarsi, e quelle che sono nemiche espugnare. Però è necessario venire a queste dimostrazioni e passare queste difficultà con quella gloria che infino a quì abbiamo militato. Però, scendendo a' particolari, dico che, se ti occorresse che assai uomini o assai popoli facessero una cosa che fusse a te utile e a loro di danno grande, come sarebbe o disfare le mura delle loro città, o mandare in esilio molti di loro, ti è necessario o ingannargli in modo che ciascuno non creda che tocchi a lui, tanto che, non sovvenendo l'uno all'altro, si truovino dipoi oppressi tutti senza rimedio; ovvero a tutti comandare quello che deggiono fare in uno medesimo giorno, acciocchè, credendo ciascuno essere solo a chi sia il comandamento fatto, pensi ad ubbidire e non a' rimedi; e così fia senza tumulto da ciascuno il tuo comandamento eseguito. Se tu avessi sospetta la fede di alcuno popolo e volessi assicurartene e occuparlo allo improvvisto, per potere colorire il disegno tuo più facilmente, non puoi far meglio che comunicare con quello alcuno tuo disegno, richiederlo di aiuto, e mostrare di voler fare altra impresa e di avere lo animo alieno da ogni pensiero di lui; il che farà che non penserà alla difesa sua, non credendo che tu pensi a offenderlo, e ti darà commodità di potere facilmente soddisfare al tuo desiderio. Quando tu presentissi che fusse nel tuo esercito alcuno che tenesse avvisato il tuo nemico de' tuoi disegni, non puoi fare meglio, a volerti valere del suo malvagio animo, che comunicargli quelle cose che tu non vuoi fare e quelle che tu vuoi fare, tacere, e dire di dubitare delle cose che tu non dubiti e, quelle di che tu dubiti, nascondere, il che farà fare al nemico qualche impresa, credendo sapere i disegni tuoi, dove facilmente tu lo potrai ingannare e opprimere. Se tu disegnassi, come fece Claudio Nerone, diminuire il tuo esercito, mandando aiuto ad alcuno amico, e che il nemico non se ne accorgesse, è necessario non diminuire gli alloggiamenti, ma mantenere i segni e gli ordini interi, faccendo i medesimi fuochi e le medesime guardie per tutto. Così se col tuo esercito si congiungesse nuova gente, e volessi che il nemico non sapesse che tu fossi ingrossato, è necessario non accrescere gli alloggiamenti; perchè, tenere secreto le azioni e i disegni suoi, fu sempre utilissimo. Donde Metello, essendo con gli eserciti in Ispagna, a uno che lo domandò quello che voleva fare l'altro giorno, rispose che se la camicia sua lo sapesse, l'arderebbe. Marco Crasso a uno che lo domandava quando moverebbe l'esercito, disse: Credi tu essere solo a non sentire le trombe? Se tu desiderassi intendere i secreti del tuo nemico e conoscere gli ordini suoi, hanno usato alcuni mandar gli ambasciadori e con quegli, sotto veste di famigli, uomini peritissimi in guerra; i quali, presa occasione di vedere l'esercito nemico e considerare le fortezze e le debolezze sue gli hanno dato occasione di superarlo. Alcuni hanno mandato in esilio uno loro familiare e, mediante quello, conosciuti i disegni dello avversario suo. Intendonsi ancora simili segreti da' nemici, quando a questo effetto ne pigliassi prigioni. Mario, nella guerra che fece co' Cimbri per conoscere la fede di quegli Franciosi che allora abitavano la Lombardia ed erano collegati col popolo Romano, mandò loro lettere aperte e suggellate; e nelle aperte scriveva che non aprissero le suggellate se non al tale tempo; e innanzi a quel tempo ridomandandole e trovandole aperte, conobbe la fede loro non essere intera. Hanno alcuni capitani, essendo assaltati, non voluto ire a trovare il nemico, ma sono iti ad assalire il paese suo e costrettolo a tornare a difendere la casa sua. Il che molte volte è riuscito bene, perchè i tuoi soldati cominciano a vincere, a empiersi di preda e di confidenza; quegli del nemico si sbigottiscono, parendo loro di vincitori diventare perditori. In modo che a chi ha fatta questa diversione, molte volte è riuscito bene. Ma solo si può fare per colui che ha il suo paese più forte che non è quel del nemico, perchè, quando fusse altrimenti, andrebbe a perdere. È stata spesso cosa utile a uno capitano che si truova assediato negli alloggiamenti dal nemico, muovere pratica d'accordo e fare triegua con seco per alcuno giorno; il che suole fare i nemici più negligenti in ogni azione, tale che, valendoti della negligenza loro, puoi avere facilmente occasione di uscire loro delle mani. Per questa via Silla si liberò due volte da' nemici, e con questo medesimo inganno Asdrubale in Ispagna uscì delle forze di Claudio Nerone, il quale lo aveva assediato. Giova ancora, a liberarsi dalle forze del nemico, fare qualche cosa, oltre alle dette, che lo tenga a bada. Questo si fa in due modi: o assaltarlo con parte delle forze, acciocchè, intento a quella zuffa, dia commodità al resto delle tue genti di potersi salvare; o fare surgere qualche nuovo accidente che, per la novità della cosa lo faccia maravigliare e per questa cagione stare dubbio e fermo; come voi sapete che fece Annibale che, essendo rinchiuso da Fabio Massimo, pose di notte facelline accese tra le corna di molti buoi, tanto che Fabio, sospeso da questa novità, non pensò impedirgli altrimenti il passo. Debbe uno capitano, tra tutte l'altre sue azioni, con ogni arte ingegnarsi di dividere le forze del nemico, o col fargli sospetti i suoi uomini ne' quali confida, o con dargli cagione ch'egli abbia a separare le sue genti e, per questo, diventare più debole. Il primo modo si fa col riguardare le cose di alcuno di quegli ch'egli ha appresso, come è conservare nella guerra le sue genti e le sue possessioni, rendendogli i figliuoli o altri suoi necessari senza taglia. Voi sapete che Annibale, avendo abbruciato intorno a Roma tutti i campi, fece solo restare salvi quegli di Fabio Massimo. Sapete come Coriolano, venendo coll'esercito a Roma, conservò le possessioni dei nobili e quelle della plebe arse e saccheggiò. Metello, avendo l'esercito contro a Iugurta, tutti gli oratori che da Iugurta gli erano mandati, erano richiesti da lui che gli dessono Iugurta prigione: e a quegli medesimi scrivendo dipoi della medesima materia lettere, operò in modo che in poco tempo Iugurta insospettì di tutti i suoi consiglieri e in diversi modi gli spense. Essendo Annibale rifuggito ad Antioco, gli oratori Romani lo praticarono tanto domesticamente, che Antioco, insospettito di lui, non prestò dipoi più fede a' suoi consigli. Quanto al dividere le genti nemiche, non ci è il più certo modo che fare assaltare il paese di parte di quelle acciocchè, essendo costrette andare a difendere quello, abbandonino la guerra. Questo modo tenne Fabio, avendo all'incontro del suo esercito le forze de' Francesi, de' Toscani, Umbri e Sanniti. Tito

Didio, avendo poche genti rispetto a quelle de' nemici e aspettando una legione da Roma e volendo i nemici ire ad incontrarla, acciò non vi andassero, dette voce per tutto il suo esercito di volere l'altro giorno fare giornata co' nemici; dipoi tenne modi che alcuni de' prigioni ch'egli aveva, ebbono occasione di fuggirsi; i quali, referendo l'ordine del Consolo di combattere l'altro giorno fecero che i nemici, per non diminuire le loro forze, non andarono ad incontrare quella Legione; e per questa via si condusse salva; il quale modo non servì a dividere le forze de' nemici, ma a duplicare le sue. Hanno usato alcuni, per dividere le sue forze, lasciarlo entrare nel paese suo e, in pruova, lasciatogli pigliare di molte terre, acciocchè, mettendo, in quelle, guardie diminuisca le sue forze; e per questa via avendolo fatto debole, assaltatolo e vinto. Alcuni altri, volendo andare in una provincia, hanno finto di volerne assaltare un'altra e usata tanta industria che, subito entrati in quella dove e' non si dubitava ch'egli entrassono, l'hanno prima vinta che il nemico sia stato a tempo a soccorrerla. Perchè il nemico tuo, non essendo certo se tu se' per tornare indietro al luogo prima da te minacciato, è costretto non abbandonare l'uno luogo e soccorrere l'altro; e così spesso non difende nè l'uno nè l'altro. Importa, oltre alle cose dette, a uno capitano, se nasce sedizione o discordia tra' soldati, saperle con arte spegnere. Il migliore modo è gastigare i capi degli errori; ma farlo in modo che tu gli abbia prima oppressi che essi se ne sieno potuti accorgere. Il modo è: se sono discosto da te, non chiamare solo i nocenti, ma insieme con loro tutti gli altri, acciocchè, non credendo che sia per cagione di punirgli, non diventino contumaci, ma dieno commodità alla punizione. Quando sieno presenti, si dee farsi forte con quegli che non sono in colpa, e, mediante lo aiuto loro, punirgli. Quando ella fusse discordia tra loro, il migliore modo è presentargli al pericolo, la quale paura gli suole sempre rendere uniti. Ma quello che sopra ogni altra cosa tiene l'esercito unito, è la reputazione del capitano, la quale solamente nasce dalla virtù sua, perchè nè sangue nè autorità la dette mai senza la virtù. E la prima cosa che a uno capitano si aspetta a fare, è tenere i suoi soldati puniti e pagati; perchè, qualunque volta manca il pagamento, conviene che manchi la punizione; perchè tu non puoi gastigare uno soldato che rubi, se tu non lo paghi, nè quello, volendo vivere, si può astenere dal rubare. Ma se tu lo paghi e non lo punisci, diventa in ogni modo insolente, perchè tu diventi di poca stima, dove chi capita non può mantenere la dignità del suo grado; e non lo mantenendo, ne seguita di necessità il tumulto e le discordie, che sono la rovina d'uno esercito. Avevano gli antichi capitani una molestia della quale i presenti ne sono quasi liberi, la quale era di interpretare a loro proposito gli auguri sinistri; perchè se cadeva una saetta in uno esercito, s'egli scurava il sole o la luna, se veniva un tremuoto, se il capitano o nel montare o nello scendere da cavallo cadeva, era da' soldati interpretato sinistramente, e generava in loro tanta paura che, venendo alla giornata, facilmente l'arebbero perduta. E però gli antichi capitani, tosto che uno simile accidente nasceva, o e' mostravano la cagione di esso e lo riducevano a cagione naturale, o e' l'interpretavano a loro proposito. Cesare, cadendo in Affrica nello uscire di nave, disse: Affrica io t'ho presa. E molti hanno renduto la cagione dello oscurare della luna e de' tremuoti; le quali cose ne' tempi nostri non possono accadere, sì per non essere i nostri uomini tanto superstiziosi, sì perchè la nostra religione rimuove in tutto da se tali opinioni. Pure, quando egli occorresse, si dee imitare gli ordini degli antichi. Quando o fame o altra naturale necessità o umana passione ha condotto il nemico tuo ad una ultima disperazione e, cacciato da quella, venga a combattere teco, dèi starti dentro a' tuoi alloggiamenti e, quanto è in tuo potere, fuggire la zuffa. Così fecero i Lacedemoni contro a' Messeni, così fece Cesare contro ad Afranio e Petrejo. Essendo Fulvio Consolo contro a' Cimbri, fece molti giorni continui alla sua cavalleria assaltare i nemici, e considerò come quegli uscivano degli alloggiamenti per seguitargli; donde che quello pose uno agguato dietro agli alloggiamenti de' Cimbri e, fattigli assaltare da' cavalli e i Cimbri uscendo degli alloggiamenti per seguitargli, Fulvio gli occupò e saccheggiogli. È stato di grande utilità ad alcuno capitano, avendo l'esercito propinquo all'esercito nemico, mandare le sue genti con le insegne nemiche a rubare ed ardere il suo paese proprio; donde che i nemici hanno creduto che sieno genti che vengano loro in aiuto, e sono ancora essi corsi ad aiutare far loro la preda, e per questo disordinatisi, e dato facultà allo avversario loro di vincergli. Questo termine usò Alessandro di Epiro combattendo contra agli Illirici e Leptene siracusano contra a' Cartaginesi; ed all'uno ed all'altro riuscì il disegno facilmente. Molti hanno vinto il nemico, dando a quello facultà di mangiare e bere fuora di modo, simulando di avere paura e lasciando gli alloggiamenti suoi pieni di vino e di armenti; de' quali, sendosi ripieno il nemico sopra ogni uso naturale lo hanno assaltato e, con suo danno, vinto. Così fece Tamiri contra a Ciro e Tiberio Gracco contra agli Spagnuoli. Alcuni hanno avvelenati i vini e l'altre cose da cibarsi per potere più facilmente vincergli. Io dissi poco fa come io non trovavo che gli antichi tenessero la notte ascolte fuora, e stimavo lo facessero per schifare i mali che ne poteva nascere; perchè si truova che, non ch'altro, le velette che pongono il giorno a velettare il nemico, sono state cagioni della rovina di colui che ve le pose, perchè molte volte è accaduto che, essendo state prese, è stato loro fatto fare per forza il cenno col quale avevano a chiamare i suoi; i quali al segno venendo, sono stati o morti o presi. Giova ad ingannare il nemico qualche volta variare una tua consuetudine; in sulla quale fondandosi quello, ne rimane rovinato; come fece già uno capitano il quale, solendo far fare cenno a' suoi per la venuta de' nemici, la notte, col fuoco e, il dì, col fumo, comandò che senza alcuna intermissione si facesse fumo e fuoco, e dipoi, sopravvenendo il nemico, si restasse; il quale, credendo venire senza essere visto, non veggendo fare segni da essere scoperto, fece, per ire disordinato, più facile la vittoria al suo avversario. Mennone Rodio, volendo trarre de' luoghi forti l'esercito nemico mandò uno, sotto colore di fuggitivo, il quale affermava come il suo esercito era in discordia e che la maggior parte di quello si partiva; e per dare fede alla cosa, fece fare in pruova certi tumulti tra gli alloggiamenti, donde che il nemico pensando di poterlo rompere, assaltandolo, fu rotto. Debbesi, oltre alle cose dette, avere riguardo di non condurre il nemico in ultima disperazione; a che ebbe riguardo Cesare combattendo co' Tedeschi; il quale aperse loro la via, veggendo come, non si potendo fuggire, la necessità gli faceva gagliardi; e volle più tosto la fatica di seguirgli quando essi fuggivano, che il pericolo di vincergli, quando si difendevano. Lucullo, veggendo come alcuni cavalli di Macedonia ch'erano seco, se ne andavano dalla parte nemica, subito fe' sonare a battaglia e comandò che l'altre genti li seguissono; donde i nemici, credendosi che Lucullo volesse appiccare la zuffa, andarono a urtare i Macedoni con tale impeto, che quegli furono costretti difendersi; e così diventarono contra a loro voglia di fuggitivi combattitori. Importa ancora il sapersi assicurare d'una terra, quando tu dubiti della sua fede, vinta che tu hai la giornata o prima, il che t'insegneranno alcuni esempj antichi. Pompeo, dubitando de' Catinensi li pregò che fussero contenti accettare alcuni infermi ch'egli aveva nel suo esercito; mandato, sotto abito di infermi, uomini robustissimi occupò la terra. Publio Valerio, temendo della fede degli Epidauri, fece venire, come noi diremmo, un perdono a una chiesa fuor della terra, e, quando tutto il popolo era ito per la perdonanza, serrò le porte e dipoi non ricevè dentro se non quegli di chi egli confidava. Alessandro Magno, volendo andare in Asia e assicurarsi di Tracia, ne menò seco tutti i Principi di quella provincia, dando loro provvisione, e a' populari di Tracia prepose uomini vili; e così fece i Principi contenti, pagandogli, e i popolari quieti, non avendo capi che gli inquietassono. Ma tra tutte le cose con le quali i capitani si guadagnano i popoli, sono gli esempj di castità e di giustizia; come fu quello di Scipione in Ispagna, quando egli rendè quella fanciulla di corpo bellissima al padre e al marito; la quale gli fece più che coll'armi guadagnare la Ispagna. Cesare, avendo fatto pagare quelle legne ch'egli aveva adoperato per fare lo steccato intorno al suo esercito in Francia, si guadagnò tanto nome di giusto, ch'egli si facilitò lo acquisto di quella provincia. Io non so che mi resti a parlare altro sopra questi accidenti; nè ci resta sopra questa materia parte alcuna che non sia stata da noi disputata. Solo ci manca a dire del modo dell'espugnare e difendere le terre; il che sono per fare volentieri, se già a voi non rincrescesse.

BATISTA: La umanità vostra è tanta, ch'ella ci fa conseguire i desiderj nostri senza avere paura di essere tenuti prosuntuosi; poichè voi liberamente ne offerite quello che noi ci saremmo vergognati di domandarvi. Però vi diciamo solo questo: che a noi non potete fare maggiore nè più grato beneficio, che fornire questo ragionamento. Ma prima che passiate a quell'altra materia, solveteci uno dubbio: s'egli è meglio continuare la guerra ancora il verno, come si usa oggi, o farla solamente la state e ire alle stanze il verno, come gli antichi.

FABRIZIO: Ecco, che se non fusse la prudenza del domandatore, egli rimaneva indietro una parte che merita considerazione. Io vi dico, di nuovo, che gli antichi facevano ogni cosa meglio e con maggiore prudenza di noi; e se nelle altre cose si fa qualche errore, nelle cose della guerra si fanno tutti. Non è cosa più imprudente o più pericolosa a uno capitano, che fare la guerra il verno, e molto più pericolo porta colui che la fa che quello che l'aspetta. La ragione è questa: tutta la industria che si usa nella disciplina militare, si usa per essere ordinato a fare una giornata col tuo nemico, perchè questo è il fine al quale ha ad ire uno capitano, perchè la giornata ti dà vinta la guerra o perduta. Chi sa adunque meglio ordinarla; chi ha l'esercito suo meglio disciplinato, ha più vantaggio in questa e più può sperare di vincerla. Dall'altro canto non è cosa più nemica degli ordini, che sono i siti aspri o i tempi freddi e acquosi; perchè il sito aspro non ti lascia distendere le tue copie secondo la disciplina, i tempi freddi e acquosi non ti lasciano tenere le genti insieme, nè ti puoi unito presentare al nemico, ma ti conviene alloggiare disiunto di necessità e senza ordine avendo ad ubbidire a' castegli, a' borghi e alle ville che ti ricevano, in maniera che tutta quella fatica da te usata per disciplinare il tuo esercito è vana. Nè vi maravigliate se oggi guerreggiano il verno; perchè, essendo gli eserciti senza la disciplina, non conoscono il danno che fa loro il non alloggiare uniti, perchè non dà loro noia non potere tenere quegli ordini e osservare quella disciplina che non hanno. Pure e' doverrebbono vedere di quanti danni è stato cagione il campeggiare la vernata, e ricordarsi come i Francesi, l'anno millecinquecentotre, furono rotti in sul Garigliano dal verno e non dagli Spagnuoli. Perchè, come io vi ho detto, chi assalta ha ancora più disavvantaggio; perchè il mal tempo l'offende più, essendo in casa altri e volendo fare la guerra. Onde è necessitato, o, per stare insieme, sostenere la incommodità dell'acqua e del freddo, o, per fuggirla, dividere le genti. Ma colui che aspetta può eleggere il luogo a suo modo e aspettarla con le sue genti fresche; e quelle può, in uno subito unire ed andare a trovare una banda delle genti nemiche, le quali non possono resistere all'impeto loro. Così furono rotti i Francesi, e così sempre fieno rotti coloro che assalteranno la vernata uno nemico che abbia in se prudenza. Chi vuole adunque che le forze, gli ordini, le discipline e la virtù in alcuna parte non gli vaglia, faccia guerra alla campagna il verno. E perchè i Romani volevano che tutte queste cose in che eglino mettevano tanta industria valessono loro, fuggivano non altrimenti le vernate, che l'alpi aspre e i luoghi difficili e qualunque altra cosa gli impedisse a potere mostrare l'arte e la virtù loro. Sicchè questo basti alla domanda vostra, e vegnamo a trattare della difesa ed offesa delle terre e de' siti e della edificazione loro.

Book Seven

You ought to know that towns and fortresses can be strong either by nature or industry. Those are strong by nature which are surrounded by rivers or marshes, as is Mantua or Ferrara, or those situated on a rock or sloping mountain, as Monaco and San Leo; for those situated on mountains which are not difficult to climb, today are ((with respect to caves and artillery)) very weak. And, therefore, very often today a plain is sought on which to build (a city) to make it strong by industry. The first industry is, to make the walls twisted and full of turned recesses; which pattern results in the enemy not being able to approach them, as they will be able to be attacked easily not only from the front, but on the flanks. If the walls are made too high, they are excessively exposed to the blows of the artillery; if they are made too low, they are very easily scaled. If you dig ditches (moats) in front of them to make it difficult (to employ) ladders, if it should happen that the enemy fills them ((which a large army can do easily)) the wall becomes prey to the enemy. I believe, therefore, ((subject to a better judgement)) that if you want to make provision against both evils the wall ought to be made high, with the ditches inside and not outside. This is the strongest way to build that is possible, for it protects you from artillery and ladders, and does not give the enemy the faculty of filling the ditches. The wall, therefore, ought to be as high as occurs to you, and not less than three arm lengths wide, to make it more difficult to be ruined. It ought to have towers placed at intervals of two hundred arm lengths. The ditch inside ought to be at least thirty arm lengths wide and twelve deep, and all the earth that is excavated in making the ditch is thrown toward the city, and is sustained by a wall that is part of the base of the ditch, and extends again as much above the ground, as that a man may take cover behind it: which has the effect of making the depth of the ditch greater. In the base of the ditch, every two hundred arm lengths, there should be a matted enclosure, which with the artillery, causes injury to anyone who should descend into it. The heavy artillery which defends the city, are placed behind the wall enclosing the ditch; for to defend the wall from the front, as it is high, it is not possible to use conveniently anything else other than small or middle sized guns. If the enemy comes to scale your wall, the height of the first wall easily protects you. If he comes with artillery, he must first batter down the first wall: but once it is battered down, because the nature of all batterings is to cause the wall to fall toward the battered side, the ruin of the wall will result ((since it does not find a ditch which receives and hides it)) in doubling the depth of the ditch, so that it is not possible for you to pass on further as you will find a ruin that holds you back and a ditch which will impede you, and from the wall of the ditch, in safety, the enemy artillery kills you. The only remedy there exists for you, is to fill up the ditch: which is very difficult, as much because its capacity is large, as from the difficulty you have in approaching it, since the walls being winding and recessed, you can enter among them only with difficulty, for the reasons previously mentioned; and then, having to climb over the ruin with the material in hand, causes you a very great difficulty: so that I know a city so organized is completely indestructible.

BATTISTA: If, in addition to the ditch inside, there should be one also on the outside, wouldn't (the encampment) be stronger?

FABRIZIO: It would be, without doubt; but my reasoning is, that if you want to dig one ditch only, it is better inside than outside.

BATTISTA: Would you have water in the ditch, or would you leave them dry?

FABRIZIO: Opinions are different; for ditches full of water protect you from (subterranean) tunnels, the ditches without water make it more difficult for you to fill them in again. But, considering everything, I would have them without water; for they are more secure, and, as it has been observed that in winter time the ditches ice over, the capture of a city is made easy, as happened at Mirandola when Pope Julius besieged it. And to protect yourself from tunnels, I would dig them so deep, that whoever should want to go (tunnel) deeper, should find water. I would also build the fortresses in a way similar to the walls and ditches, so that similar difficulty would be encountered in destroying it I want to call to mind one good thing to anyone who defends a city. This is, that they do not erect bastions outside, and they be distant from its wall. And another to anyone who builds the fortresses: And this is, that he not build any redoubts in them, into which whoever is inside can retire when the wall is lost. What makes me give the first counsel is, that no one ought to do anything, through the medium of which, you begin to lose your reputation without any remedy, the loss of which makes others esteem you less, and dismay those who undertake your defense. And what I say will always happen to you if you erect bastions outside the town you have to defend, for you will always lose them, as you are unable to defend small things when they are placed under the fury of the artillery; so that in losing them, they become the beginning and the cause of your ruin. Genoa, when it rebelled from King Louis of France, erected some bastions on the hills outside the City, which, as soon as they were lost, and they were lost quickly, also caused the city to be lost. As to the second counsel, I affirm there is nothing more dangerous concerning a fortress, than to be able to retire into it, for the hope that men have (lose) when they abandon a place, cause it to be lost, and when it is lost, it then causes the entire fortress to be lost. For an example, there is the recent loss of the fortress of Forli when the Countess Catherine defended it against Caesare Borgia, son of Pope Alexander the Sixth, who had led the army of the King of France. That entire fortress was full of places by both of them: For it was originally a citadel. There was a moat before coming to the fortress, so that it was entered by means of a draw bridge. The fortress was divided into three parts, and each part separated by a ditch, and with water between them; and one passed from one place to another by means of bridges: whence the Duke battered one of those parts of the fortress with artillery, and opened up part of a wall; whence Messer Giovanni Da Casale, who was in charge of the garrison, did not think of defending that opening, but abandoned to retire into the other places; so that the forces of the Duke, having entered that part without opposition, immediately seized all of it, for they became masters of the bridges that connected the members (parts) with each other. He lost the fort which was held to be indestructible because of two mistakes: one, because it had so many redoubts: the other, because no one was made master of his bridges (they were unprotected). The poorly built fortress and the little prudence of the defender, therefore, brought disgrace to the magnanimous enterprise of the Countess, who had the courage to face an army which neither the King of Naples, nor the Duke of Milan, had faced. And although his (the Duke) efforts did not have a good ending, none the less, he became noted for those honors which his virtu merited. Which was testified to by the many epigrams made in those times praising him. If I should therefore have to build a fortress, I would make its walls strong, and ditches in the manner we have discussed, nor would I build anything else to live in but houses, and they would be weak and low, so that they would not impede the sight of the walls to anyone who might be in the plaza, so that the Captain should be able to see with (his own) eyes where he could be of help, and that everyone should understand that if the walls and the ditch were lost, the entire fortress would be lost. And even if I should build some redoubts, I would have the bridges so separated, that each part should be master of (protect) the bridge in its own area, arranging that it be buttressed on its pilasters in the middle of the ditch.

BATTISTA: You have said that, today, the little things can not be defended, and it seems to me I have understood the opposite, that the smaller the thing was, the better it was defended.

FABRIZIO: You have not understood well, for today that place can not be called strong, where he who defends it does not have room to retire among new ditches and ramparts: for such is the fury of the artillery, that he who relies on the protection of only one wall or rampart, deceives himself. And as the bastions ((if you want them not to exceed their regular measurements, for then they would be terraces and castles)) are not made so that others can retire into them, they are lost quickly. And therefore it is a wise practice to leave these bastions outside, and fortify the entrances of the terraces, and cover their gates with revets, so that one does not go in or out of the gate in a straight line, and there is a ditch with a bridge over it from the revet to the gate. The gates are also fortified with shutters, so as to allow your men to reenter, when, after going out to fight, it happens that the enemy drives them back, and in the ensuing mixing of men, the enemy does not enter with them. And therefore, these things have also been found which the ancients called "cataracts", which, being let down, keep out the enemy but saves one's friends; for in such cases, one can not avail himself of anything else, neither bridges, or the gate, since both are occupied by the crowd.

BATTISTA: I have seen these shutters that you mention, made of small beams, in Germany, in the form of iron grids, while those of ours are made entirely of massive planks. I would want to know whence this difference arises, and which is stronger.

FABRIZIO: I will tell you again, that the methods and organizations of war in all the world, with respect to those of the ancients, are extinct; but in Italy, they are entirely lost, and if there is something more powerful, it results from the examples of the Ultramontanes. You may have heard, and these others can remember, how weakly things were built before King Charles of France crossed into Italy in the year one thousand four hundred ninety four (1494). The battlements were made a half arm length thin (wide), the places for the cross-bowmen and bombardiers (gunners) were made with a small aperture outside and a large one inside, and with many other defects, which I will omit, not to be tedious; for the defenses are easily taken away from slender battlements; the (places for) bombardiers built that way are easily opened (demolished). Now from the French, we have learned to make the battlements wide and large, and also to make the (places of the) bombardiers wide on the inside, and narrow it at the center of the wall, and then again widen it up to the outside edge: and this results in the artillery being able to demolish its defenses only with difficulty, The French, moreover, have many other arrangements such as these, which, because they have not been seen thus, have not been given consideration. Among which, is this method of the shutters made in the form of a grid, which is by far a better method than yours; for if you have to repair the shutters of a gate such as yours, lowering it if you are locked inside, and hence are unable to injure the enemy, so that they can attack it safely either in the dark or with a fire. But if it is made in the shape of a grid, you can, once it is lowered, by those weaves and intervals, to be able to defend it with lances, cross-bows, and every other kind of arms.

BATTISTA: I have also seen another Ultramontane custom in Italy, and it is this, making the carriages of the artillery with the spokes of the wheels bent toward the axles. I would like to know why they make them this way, as it seems to me they would be stronger straight, as those of our wheels.

FABRIZIO: Never believe that things which differ from the ordinary are made at home, but if you would believe that I should make them such as to be more beautiful, you would err; for where strength is necessary, no account is taken of beauty; but they all arise from being safer and stronger than ours. The reason is this. When the carriage is loaded, it either goes on a level, or inclines to the right or left side. When it goes level, the wheels equally sustain the weight, which, being divided equally between them, does not burden them much; when it inclines, it comes to have all the weight of the load upon that wheel on which it inclines. If its spokes are straight, they can easily collapse, since the wheel being inclined, the spokes also come to incline, and do not sustain the weight in a straight line. And, thus, when the carriage rides level and when they carry less weight, they come to be stronger; when the carriage rides inclined and when they carry more weight, they are weaker. The contrary happens to the bent spokes of the French carriages; for when the carriage inclines to one side, it points (leans straight) on them, since being ordinarily bent, they then come to be (more) straight (vertical), and can sustain all the weight strongly; and when the carriage goes level and they (the spikes) are bent, they sustain half the weight.

But let us return to our Cities and Fortresses. The French, for the greater security of their towns, and to enable them during sieges to put into and withdraw forces from them more easily, also employ, in addition to the things mentioned, another arrangement, of which I have not yet seen any example in Italy: and it is this, that they erect two pilasters at the outside point of a draw-bridge, and upon each of them they balance a beam so that half of it comes over the bridge, and the other half outside. Then they join small beams to the part outside, which are woven together from one beam to another in the shape of a grid, and on the inside they attach a chain to the end of each beam. When they want to close the bridge from the outside, therefore, they release the chains and allow all that gridded part to drop, which closes the bridge when it is lowered, and when they want to open it, they pull on the chains, and they (gridded beams) come to be raised; and they can be raised so that a man can pass under, but not a horse, and also so much that a horse with the man can pass under, and also can be closed entirely, for it is lowered and raised like a lace curtain. This arrangement is more secure than the shutters: for it can be impeded by the enemy so that it cannot come down only with difficulty, (and) it does not come down in a straight line like the shutters which can easily be penetrated. Those who want to build a City, therefore, ought to have all the things mentioned installed; and in addition, they should want at least one mile around the wall where either farming or building would not be allowed, but should be open field where no bushes, embankments, trees, or houses, should exist which would impede the vision, and which should be in the rear of a besieging enemy. It is to be noted that a town which has its ditches outside with its embankments higher than the ground, is very weak; for they provide a refuge for the enemy who assaults you, but does not impede him in attacking you, because they can be easily forced (opened) and give his artillery an emplacement.

But let us pass into the town. I do not want to waste much time in showing you that, in addition to the things mentioned previously, provisions for living and fighting supplies must also be included, for they are the things which everyone needs, and without them, every other provision is in vain. And, generally, two things ought to be done, provision yourself, and deprive the enemy of the opportunity to avail himself of the resources of your country. Therefore, any straw, grain, and cattle, which you cannot receive in your house, ought to be destroyed. Whoever defends a town ought to see to it that nothing is done in a tumultuous and disorganized manner, and have means to let everyone know what he has to do in any incident. The manner is this, that the women, children, aged, and the public stay at home, and leave the town free to the young and the brave: who armed, are distributed for defense, part being on the walls, part at the gates, part in the principal places of the City, in order to remedy those evils which might arise within; another part is not assigned to any place, but is prepared to help anyone requesting their help. And when matters are so organized, only with difficulty can tumults arise which disturb you. I want you to note also that in attacking and defending Cities, nothing gives the enemy hope of being able to occupy a town, than to know the inhabitants are not in the habit of looking for the enemy; for often Cities are lost entirely from fear, without any other action. When one assaults such a City, he should make all his appearances (ostentatious) terrible. On the other hand, he who is assaulted ought to place brave men, who are not afraid of thoughts, but by arms, on the side where the enemy (comes to) fight; for if the attempt proves vain, courage grows in the besieged, and then the enemy is forced to overcome those inside with his virtu and his reputation.

The equipment with which the ancients defended the towns were many, such as, Ballistas, Onagers, Scorpions, Arc-Ballistas, Large Bows, Slingshots; and those with which they assaulted were also many, such as, Battering Rams, Wagons, Hollow Metal Fuses (Muscoli), Trench Covers (Plutei), Siege Machines (Vinee), Scythes, Turtles (somewhat similar to present day tanks). In place of these things, today there is the artillery, which serves both attackers and defenders, and, hence, I will not speak further about it. But let us return to our discussion, and come to the details of the siege (attack). One ought to take care not to be able to be taken by hunger, and not to be forced (to capitulate) by assaults. As to hunger, it has been said that it is necessary, before the siege arrives, to be well provided with food. But when it is lacking during a long siege, some extraordinary means of being provided by friends who want to save you, have been observed to be employed, especially if a river runs in the middle of the besieged City, as were the Romans, when their castle of Casalino was besieged by Hannibal, who, not being able to send them anything else by way of the river, threw great quantities of nuts into it, which being carried by the river without being able to be impeded, fed the Casalinese for some time. Some, when they were besieged, in order to show the enemy they had grain left over, and to make them despair of being able to besiege (defeat) them by hunger, have either thrown bread outside the walls, or have given a calf grain to eat, and then allowed it to be taken, so that when it was killed, and being found full of grain, gave signs of an abundance which they do not have. On the other hand, excellent Captains have used various methods to enfamish the enemy. Fabius allowed the Campanians to sow so that they should lack that grain which they were sowing. Dionysius, when he was besieged at Reggio, feigned wanting to make an accord with them, and while it was being drawn, had himself provided with food, and then when, by this method, had depleted them of grain, pressed them and starved them. Alexander the Great, when he wanted to capture Leucadia, captured all the surrounding castles, and allowed the men from them to take refuge in it (the City), and thus by adding a great multitude, he starved them. As to assaults, it has been said that one ought to guard against the first onrush, with which the Romans often occupied many towns, assaulting them all at once from every side, and they called it attacking the city by its crown: as did Scipio when he occupied new Carthage in Spain. If this onrush is withstood, then only with difficulty will you be overcome. And even if it should occur that the enemy had entered inside the city by having forced the walls, even the small terraces give you some remedy if they are not abandoned; for many armies have, once they have entered into a town, been repulsed or slain. The remedy is, that the towns people keep themselves in high places, and fight them from their houses and towers. Which thing, those who have entered in the City, have endeavored to win in two ways: the one, to open the gates of the City and make a way for the townspeople by which they can escape in safety: the other, to send out a (message) by voice signifying that no one would be harmed unless armed, and whoever would throw his arms on the ground, they would pardon. Which thing has made the winning of many Cities easy. In addition to this, Cities are easy to capture if you fall on them unexpectedly, which you can do when you find yourself with your army far away, so that they do not believe that you either want to assault them, or that you can do it without your presenting yourself, because of the distance from the place. Whence, if you assault them secretly and quickly, it will almost always happen that you will succeed in reporting the victory. I unwillingly discuss those things which have happened in our times, as I would burden you with myself and my (ideas), and I would not know what to say in discussing other things. None the less, concerning this matter, I can not but cite the example of Cesare Borgia, called the Duke Valentine, who, when he was at Nocera with his forces, under the pretext of going to harm Camerino, turned toward the State of Urbino, and occupied a State in one day and without effort, which some other, with great time and expense, would barely have occupied. Those who are besieged must also guard themselves from the deceit and cunning of the enemy, and, therefore, the besieged should not trust anything which they see the enemy doing continuously, but always believe they are being done by deceit, and can change to injure them. When Domitius Calvinus was besieging a town, he undertook habitually to circle the walls of the City every day with a good part of his forces. Whence the townspeople, believing he was doing this for exercise, lightened the guard: when Domitius became aware of this, he assaulted them, and destroyed them. Some Captains, when they heard beforehand that aid was to come to the besieged, have clothed their soldiers with the insignia of those who were to come, and having introduced them inside, have occupied the town. Chimon, the Athenian, one night set fire to a Temple that was outside the town, whence, when the townspeople arrived to succor it, they left the town to the enemy to plunder. Some have put to death those who left the besieged castle to blacksmith (shoe horses), and redressing their soldiers with the clothes of the blacksmiths, who then surrendered the town to him. The ancient Captains also employed various methods to despoil the garrisons of the towns they want to take. Scipio, when he was in Africa, and desiring to occupy several castles in which garrisons had been placed by Carthaginians, feigned several times wanting to assault them, but then from fear not only abstained, but drew away from them. Which Hannibal believing to be true, in order to pursue him with a larger force and be able to attack him more easily, withdrew all the garrisons from them: (and) Scipio becoming aware of this, sent Maximus, his Captain, to capture them. Pyrrhus, when he was waging war in Sclavonia, in one of the Chief Cities of that country, where a large force had been brought in to garrison it, feigned to be desperate of being able to capture it, and turning to other places, caused her, in order to succor them, to empty herself of the garrison, so that it became easy to be forced (captured). Many have polluted the water and diverted rivers to take a town, even though they then did not succeed. Sieges and surrenders are also easily accomplished, by dismaying them by pointing out an accomplished victory, or new help which is come to their disfavor. The ancient Captains sought to occupy towns by treachery, corrupting some inside, but have used different methods. Some have sent one of their men under the disguise of a fugitive, who gained authority and confidence with the enemy, which he afterward used for his own benefit. Many by this means have learned the procedures of the guards, and through this knowledge have taken the town. Some have blocked the gate so that it could not be locked with a cart or a beam under some pretext, and by this means, made the entry easy to the enemy. Hannibal persuaded one to give him a castle of the Romans, and that he should feign going on a hunt at night, to show his inability to go by day for fear of the enemy, and when he returned with the game, placed his men inside with it, and killing the guard, captured the gate. You also deceive the besieged by drawing them outside the town and distant from it, by feigning flight when they assault you. And many ((among whom was Hannibal)) have, in addition, allowed their quarters to be taken in order to have the opportunity of placing them in their midst, and take the town from them. They deceive also by feigning departure, as did Forminus, the Athenian, who having plundered the country of the Calcidians, afterwards received their ambassadors, and filled their City with promises of safety and good will, who, as men of little caution, were shortly after captured by Forminus. The besieged ought to look out for men whom they have among them that are suspect, but sometimes they may want to assure themselves of these by reward, as well as by punishment. Marcellus, recognizing that Lucius Bancius Nolanus had turned to favor Hannibal, employed so much humanity and liberality toward him, that, from an enemy, he made him a very good friend. The besieged ought to use more diligence in their guards when the enemy is distant, than when he is near. And they ought to guard those places better which they think can be attacked less; for many towns have been lost when the enemy assaulted them on a side from which they did not believe they would be assaulted. And this deception occurs for two reasons: either because the place is strong and they believe it is inaccessible, or because the enemy cunningly assaults him on one side with feigned uproars, and on the other silently with the real assaults. And, therefore, the besieged ought to have a great awareness of this, and above all at all times, but especially at night, have good guards at the walls, and place there not only men, but dogs; and keep them ferocious and ready, which by smell, detect the presence of the enemy, and with their baying discover him. And, in addition to dogs, it has been found that geese have also saved a City, as happened to the Romans when the Gauls besieged the Capitol. When Athens was besieged by the Spartans, Alcibiades, in order to see if the guards were awake, arranged that when a light was raised at night, all the guards should rise, and inflicted a penalty on those who did not observe it. Hissicratus, the Athenian, slew a guard who was sleeping, saying he was leaving him as he had found him. Those who are besieged have had various ways of sending news to their friends, and in order not to send embassies by voice, wrote letters in cipher, and concealed them in various ways. The ciphers are according to the desires of whoever arranges them, the method of concealment is varied. Some have written inside the scabbard of a sword. Others have put these letters inside raw bread, and then baked it, and gave it as food to him who brought it. Others have placed them in the most secret places of the body. Others have put them in the collar of a dog known to him who brings it. Others have written ordinary things in a letter, and then have written with water (invisible ink) between one line and another, which afterwards by wetting or scalding (caused) the letter to appear. This method has been very astutely observed in our time, where some wanting to point out a thing which was to be kept secret to their friends who lived inside a town, and not wanting to trust it in person, sent communications written in the customary manner, but interlined as I mentioned above, and had them hung at the gates of a Temple; which were then taken and read by those who recognized them from the countersigns they knew. Which is a very cautious method, because whoever brings it can be deceived by you, and you do not run any danger. There are infinite other ways by which anyone by himself likewise can find and read them. But one writes with more facility to the besieged than the besieged do to friends outside, for the latter can not send out such letters except by one who leaves the town under the guise of a fugitive, which is a doubtful and dangerous exploit when the enemy is cautious to a point. But as to those that are sent inside, he who is sent can, under many pretexts, go into the camp that is besieged, and from here await a convenient opportunity to jump into the town.

But let us come to talk of present captures, and I say that, if they occur when you are being fought in your City, which is not arranged with ditches inside, as we pointed out a little while ago, when you do not want the enemy to enter by the breaks in the wall made by artillery ((as there is no remedy for the break which it makes)), it is necessary for you, while the artillery is battering, to dig a ditch inside the wall that is being hit, at least thirty arm lengths wide, and throw all (the earth) that is excavated toward the town, which makes embankments and the ditch deeper: and you must do this quickly, so that if the wall falls, the ditch will be excavated at least five or six arm lengths deep. While this ditch is being excavated, it is necessary that it be closed on each side by a block house. And if the wall is so strong that it gives you time to dig the ditches and erect the block houses, that part which is battered comes to be stronger than the rest of the City, for such a repair comes to have the form that we gave to inside ditches. But if the wall is weak and does not give you time, then there is need to show virtu, and oppose them with armed forces, and with all your strength. This method of repair was observed by the Pisans when you went to besiege them, and they were able to do this because they had strong walls which gave them time, and the ground firm and most suitable for erecting ramparts and making repairs. Which, had they not had this benefit, would have been lost. It would always be prudent, therefore, first to prepare yourself, digging the ditches inside your City and throughout all its circuit, as we devised a little while ago; for in this case, as the defenses have been made, the enemy is awaited with leisure and safety. The ancients often occupied towns with tunnels in two ways: either they dug a secret tunnel which came out inside the town, and through which they entered it, in the way in which the Romans took the City of the Veienti: or, by tunnelling they undermined a wall, and caused it to be ruined. This last method is more effective today, and causes Cities located high up to be weaker, for they can be undermined more easily, and then when that powder which ignites in an instant is placed inside those tunnels, it not only ruins the wall, but the mountains are opened, and the fortresses are entirely disintegrated into several parts. The remedy for this is to build on a plain, and make the ditch which girds your City so deep, that the enemy can not excavate further below it without finding water, which is the only enemy of these excavations. And even if you find a knoll within the town that you defend, you cannot remedy it otherwise than to dig many deep wells within your walls, which are as outlets to those excavations which the enemy might be able to arrange against it. Another remedy is to make an excavation opposite to where you learn he is excavating: which method readily impedes him, but is very difficult to foresee, when you are besieged by a cautious enemy. Whoever is besieged, above all, ought to take care not to be attacked in times of repose, as after having engaged in battle, after having stood guard, that is, at dawn, the evening between night and day, and, above all, at dinner time, in which times many towns have been captured, and many armies ruined by those inside. One ought, therefore, to be always on guard with diligence on every side, and in good part well armed. I do not want to miss telling you that what makes defending a City or an encampment difficult, is to have to keep all the forces you have in them disunited; for the enemy being able all together to assault you at his discretion, you must keep every place guarded on all sides, and thus he assaults you with his entire force, and you defend it with part of yours. The besieged can also be completely overcome, while those outside cannot unless repulsed; whence many who have been besieged either in their encampment or in a town, although inferior in strength, have suddenly issued forth with all their forces, and have overcome the enemy. Marcellus did this at Nola, and Caesar did this in Gaul, where his encampment being assaulted by a great number of Gauls, and seeing he could not defend it without having to divide this forces into several parts, and unable to stay within the stockade with the driving attack of the enemy, opened the encampment on one side, and turning to that side with all his forces, attacked them with such fury, and with such virtu, that he overcame and defeated them. The constancy of the besieged has also often displeased and dismayed the besieger. And when Pompey was affronting Caesar, and Caesar's army was suffering greatly from hunger, some of his bread was brought to Pompey, who, seeing it made of grass, commanded it not be shown to his army in order not to frighten it, seeing what kind of enemies he had to encounter.

Nothing gave the Romans more honor in the war against Hannibal, as their constancy; for, in whatever more inimical and adverse fortune, they never asked for peace, (and) never gave any sign of fear: rather, when Hannibal was around Rome, those fields on which he had situated his quarters were sold at a higher price than they would ordinarily have been sold in other times; and they were so obstinate in their enterprises, that to defend Rome, they did not leave off attacking Capua, which was being besieged by the Romans at the same time Rome was being besieged.

I know that I have spoken to you of many things, which you have been able to understand and consider by yourselves; none the less, I have done this ((as I also told you today)) to be able to show you, through them, the better kind of training, and also to satisfy those, if there should be any, who had not had that opportunity to learn, as you have. Nor does it appear to me there is anything left for me to tell you other than some general rules, with which you should be very familiar: which are these. What benefits the enemy, harms you; and what benefits you, harm the enemy. Whoever is more vigilant in observing the designs of the enemy in war, and endures much hardship in training his army, will incur fewer dangers, and can have greater hope for victory. Never lead your soldiers into an engagement unless you are assured of their courage, know they are without fear, and are organized, and never make an attempt unless you see they hope for victory. It is better to defeat the enemy by hunger than with steel; in such victory fortune counts more than virtu. No proceeding is better than that which you have concealed from the enemy until the time you have executed it. To know how to recognize an opportunity in war, and take it, benefits you more than anything else. Nature creates few men brave, industry and training makes many. Discipline in war counts more than fury. If some on the side of the enemy desert to come to your service, if they be loyal, they will always make you a great acquisition; for the forces of the adversary diminish more with the loss of those who flee, than with those who are killed, even though the name of the fugitives is suspect to the new friends, and odious to the old. It is better in organizing an engagement to reserve great aid behind the front line, than to spread out your soldiers to make a greater front. He is overcome with difficulty, who knows how to recognize his forces and those of the enemy. The virtu of the soldiers is worth more than a multitude, and the site is often of more benefit than virtu. New and speedy things frighten armies, while the customary and slow things are esteemed little by them: you will therefore make your army experienced, and learn (the strength) of a new enemy by skirmishes, before you come to an engagement with him. Whoever pursues a routed enemy in a disorganized manner, does nothing but become vanquished from having been a victor. Whoever does not make provisions necessary to live (eat), is overcome without steel. Whoever trusts more in cavalry than in infantry, or more in infantry than in cavalry, must settle for the location. If you want to see whether any spy has come into the camp during the day, have no one go to his quarters. Change your proceeding when you become aware that the enemy has foreseen it. Counsel with many on the things you ought to do, and confer with few on what you do afterwards. When soldiers are confined to their quarters, they are kept there by fear or punishment; then when they are led by war, (they are led) by hope and reward. Good Captains never come to an engagement unless necessity compels them, or the opportunity calls them. Act so your enemies do not know how you want to organize your army for battle, and in whatever way you organize them, arrange it so that the first line can be received by the second and by the third. In a battle, never use a company for some other purpose than what you have assigned it to, unless you want to cause disorder. Accidents are remedied with difficulty, unless you quickly take the facility of thinking. Men, steel, money, and bread, are the sinews of war; but of these four, the first two are more necessary, for men and steel find find money and bread, but money and bread do not find men and steel. The unarmed rich man is the prize of the poor soldier. Accustom your soldiers to despise delicate living and luxurious clothing.

This is as much as occurs to me generally to remind you, and I know I could have told you of many other things in my discussion, as for example, how and in how many ways the ancients organized their ranks, how they dressed, and how they trained in many other things; and to give you many other particulars, which I have not judged necessary to narrate, as much because you are able to see them, as because my intention has not been to show you in detail how the ancient army was created, but how an army should be organized in these times, which should have more virtu than they now have. Whence it does not please me to discuss the ancient matters further than those I have judged necessary to such an introduction. I know I should have enlarged more on the cavalry, and also on naval warfare; for whoever defines the military, says, that it is an army on land and on the sea, on foot and on horseback. Of naval matters, I will not presume to talk, not because of not being informed, but because I should leave the talk to the Genoese and Venetians, who have made much study of it, and have done great things in the past. Of the cavalry, I also do not want to say anything other than what I have said above, this part being ((as I said)) less corrupted. In addition to this, if the infantry, who are the nerve of the army, are well organized, of necessity it happens that good cavalry be created. I would only remind you that whoever organizes the military in his country, so as to fill (the quota) of cavalry, should make two provisions: the one, that he should distribute horses of good breed throughout his countryside, and accustom his men to make a round-up of fillies, as you do in this country with calves and mules: the other, ((so that the round-up men find a buyer)) I would prohibit anyone to keep mules who did not keep a horse; so that whoever wanted to keep a mount only, would also be constrained to keep a horse; and, in addition, none should be able to dress in silk, except whoever keeps a horse. I understand this arrangement has been done by some Princes of our times, and to have resulted in an excellent cavalry being produced in their countries in a very brief time. About other things, how much should be expected from the cavalry, I will go back to what I said to you today, and to that which is the custom. Perhaps you will also desire to learn what parts a Captain ought to have. In this, I will satisfy you in a brief manner; for I would not knowingly select any other man than one who should know how to do all those things which we have discussed today. And these would still not be enough for him if he did not know how to find them out by himself, for no one without imagination was ever very great in his profession; and if imagination makes for honor in other things, it will, above all, honor you in this one. And it is to be observed, that every creation (imagination), even though minor, is celebrated by the writers, as is seen where they praised Alexander the Great, who, in order to break camp more secretly, did not give the signal with the trumpet, but with a hat on the end of a lance. He is also praised for having ordered his soldiers, when coming to battle with the enemy, to kneel with the left foot (knee) so that they could more strongly withstand the attack (of the enemy); which not only gave him victory, but also so much praise that all the statues erected in his honor show him in that pose.

But as it is time to finish this discussion, I want to return to the subject, and so, in part, escape that penalty which, in this town, custom decrees for those who do not return. If you remember well, Cosimo, you said to me that I was, on the one hand, an exalter of antiquity, and a censurer of those who did not imitate them in serious matters, and, on the other (hand), in matters of war in which I worked very hard, I did not imitate them, you were unable to discover the reason: to that I replied, that men who want to do something must first prepare themselves to know how to do it in order to be able afterwards to do it when the occasion permits it. whether or not I would know how to bring the army to the ancient ways, I would rather you be the judge, who have heard me discuss on this subject at length; whence you have been able to know how much time I have consumed on these thoughts, and I also believe you should be able to imagine how much desire there is in me to put them into effect. Which you can guess, if I was ever able to do it, or if ever the opportunity was given to me. Yet, to make you more certain, and for my greater justification, I would like also to cite you the reasons, and in part, will observe what I promised you, to show you the ease and the difficulty that are present in such imitation. I say to you, therefore, that no activity among men today is easier to restore to its ancient ways than the military; but for those only who are Princes of so large a State, that they are able to assemble fifteen or twenty thousand young men from among their own subjects. On the other hand, nothing is more difficult than this to those who do not have such a convenience. And, because I want you to understand this part better, you have to know that Captains who are praised are of two kinds. The one includes those, who, with an army (well) ordered through its own natural discipline, have done great things, such as were the greater part of the Roman Citizens, and others, who have led armies, who have not had any hardship in maintaining them good, and to see to it that they were safely led. The other includes those who not only had to overcome the enemy, but before they came to this, had been compelled to make their army good and well ordered, (and) who, without doubt, deserve greater praise that those others merited who with a army which was (naturally) good have acted with so much virtu. Such as these were Pelopidas, Epaminondas, Tullus Hostilius, Phillip of Macedonia father of Alexander, Cyrus King of the Persians, and Gracchus the Roman. All these had first to make the army good, and then fight with it. All of these were able to do so, as much by their prudence, as by having subjects capable of being directed in such practices. Nor would it have been possible for any of them to accomplish any praiseworthy deed, no matter how good and excellent they might have been, should they have been in an alien country, full of corrupt men, and not accustomed to sincere obedience. It is not enough, therefore, in Italy, to govern an army already trained, but it is necessary first to know how to do it, and then how to command it. And of these, there need to be those Princes, who because they have a large State and many subjects, have the opportunity to accomplish this. Of whom, I cannot be one, for I have never commanded, nor can I command except armies of foreigners, and men obligated to others and not to me. Whether or not it is possible to introduce into them (those Princes) some of the things we discussed today, I want to leave to your judgement. Would I make one of these soldiers who practice today carry more arms than is customary, and in addition, food for two or three days, and a shovel? Should I make him dig, or keep him many hours every day under arms in feigned exercises, so that in real (battles) afterward he could be of value to me? Would they abstain from gambling, lasciviousness, swearing, and insolence, which they do daily? Would they be brought to so much discipline, obedience, and respect, that a tree full of apples which should be found in the middle of an encampment, would be left intact, as is read happened many times in the ancient armies? What can I promise them, by which they well respect, love, or fear me, when, with a war ended, they no longer must come to me for anything? Of what can I make them ashamed, who are born and brought up without shame? By what Deity or Saints do I make them take an oath? By those they adore, or by those they curse? I do not know any whom they adore; but I well know that they curse them all. How can I believe they will observe the promises to those men, for whom they show their contempt hourly? How can those who deprecate God, have reverence for men? What good customs, therefore, is it possible to instill in such people? And if you should tell me the Swiss and the Spaniards are good, I should confess they are far better than the Italians: but if you will note my discussion, and the ways in which both proceeded, you will see that there are still many things missing among them (the Swiss and Spaniards) to bring them up to the perfection of the ancients. And the Swiss have been good from their natural customs, for the reasons I told you today, and the others (Spaniards) from necessity; for when they fight in a foreign country, it seems to them they are constrained to win or die, and as no place appeared to them where they might flee, they became good. But it is a goodness defective in many parts, for there is nothing good in them except that they are accustomed to await the enemy up to the point of the pike and of the sword. Nor would there be anyone suitable to teach them what they lack, and much less anyone who does not (speak) their language.

But let us turn to the Italians, who, because they have not wise Princes, have not produced any good army; and because they did not have the necessity that the Spaniards had, have not undertaken it by themselves, so that they remain the shame of the world. And the people are not to blame, but their Princes are, who have been castigated, and by their ignorance have received a just punishment, ignominously losing the State, (and) without any show of virtu. Do you want to see if what I tell you is true? Consider how many wars have been waged in Italy, from the passage of King Charles (of France) until today; and wars usually make men warlike and acquire reputations; these, as much as they have been great (big) and cruel, so much more have caused its members and its leaders to lose reputation. This necessarily points out, that the customary orders were not, and are not, good, and there is no one who know how to take up the new orders. Nor do you ever believe that reputation will be acquired by Italian arms, except in the manner I have shown, and by those who have large States in Italy, for this custom can be instilled in men who are simple, rough, and your own, but not to men who are malignant, have bad habits, and are foreigners. And a good sculptor will never be found who believes he can make a beautiful statue from a piece of marble poorly shaped, even though it may be a rough one. Our Italian Princes, before they tasted the blows of the ultramontane wars, believed it was enough for them to know what was written, think of a cautious reply, write a beautiful letter, show wit and promptness in his sayings and in his words, know how to weave a deception, ornament himself with gems and gold, sleep and eat with greater splendor than others, keep many lascivious persons around, conduct himself avariciously and haughtily toward his subjects, become rotten with idleness, hand out military ranks at his will, express contempt for anyone who may have demonstrated any praiseworthy manner, want their words should be the responses of oracles; nor were these little men aware that they were preparing themselves to be the prey of anyone who assaulted them. From this, then, in the year one thousand four hundred ninety four (1494), there arose the great frights, the sudden flights, and the miraculous (stupendous) losses: and those most powerful States of Italy were several times sacked and despoiled in this manner. But what is worse is, that those who remained persist in the same error, and exist in the same disorder: and they do not consider that those who held the State anciently, had done all those things we discussed, and that they concentrated on preparing the body for hardships and the mind not to be afraid of danger. Whence it happened that Caesar, Alexander, and all those excellent men and Princes, were the first among the combatants, went around on foot, and even if they did lose their State, wanted also to lose their lives; so that they lived and died with virtu. And if they, or part of them, could be accused of having too much ambition to rule, there never could be found in them any softness or anything to condemn, which makes men delicate and cowardly. If these things were to be read and believed by these Princes, it would be impossible that they would not change their way of living, and their countries not change in fortune. And as, in the beginning of our discussion, you complained of your organization, I tell you, if you had organized it as we discussed above, and it did not give a good account for itself, then you have reason to complain; but if it is not organized and trained as I have said, (the Army) it can have reason to complain of you, who have made an abortion, and not a perfect figure (organization). The Venetians also, and the Duke of Ferrara, begun it, but did not pursue it; which was due to their fault, and not of their men. And I affirm to now, that any of them who have States in Italy today, will begin in this way, he will be the

Lord higher than any other in this Province; and it will happen to his State as happened to the Kingdom of the Macedonians, which, coming under Phillip, who had learned the manner of organizing the armies from Epaminondas, the Theban, became, with these arrangements and practices ((while the rest of Greece was in idleness, and attended to reciting comedies)) so powerful, that in a few years, he was able to occupy it completely, and leave such a foundation to his son, that he was able to make himself Prince of the entire world. Whoever disparages these thoughts, therefore, if he be a Prince, disparages his Principality, and if he be a Citizen, his City. And I complain of nature, which either ought to make me a recognizer of this, or ought to have given me the faculty to be able to pursue it. Nor, even today when I am old, do I think I can have the opportunity: and because of this, I have been liberal with you, who, being young and qualified, when the things I have said please you, could, at the proper time, in favor of your Princes, aid and counsel them. I do not want you to be afraid or mistrustful of this, because this country appears to be born (to be destined) to resuscitate the things which are dead, as has been observed with Poetry, Painting, and Sculpture. But as for waiting for me, because of my years, do not rely on it. And, truly, if in the past fortune had conceded to me what would have sufficed for such an enterprise, I believe I would, in a very brief time, have shown the world how much the ancient institutions were of value, and, without doubt, I would have enlarged it with glory, or would have lost it without shame.

Libro Settimo

Voi dovete sapere come le terre e le rocche possono essere forti o per natura o per industria. Per natura sono forti quelle che sono circondate da fiumi o da paludi, come è Mantova e Ferrara, o che sono poste sopra uno scoglio o sopra uno monte erto, come Monaco e Santo Leo; perchè quelle poste sopra a' monti, che non sieno molto difficili a salirgli, sono oggi, rispetto alle artiglierie e le cave, debolissime. E però, il più delle volte nello edificare si cerca oggi uno piano, per farlo forte con la industria. La prima industria è fare le mura ritorte e piene di volture e di ricetti; la quale cosa fa che il nemico non si può accostare a quelle, potendo facilmente essere ferito non solamente a fronte, ma per fianco. Se le mura si fanno alte, sono troppo esposte a' colpi dell'artiglieria; s'elle si fanno basse, sono facili a scalare. Se tu fai i fossi innanzi a quelle per dare difficoltà alle scale, se avviene che il nemico gli riempia, il che può uno grosso esercito fare facilmente, resta il muro in preda del nemico. Pertanto io credo, salvo sempre migliore giudicio, che a volere provvedere all'uno e all'altro inconveniente, si debba fare il muro alto e con fossi di dentro e non di fuora. Questo è il più forte modo di edificare che si faccia, perchè ti difende dall'artiglierie e dalle scale, e non da facilità al nemico di riempiere il fosso. Debbe essere adunque il muro alto di quale altezza vi occorre maggiore, e grosso non meno di tre braccia, per rendere più difficile il farlo rovinare. Debbe avere poste le torri con gli intervalli di dugento braccia; debbe il fosso dentro essere largo almeno trenta braccia e fondo dodici; e tutta la terra che si cava per fare il fosso, sia gettata di verso la città, e sia sostenuta da uno muro che si parta dal fondo del fosso e vadia tanto alto sopra la terra che uno uomo si cuopra dietro a quello: la quale cosa farà la profondità del fosso maggiore. Nel fondo del fosso ogni dugento braccia vuole essere una casamatta che, con l'artiglierie, offenda qualunque scendesse in quello. L'artiglierie grosse che difendono la città, si pongano dietro al muro che chiude il fosso; perchè, per difendere il muro davanti, sendo alto, non si possono adoperare commodamente altro che le minute o mezzane. Se il nemico ti viene a scalare, l'altezza del primo muro facilmente ti difende. Se viene con l'artiglierie, gli conviene prima battere il muro primo; ma battuto ch'egli è, perchè la natura di tutte le batterie è fare cadere il muro di verso la parte battuta, viene la rovina del muro, non trovando fosso che la riceva e nasconda, a raddoppiare la profondità del fosso; in modo che passare più innanzi non ti è possibile, per trovare una rovina che ti ritiene, uno fosso che ti impedisce e l'artiglierie nemiche che dal muro del fosso sicuramente ti ammazzano. Solo vi è questo rimedio: riempire il fosso; il che è difficilissimo, sì perchè la capacità sua è grande, sì per la difficoltà che è nello accostarvisi, essendo le mura sinuose e concave; tra le quali, per le ragioni dette, con difficoltà si può entrare, e dipoi avendo a salire con la materia su per una rovina che ti dà difficoltà grandissima; tantochè io fo una città così ordinata al tutto inespugnabile.

BATISTA: Quando si facesse, oltre al fosso di dentro, ancora uno fosso di fuora, non sarebbe ella più forte?

FABRIZIO: Sarebbe senza dubbio, ma il ragionamento mio è, volendo fare uno fosso solo, ch'egli sta meglio dentro che fuora.

BATISTA: Vorresti voi che ne' fossi fusse acqua, o gli ameresti asciutti?

FABRIZIO: Le opinioni sono diverse; perchè i fossi pieni d'acqua ti guardano dalle cave sutterranee, i fossi senza acqua ti fanno più difficile il riempierli. Ma io considerato tutto, li farei senza acqua, perchè sono più sicuri; e si è visto di verno ghiacciare i fossi e fare facile la espugnazione di una città, come intervenne alla Mirandola, quando papa Iulio la campeggiava. E per guardarmi dalle cave, gli farei profondi tanto che chi volesse andare più sotto trovasse l'acqua. Le rocche ancora edificherei, quanto a' fossi e alle mura, in simile modo, acciocch'elle avessero la simile difficoltà a espugnarle. Una cosa bene voglio ricordare a chi difende le città: e questo è, che non facciano bastioni fuora e che sieno discosto dalle mura di quelle, ed un'altra a chi fabbrica le rocche: e questo è, che non faccia ridotto alcuno in quelle, nel quale chi vi è dentro, perduto il primo muro, si possa ritirare. Quello che mi fa dare il primo consiglio è che niuno debbe fare cosa mediante la quale, senza rimedio, tu cominci a perdere la tua prima riputazione; la quale, perdendosi, fa stimare meno gli altri ordini tuoi e sbigottire coloro che hanno preso la tua difesa. E sempre t'interverrà questo che io dico, quando tu faccia bastioni fuora della terra che tu abbia a difendere; perchè sempre gli perderai, non si potendo oggi le cose piccole difendere, quando che sieno sottoposte al furore delle artiglierie; in modo che, perdendoli, fieno principio e cagione della tua rovina. Genova, quando si ribellò dal Re Luigi di Francia, fece alcuni bastioni su per quegli colli che gli sono d'intorno; i quali, come furono perduti, che si perderono subito, fecero ancora perdere la città. Quanto al consiglio secondo, affermo niuna cosa essere ad una rocca più pericolosa, che essere in quella ridotti da potersi ritirare; perchè la speranza che gli uomini hanno, abbandonando uno luogo, fa che egli si perde, e quello perduto fa perdere poi tutta la rocca. Di esemplo ci è fresco la perdita della rocca di Furlì, quando la Contessa Caterina la difendeva contra a Cesare Borgia, figliuolo di papa Alessandro VI il quale vi aveva condotto l'esercito dei Re di Francia. Era tutta quella fortezza piena di luoghi da ritirarsi dall'uno nell'altro; perchè vi era prima la cittadella; da quella alla rocca era uno fosso, in modo che vi si passava per uno ponte levatoio; la rocca era partita in tre parti, e ogni parte era divisa con fossi e con acque dall'altra, e con ponti da quello luogo a quell'altro si passava. Donde che il duca battè coll'artiglieria una di quelle parti della rocca e aperse parte del muro; donde messer Giovanni da Casale, che era preposto a quella guardia, non pensò di difendere quella apertura, ma l'abbandonò per ritirarsi negli altri luoghi; talchè, entrate le genti del duca senza contrasto in quella parte, in uno subito la presero tutta, perchè diventarono signori de' ponti che andavano dall'uno membro all'altro. Perdessi adunque questa rocca, ch'era tenuta inespugnabile, per due difetti: l'uno per avere tanti ridotti, l'altro per non essere ciascuno ridotto signore de' ponti suoi. Fece, dunque, la mala edificata fortezza e la poca prudenza di chi la difendeva, vergogna alla magnanima impresa della Contessa; la quale aveva avuto animo ad aspettare uno esercito, il quale nè il Re di Napoli nè il duca di Milano aveva aspettato. E benchè gli suoi sforzi non avessero buono fine, nondimeno ne riportò quello onore che aveva meritata la sua virtù. Il che fu testificato da molti epigrammi in quegli tempi in sua lode fatti. Se io avessi pertanto ad edificare rocche, io farei loro le mura gagliarde e i fossi nel modo abbiamo ragionato; nè vi farei dentro altro che case per abitare, e quelle farei deboli e basse di modo ch'elle non impedissero, a chi stesse nel mezzo della piazza, la vista di tutte le mura, acciocchè il capitano potesse vedere coll'occhio dove potesse soccorrere e che ciascuno intendesse che perdute le mura e il fosso, fusse perduta la rocca. E quando pure io vi facessi alcuno ridotto, farei i ponti divisi in tal modo che ciascuna parte fusse signore de' ponti dalla banda sua, ordinando che battessero in su' pilastri nel mezzo del fosso.

BATISTA: Voi avete detto che le cose piccole oggi non si possono difendere; ed egli mi pareva avere inteso al contrario: che quanto minore era una cosa, meglio si difendeva.

FABRIZIO: Voi non avevi inteso bene; perchè egli non si può chiamare oggi forte quello luogo dove, chi lo difende non abbia spazio da ritirarsi con nuovi fossi e con nuovi ripari; perchè egli è tanto il furore delle artiglierie, che quello che si fonda in sulla guardia d'uno muro e d'uno riparo solo, s'inganna; e perchè i bastioni, volendo che non passino la misura ordinaria loro, perchè poi sarebbono terre e castella, non si fanno in modo che altri si possa ritirare, si perdono subito. È adunque savio partito lasciare stare questi bastioni di fuora e fortificare l'entrate delle terre e coprire le porte di quelle con rivellini, in modo che non si entri o esca della porta per linea retta, e dal rivellino alla porta sia uno fosso con uno ponte. Affortificansi ancora le porte con le saracinesche, per potere mettere dentro i suoi uomini quando sono usciti fuora a combattere e occorrendo che i nemici gli caccino, ovviare che alla mescolata non entrino dentro con loro. E però sono trovate queste, le quali gli antichi chiamano cateratte, le quali, calandosi, escludono i nemici e salvono gli amici; perchè in tale caso altri non si può valere nè de' ponti nè della porta, sendo l'uno e l'altra occupata dalla calca.

BATISTA: Io ho vedute queste saracinesche che voi dite, fatte nella Magna di travette in forma d'una graticola di ferro, e queste nostre sono fatte di panconi tutte massicce. desidererei intendere donde nasca questa differenza e quali sieno più gagliarde.

FABRIZIO: Io vi dico di nuovo che i modi e ordini della guerra in tutto il mondo, rispetto a quegli degli antichi, sono spenti; ma in Italia sono al tutto perduti; e se ci è cosa un poco più gagliarda, nasce dallo esemplo degli oltramontani. Voi potete avere inteso, e quest'altri se ne possono ricordare, con quanta debolezza si edificava innanzi che il Re Carlo di Francia nel mille quattrocento novantaquattro passasse in Italia. I merli si facevano sottili un mezzo braccio, le balestriere e le bombardiere si facevano con poca apertura di fuora e con assai dentro, e con molti altri difetti che, per non essere tedioso, lascerò; perchè da' merli sottili facilmente si lievano le difese, e le bombardiere edificate in quel modo facilmente si aprono. Ora da' Francesi si è imparato a fare il merlo largo e grosso, e che ancora le bombardiere sieno larghe dalla parte di dentro e ristringano infino alla metà del muro e poi, di nuovo, rallarghino infino alla corteccia di fuora; questo fa che l'artiglieria con fatica può levare le difese. Hanno pertanto i Francesi, come questi, molti altri ordini i quali, per non essere stati veduti da' nostri, non sono stati considerati. Tra' quali è questo modo di saracinesche fatte ad uso di graticola, il quale è di gran lunga migliore modo che il vostro; perchè, se voi avete per riparo d'una porta una saracinesca soda come la vostra, calandola, voi vi serrate dentro e non potete per quella offendere il nemico; talmente che quello con scure o con fuoco la può combattere sicuramente. Ma s'ella è fatta ad uso di graticola, potete, calata ch'ella è, per quelle maglie e per quegli intervalli difenderla con lance, con balestre e con ogni altra generazione d'armi.

BATISTA: Io ho veduto in Italia un altra usanza oltramontana, e questo è fare i carri delle artiglierie co' razzi delle ruote torti verso i poli. Io vorrei sapere perchè gli fanno così, parendomi che sieno più forti diritti, come quegli delle ruote nostre.

FABRIZIO: Non crediate mai che le cose che si partono da modi ordinarj sieno fatte a caso; e se voi credeste che gli facessero così per essere più begli, voi erreresti, perchè dove è necessaria la fortezza, non si fa conto della bellezza, ma tutto nasce perchè sono assai più sicuri e più gagliardi che i vostri. La ragione è questa: il carro, quando egli è carico, o e' va pari, o e' pende sopra il destro o sopra il sinistro lato. Quando egli va pari, le ruote parimente sostengono il peso, il quale, sendo diviso ugualmente tra loro, non le aggrava molto, ma, pendendo, viene ad avere tutto il pondo del carro addosso a quella ruota, sopra la quale egli pende. Se i razzi di quella sono diritti, possono facilmente fiaccarsi, perchè, pendendo la ruota, vengono i razzi a pendere ancora loro e a non sostenere il peso per il ritto. E così quando il carro va pari e quando eglino hanno meno peso, vengono ad essere più forti; quando il carro va torto e che vengono ad avere più peso, e' sono più deboli. Al contrario appunto interviene a' razzi torti de' carri Francesi; perchè, quando il carro, pendendo sopra una banda, ponta sopra di loro, per essere ordinariamente torti, vengono allora ad essere diritti e potere sostenere gagliardamente tutto il peso; che quando il carro va pari e che sono torti lo sostengono mezzo. Ma torniamo alle nostre città e rocche. Usano ancora i Francesi, per più sicurtà delle porte delle terre loro e per potere nelle ossidioni più facilmente mettere e trarre genti di quelle, oltre alle cose dette, un altro ordine, del quale io non ne ho veduto ancora in Italia alcuno esemplo; e questo è che rizzano dalla punta di fuora del ponte levatoio due pilastri, e sopra ciascuno di quegli bilicono una trave; in modo che le metà di quelle vengano sopra il ponte, l'altre metà di fuora. Dipoi tutta quella parte che viene di fuora congiungono con travette, le quali tessono dall'una trave all'altra ad uso di graticola, e dalla parte di dentro appiccano alla punta di ciascuna trave una catena. Quando vogliono adunque chiudere il ponte dalla parte di fuora, eglino allentano le catene e lasciano calare tutta quella parte ingraticolata la quale, abbassandosi, chiude il ponte; e quando lo vogliono aprire, tirano le catene, e quella si viene ad alzare; e puossi alzare tanto che vi passi sotto uno uomo e non uno cavallo, e tanto che vi passi il cavallo e l'uomo, e chiuderla ancora affatto, perch'ella si abbassa ed alza come una ventiera di merlo. Questo ordine è più sicuro che la saracinesca, perchè difficilmente può essere dal nemico impedito in modo che non cali, non calando per una linea retta come la saracinesca, che facilmente si può puntellare. deggiono adunque coloro che vogliono fare una città, fare ordinare tutte le cose dette; e di più si vorrebbe, almeno uno miglio intorno alle mura, non vi lasciare nè cultivare, nè murare, ma fusse tutta campagna dove non fusse nè macchia, nè argine, nè arbori, nè casa che impedisse la vista e che facesse spalle al nemico che si accampa. E notate che una terra che abbia i fossi di fuora con gli argini più alti che il terreno, è debolissima; perchè quegli fanno riparo al nemico che ti assalta e non gli impediscono l'offenderti, perchè facilmente si possono aprire e dare luogo alle artiglierie di quello. Ma passiamo dentro nella terra. Io non voglio perdere molto tempo in mostrarvi come, oltre alle cose predette, conviene avere munizioni da vivere e da combattere, perchè sono cose che ciascuno se le intende e, senza esse, ogni altro provvedimento è vano. E generalmente si dee fare due cose: provvedere se e torre commodità al nemico di valersi delle cose del tuo paese. Però gli strami, il bestiame, il frumento che tu non puoi ricevere in casa, si dee corrompere. Debbe ancora, chi difende una terra, provvedere che tumultuariamente e disordinatamente non si faccia alcuna cosa, e tenere modi che in ogni accidente ciascuno sappia quello abbia a fare. Il modo è questo: che le donne, i vecchi, i fanciugli e i deboli si stieno in casa e lascino la terra libera a' giovani e gagliardi; i quali armati si distribuiscano alla difesa, stando parte di quegli alle mura, parte alle porti, parte ne' luoghi principali della città, per rimediare a quegli inconvenienti che potessero nascere dentro; un'altra parte non sia obligata ad alcuno luogo, ma sia apparecchiata a soccorrere a tutti, richiedendolo il bisogno. Ed essendo le cose ordinate così, possono con difficoltà nascere tumulti che ti disordinino. Ancora voglio che notiate questo nelle offese e difese delle città: che niuna cosa dà tanta speranza al nemico di potere occupare una terra, quanto il sapere che quella non è consueta a vedere il nemico; perchè molte volte, per la paura solamente, senza altra esperienza di forze, le città si perdono. Però debbe uno, quando egli assalta una città simile, fare tutte le sue ostentazioni terribili. Dall'altra parte chi è assaltato debba preporre, da quella parte che il nemico combatte uomini forti e che non gli spaventi l'opinione ma l'arme; perchè se la prima pruova torna vana, cresce animo agli assediati, e dipoi il nemico è forzato a superare chi è dentro con la virtù e non con la reputazione. Gli instrumenti co' quali gli antichi difendevano le terre erano molti, come baliste, onagri, scorpioni, arcubaliste, fustibali, funde; ed ancora erano molti quegli co' quali le assaltavano, come arieti, torri, musculi, plutei, vinee, falci, testudini. In cambio delle quali cose sono oggi l'artiglierie, le quali servono a chi offende e a chi si difende; e però io non ne parlerò altrimenti. Ma torniamo al ragionamento nostro, e vegnamo alle offese particolari. Debbesi avere cura di non potere essere preso per fame e di non essere sforzato per assalti. Quanto alla fame, si è detto che bisogna, prima che la ossidione venga, essersi munito bene di viveri. Ma quando ne manca per la ossidione lunga, si è veduto usare qualche volta qualche modo estraordinario ad essere provvisto dagli amici che ti vorrebbero salvare, massime se per il mezzo della città assediata corre uno fiume, come ferno i Romani essendo assediato Casalino loro castello da Annibale, che, non potendo per il fiume mandare loro altro, gittorno in quello gran quantità di noci, le quali, portate dal fiume senza potere essere impedite, ciborno più tempo i Casalinesi. Alcuni assediati, per mostrare al nemico che gli avanza loro grano e per farlo disperare che non possa per fame assediargli, hanno o gittato pane fuora delle mura, o dato mangiare grano ad uno giovenco, e quello dipoi lasciato pigliare, acciocchè, morto e trovatolo pieno di grano, mostri quella abbondanza che non hanno. Dall'altra parte, i capitani eccellenti hanno usato vari termini per affamare il nemico. Fabio lasciò seminare a' Campani, acciocchè mancassero di quel frumento che seminavano. Dionisio, essendo a campo a Reggio, finse di volere fare con loro accordo, e durante la pratica si faceva provvedere da vivere, e quando poi gli ebbe per questo modo voti di frumento, gli ristrinse ed affamogli. Alessandro Magno, volendo espugnare Leucadia, espugnò tutti i castegli allo intorno, e gli uomini di quegli lasciò rifuggire in quella; e così, sopravvenendo assai moltitudine, l'affamò. Quanto agli assalti, si è detto che altri si debbe guardare dal primo impeto, col quale i Romani occuparono molte volte di molte terre, assaltandole ad un tratto e da ogni parte, e chiamavanlo «Aggredi urbem corona», come fece Scipione quando occupò Cartagine Nuova in Ispagna. Il quale impeto se si sostiene, con difficoltà sei poi superato. E se pure egli occorresse che il nemico fusse entrato dentro nella città per avere sforzate le mura, ancora i terrazzani vi hanno qualche rimedio, se non si abbandonano; perchè molti eserciti sono, poi che sono entrati in una terra, stati o ributtati o morti. Il rimedio è che i terrazzani si mantengano ne' luoghi alti e dalle case e dalle torri gli combattano. La quale cosa coloro che sono entrati nelle città si sono ingegnati vincere in due modi: l'uno, con aprire le porte della città e fare la via a' terrazzani che sicuramente si possano fuggire; l'altro, col mandare fuora una voce che significhi che non si offenda se non gli armati, e a chi getta l'armi in terra si perdoni. La quale cosa ha renduta facile la vittoria di molte città. Sono facili, oltre a questo, le città ad espugnarle, se tu giugni loro addosso imprevisto; il che si fa, trovandosi con l'esercito discosto, in modo che non si creda o che tu le voglia assaltare, o che tu possa farlo senza che si presenta per la distanza del luogo. Donde che se tu secretamente e sollecitamente le assalti, quasi sempre ti succederà di riportarne la vittoria. Io ragiono male volentieri delle cose successe de' nostri tempi, perchè di me e de' miei mi sarebbe carico a ragionare; d'altri non saprei che mi dire. Nondimeno non posso a questo proposito non addurre lo esemplo di Cesare Borgia, chiamato duca Valentino; il quale, trovandosi a Noc-era con le sue genti, sotto colore di andare a' danni di Camerino si volse verso lo stato d'Urbino, ed occupò uno stato in uno giorno e senza alcuna fatica, il quale un altro con assai tempo e spesa non avrebbe appena occupato. Conviene ancora, a quegli che sono assediati, guardarsi dagli inganni e dalle astuzie del nemico; e però non si deggiono fidare gli assediati d'alcuna cosa che veggano fare al nemico continuamente, ma credano sempre che vi sia sotto lo inganno e che possa a loro danno variare. Domizio Calvino, assediando una terra, prese per consuetudine di circuire ogni giorno, con buona parte delle sue genti, le mura di quella. Donde credendo i terrazzani lo facesse per esercizio, allentarono le guardie; di che accortosi Domizio, gli assaltò ed espugnogli. Alcuni capitani, avendo presentito che doveva venire aiuto agli assediati, hanno vestiti loro soldati sotto le insegne di quegli che dovevano venire, ed essendo stati intromessi hanno occupato la terra. Cimone ateniese messe fuoco una notte in uno tempio che era fuora della terra, onde i terrazzani, andando a soccorrerlo, lasciarono in preda la terra al nemico. Alcuni hanno morti quegli che del castello assediato vanno a saccomanno e rivestiti i suoi soldati con la veste de' saccomanni; i quali dipoi gli hanno dato la terra. Hanno ancora usato gli antichi capitani vari termini da spogliare di guardie le terre che vogliono pigliare. Scipione, sendo in Affrica e desiderando occupare alcuni castegli ne' quali erano messe guardie da' Cartaginesi, finse più volte di volergli assaltare, ma poi per paura non solamente astenersi, ma discostarsi da quegli. Il che credendo Annibale essere vero, per seguirlo con maggiore forze e per potere più facilmente opprimerlo, trasse tutte le guardie di quegli; il che Scipione conosciuto, mandò Massinissa suo capitano ad espugnargli. Pirro, faccendo guerra in Schiavonia ad una città capo di quello paese, dove era ridotta assai gente in guardia, finse di essere disperato di poterla espugnare e, voltatosi agli altri luoghi, fece che quella per soccorrergli si votò di guardie e diventò facile ad essere sforzata. Hanno molti corrotte l'acque e derivati i fiumi per pigliare le terre, ancora che dipoi non riuscisse. Fannosi facili ancora gli assediati ad arrendersi, spaventandogli con significare loro una vittoria avuta o nuovi aiuti che vengano in loro disfavore. Hanno cerco gli antichi capitani occupare le terre per tradimento, corrompendo alcuno di dentro; ma hanno tenuti diversi modi. Alcuno ha mandato uno suo che, sotto nome di fuggitivo, prenda autorità e fede co' nemici, la quale dipoi usi in benificio suo. Alcuno per questo mezzo ha inteso il modo delle guardie e, mediante quella notizia, presa la terra. Alcuno ha impedito la porta, ch'ella non si possa serrare, con uno carro e con travi sotto qualche colore, e per questo modo fatto l'entrare facile al nemico. Annibale persuase ad uno che gli desse uno castello de' Romani e che fingesse di andare a caccia la notte, mostrando non potere andare di giorno per paura de' nemici, e, tornando dipoi con la cacciagione, mettesse dentro con seco de' suoi uomini e, ammazzata la guardia, gli desse la porta. Ingannansi ancora gli assediati col tirargli fuora della terra e discostargli da quella, mostrando, quando essi ti assaltano, di fuggire. E molti, tra' quali fu Annibale, hanno non ch'altro, lasciatosi torre gli alloggiamenti per avere occasione di mettergli in mezzo e torre loro la terra. Ingannansi ancora col fingere di partirsi, come fece Formione ateniese; il quale, avendo predato il paese de' Calcidensi, ricevè dipoi i loro ambasciadori, riempiendo la loro città di sicurtà e di buone promesse sotto le quali, come uomini poco cauti, furono poco dipoi da Formione oppressi. Debbonsi gli assediati guardare dagli uomini che egli hanno fra loro sospetti; ma qualche volta si suole così assicurarsene col merito come con la pena. Marcello, conoscendo come Lucio Banzio Nolano era volto a favorire Annibale, tanta umanità e liberalità usò verso di lui, che di nemico se lo fece amicissimo. deggiono gli assediati usare più diligenza nelle guardie, quando il nemico si è discostato, che quando egli è propinquo; e deggiono guardare meglio quegli luoghi i quali pensano che possano essere offesi meno; perchè si sono perdute assai terre quando il nemico le assalta da quella parte donde essi non credono essere assaltati. E questo inganno nasce da due cagioni: o per essere il luogo forte e credere che sia inaccessibile, o per essere usata arte dal nemico di assaltargli da uno lato, con romori finti e, dall'altro, taciti e con assalti veri. E però deggiono gli assediati avere a questo grande avvertenza, e sopra tutto d'ogni tempo, e massime la notte, fare buone guardie alle mura; e non solamente preporvi uomini, ma i cani, e torgli feroci e pronti, i quali col fiuto presentano il nemico e con lo abbaiare lo scuoprano. E non che i cani, si è trovato che l'oche hanno salvo una città, come intervenne a' Romani quando i Francesi assediavano il Campidoglio. Alcibiade, per vedere se le guardie vigilavano, essendo assediata Atene dagli Spartani, ordinò che, quando la notte egli alzasse uno lume, tutte le guardie lo alzassero, constituendo pena a chi non lo osservasse. Ificrate ateniese ammazzò una guardia che dormiva, dicendo di averlo lasciato come l'aveva trovato. Hanno coloro che sono assediati tenuti vari modi a mandare avvisi agli amici loro; e per non mandare imbasciate a bocca, scrivono lettere in cifera e nascondonle in vari modi: le cifere sono secondo la volontà di chi l'ordina, il modo del nasconderle è vario. Chi ha scritto il fodero, dentro, d'una spada; altri hanno messe le lettere in uno pane crudo, e dipoi cotto quello e datolo come per suo cibo a colui che le porta. Alcuni se le sono messe ne' luoghi più secreti del corpo. Altri le hanno messe in un collare d'uno cane che sia familiare di quello che le porta. Alcuni hanno scritto in una lettera cose ordinarie, e dipoi, tra l'uno verso e l'altro, scritto con acque che, bagnandole e scaldandole, poi le lettere appariscano. Questo modo è stato astutissimamente osservato ne' nostri tempi; dove che, volendo alcuno significare cose da tenere secrete a' suoi amici che dentro a una terra abitavano, e non volendo fidarsi di persona, mandava scomuniche scritte secondo la consuetudine ed interlineate, come io dico di sopra, e quelle faceva alle porte de' templi suspendere; le quali conosciute da quegli che per gli contrassegni le conoscevano, erano spiccate e lette. Il quale modo è cautissimo, perchè chi le porta vi può esser ingannato e non vi corre alcuno pericolo. Sono infiniti altri modi che ciascuno per se medesimo può fingere e trovare. Ma con più facilità si scrive agli assediati, che gli assediati agli amici di fuora, perchè tali lettere non le possono mandare, se non per uno che sotto ombra di fuggitivo esca della terra; il che è cosa dubbia e pericolosa quando il nemico è punto cauto. Ma quelli che mandono dentro, può quello che è mandato, sotto molti colori andare nel campo che assedia, e di quivi, presa conveniente occasione, saltare nella terra. Ma vegnamo a parlare delle presenti espugnazioni; e dico che s'egli occorre che tu sia combattuto nella tua città, che non sia ordinata co' fossi dalla parte di dentro, come poco fa dimostrammo, a volere che il nemico non entri per le rotture del muro che l'artiglieria fa, perchè alla rottura ch'ella non si faccia non è rimedio, , ti è necessario, mentre che l'artiglieria batte, muovere uno fosso dentro al muro che è percosso, largo almeno trenta braccia, e gittare tutto quello che si cava di verso la terra, che faccia argine e più profondo il fosso; e ti conviene sollecitare questa opera in modo che, quando il muro caggia, il fosso sia cavato almeno cinque o sei braccia. Il quale fosso è necessario, mentre che si cava, chiudere da ogni fianco con una casamatta. E quando il muro è sì gagliardo che ti dia tempo a fare il fosso e le casematte, viene ad essere più forte quella parte battuta che il resto della città; perchè tale riparo viene ad avere la forma che noi demmo a' fossi di dentro. Ma quando il muro è debole e che non ti dia tempo, allora è che bisogna mostrare la virtù, ed opporvisi con le genti armate e con tutte le forze tue. Questo modo di riparare fu osservato da' Pisani, quando voi vi andavi a campo; e poterono farlo, perchè avevano le mura gagliarde, che davano loro tempo, e il terreno tenace e attissimo a rizzare argini e fare ripari. Che se fussono mancati di questa commodità, si sarebbero perduti. Pertanto si farà sempre prudentemente a provvedersi prima, faccendo i fossi dentro alla sua città e per tutto il suo circuito, come poco fa divisammo, perchè in questo caso si aspetta ozioso e sicuro il nemico, essendo i ripari fatti. Occupavano gli antichi molte volte le terre con le cave sutterranee in due modi: o e' facevano una via sotterra segretamente che riusciva nella terra, e per quella entravano, nel quale modo i Romani presono la città de' Veienti, o con le cave scalzavano uno muro e facevanlo rovinare. Questo ultimo modo è oggi più gagliardo e fa che le città poste alto sieno più deboli, perchè si possono meglio cavare; e mettendo dipoi nelle cave di quella polvere che in istante si accende, non solamente rovina uno muro, ma i monti si aprono e le fortezze tutte in più parti si dissolvono. Il rimedio a questo è edificare in piano e fare il fosso che cigne la tua città tanto profondo, che il nemico non possa cavare più basso di quello che non trovi l'acqua, la quale è solamente nemica di queste cave. E se pure ti truovi con la terra che tu difendi in poggio, non puoi rimediarvi con altro che fare dentro alle tue mura assai pozzi profondi, i quali sono come sfogatoi a quelle cave che il nemico ti potesse ordinare contra. Un altro rimedio è fargli una cava all'incontro, quando ti accorgessi donde quello cavasse; il quale modo facilmente lo impedisce, ma difficilmente si prevede, essendo assediato da uno nemico cauto. Deve sopra tutto avere cura, quello che è assediato, di non essere oppresso ne' tempi del riposo, come è dopo una battaglia avuta, dopo le guardie fatte, che è la mattina al fare del giorno, la sera tra dì e notte, e sopra tutto quando si mangia; nel quale tempo molte terre sono espugnate e molti eserciti sono stati da quegli di dentro rovinati. Però si debbe con diligenza da ogni parte stare sempre guardato e in buona parte armato. Io non voglio mancare di dirvi come quello che fa difficile il difendere una città o uno alloggiamento è lo avere a tenere disunite tutte le forze che tu hai in quegli; perchè, potendoti il nemico assalire a sua posta tutto insieme da qualunque banda, ti conviene tenere ogni luogo guardato; e così quello ti assalta con tutte le forze e tu con parte di quelle ti difendi. Può ancora lo assediato essere vinto in tutto, quello di fuora non può essere se non ributtato; onde che molti che sono stati assediati o nello alloggiamento o in una terra, ancora che inferiori di forze sono usciti con tutte le loro genti ad un tratto fuora e hanno superato il nemico. Questo fece Marcello a Nola; questo fece Cesare in Francia, che, essendogli assaltati gli alloggiamenti da uno numero grandissimo di Francesi e veggendo non gli potere difendere per avere a dividere le sue forze in più parti, e non potere, stando dentro agli steccati, con empito urtare il nemico, aperse da una banda lo alloggiamento, e, rivoltosi in quella parte con tutte le forze, fece tanto impeto loro contra e con tanta virtù che gli superò e vinse. La costanza ancora degli assediati fa molte volte disperare e sbigottire coloro che assediano. Essendo Pompeo a fronte di Cesare e patendo assai l'esercito Cesariano per la fame, fu portato del suo pane a Pompeo; il quale vedendo fatto di erbe comandò che non si mostrasse al suo esercito per non lo fare sbigottire, vedendo quali nemici aveva all'incontro. Niuna cosa fece tanto onore a' Romani nella guerra di Annibale quanto la costanza loro, perchè in qualunque più nemica e avversa fortuna mai non domandorono pace, mai fecero alcun segno di timore; anzi, quando Annibale era allo intorno di Roma, si venderono quegli campi dove egli aveva posti i suoi alloggiamenti, più pregio che per l'ordinario per altri tempi venduti non si sarebbono; e stettero in tanto ostinati nelle imprese loro, che, per difendere Roma, non vollero levare le offese da Capua, la quale, in quel medesimo tempo che Roma era assediata, i Romani assediavano. Io so che io vi ho detto di molte cose le quali per voi medesimi avete potuto intendere e considerare; nondimeno l'ho fatto, come oggi ancora vi dissi, per potervi mostrare, mediante quelle, meglio la qualità di questo esercizio e ancora per soddisfare a quegli, se alcuno ce ne fusse, che non avessero avuta quella commodità di intenderle che voi. Nè mi pare che ci resti altro a dirvi che alcune regole generali, le quali voi averete famigliarissime; che sono queste: Quello che giova al nemico nuoce a te, e quel che giova a te nuoce al nemico. Colui che sarà nella guerra più vigilante a osservare i disegni del nemico e più durerà fatica ad esercitare il suo esercito, in minori pericoli incorrerà e più potrà sperare della vittoria. Non condurre mai a giornata i tuoi soldati, se prima non hai confermato l'animo loro e conosciutogli senza paura e ordinati, nè mai ne farai pruova, se non quando vedi ch'egli sperano di vincere. Meglio è vincere il nemico con la fame che col ferro, nella vittoria del quale può molto più la fortuna che la virtù. Niuno partito è migliore che quello che sta nascoso al nemico infino che tu lo abbia eseguito. Sapere nella guerra conoscere l'occasione e pigliarla, giova più che niuna altra cosa. La natura genera pochi uomini gagliardi; la industria e l'esercizio ne fa assai. Può la disciplina nella guerra più che il furore. Quando si partono alcuni dalla parte nemica per venire a' servizj tuoi, quando sieno fedeli vi sarà sempre grandi acquisti; perchè le forze degli avversari più si minuiscono con la perdita di quegli che si fuggono, che di quegli che sono ammazzati, ancora che il nome de' fuggitivi sia a' nuovi amici sospetto, a' vecchi odioso. Meglio è, nell'ordinare la giornata, riserbare dietro alla prima fronte assai aiuti, che, per fare la fronte maggiore, disperdere i suoi soldati. Difficilmente è vinto colui che sa conoscere le forze sue e quelle del nemico. Più vale la virtù de' soldati che la moltitudine; più giova alcuna volta il sito che la virtù. Le cose nuove e subite sbigottiscono gli eserciti; le cose consuete e lente sono poco stimate da quegli; però farai al tuo esercito praticare e conoscere con piccole zuffe un nemico nuovo, prima che tu venga alla giornata con quello. Colui che seguita con disordine il nemico poi ch'egli è rotto, non vuole fare altro che diventare, di vittorioso, perdente. Quello che non prepara le vettovaglie necessarie al vivere è vinto senza ferro. Chi confida più ne' cavalli che ne' fanti, o più ne' fanti che ne' cavalli, si accomodi col sito. Quando tu vuoi vedere se, il giorno, alcuna spia è venuta in campo, fa' che ciascuno ne vadia al suo alloggiamento. Muta partito, quando ti accorgi che il nemico l'abbia previsto. Consigliati, delle cose che tu dèi fare, con molti; quello che dipoi vuoi fare conferisci con pochi. I soldati, quando dimorano alle stanze, si mantengano col timore e con la pena; poi, quando si conducono alla guerra, con la speranza e col premio. I buoni capitani non vengono mai a giornata se la necessità non gli strigne o la occasione non gli chiama. Fa' che i tuoi nemici non sappiano come tu voglia ordinare l'esercito alla zuffa: e in qualunque modo l'ordini, fa' che le prime squadre possano essere ricevute dalle seconde e dalle terze. Nella zuffa non adoperare mai una battaglia ad un'altra cosa che a quella per che tu l'avevi deputata, se tu non vuoi fare disordine. Agli accidenti subiti con difficoltà si rimedia, a' pensati con facilità. Gli uomini, il ferro, i danari e il pane sono il nervo della guerra; ma di questi quattro sono più necessarj i primi due, perchè gli uomini e il ferro truovano i danari e il pane, ma il pane e i danari non truovano gli uomini e il ferro. Il disarmato ricco è premio del soldato povero. Avvezza i tuoi soldati a spregiare il vivere delicato e il vestire lussurioso. Questo è quanto mi occorre generalmente ricordarvi; e so che si sarebbero possute dire molte altre cose in tutto questo mio ragionamento, come sarebbero: come e in quanti modi gli antichi ordinavano le schiere; come vestivano e come in molte altre cose si esercitavano, e aggiugnervi assai particolari i quali non ho giudicati necessarj narrare, sì perchè per voi medesimi potete vederli, sì ancora perchè la intenzione mia non è stata mostrarvi appunto come l'antica milizia era fatta, ma come in questi tempi si potesse ordinare una milizia che avesse più virtù che quella che si usa. Donde che non mi è parso delle cose antiche ragionare altro che quello che io ho giudicato a tale introduzione necessario. So ancora che io mi arei avuto ad allargare più sopra la milizia a cavallo e dipoi ragionare della guerra navale, perchè chi distingue la milizia dice come egli è uno esercizio di mare e di terra, a piè e a cavallo. Di quello di mare io non presumerei parlare, per non ne avere alcuna notizia; ma lascieronne parlare a' Genovesi e a' Viniziani, i quali con simili studi hanno per lo addietro fatto gran cose. De' cavalli ancora non voglio dire altro che di sopra mi abbia detto, essendo, come io dissi, questa parte corrotta meno. Oltre a questo, ordinate che sono bene le fanterie, che sono il nervo dell'esercito, si vengono di necessità a fare buoni cavalli. Solo ricorderei a chi ordinasse la milizia nel paese suo per riempierlo di cavalli, facesse due provvedimenti: l'uno, che distribuisse cavalle di buona razza per il suo contado e avvezzasse i suoi uomini a fare incette di puledri come voi in questo paese fate de' vitegli e de' muli; l'altro, acciocchè gli incettanti trovassero il comperatore, proibirei il potere tenere mulo ad alcuno che non tenesse cavallo, talmente che chi volesse tenere una cavalcatura sola fusse costretto tenere cavallo; e di più, che non potesse vestire di drappo se non chi tenesse cavallo. Questo ordine intendo essere stato fatto da alcuno principe ne' nostri tempi, e in brevissimo tempo avere nel paese suo ridotto una ottima cavalleria. Circa alle altre cose, quanto si aspetta a' cavalli, mi rimetto a quanto oggi vi dissi e a quello che si costuma. Desidereresti forse ancora intendere quali parte debbe avere uno capitano? A che io vi soddisfarò brevissimamente, perchè io non saprei eleggere altro uomo che quello che sapesse fare tutte quelle cose che da noi sono state oggi ragionate; le quali ancora non basterebbero, quando non ne sapesse trovare da se, perchè niuno senza invenzione fu mai grande uomo nel mestiero suo; e se la invenzione fa onore nell'altre cose, in questo sopra tutto ti onora. E si vede ogni invento, ancora che debole, essere dagli scrittori celebrato; come si vede che lodano Alessandro Magno, che, per disalloggiare più segretamente, non dava il segno con la tromba, ma con uno cappello sopra una lancia. È laudato ancora per avere ordinato agli suoi soldati che, nello appiccarsi con gli nemici, s'inginocchiassero col piè manco, per potere più gagliardamente sostenere l'impeto loro; il che avendogli dato la vittoria, gli dette ancora tanta lode, che tutte le statue, che si rizzavano in suo onore, stavano in quella guisa. Ma perch'egli è tempo di finire questo ragionamento, io voglio tornare a proposito; e parte fuggirò quella pena in che si costuma condannare in questa terra coloro che non vi tornano. Se vi ricorda bene, Cosimo, voi mi dicesti che, essendo io dall'uno canto esaltatore della antichità e biasimatore di quegli che nelle cose gravi non la imitano, e, dall'altro, non la avendo io nelle cose della guerra, dove io mi sono affaticato, imitata, non ne potevi ritrovare la cagione; a che io risposi come gli uomini che vogliono fare una cosa, conviene prima si preparino a saperla fare, per potere poi operarla quando l'occasione lo permetta. Se io saprei ridurre la milizia ne' modi antichi o nò, io ne voglio per giudici voi che mi avete sentito sopra questa materia lungamente disputare; donde voi avete potuto conoscere quanto tempo io abbia consumato in questi pensieri, e ancora credo possiate immaginare quanto desiderio sia in me di mandargli ad effetto. Il che se io ho potuto fare, o se mai me ne è stata data occasione, facilmente potete conietturarlo. Pure per farvene più certi, e per più mia giustificazione, voglio ancora addurne le cagioni; e parte vi osserverò quanto promissi di dimostrarvi: le difficoltà e le facilità che sono al presente in tali imitazioni. Dico pertanto come niuna azione che si faccia oggi tra gli uomini, è più facile a ridurre ne' modi antichi che la milizia, ma per coloro soli che sono Principi di tanto stato, che potessero almeno di loro suggetti mettere insieme quindici o ventimila giovani. Dall'altra parte, niuna cosa è più difficile che questa a coloro che non hanno tale commodità. E perchè voi intendiate meglio questa parte, voi avete a sapere come e' sono di due ragioni capitani lodati. L'una è quegli che con uno esercito ordinato per sua naturale disciplina hanno fatto grandi cose, come furono la maggior parte de' cittadini Romani e altri che hanno guidati eserciti; i quali non hanno avuto altra fatica che mantenergli buoni e vedere di guidargli sicuramente. L'altra è quegli che non solamente hanno avuto a superare il nemico, ma, prima ch'egli arrivino a quello, sono stati necessitati fare buono e bene ordinato l'esercito loro, i quali senza dubbio meritono più lode assai che non hanno meritato quegli che con gli eserciti antichi e buoni hanno virtuosamente operato. Di questi tali fu Pelopida ed Epaminonda, Tullo Ostilio, Filippo di Macedonia padre d'Alessandro, Ciro Re de' Persi, Gracco Romano. Costoro tutti ebbero prima a fare l'esercito buono, e poi combattere con quello. Costoro tutti lo poterono fare, sì per la prudenza loro, sì per avere suggetti da potergli in simile esercizio indirizzare. Nè mai sarebbe stato possibile che alcuno di loro, ancora che uomo pieno d'ogni eccellenza, avesse potuto in una provincia aliena, piena di uomini corrotti, non usi ad alcuna onesta ubbidienza, fare alcuna opera lodevole. Non basta adunque in Italia il sapere governare uno esercito fatto, ma prima è necessario saperlo fare e poi saperlo comandare. E di questi bisogna sieno quegli Principi che, per avere molto stato e assai suggetti, hanno commodità di farlo. De' quali non posso essere io che non comandai mai, nè posso comandare se non a eserciti forestieri e a uomini obligati ad altri e non a me. Ne' quali s'egli è possibile o nò, introdurre alcuna di quelle cose da me oggi ragionate, lo voglio lasciare nel giudicio vostro. Quando potrei io fare portare a uno di questi soldati che oggi si praticano, più armi che le consuete, e, oltra alle armi, il cibo per due o tre giorni e la zappa? Quando potrei io farlo zappare o tenerlo ogni giorno molte ore sotto l'armi negli esercizj finti, per potere poi ne' veri valermene? Quando si asterrebbe egli da' giuochi, dalle lascivie, dalle bestemmie, dalle insolenze che ogni dì fanno? Quando si ridurrebbero eglino in tanta disciplina e in tanta ubbidienza e reverenza, che uno arbore pieno di pomi nel mezzo degli alloggiamenti vi si trovasse e lasciasse intatto come si legge che negli eserciti antichi molte volte intervenne? Che cosa posso io promettere loro, mediante la quale e' mi abbiano con reverenza ad amare o temere, quando, finita la guerra, e' non hanno più alcuna cosa a convenire meco? Di che gli ho io a fare vergognare, che sono nati e allevati senza vergogna? Perchè mi hanno eglino ad osservare che non mi conoscono? Per quale Iddio, o per quali santi gli ho io a fare giurare? Per quei ch'egli adorano, o per quei che bestemmiano? Che ne adorino non so io alcuno, ma so bene che li bestemmiano tutti. Come ho io a credere ch'egli osservino le promesse a coloro che ad ogni ora essi dispregiano? Come possono coloro che dispregiano Iddio, riverire gli uomini? Quale adunque buona forma sarebbe quella che si potesse imprimere in questa materia? E se voi mi allegassi che i Svizzeri e gli Spagnuoli sono buoni, io vi confesserei come eglino sono di gran lunga migliori che gli Italiani; ma se voi noterete il ragionamento mio e il modo del procedere d'ambidue, vedrete come e' manca loro di molte cose ad aggiugnere alla perfezione degli antichi. E i Svizzeri sono fatti buoni da uno loro naturale uso causato da quello che oggi vi dissi, quegli altri da una necessità; perchè, militando in una provincia forestiera e parendo loro essere costretti o morire o vincere, per non parere loro avere luogo alla fuga, sono diventati buoni. Ma è una bontà in molte parti defettiva, perchè in quella non è altro di buono, se non che si sono assuefatti ad aspettare il nemico infino alla punta della picca e della spada. Nè quello che manca loro, sarebbe alcuno atto ad insegnarlo, e tanto meno chi non fusse della loro lingua. Ma torniamo agli Italiani, i quali, per non avere avuti i Principi savi, non hanno preso alcuno ordine buono, e, per non avere avuto quella necessità che hanno avuta gli Spagnuoli, non gli hanno per loro medesimi presi; tale che rimangono il vituperio del mondo. Ma i popoli non ne hanno colpa, ma sì bene i Principi loro; i quali ne sono stati gastigati, e della ignoranza loro ne hanno portate giuste pene perdendo ignominiosamente lo stato, e senza alcuno esemplo virtuoso. Volete voi vedere se questo che io dico è vero? Considerate quante guerre sono state in Italia dalla passata del Re Carlo ad oggi; e solendo le guerre fare uomini bellicosi e riputati, queste quanto più sono state grandi e fiere, tanto più hanno fatto perdere di riputazione alle membra e a' capi suoi. Questo conviene che nasca che gli ordini consueti non erano e non sono buoni; e degli ordini nuovi non ci è alcuno che abbia saputo pigliarne. Nè crediate mai che si renda riputazione alle armi italiane, se non per quella via che io ho dimostra e mediante coloro che tengono stati grossi in Italia; perchè questa forma si può imprimere negli uomini semplici, rozzi e proprj, non ne' maligni, male custoditi e forestieri. Nè si troverrà mai alcuno buono scultore che creda fare una bella statua d'un pezzo di marmo male abbozzato, ma sì bene d'uno rozzo. Credevano i nostri Principi italiani, prima ch'egli assaggiassero i colpi delle oltramontane guerre, che a uno principe bastasse sapere negli scrittoi pensare an'acuta risposta, scrivere una bella lettera, mostrare ne' detti e nelle parole arguzia e prontezza, sapere tessere una fraude, ornarsi di gemme e d'oro, dormire e mangiare con maggiore splendore che gli altri, tenere assai lascivie intorno, governarsi co' sudditi avaramente e superbamente, marcirsi nello ozio, dare i gradi della milizia per grazia, disprezzare se alcuno avesse loro dimostro alcuna lodevole via, volere che le parole loro fussero responsi di oraculi; nè si accorgevano i meschini che si preparavano ad essere preda di qualunque gli assaltava. Di quì nacquero poi nel mille quattrocento novantaquattro i grandi spaventi, le subite fughe e le miracolose perdite; e così tre potentissimi stati che erano in Italia, sono stati più volte saccheggiati e guasti. Ma quello che è peggio, è che quegli che ci restano stanno nel medesimo errore e vivono nel medesimo disordine, e non considerano che quegli che anticamente volevano tenere lo stato, facevano e facevano fare tutte quelle cose che da me si sono ragionate, e che il loro studio era preparare il corpo a' disagi e lo animo a non temere i pericoli. Onde nasceva che Cesare, Alessandro e tutti quegli uomini e Principi eccellenti, erano i primi tra' combattitori, andavano armati a piè, e se pure perdevano lo stato, e' volevano perdere la vita; talmente che vivevano e morivano virtuosamente. E se in loro, o in parte di loro, si poteva dannare troppa ambizione di regnare, mai non si troverrà che in loro si danni alcuna mollizia o alcuna cosa che faccia gli uomini delicati e imbelli. Le quali cose, se da questi Principi fussero lette e credute, sarebbe impossibile che loro non mutassero forma di vivere e le provincie loro non mutassero fortuna. E perchè voi, nel principio di questo nostro ragionamento, vi dolesti della vostra ordinanza, io vi dico che, se voi la avete ordinata come io ho di sopra ragionato ed ella abbia dato di se non buona esperienza, voi ragionevolmente ve ne potete dolere; ma s'ella non è così ordinata ed esercitata come ho detto, ella può dolersi di voi che avete fatto uno abortivo, non una figura perfetta. I Viniziani ancora e il duca di Ferrara la cominciarono e non la seguirono, il che è stato per difetto loro, non degli uomini loro. E io vi affermo che qualunque di quelli che tengono oggi stati in Italia prima entrerrà per questa via, fia, prima che alcuno altro, signore di questa provincia; e interverrà allo stato suo come al Regno de' Macedoni, il quale, venendo sotto a Filippo che aveva imparato il modo dello ordinare gli eserciti da Epaminonda tebano, diventò, con questo ordine e con questi esercizi, mentre che l'altra Grecia stava in ozio e attendeva a recitare commedie, tanto potente che potette in pochi anni tutta occuparla, e al figliuolo lasciare tale fondamento, che potèo farsi principe di tutto il mondo. Colui adunque che dispregia questi pensieri, s'egli è principe, dispregia il principato suo; s'egli è cittadino, la sua città. E io mi dolgo della natura, la quale o ella non mi dovea fare conoscitore di questo, o ella mi doveva dare facultà a poterlo eseguire. Nè penso oggimai, essendo vecchio, poterne avere alcuna occasione; e per questo io ne sono stato con voi liberale, che, essendo giovani e qualificati, potrete, quando le cose dette da me vi piacciano, ai debiti tempi, in favore de' vostri Principi, aiutarle e consigliarle. Di che non voglio vi sbigottiate o diffidiate, perchè questa provincia pare nata per risuscitare le cose morte, come si è visto della poesia, della pittura e della scultura. Ma quanto a me si aspetta, per essere in là con gli anni, me ne diffido. E veramente, se la fortuna mi avesse conceduto per lo addietro tanto stato quanto basta a una simile impresa, io crederei, in brevissimo tempo, avere dimostro al mondo quanto gli antichi ordini vagliono; e senza dubbio o io l'arei accresciuto con gloria o perduto senza vergogna.

Made in the USA
Las Vegas, NV
11 August 2024